# INTERNAL WAR

## PROBLEMS AND APPROACHES

HARRY ECKSTEIN, *Editor*

The Free Press of Glencoe
Collier-Macmillan Limited, London

## ACKNOWLEDGMENT

This book is an early product of a general inquiry into internal wars that is being carried on at Princeton University's Center of International Studies. I wish here to express the gratitude of the Center, the contributors, and myself to the Carnegie Foundation, which has substantially supported this inquiry.

HARRY ECKSTEIN

Princeton, N.J.
May 1963

# CONTRIBUTORS

Professor Harry Eckstein
*Princeton University*

Professor Talcott Parsons
*Harvard University*

Mr. Thomas P. Thornton
*Princeton University*

Professor Karl Deutsch
*Yale University*

Professor Arnold S. Feldman
*Northwestern University*

Professor Andrew C. Janos
*University of California, Berkeley*

Professor William Kornhauser
*University of California, Berkeley*

Professor Lucian W. Pye
*Massachusetts Institute of Technology*

Professor Alexander Gerschenkron
*Harvard University*

Professor Sidney Verba
*Princeton University*

Professor Gabriel A. Almond
*Stanford University*

Professor Marion J. Levy, Jr.
*Princeton University*

Professor S. M. Lipset
*University of California, Berkeley*

# CONTENTS

Introduction. Toward the Theoretical Study of
Internal War                                                      1
  HARRY ECKSTEIN

Some Reflections on the Place of Force in Social Process          33
  TALCOTT PARSONS

Terror as a Weapon of Political Agitation                         71
  THOMAS PERRY THORNTON

External Involvement in Internal War                             100
  KARL W. DEUTSCH

Violence and Volatility: The Likelihood of Revolution            111
  ARNOLD S. FELDMAN

Authority and Violence:
  The Political Framework of Internal War                        130
  ANDREW C. JANOS

Rebellion and Political Development                              142
  WILLIAM KORNHAUSER

The Roots of Insurgency and
  the Commencement of Rebellions                                 157
  LUCIAN W. PYE

Reflections on Economic Aspects of Revolutions                   180
  ALEXANDER GERSCHENKRON

National Revolutions and Political Commitment                    205
  SIDNEY VERBA AND GABRIEL A. ALMOND

Contents

A *Revision of the* Gemeinschaft-Gesellschaft *Categories
and Some Aspects of the Interdependencies of
Minority and Host Systems*     233
    Marion J. Levy, Jr.

*Democracy and the Social System*     267
    Seymour Martin Lipset

*Index*     335

# INTERNAL WAR

*Harry Eckstein*

## INTRODUCTION. TOWARD THE

## THEORETICAL STUDY OF INTERNAL WAR

*Internal War and Social Science Theory*

When today's social science has become intellectual history, one question will almost certainly be asked about it: Why did social science, which has produced so many studies of so many subjects, produce so few on violent political disorder—internal war?* Here indeed will be a problem for future sociologists of knowledge, for by any common-sense reckoning the contemporary literature of social science should be brimming over with such studies.

After all, interest in the subject has always been intense. Revolution is one of the classic themes of social thought; among the great thinkers there is scarcely one who has failed to come to grips with it. Of course, approaches vary. Some deal with it mainly from a normative point of view, seeking to demonstrate or deny the justifiability of political violence. Others are interested in formulating generalizations about its causes, course, or consequences. Still others put themselves into the place of the participants and try to find prudential rules for making, avoiding, or winning revolutionary conflicts.

In the history of social thought we find almost every conceivable perspective on internal war, with almost every conceivable difference of nuance or emphasis. But we do not find

---

* The meaning of the term "internal war" is dealt with below. Broadly speaking, ⌐internal wars are attempts to change by violence, or threat of violence, a government's policies, rulers, or organization. ⌐

any considerable social thinker who does not hold the subject worth the bother or does not indeed accord it a central place in his reflections. Yet in a recently published anthology of social theory, compiled by several notable contemporary social theorists, running to some 1,400 large, print-saturated pages, and purporting to present the "foundations" of sociological theory, no special section is devoted to revolution, and hardly a single extensive reference to it is to be found.\* This omission constitutes a serious gap in that mammoth (and useful) work, a misrepresentation of the history of social theory, and a good measure of the status currently accorded in social science to studies of internal war.

The omission would be more comprehensible if there had been a long decline of interest in political violence. But the truth is just the reverse. In the immediate environs of contemporary social thought, one finds not merely interest in social force and war, but obsession. One also finds there most of those few social theorists who regard revolutions as forces of progress, agencies of social adjustment, and suitable activities for moral men. Adherents of Marxism, of course, are the most conspicuous example. Less obvious perhaps are the political evolutionists, with their glorification of force as an agency of social consolidation and a means for recruiting to power the true élites of society. There is also the social romantics' love of violence— demonstrated by condottiere-worshippers like D'Annunzio and Malaparte or ferocious revolutionaries like Blanqui and Sorel. Even those men who, according to Talcott Parsons' monumental *Structure of Social Action*, compounded the main lines of contemporary sociological theory—Pareto, Durkheim, Weber (and, one could add, Comte and Mosca)—had plenty to say about social violence. How, after all, could one have missed the import of revolutionary disorders in so revolutionary a period as the nineteenth and early twentieth centuries? Not even Durkheim, with his pervasive emphasis on social solidarity, disdains the subject. His whole work, in fact, could be interpreted as a search

---

\* I refer to T. Parsons, E. Shils, K. D. Naegele, and J. R. Pitts (eds.), *Theories of Society: Foundations of Modern Sociological Theory* (New York: The Free Press of Glencoe, 1961). This book's omission is, of course, only one of several indicators of the neglect of the subject.

for the conditions of solidarity in a world of increasing, and apparently increasingly antagonistic, social fragmentation.

Yet perhaps it is not so difficult to miss the obvious. Contemporary social scientists have managed to do it very well. For if internal war was commonplace in the nineteenth and early twentieth centuries, it is practically the essence of contemporary political life. The Russian Revolution was an event at least as decisive and arresting as the French. It has been followed by wave upon wave of internal war—fascist, Nazi, communist, colonial, militarist, modernizing, reactionary, populist, élitist, middle class, proletarian, spontaneous, and conspiratorial. *The New York Times* alone reported well over 1,200 unequivocal examples between 1946 and 1959 (civil wars, including guerrilla wars, localized rioting, widely dispersed turmoil, organized and apparently unorganized terrorism, mutinies, and *coups d'état*). And it is unlikely to have covered all those that occurred—not to mention hundreds of equivocal cases, such as forestalled "plots" that may or may not actually have been fomented. Only a handful of societies have managed to remain highly tranquil in the general commotion, and, while it is precisely these societies that produce most of today's social science, it is hard to believe that social scientists could be so oblivious to social occurrences outside their immediate environment.

Surely nothing in the world of political events can account for the relative neglect of internal war studies.* One is tempted, therefore, to look to the intellectual world of the social scientist for explanations. But here the mystery only deepens. What, after all, have been the key problems of contemporary sociology? Social development, discontinuity, integration, deviance, delinquency, conflict and its resolution, and Durkheim's old problem of the conditions of social solidarity and viability. Conflict and change, as Arnold Feldman points out in this book, have been "persistent themes" in modern social studies—and what are the great con-

---

* Lucian Pye, on p. 162 below, makes a contrary point worth considering. He suggests that perhaps the very seriousness of much modern internal war accounts for the relative neglect of internal war studies—that this neglect constitutes a kind of sublimation of traumatic social experiences. This theory hardly explains, however, the neglect of such studies in the more peaceful countries, those whose major internal wars lie far back in their histories.

ceptual schemes of contemporary social science if not designs for discovering and accounting for the presence or absence of these conditions? Rarely, it seems, have social thinkers been so well equipped with basic concepts, perspectives, and analytical approaches designed to make sense of the phenomena of internal war. Their literature teems with requisites for social order, functional imperatives for solidary social life, and theories of social interaction and communication, effective and ineffective socialization, alienation and aggression. One would think that anyone interested in social solidarity, integration, equilibrium, and conformity—the grand theoretical problems of contemporary social science—would be consumingly interested in their ultimate negation in revolutionary conflict. And one would have thought as well that any theory meant to illuminate the one set of conditions could be applied, without much change and difficulty, to its opposite.

Then too there is the fact that contemporary social science offers an abundance of empirical works highly relevant to any general study of internal war. There are studies of mass movements, of the appeals and techniques of communism and such specific social tensions as intergenerational conflicts, industrial conflicts, role conflicts in general, and the strains attending processes of social transition. These studies often come close to being studies of internal war, yet the great majority of them are not aimed directly and intentionally at that target.

It is tempting to conclude that social scientists have lately neglected the subject of internal war for no reason at all, but simply because they have been preoccupied with other matters. At any rate, that was the hopeful guess that led the Center of International Studies at Princeton University to convene, late in 1961, a symposium of social scientists to write about and discuss internal war. Many—but not all—were selected for their knowledge of and contributions to the theoretical foundations of present-day social science. Their task was to write papers "on the application of contemporary social theories to the study of internal wars, including, for example, functional theory, action theory, communications theory, theories of group dynamics, theories of attitude formation, and the like." We felt that in all these fields and theories important insights into the problems of internal war might lie not too deeply hidden, that each might provide powerful tools for dealing incisively with old and fuzzy but now extremely urgent problems. The essays in this book are the result.*

What answer to our problem do they suggest? Certainly not that it is merely an accidental lack of attention that has kept contemporary social scientists from writing internal war studies and improving upon the results of earlier thought about the subject. Whatever their merits in other respects, there is no use pretending that the essays here achieve the end intended. Some of them avoid any substantial, direct confrontation of the subject; others attack it, but without any considerable use of social science theory. Indeed, the greater the author's concern with internal war itself, the less he seems to use social science equipment. This remark is not true of all the essays, but it is true of a sufficient number to make one wonder. Obviously, merely asking contemporary social scientists to write about internal war is not enough to produce a real wedding of contemporary theory with long-standing problems.

Why then the recent neglect of internal war studies? What explanation remains? Future sociologists of knowledge may think differently, but I should like to suggest an answer, or, rather, two. To make substantive use of formal theories, to derive empirical knowledge from abstract theoretical approaches, to apply general conceptual schemes to particular subjects, it is not enough merely to confront the theorist with a concrete subject. The subject itself must first be processed theoretically; there must be a certain equivalence, as it were, between the tools and the material. One does not build physical structures simply by using tools directly upon raw materials; first, one processes the materials to make them usable for building. In the case of internal war, as in the case of many other concrete subjects in contemporary social science, such processing is conspicuously lacking. In consequence, social theorists confronted by the subject are understandably at sea—like shoemakers working not on leather but an ox. Social science in general has been too much concerned with

---

* Or, rather, most of the result. Some of the papers prepared for the symposium were, at their authors' requests, withdrawn; one has since been added.

fashioning tools that might be used for diverse substantive purposes, too little with the direct processing of concrete experience in order to prepare it for theoretical contrivance by the abstract systems now in vogue. That is why in general an enormous gulf still exists in social science between theoretical schemata and empirical work and why, confronted with a concrete subject like internal war, even the more illustrious masters of social theory are visibly ill at ease.

As I have said, this point applies generally to social studies. Still, it undoubtedly applies more emphatically to the study of internal war than to many other problem areas. The reason lies, in my view, in the methodological conscience rather than the pretheoretical concerns of social scientists (although the two are related). Social scientists, in recent times, have seemed to feel acutely guilty about their apparent lack of rigor. They have been widely criticized and have widely criticized themselves for it. A concern with general analytical approaches has been one result, for the ambiguities of social science can be attributed, at least in some degree, to the imprecision of conventional concepts and perspectives. Another consequence has been a preoccupation with methodological precision, which has been widely identified with two areas: the study of subjects for which ready-made and large-scale quantitative data are easily obtained and the use of certain complicated techniques to elicit trustworthy and replicable data that are not presented directly by the social environment—techniques like social-survey analysis, experimentation in controlled situations, and "field work." Internal wars, unfortunately, are not very suitable for these kinds of work. Many of them do occur, but nowhere near enough to provide the number of cases one deals with, say, in voting studies. They can hardly be staged experimentally, and tend, for obvious reasons, to deter field workers, interviewers, and pollsters.

This point must be considered with the earlier argument about lack of processing if one is to make sense of the general neglect of internal war studies in contemporary social science. For the present purpose, however, the earlier argument is much more important. After all, the social scientists who have contributed to this book were not asked to supply rigorously tested empirical generalizations about internal wars but only to indicate what ideas on the subject their various theoretical perspectives and schema might imply. And most of them are not themselves social scientists of the sort who worship numbers or trust only experimental data.

What I am saying, in effect, is that the purpose of the symposium, of which this book is the product, was misconceived.* Rather than being asked to apply their theoretical equipment directly to the subject of internal war, these social theorists should have been requested, at this stage, to reflect on how the subject could be shaped for theoretical processing. General social science theories do not, in this or any other case, make theoretical reflection directly upon concrete experience unnecessary.

No great harm was done, however. Most of the essays here, despite contrary directions, do precisely what is needed, at least implicitly. Their theoretical concern, as often as not and so far as they deal directly with internal war, is to come to grips speculatively with the phenomenon of internal war itself, rather than to attempt clarification of the inchoate subject with the ordered theories of social science. On the basis of these essays, it is at least easier to indicate what theoretical preparation of the subject requires. The essays should be read mainly (though not only) from that point of view.

### Pre-theoretical Concerns in the Study of Internal War

To prepare a concrete subject for theoretical processing, certain operations must always be performed. These operations are not, in the absolutely literal sense, preliminary to theory—that is, they need not be (and rarely are) definitive and complete before fruitful theorizing can start. Actually, one works on them continuously throughout theoretical study; the preliminary operations inform the studies, and the studies, in turn, change the earlier results of the preliminary operations. Nevertheless, theoretical study is hardly possible at all unless the preliminary operations are carried out, at least in tentative form.†

---

* It is only fair to add, by myself, as its organizer.
† Since the term "theory" has neither a single technical nor ambiguous

No common vocabulary for these operations exists, but the terms "delimitation," "classification," "analysis," and "problematization" will probably do well enough. In the rest of this essay, I shall try to explain what they mean, what issues they raise, and how the essays that follow touch on them. I should stress that, in the nature of the study, nothing in this introduction (or book) is meant to settle anything. Its purpose is to raise issues and make suggestions.

DELIMITATION. To carry on theoretical study, one must first have a subject to study. The task of delimitation is, in a nutshell, to state unambiguously what that subject is.

Nothing might seem simpler or more arbitrary, and therefore less worth talking about, than stating a subject. It seems necessary, at first glance, only to declare one's interests. In the case of internal war, for example, it might seem enough to say (in the manner of Alexander Gerschenkron in this book) that one is interested in certain events—like the Hungarian uprising of 1956, the Potemkin mutiny, and guerrilla warfare in Laos. But the matter cannot be allowed to rest there. Since theory always consists of generalizations, two problems are raised by such a statement: Can these phenomena in fact be generalized about, and what other concrete events must valid generalizations about them fit? In other words, are the phenomena alike, and how can we know what other phenomena are like them?

The point is that while a subject usually originates in an interest, the interest does not constitute the subject. A theoretical subject is a set of phenomena about which one can develop informative, testable generalizations that hold for all instances of the subject, and some of which apply to those instances alone.

The nature of such a set depends, of course, on the level and kind of generalization sought. For example, a theorist interested in discovering general functional requisites for social systems will have to cast his net much wider than one interested in finding the antecedent conditions of a particular category of social events like

conventional meaning, I should state how I use the term here. Theories, for the present purpose, are testable (that is, falsifiable) generalizations stating relations among concrete phenomena or, more broadly, abstract forms approximated in concrete experience. Operations preliminary to theory (pretheories) are those required for the formulation of such generalizations.

international wars. Furthermore, the kind of theory one decides to seek is an arbitrary matter. Determining whether a certain set of phenomena is a universe for *any* kind of theory or a particular kind of theory is, however, not arbitrary. Someone interested in the Hungarian uprising, the Potemkin mutiny, and Laotian guerrilla war has a topic, or possibly three, but he still has to determine whether any theories about all three can be constructed, what kinds, and in what other cases they should or should not hold. He must discover the boundaries of his subject—i.e., delimit it.

Once one conceives of a subject as a universe of phenomena amenable to theory in that sense, it is possible to distinguish between the delimitation of a subject and the definition of a concept. A definition states the meaning of a word in other words, but the word defined may or may not denote a theoretical universe. We could easily define "internal war" so that it would cover the three cases mentioned, but that would not necessarily help us to discover valid theories. Nevertheless, delimitations and definitions are not entirely unrelated. Not only can one define a concept in terms of its delimitation but, more important, at the beginning of inquiry one may have little more than a definition to serve as a delimitation of a subject. One of the objects of theoretical study itself is to help transform defined words into theoretical subjects, in such a way that the events belonging or not belonging to the subject can be readily identified.

The necessity for this process is plain. It matters a great deal at the earliest stage of inquiry, when one examines cases in order to get theoretical ideas about the category to which they belong (the "natural history stage of inquiry," as Northrop calls it), and it is absolutely crucial when one comes to testing generalizations. If, for example, we want ideas about the dynamics of leadership in modern political parties, it will probably do little good to make a close case study of "organizational weapons" like the Communist Party or of those informal associations of parliamentary notables that used to be called parties in Western countries. It may turn out that such parties are parties in name only, structures so different from those that really interest us that nothing (or very little) we want to know can be learned from them. And we would really be in trouble if we supposed that generalizations about, say, contemporary American, British, and

German parties should be discarded if they did not fit the Tory party in eighteenth-century Britain or the Chinese Communist Party or the old Bavarian Peasants Party. If a generalization about eggs is considered invalid because it fails to cover oranges, valid generalizations are unlikely ever to be discovered. Here too a mere verbal definition will not be very helpful. To be told, for instance, that a party is "a number of men joined to achieve some object on which they are all agreed" might lead only to the discovery that no such thing exists at all or that the cases included are too disparate for generalization. At any rate, whether or not they are is not settled by the definition. "Party" as a theoretical subject must be delimited by the two criteria I have mentioned: that some generalizations apply to all the cases included and only to these cases.

In the delimitation of theoretical subjects, two problems really arise. The first is to find a homogeneous set of cases. The second, which becomes very troublesome once one starts making close distinctions, is somehow to limit the degree of homogeneity required. For no two concrete objects or events are ever really alike. Each has unique aspects. If, consequently, we start with an interest in a concrete event—the French Revolution perhaps— and specify its attributes in exhaustive detail as the nature of our subject, we will find in the end that we have a case on our hands but not a subject. Even if we are not exhaustive but merely very detailed, the number of other cases falling into our conception of the subject may be so small as to make generalization worthless. The same result may occur if we start not with a concrete case but with a very complicated abstract definition. While, to be sure, a statement about two or three cases is certainly a generalization in the dictionary sense, a generalization in the methodological sense must usually be based on more; it ought to cover a number of cases large enough for certain rigorous testing procedures like statistical analysis to be used. Finally, it must not be possible to "save" any hypothesis about a subject by claiming that a case it fails to cover is simply beyond its scope because it is, somehow, a different case. A proper delimitation of a subject must strike a fine balance between inclusion and exclusion. At one extreme lurks the danger of unfalsifiable interpretation, at the other that of triviality or of generalizations that cannot fail to prove invalid.

In consequence, two approaches to delimitation can be imagined. One starts from particular cases but deliberately ignores most of their particular attributes to arrive at some kernel of similarity; the other starts with very broadly inclusive abstract conceptions, then distinguishes within them narrower categories differing in essential aspects and requiring narrower generalizations.

An example of the latter approach is provided by the first essay in this volume, Parsons' essay on "The Place of Force in Social Process." Parsons' approach is, first, to put his subject into certain larger sets of cases of which it is a part and then to distinguish it from phenomena within these sets requiring different generalizations. Force, in social life, he points out, is an "interaction," so that generalizations about interactions as such should also apply to it; yet not all interactions involve force, so that special generalizations about force are needed, and need not apply to the other interactions. Force belongs to that particular family of interactions aiming at social control, yet social control can also be achieved by other means: inducements, persuasion, and the "activation of commitments." Force is then conceived as an interaction aiming at social control through a particular process and by particular means, and these means are specified at some length in Parsons' essay. This narrowing is still fairly definitional, but those who follow Parsons' exposition (rather than the extreme summary here) will have much less difficulty than before in determining what to include or exclude in studies of force in society.

In delimiting the phenomenon of force from other social interactions, Parsons brings us much closer to a delimitation of our own subject, internal war, which is how his essay relates to the others in this volume. As he would certainly admit, however, we need to go much further—in a sense, we must begin where he stops. Since all social force is not internal war, a further delimitation of the broader subject is required. To a degree, it is provided by Janos' essay. Janos distinguishes between "military" force and "civic" force (force in Parsons' sense), identifying the two with struggle according to or not according to the norms and expectations of society. This is at least the bare beginning of a useful charting of the area of social force, within which the boundaries of internal war could be precisely located. Actually, however, the problem of delimiting internal war as a theoretical subject is more complicated. The great difficulty is that internal war belongs simultaneously to a number of larger theoretical subjects, from all of which it requires delimitation.

Internal wars belong to the realm not only of *social force* but also to *political competition,* since their object is to obtain political outputs advantageous to the groups that urge them—favorable policies, offices, or general control of the political structure of society. As Janos himself argues, internal war is part of the general struggle of individuals, groups, parties, and movements for "authority," despite "rationalist" conceptions that place it somehow outside of the universe of "political" struggle. Internal wars belong as well to the larger universe of *social deviance,* since their occurrence violates institutionalized norms of social behavior (in the language suggested by Marion J. Levy in this volume, they involve challenges by "minority systems" to the "*Gemeinschaft* set" of values in a society). They belong, furthermore, to the general universe of *social instability,* a segment of which S. M. Lipset treats in this volume, since they involve breakdowns in previously settled institutional patterns. Not least, they are part of the general subject of *war,* if by war we mean violent social conflict waged with very few shared normative rules or no rules at all.

The subject of internal war is therefore one of the great synthetic subjects of social science. It can be approached directly and through many circumlocutions, Parsons' and Lipset's essays here being examples. To shed light on internal war, both of these essays undoubtedly need extension, yet there can be little doubt, at least in principle, that they could be extended to the point desired.

The question still remains: What are the boundaries of internal war as a theoretical subject? To what cases do these essays need extension to be essays about internal war itself?

One possible answer is that internal war is that part of each of the five subjects I have mentioned that overlaps with all the others. It is a kind of social force that is exerted in the process of political competition, deviating from previously shared social norms, "warlike" in character (that is, conducted practically without mutually observed normative rules), and involving the serious disruption of settled institutional patterns.

Such a delimitation of the subject of internal war seems to meet the two essential purposes of any delimitation. It is general enough to permit even the most exacting methodologist to develop informative and testable generalizations; even if many cases of internal war that one might intuitively want to cover are excluded by this formulation, literally hundreds remain. And it apparently does not encompass a motley universe, composed of cases so disparate that validated generalizations about them are unlikely to be found. This latter characteristic is suggested by two things. First, it is relatively easy, on the basis of this delimitation, to determine when a case is one of internal war, particularly if "force" is used as Parsons uses it, not simply to denote direct compulsion but also coercion, threat, and warning.* Such phenomena as *coups d'état*, which may succeed with little or no bloodshed, or terrorism, as it is discussed in Thomas Thornton's paper, then fall readily into place (even though not all cases of what conventional language terms *coups d'état* or terror may belong to the universe of internal wars). Second, and perhaps still more important, cases likely to lead to the falsification of valid theories about internal war are clearly excluded from the subject, so that such theories may have at least a decent chance of survival. Let me give some examples of such cases.

A generalization about the causes of internal war will certainly founder if it is expected to account simultaneously for such disparate phenomena as, say, the outbreak of political violence in late eighteenth-century France and ethnic strife in a newly created contemporary state. The French Revolution falls clearly into the subject of internal war as I have delimited it; it involved warlike and deviant social force for purposes of political competition, and it seriously disrupted settled institutional patterns. In the case of the new state, however, there was, in all probability, no previously shared system of norms from which to deviate and, even more probably, no previously settled institutional pattern; there can therefore be no speaking of internal war in the proper sense. Or take the case of violence attending a succession crisis in a dictatorship. Here too the lack of a settled institutional pattern distinguishes the case from one like the French Revolution; the use of force in such a case may indeed be due to nothing

---

* For Parsons' definitions, see pp. 36-37.

more than the absence of an institutional pattern for settling conflict. The occurrence of violent political competition in a country where such competition is practically a way of life, as it seems to be in some Latin American and Asian countries (Burma and Indonesia are mentioned in this connection in Pye's essay), can be similarly differentiated. In such cases, it is not the absence of institutional patterns but the very fact that social force is, as Pye points out, highly institutionalized (and probably not exercised in a warlike manner but with a nice observance of clearly understood norms, as in most feudal warfare) that is the decisive point. Certainly it is not reasonable on the face of it to expect a theory about the causes of internal war in previously peaceable societies to fit as well all cases where political violence is endemic and expected.

Other phenomena that have troubled writers on internal war in the past—purges, partisan activities against a military occupation, wars of independence, spontaneous clashes between demonstrators and police—can be dealt with in the same way. That does not mean, however, that all cases commonly given one label or another will fall into or outside the subject of internal wars; conventional categories are usually filled with ill-assorted cases. Nor does it mean that to determine whether any case is or is not an internal war does not require taking pains; at the very least one must take trouble to understand the case. The only claim I make is that anyone who does take pains is likely, with the delimitation suggested here, to get a clear result, while his efforts might otherwise be wasted.

This formulation of the subject of internal war must necessarily, however, be treated as tentative at this stage. It may be found upon inquiry, for instance, that the subject so delimited is not really a proper subject. It may be either too constricting for the formulation and testing of theories or still too heterogeneous for the kinds of theory one seeks. In that case, the formulation must either be revised or the theoretical study of internal war abandoned. Or it may be found that generalizations developed to fit the cases in the universe fit many other cases equally—perhaps all cases of force exerted in political competition, however they occur. In that event, a conclusive reason exists for widening the original delimitation of the subject. In this sense, delimitation is an end of theoretical study, as well as its beginning.

Two further points should be made before we leave the matter. (1) However carefully a subject may be delimited, some ambiguities will remain. Delimitation reduces ambiguity but rarely eliminates it altogether. An example arises from Karl Deutsch's flat assertion, in his essay here, that wars apparently internal to a society may not be "authentic" internal wars at all but rather "wars by proxy," depending on the extent of external involvement in them. He then provides suggestions on how to assess the extent of external involvement. I confess that I am stumped by the difficulty he raises. Clearly the extent of external involvement makes a difference. It may help to precipitate internal war, affect its duration, and determine its outcome. This possibility does not necessarily, however, make the internal war "inauthentic" from a theoretical point of view (unless the actors are actually externals in disguise); it may merely mean that external factors should be considered together with purely internal ones in the study of internal war. There is the further problem of determining what should be considered internal and external, a problem raised in this volume by Parsons as well as Deutsch. Is an "internal" event one occurring in a state recognized as sovereign by the criteria of international law, or is it, in Parsons' language, something that happens in a "moral community"—one that shares common norms, values, and culture? Both conceptions raise difficulties. While moral community may be a prerequisite for a stable polity, not every such community expresses itself in a polity—ancient Greece, for example, or Latin Christendom. On the other hand, not every legal state need be a moral community; the Congo is an obvious example. What appears internal from the legal point of view, therefore, may be external from the cultural point of view and vice versa. Perhaps we can cope with this difficulty by defining "internal" in terms of legal polity *plus* moral community, but that step does not solve the original problem: how to regard cases involving large-scale external involvement in that sense. Probably there is no logical way to settle the issue in the abstract. It can surely be settled, however, by a practical procedure. One can arbitrarily begin study by ruling out cases not preponderantly internal to legal and moral social entities (preponderantly rather than exclusively, because internal wars without any external involvement are unlikely to be found). It is then possible to see whether generalizations developed for such cases also apply, entirely or in part, to other cases—"wars by proxy," in Deutsch's sense, or ethnic violence and colonial conflicts—cases in which the actors are in some sense internally, in another externally, related. In that way, the significance of external involvement could also be precisely assessed. This procedure does comply with Deutsch's conclusion that cases in which heavy external involvement occurs be left out of the universe of internal war, but initially rather than permanently—and certainly not by definition. In either case, of course, such indices of external involvement as Deutsch proposes are needed.

(2) What has been said here should not be taken to imply that whenever internal wars are studied, for whatever purpose, the boundaries of study should be drawn as has been suggested. Certain theoretical interests, even if they begin in studies of internal war, may best be pursued in different universes. If, for example, one is interested in irregular warfare (guerrilla war, partisan fighting, etc.) it is advisable to look much further than internal war and necessary to leave many internal wars unexamined, for irregular warfare occurs also in other contexts and does not necessarily occur in all internal wars. The same is true of an interest in fights or deviance or any of the universes to which internal wars belong.

By the same token, one can learn a great deal about internal war in studying other subjects. General studies of warfare, regular or irregular, obviously pertain to internal no less than external warfare, as the genius of war studies, Clausewitz, well realized. And general studies of political stability or instability, like Lipset's paper in this volume, are equally pertinent, even if they do not go so far as to tell us when political instability takes the form of deviant, warlike social force.

CLASSIFICATION. I have discussed the problem of delimitation at some length and suggested a solution to it for several reasons. It is the most fundamental problem one faces prior to theoretical inquiry; it is nevertheless rarely discussed; few writings on internal war deal with it except by the most arbitrary definitions; the present essays barely touch on it; and, above all, it happens to

be a matter that *can* be constructively discussed in relatively brief compass. The other kinds of pre-theory must be dealt with less comprehensively and without serious substantive suggestions on my part, mainly because they are far more difficult and complex matters, requiring more thorough study and lengthy treatment than can be accorded them in one section of a symposium introduction. I shall try only to relate this set of essays to the pre-theoretical tasks involved. For this purpose, we must, of course, understand the tasks.

However much it may be possible and informative to generalize about the whole universe of instances comprehended in a subject, it is likely that some generalizations will apply only to a segment of it or with more force or fewer qualifications to some instances than others. The process of sub-delimiting a subject for such narrower generalizations is termed "classification." Its object is to divide a subject into classes distinct from one another —classes about which both common and separate generalizations can and ought to be formulated. This process hardly needs to be discussed at length in the abstract, since it is very familiar, although rarely done well.

The essays most concerned with classification here are those by Janos (who lists seven techniques of internal war—strikes, demonstrations, terrorism, guerrilla warfare, civil war, insurrection, and *coup de force*), by Thornton (who discusses at length one type of internal war—terror—but also distinguishes it briefly from two others, one involving conventional warfare, the other guerrilla warfare), and by Kornhauser (who classifies cases according to the authority structures in which internal wars arise and toward which they tend). Thornton's essay also illustrates the fact that a category or type of internal war may not describe whole events (or at least what we usually think of as whole events—for example, the French Revolution) but only parts of events, either phases in their development or concurrent but distinguishable phenomena.

Like the delimitation of a subject, classification often seems essentially arbitrary—a matter merely of stating concepts and defining them. That is precisely the approach to classification one finds in the literature on internal war (this volume not excepted).

Writings on internal war abound in disparate classificatory

schemes, some completely unique to a particular writer, others overlapping, still others using much the same concepts to denote different events. Obviously this situation is not desirable. For one thing, it means that one must suffer, without discernible reason, the imposition of a new, often ill-defined, language practically every time one reads a piece on internal war. Worse than that, findings gathered and reported in terms of so various a set of concepts can hardly be made cumulative or used to check on one another. The variety of classificatory schemes now in use not only increases misunderstanding but is a positive barrier to the development of knowledge.

Apart from the possibility of persuading writers on internal war to use one writer's arbitrary classificatory concepts instead of their own, is there any way out of this impasse, any basis on which the adequacy of classificatory schemes can be assessed? In my view, there is—although I am not prepared to say at this point what an adequate scheme might be.

The first point to realize is that classification is no more or less arbitrary a process than delimitation, since, logically, it is the same process taken a step further. Classificatory schemes also must strike a reasonable balance between inclusion and exclusion, so that both valid generalizations about phenomena and convincing falsification are possible; they too must reduce as much as possible the ambiguities surrounding the theoretical treatment of concrete events. These requirements give us at least a broad criterion for evaluating such schemes, as well as for using research itself to alter them and make them more definite.

A second important point emerges if we ask why the classifications of internal war currently in use are so disparate. Surely this disparity is due to the fact that every writer on internal war bases his classifications on some one element of internal war or some small combination of elements that happens particularly to interest him or that, often for reasons not even intimated, he feels is particularly crucial—perhaps a determinant variable in a world of dependent variables. In Thornton's essay, for example, the basis of classification seems to be the type of destructive force; in Janos' it is the amount of physical violence and the objectives of the insurgents (annihilation of the enemy or achieving "authority"). For another inquirer, it may be the comprehensiveness of the objective, rather than its type, that distinguishes internal wars. Blanksten, for example, has suggested that national independence movements need distinction from "social revolutions," since the latter aim at comprehensive social change, the former at almost no social change at all, while still a third type, "nonconstitutional changes in government," seem to fall somewhere in between. Harold Lasswell's and Abraham Kaplan's classification uses the structure of participation in the insurgent movement as the touchstone; Samuel Huntington singles out the duration of the war and the nature of the participants; and so forth.

In a sense, this state of affairs is unavoidable. Internal wars are complex, and different people will and should be more interested in some aspects than in others. Nothing is wrong with these variations if one's concern is a particular element of internal war. Everything is wrong with it, however, if one does not know whether one element of internal war is more crucial than another. Some day, conceivably, we may discover that, once the objective or participant structure or destructiveness or some other feature of an internal war is known, everything else about it is known as well. That is one way in which theoretical study can inform classification. Until then, however, classifications based upon these elements are classifications of the elements and not of internal wars. From this point of view, we do not at present possess too many classifications of internal war, but none at all.

The problem is similar to that of contemporary classifications of social systems like the traditional-modern dichotomy now so much in vogue (or for that matter the *Gemeinschaft-Gesellschaft* dichotomy discussed in this volume by Levy, which used to be so much in vogue). For one man, the distinction may rest on industrialization; for another, on norms of rationality and the scientific spirit; for still others, on mobility, the substitutability of men and empathy, functional specificity, universalistic standards, nationalism, democratization, bureaucratization, political and economic centralization, the prevalence of contracts, mass consumption, largeness of scale in social organization, the capacity to sustain and absorb growth, urbanization, rapid and voluminous communication, secularism, mass education, or any of the many other aspects of prototypical "modern" societies. The assumption that usually underlies these divergent emphases is that all elements of society cluster in dependence on whatever one is singled out as crucial, when in fact that may not be true or, at least, has not yet been demonstrated. The consequence, more often than not, is that a society that seems traditional in one sense to one observer will seem modern in another sense to another observer. Or all societies may seem "transitional" to everyone upon close examination, no matter what their differences.

The moral is simply that classification of complex phenomena must be based on their various elements, at least until relations of covariance for these elements have been established. Such classifications can be of two kinds. They can denote "concrete types"—combinations of elements frequently found in concrete experience. Theory is then developed for these types that can also be applied to nontypical cases to the extent that they resemble the types in question. Or classifications can denote "ideal (or pure) types"—combinations of elements that seem to fit logically from the theorist's point of view. Theories are then developed about the constructs of the types and can be applied to concrete cases to the extent that they resemble the "ideal."

By constructing classificatory categories in this manner, one not only avoids presupposing what only theoretical study can establish, but one also gains, as should be clear from what I have just said, another important advantage: the ability to account for atypical cases with theories developed for the typical ones. If one can establish how far any given case diverges from type, one can also determine to what extent a generalization about the type can apply to it. The most obvious means for assessing degrees of divergence from type is of course a close comparison of the elements of the cases involved. One case may have six of the seven elements of a type, another five; one case may have one element of a type in impure form, another two; and so forth. The more such typical elements are present in pure form, the less a theory about the type should need modification to fit the atypical case. And in the world of phenomena there will always be atypical cases to plague the theorist. Such extensions of theories about types to atypical cases (and thus to the whole of one's subject) are not possible at all unless one constructs typologies from a proper analysis of the elements in a complex phenomenon.

ANALYSIS. Classification and analysis are therefore closely related; the first presupposes the other. I use the term "analysis" here in the strict sense, not as it is often employed, to denote practically any kind of study other than bare natural history. Analysis, literally, is the division of a subject into its basic components. Its counterpart is synthesis, the combination of the components into typological classes or to represent particular cases. The chemical table of elements is probably the most familiar example of an analytical construct in this sense.

Few social sciences have carried analysis of any subject very far, and social science has undoubtedly been the worse for it. The signal exception, if indeed it qualifies as a social science, is structural linguistics (although social anthropology also has some claims in this direction). In structural linguistics, a very detailed scheme of the basic elements of speech exists, based upon the positions of the organs of speech in making sounds. This procedure avoids identifying sounds with those made in any particular language, and even enables one to speak a language tolerably well on the basis of a generalized structural description of its sounds. In other words, structural linguists can create a reasonably close model of the concrete phenomena of speech through a synthesis of its general structural elements. The categories of the fundamental general elements of speech serve structural linguists as a basis for all comparative studies—for example, studies of the similarities of language in order to establish the probability or improbability of common origins.*

The structural abstractions of linguistics are certainly far more informative (i.e., detailed and complete, as well as general) than the structural categories now employed in other social sciences. To say, for example, that a society is "modern" or a

---

* To illustrate, a widely used scheme of structural categories for analyzing speech divides consonants into the following classes: nonnasal labials, including such sounds as those indicated by our p, b, and w; nonnasal dentals (t, d, th); bilabial nasals (m); dental nasals (n); velars (k, g); midpalatal semivowels (y); midpalatal occlusives (ch, j); sibilant fricatives (s, sh, z); liquids (l, r,); aspirates (h); velar nasals (ng); clusters and clicks. Vowels are grouped in three categories: low vowels (a); high front vowels (e, i); and high back vowels (o, u).

"democracy"—or that it has had a "revolution" or has a "stable *Gemeinschaft* set"—is little more revealing than to say that the Swahili word for mother contains a vowel and a consonant.* This analogy is not meant to ridicule such statements, but it *is* meant to belittle them—to convey how little they tell us, even though they do, of course, contain some information. Undoubtedly it is easier to analyze the basic elements of speech and group them in meaningful descriptive "classes" than to do the same for social phenomena like internal war, but difficulty is a bad reason for not trying.

An example of how one might begin to analyze a subject like internal war is provided by Thornton's essay on terror. The paper uses five categories roughly on the same level of discrimination as the concepts "vowels" and "consonants." These categories are the *actors* in terror, their *acts*, the *targets* of their acts, their *objectives*, and the *responses* they achieve. Some of these are then classified further—objectives, for example, into morale-building, advertising, disorientation, the elimination of opponents, and provocation; responses into enthusiasm, fright, and despair. This breakdown is certainly not a definitive "analysis," as Thornton would agree, but it is not inconceivable that it could be elaborated to the point required. Another example on a similar level is provided by Deutsch's paper. Restricting himself to aspects of internal wars that he thinks are quantifiable, he dissects them into a long list of descriptive components—duration, extent (territorial and in terms of participation), and, in regard to participant structures, recruitment rates and rates of attrition, morale, intensity of commitment, coordination, and so forth.† Deutsch's paper does not go so far toward a complete analysis as Thornton's, but, again, it is at least a beginning. So also is the essay by Pye, which recommends five categories as the basis of an analytical dissection and classification of internal wars: the goals they involve, methods of recruitment to the participant structures, methods of indoctrination of the participants, organizational characteristics of the structures, and propensities in decision-making and action of the participants.

---

* Some analytical schema in the social sciences, e.g., Parsons' "pattern variables," come closer to what is wanted.

† See p. 106 for further categories.

One finds such analytical constructs in most writings on internal war. In practically all cases, however, the matter is incipient at best. Discrimination is not carried very far or done very comprehensively. As in classification, the usual procedure in analysis is to pick out some aspects of internal war that arrest one's interest and ignore the rest. This method clearly is not good enough.

Despite the fact that this volume contains much relevant material, I have no analysis of internal war to offer here for which even the possibility of adequacy could be claimed. Social analyses, like those of chemistry and structural linguistics, are not developed by one man or in one set of essays. It seems to me vitally important, however, at least to call attention to the matter. The most urgent pre-theoretical need in internal war studies today is the development, even if only tentative, of basic descriptive categories in terms of which the basic features of internal wars can be identified, in terms of which their nuances and broader features can be depicted in general structural concepts, classes (or types) constructed, and resemblances of cases to one another or to types accurately assessed. Without such categories, one cannot even do work that is itself preliminary to theoretical study, let alone theoretical study proper.

PROBLEMATION. Delimitation, classification, and analysis are all closely related requirements of theory-construction. Equally basic is a requirement of a rather different order. To theorize, it is necessary to have problems to solve. This aspect of pre-theoretical study—which, like other pre-theoretical exercises, occurs in practice during the whole course of theorizing—I call "problemation." The word, admittedly, is ugly and does not exist in common speech. I use it for a purpose, however: to indicate that formulating problems for theory-construction is not simply what it is commonly thought to be, a mere matter of stating interesting interrogative sentences, but a more complicated process that, like other pre-theoretical operations, is not quite as arbitrary as it may seem.

This statement, however, does not apply to the first step in problemation, raising questions. Undoubtedly questions are matters of arbitrary interest; methodological precepts can contribute little to raising them. The ability to put them is a gift, a matter of being imaginative enough to see unresolved issues in empirical experience. It is perhaps this gift above all that divides talented from mediocre social scientists. Having few questions or questions that do not penetrate far or are highly conventional is the mark of the dullard in any field. It is not necessary, however, for every theorist to question entirely for himself. Paradigms and theoretical "approaches" can, to an extent, assist his imagination—that, perhaps, is the ultimate *raison d'être* of the abstract schemes we had hoped the essayists would apply to internal war. In fact, the corpus of any field of study is, in the first instance, an accumulation of issues, resolved or unresolved. From this point of view, at the very least, the present volume is an important contribution to internal war studies.

The questions that are raised in it can be arranged best, perhaps, in relation to the phases through which every internal war must pass.

First of all, the essays contain questions about prerevolutionary conditions. Surprisingly enough, these questions are not in the main concerned with the causes of internal war, at any rate in the sense we usually think of causes. For example, Feldman's paper raises, first and foremost, the question of how one might conceive social structures in order to be able to account for internal wars at all. In other words, he wants to know what image, or model, of a social system allows one to account for violent conflict, as well as for peaceful integration. Some of the basic conceptions of society now employed, he feels, can explain only the latter; in consequence, internal war is conceived as a "pathological" event that must either be explained by exogenous variables or, much more likely, explained away as not "social" at all. Given the sheer frequency of internal wars, this approach seems to him unsatisfactory, and he proposes a model of society than can be used to account for either case—and to shed light on the fact that internal wars occur so frequently, yet not more frequently than they do. This model says nothing directly about the causes of internal war; rather it provides a general frame of reference within which these causes are to be sought. The question to which it is a response is certainly the most basic one that can be raised about the preconditions of internal war or any other social event.

Feldman also makes another point crucial to the treatment of prerevolutionary conditions. He distinguishes between revolutionary "potential" and the actual occurrence of internal wars. The basic point here seems to be that the outbreak of internal wars may be triggered or prevented by a large variety of circumstances, perhaps fortuitous and not susceptible to theoretical study, and that, in consequence, the social scientist should concentrate on revolutionary potential rather than actual revolutions.

How he might do so is another question, but the point itself is important. It implies many other questions not directly posed in Feldman's paper. Is it possible, for example, to find in the study of prerevolutionary societies (as L. P. Edwards and Crane Brinton seem to think) certain "symptoms" of revolutionary potential, conditions that indicate the extent of a society's ripeness for internal war, even if they do not themselves bring about internal war? What can be said about processes that appear necessary to transform revolutionary potential into actuality—for example, about the nucleation of insurgent organizations? Are there conditions that generally facilitate or inhibit the translation of unrest into violence? Do such conditions include, for example, those that affect the capabilities of insurgents or incumbents—terrain, or the network of communications, the attitudes of armies or other social organizations with a great capacity for violence, previous experience in the techniques of internal war, the availability of qualified leadership from indigenous élites or other sources, the support of external forces; or those that tend to turn frustrations into aggression—such important system failures by the established government as defeat in war or such policies by authorities whose existence is precarious as concessions, repression, or diversionary maneuvers; or the very existence or lack of alternative channels for the redress of grievances? Not least, of course, what produces internal war potential—specific social conditions like economic immiseration and a low rate of élite circulation or general social processes like rapid and erratic change of any kind?

William Kornhauser's paper suggests an answer to the last question. Since internal wars are political events, he locates their preconditions (implicitly, anyway) in the political sector of society, specifically in political performance, and relates that to levels of "political development." His paper, however, like that of Janos, is more concerned with the next phase of internal war: its course. The main question in both papers involves the form internal wars are likely to take in particular contexts. For Kornhauser, this question is basically one of whether social struggle centers about the creation of a political identity, centralized authority, "constitutionalism," or equality of political status; and that question in turn is determined by the level of political development in a society. For Janos, the crucial determinant appears to be the power capabilities of the conflicting parties (provided that they act "rationally"). Thornton too raises this question, but in a more limited form, in regard to the conditions under which one kind of internal war, terror, is likely to occur. (For dealing with questions of this sort, it might be noted, the use of an adequate set of classifications is particularly important.)

There are many other questions one can raise about the course of internal wars. The largest number involve, not their general forms, but the sequence of events that takes place in them. Perhaps the classic question of all comparative studies of revolutions is whether or not they follow a predictable course —whether, using Brinton's metaphor, they progress from preliminary symptoms through fever, delirium, convalescence, and finally recovery; or whether they follow the course Sorokin once posited, from a particular degree of control in the prerevolutionary society through uncontrolled anarchical autonomy, a vastly greater amount of control than existed before the revolution, and ultimate restoration of the old level of control. Or does each instance of internal war, or each type, have a sequential pattern of its own, as others (Janos here and Huntington elsewhere) have argued? Even if internal wars themselves do not follow predictable sequences, is it possible to discover such sequences in certain of their aspects? Is it true, for example, that leadership structures become increasingly hierarchical in their course; that in the different phases of internal war different skill groups tend to take over leadership (as Harold Lasswell and Abraham Kaplan suggest)—perhaps ideological skill groups in the initial formation of an insurgent movement, organizational skill groups and masters of violence in the fighting phase, demagogic skill groups in the period when a revolutionary regime must implant itself, administrative skill groups when the regimes become routinized? Is it true that revolutionary aims become increasingly more radical in the course of internal war; that masses and élites on the insurgent side become increasingly differentiated; that the revolutionary struggle necessarily turns from attack on established authorities to conflict among the insurgent groups because of the lack of institutionalized means for settling their disputes?

In this set of essays, such questions appear in rather more modest form. Thornton, for example, conceptualizes the formal phases of internal war without going into their probable content (he writes about the preparatory phase, initial violence, expansion, victory, and consolidation). He also makes a substantive point, however. Terror, he argues, in addition to being a distinguishable type of internal war, tends to play a particularly crucial role in the initial phases of revolutionary conflict—thus illustrating, by the way, how a set of static types can be used to construct a theory of dynamic sequence. The most directly relevant of all the papers, that by Pye, goes into an even more modest, though important and, as far as I know, previously unexplored problem: how the course of events in internal war is conditioned by the initial response that established authorities make to revolutionary threats.

After questions about the courses of internal wars come questions about their outcomes. In the form such questions are usually put—what determines who wins or loses?—this issue is hardly dealt with at all in the essays here. It is, however, raised in a much more sophisticated form by Levy. His argument implies—if I have understood it—that the question of outcome cannot be settled simply by looking at who appears to win or lose. The possibilities he raises are that insurgents may win as individuals, yet fail in their objectives through the persistence of the old order; or that they may be defeated, yet succeed in transforming the social structure in the direction they desire, or some other. Either possibility could be proposed as a serious generalization about all internal wars. Indeed, Levy himself seems to do so; his argument clearly implies that internal wars always succeed in changing societies, regardless of who wins them, even if the changes do not accord with anyone's intentions

—the opposite of one of de Tocqueville's more famous theses. This view also raises the possibility that internal wars, or some types of internal war, may have determinate concrete outcomes, no matter who wins them in the conventional sense. In any event, it seems clear, in the light of Levy's paper, that studies of the outcomes of internal wars must be much more subtle, even in their basic conception of what constitutes an "outcome."

A final set of questions can be raised about the longer-run consequences of internal war, in the manner of Gerschenkron's essay and that by Almond and Verba. The latter explores the impact of internal war on later political attitudes. Gerschenkron discusses certain long-run economic consequences of two great modern revolutions in order to test the Marxian notions that the consequences of revolution can be identified with the program or ideology of the successful revolutionists and that revolutions play a decisive role in economic development, marking, as it were, the real dividing-lines between economic stages. Such an exercise in tracing the repercussions of internal war could of course be carried out in other sectors of social life or, as Deutsch's essay suggests, in the international sphere—note Deutsch's discussion of the spill-over effects of internal wars and their possible conversion into international conflicts. Conceivably one might also be able to draw up a fairly exact balance sheet of the costs and benefits of revolutions (at any rate, assuming certain value preferences) and thus deal more precisely with an age-old issue between radicals and conservatives: whether or not revolutions are worthwhile.

No questions about internal war have been more thoroughly neglected by social scientists, in any generation, than these long-run ones—that perhaps is why only two of the present essays go into them at all. This neglect is most serious in what may well be the most crucial practical question that can be asked about internal war, a question made more pointed by the findings that Almond and Verba report here: How is it possible to re-establish truly legitimate authority after a society has been rent by a revolutionary convulsion? How does one go from a "politics of aspiration" to a settled civic order? It is extremely common for internal war to grow into an institutional pattern of political competition by force, less common for a truly "civil" society to emerge from a major internal war, except in the very long run. What then are the circumstances under which the self-renewing aspects of internal war become, or may become, muted?

These questions are a few of those posed or prompted by the essays in this volume. The list is by no means exhaustive. In particular, we have not yet touched upon any of the "operational" questions raised in the papers, particularly in Pye's—attempts to establish maxims of prudence in regard to internal wars. These questions are better discussed in connection with the next step in problemation.

What, besides stating questions, is needed to formulate problems for theoretical study? One additional requirement is the assessment of questions, to determine whether they are amenable to theoretical treatment. Questions, like subjects, are not all equal. For purposes of theory, it is essential, for example, [that they be really answerable—]and not all questions are. To be sure, whether they are answerable or not is undoubtedly difficult to decide in advance of the attempt to answer them. One test at least, however, can be applied to any question before one tries to answer it (apart from such obvious tests as whether or not it has been clearly put): Is it likely that reliable data concerning the question will be discovered? If not, it is certainly prudent not to raise it, unless the course of inquiry absolutely forces one to do so. Examples include questions about attitudes or culture, wherever extensive survey analysis necessary to get at them cannot be carried out, or questions answerable only on the basis of historical materials that are unavailable, or beyond the reach of the time and skill that social scientists command.

Questions for theoretical study must fulfill another requirement as well—they must concern phenomena that occur frequently enough to permit testable generalization; they must be about theoretical subjects or classes of events. It is surely this point that underlies Feldman's argument that social scientists should study revolutionary "potential" rather than conditions that tend to actualize it. As I have said, the "precipitants" of internal war may be so various that they will defy theoretical treatment. If so, one has no choice but to leave them to the narrative historian, however important they may be.

This requirement is closely related to a third. The questions one raises must be such that *generalizations* (not any kind of statement) can really answer them. It is here that operational questions enter the picture. On the whole, they are, in the light of this third requirement, of somewhat dubious theoretical concern (which is not to say of dubious concern for everyone). There is, to be sure, no hard and fast dividing line between operational and other questions. Certainly it is always possible to derive nonoperational questions from operational ones. Pye's essay, for instance, clearly originates in an operational interest (what can one advise rulers to do about insurgency?) but this interest immediately pushes him to raise nonoperational questions, particularly the question of how initial reactions to insurgency condition subsequent events. It is absolutely essential, however, to go through this process of translation and to realize that answers to questions derived from operational difficulties are not necessarily ways out of the operational difficulties. Pye himself makes this clear. Policy, he points out, must always cope with particular cases, and particular cases may have important unique as well as shared features. Where the unique features are minimal—as Pye claims they are in the case of international wars—prudential maxims may certainly be derived directly from theories; the two are practically equivalent. But where they are considerable, as (still according to Pye) in the case of internal wars, policy cannot be a matter of "doctrines." For this reason, Pye's own paper does not arrive at a set of operational maxims, despite the operational "interests" underlying it. He merely outlines a series of typical policy difficulties that arise in the initial stages of internal war and tend to shape its later course, more to illustrate the irrelevance of the kind of advice usually given governments faced by insurgency than to provide nostrums for them to employ.

It is always prudent to think about one's questions in the light of these criteria (and perhaps others) prior to research. Speculation alone, however, may not suffice. Large-scale research itself may be necessary—not so much to answer the questions as to establish that they are potentially answerable in the form of theories. Hence, this pre-theoretical concern, like the others we have discussed, persists throughout research.

After assessing a question, one more step is required in problemation. This step is much more difficult to discuss abstractly than the others, but it is perhaps even more crucial to the adequacy of the final result of inquiry. It consists of determining what problem must be solved if a question is to be answered. One must always try to discover what is really puzzling about a question, to analyze it to the point where its crucial elements are revealed.

As an example, take Weber's famous question about the origins of modern capitalism in the West. Far from plunging immediately into generalization or empirical study, he first analyzes his question in order to discover what he must generalize about in order to answer it. He does so by first isolating the elements of action characteristic of modern capitalism. He then reflects upon the logical prerequisites of these characteristics, arriving at the conclusion that there are three—a certain level of technology, the modern state system, and certain normative attitudes toward acquisition. He proceeds to initiate comparative empirical inquiry into whether any combination of these prerequisites has existed elsewhere or before modern times and discovers that the requisite technology and governmental system have existed in combination without the consequence of modern capitalism. He therefore concludes that the crucial puzzle raised by his question is, What produced the peculiar attitudes toward acquisition that, like early modern capitalism itself, developed only in certain parts of the West? At this point, he is already very close to his ultimate, and justly famed, solution—but without such an involved process of problemation, including analysis, logical reflection, and empirical inquiry, it is doubtful that he could ever have found it.

In the present volume, perhaps the only example of problemation in this sense is Gerschenkron's essay. The way in which it formulates the problem of assessing the economic consequences of revolution is, in the present writer's view, at least as important as its substantive finding. One of the recurrent themes of the search for puzzles within questions does, however, pervade the other essays: the concern with crucial setting variables. Social life has many facets that are closely intertwined. Much of the art of theoretical study in social science, consequently, is to disentangle these facets and to find the strands crucial to one's own concern. The present volume does not succeed in doing so for the whole subject of internal war. It does, however, go some distance toward preparing the ground—toward clarifying what setting variables might be considered crucial to questions about internal war and how they vary. Those treated at length include social value systems (Lipset and Levy), the degree and rate of social differentiation (Feldman), political development (Kornhauser), structures of authority (Janos), and the "integration" of the political and social spheres (Pye).

At the present stage of inquiry into internal war, the crucial issues, in my view, are all of the order of those I have discussed —pre-theoretical issues (although many of them, fortunately, can be combined with, and indeed require, substantive inquiries). I have been at pains to emphasize this point above all because the understandable desire for substantive findings has tended to inhibit adequate consideration of such issues—and thereby achievement of the results desired. And I have done so at some length mainly in order to clarify in detail how the present papers, while not intended to deal directly with these concerns, relate to them.

The papers should not, of course, be read exclusively from the point of view set forth in this introduction. Because they were written from many other perspectives and for many other purposes, they contain much else of interest. For the same reason, I regret that this introduction may seem, at some points, to belittle them. Wherever that may be the case, the reasons are that the issue before me was not that before the authors (however relevant their remarks) and that I particularly want to stress how much remains to be done before we can be reasonably confident of our approaches to the theoretical study of internal war.

*Talcott Parsons*

## SOME REFLECTIONS ON

## THE PLACE OF FORCE

## IN SOCIAL PROCESS

Considering the scope of this volume, it has seemed to me that the most useful contribution I could make would be to attempt a general analytical approach to examining the place of force in the operation of social systems. This theme, of course, runs through, not only the whole of the present volume, but a vast body of literature in the political field. There seems, however, to be a notable lack of concerted attempts at a general theoretical attack on the problem. This essay may, it is hoped, provide reference points that will help make some of the more empirical analyses more meaningful in terms of their theoretical premises and implications.

It is conceived as an application and further development of a general conceptual scheme for the analysis of social systems. The whole scheme cannot be presented here, but an attempt will be made to present the essential assumptions on which the more circumstantial discussion is based. It should also be kept in mind that the scheme is in process of continuing development, and reference to the author's previous writings probably cannot therefore provide full elucidation of the present bases of the argument in the scheme.[1]

### Force and Systems of Normative Order

This volume's concern is with internal war, and of course the hallmark of war of any sort is violence. It is perhaps worth

[ 33 ]

remarking initially that the line between internal and external war is theoretically a gradual one. A relatively established "politically organized society" is clearly a "moral community" to some degree, its members sharing common norms, values, and culture—which is to say that I start with a view that repudiates the idea that any political system that rests *entirely* on self-interest, force, or a combination of them, can be stable over any considerable period of time. If the politically organized community is a moral community, however, it is equally important that at least *some* elements of moral community have generally transcended the area of political sovereignty, in the usual sense. To give only essentially trite examples, certainly the Greeks who so self-consciously distinguished themselves from barbarians constituted such a community, so that the very prevalent wars between the *polis* units were in a sense "civil wars." In more recent times, the conception of Christendom has not been a totally meaningless one, yet we are all too familiar with the prevalence of war in modern European history. Hence there is good reason to believe that a general treatment of the use of force in society will not be inapplicable simply because the internal and the external contexts of its use are radically different.

The primary reference for the concept of force—a term that I prefer, on the whole, to "violence"—is as an aspect of social interaction. Force is a "way" not necessarily always a "means"— in which one unit in a system of social interaction may act toward another, whether the unit be an individual or a collectivity. Within this framework, then, force is the use of control of the situation in which "alter"—the unit that is the object of "ego's" action—is subjected to *physical* means to prevent him from doing something ego does not wish him to do, to "punish" him for doing something that, from ego's point of view, he should not have done (which may in turn be intended to deter him from doing similar things in the future), or to demonstrate "symbolically" the capacity of ego to control the situation, even apart from ego's specific expectations that alter may desire to do things that are undesirable from ego's point of view. I do not speak of the use of force unless the action or its "threat" is "oriented" to an alter on whom it is expected to have an impact, e.g., by frightening him or of making it impossible for him to carry out his own actual or conceivable intentions.

Seen in this perspective, the concept of force as a "way" of acting is inherently negative in its meaning to alter. It always concerns the *undesired* consequences (although from *some* points of view not taken in this discussion, they may also be desired, as in the case of martyrdom)—that alter would on the face of it like to avoid—of *his* actually or potentially acting in a certain way. Thus if ego conducts certain physical operations in his environment that may unintentionally have an injurious effect on an alter—an accident caused by negligently fast driving of a car, for example—his action does not constitute "use of force" in social action, in the present sense. Nor would we, for present purposes, treat the "forcible" holding of a child for a hypodermic injection as a use of force; it is at most only a completely marginal case.

It is the "intention" of the actor in actually using or threatening force that is our central criterion, and such intentions we have classified in three types: *deterrence* from undesired action; *punishment* for negatively valued acts actually committed; and symbolic *demonstration* of capacity to act, without orientation to specific contexts of either deterrence or intention to punish.* It has already become evident that this classification, important as it is, is cut across by another that we must keep clearly in mind.

We have stated the problem of force in the frame of reference of social interaction. Interaction, however, is a process that occurs over time, and one of its most important characteristics is that an act of ego will be a stimulus to a reaction of alter, which will in turn be the stimulus to the next act of ego, and so forth. If ego then has an ultimate intention he hopes to realize, what we usually call a "goal," he will envisage a series of "interacts" between himself and alter in the period intervening between his initiation of the process and the possible consum-

---

* We have spoken of both actors and objects as either individual or collective. When we refer to a collectivity as having "intentions," they are, of course, in the *psychological* sense, the intentions of individual persons acting in roles by virtue of which their decisions can bind the collectivity. Thus a general's decision to attack may be interpreted as activating a process involving the whole collectivity—the military units he commands. For most of our purposes, it is not necessary to pursue these problems of mechanism in the relation between collectivities and individual personalities—to say that "the Third Army Group intends to attack" is not merely metaphorical.

mation of his goal. The problem of how he intends to take account of the reciprocal intentions of alter and his actions in the intermediate stages thus becomes one of the central problems.

If we take deterrence as the simplest and, in many ways, the most important of the three meanings of force, another basic distinction immediately becomes evident. On the one hand, ego may attempt to deter alter by acting so as to make his carrying out undesired intentions realistically impossible—or nearly so. We would refer to this behavior as *compulsion*. A classic example would be the arrest and imprisonment of persons whose future action is feared, without giving them any choice in the matter. The alternative to compulsion in this respect is *coercion*. By this term, we mean "threatening" to use force *if* alter carries through the presumed undesired (by ego) intentions. If alter then disregards the threat and carries out his act, the use of force against him becomes a punishment, although the primary intention of ego may still be deterrence and he may be deeply regretful at having to carry out his threats and actually to resort to force. Conversely, of course, the actual implementation of force may, although it is a punishment in the particular case, be thought of more broadly as a deterrent, both for alter's future action—he may have been "taught a lesson"—and for third parties who thereby find out what happens to noncompliers, including the lesson that ego "means it" when he says the forbidden act should not be performed. There is an important relativity between the positive and the negative here. The last statement has been phrased in terms of the performance of acts that have been forbidden. For most of the purposes of our discussion, however, it would not matter if it were an omission of acts that had been prescribed. Thus failing to pay assessed taxes is as punishable as parking under a no-parking sign. For some purposes, however, it is important to distinguish these cases, since coercive threats may not be able to motivate new commitments in exactly the same way that they can deter from abandonment of those already assumed. This problem belongs in the general context of asymmetry between positive and negative motivation, which we will take up presently.

What we will call the "demonstration case," which in this particular context is a "show of force," clearly must have the

meaning of intended deterrence and not immediately of punishment. It is not, however, made contingent on specific forbidden
or disapproved acts. It may then be said to be of the nature of
a *warning* rather than a threat, if the distinction may be made
in terms of relative diffuseness *vs.* specificity. A threat then is
a direct expression of intention to impose a specific negative
sanction, contingent on performance of a forbidden or disapproved act; a warning is a demonstration of the capacity and
readiness to act should alter perform any of a much wider
range of actions undesired by ego. The appropriate "emotion"
on alter's part, in response to a threat, is fear—to a warning,
anxiety. In either case, of course, the negative emotion may be
overcome by "courage" or "resolution." In popular speech, we
often use unrealistic absolutes—we say he had no fear at all,
when we really mean that his courage was sufficient to overcome
his fear.

### Force and the Problem of Social Control

It is implicit in the way we have approached the problem
of the use of force that the primary common element of the
three components of meaning we have distinguished is *control*,
to which, because of the context of interaction, we may add the
adjective "social." Force is a way of trying to "make sure" that
alter acts in a desired manner or refrains from acting in an undesired one. We have formulated the approach in terms of ego,
conceived as a *unit* in a social system, that exercises control over
the actions of other units, here called "alters." One highly relevant problem is, however, to determine how this formulation is
related to the mechanisms by which the actions of all units in
a system are controlled—or fail to be controlled—from the point
of view of the operation of the system as a system. Before approaching this problem, it is necessary to place the problem of
the use of force in a more general context at the level of the
interaction of units of a system.

From this point of view of control, clearly the primary meaning of force is as deterrent. Indeed, from various points of view,
it can be said to be the ultimate deterrent. This statement, how-

ever, clearly refers to the context we have called "compulsion." Truly effective imprisonment, which makes escape literally impossible—a limiting case—and blocks all communication between the prisoner and possible associates, can prevent his acting as he intended. Even more drastic is the killing of alter, since dead men do not act, in our sense—at least the possibilities of escape and of communication leaks are closed by "liquidation." The indirect consequences for the actions of others of knowledge that this compulsion has been exercised, introduces many complications, of course, so that groups perfectly able to use compulsion, and ardently desiring to do so, often refrain through consideration of the indirect consequences. But this point is aside from the main argument.

The use of force as threat or warning is, of course, much more problematical even in its more immediate consequences. As threat, alter may view it in terms of cost and he may consider noncompliance quite worthwhile. As warning it may be discounted in various ways or serve only to activate resistance. In the light of these complications, it becomes imperative to consider the problem of these possibilities, of compulsion as well as of deterrence, in a wider context. The essential point is that force is only one among a number of means of controlling the action of alters coercively and, furthermore, that coercion— even by other threats than those of force—is itself only one of several modes of controlling such action at the unit-to-unit level.

Let us approach the latter problem first. We presume here a paradigm in which, on the one hand, there are two main *channels* through which ego may seek to control alter's action and, on the other hand, there are two main *modes* of such control, modes that may in turn be subdivided according to whether or not options are left open to alter.

The channels are the exercise of control over the *situation* in which alter is placed and, control over his "intentions." The second dimension, which we have called a "mode" of control, is a matter of whether ego's actual or proposed action toward alter is favorable or unfavorable from alter's point of view. On the basis of *contingency* of ego's act on alter's response to his "definition of the situation"—through a threat, for example—we may distinguish four types of attempted control:

1. Situational channel, positive sanction: the offer of positive advantages to alter, conditional on his compliance with ego's wishes or "suggestions." We call this process *inducement*. Economic exchange is the prototypical case.

2. Situational channel, negative sanction: the threat of disadvantage, imposed through ego's control of alter's situation, conditional on alter's *non*compliance with ego's wishes or suggestions. This approach is what we have called *coercion*. The use of power is the prototypical case.

3. Intentional channel, positive sanction: the offer of "good reasons" why, in the circumstances and without either offer of contingent advantages or the threat of contingent disadvantages, ego argues that it is to the "interest" of alter to comply with ego's wishes or suggestions. This mode of control we will call *persuasion*. It includes transmitting information, in addition to an appeal to alter to do what he "really wants to do."

4. Intentional channel, negative sanction: the threat or warning that, independently of any advantageous or disadvantageous changes in the situation imposed contingently by ego, it would not be "right" for alter to fail to comply with ego's suggestions on how he should act, in terms of alter's *own* standards of right action. This mode we may call *activation of commitments*. Appeal to "conscience" is the prototypical case.

Each of these types can—with respect to the time left open to alter to make a decision, ego's "tolerance" of his position and hence willingness to hear his case, etc.—be "foreshortened" in the same basic sense in which compulsion, as we have discussed it, foreshortens coercion. Compulsion thus is the limiting case where alter is in principle left no alternative; "compliance" is simply "being compelled." In the case of inducement, the element of contingency may be constricted, or even eliminated, by ego "insisting" on "doing something for" alter, whether alter likes it or not. The *gift* in the ideal-type sense, which leaves no option of refusal open, is the prototypical case. To fit our paradigm, a gift in this sense must be something of situational value, rather than a purely symbolic expression of sentiment.

As a corresponding limit to contingency in case 4, we may speak of "moral compulsion"—putting alter in such an acute "dilemma of conscience" that it is "unthinkable" for him to choose an alternative other than the one ego desires. A suitable if extreme example would be the use of hostages to control the action of an alter beyond the range of physical control. Thus if a citizen of a totalitarian society is abroad, the totalitarian authorities may try to control him by threatening to kill or torture his next of kin, whom they do physically control, unless he complies with their wishes. Bringing about the torture or death of a spouse or child by failing to comply would be, at the level in question, "unthinkable."

For reasons that we will develop later, there is a special relation between what we have called persuasion and member-ship in solidary groups. If this relation is accepted, we may infer that, at the *social* level with which we are directly concerned, the limit of persuasion is simply assertion of the imperative meaning of the "we" that comprises ego and alter together. At that point persuasion is no longer merely the argument that, since you are a "such-and-such," you should comply with ego's wishes, that it is to your interest to "do so and so." The pressure is sharpened instead to the point where the assertion is that "we such-and-suches *do* so and so," with the clear implication that, if you do not, you are not "really" a such-and-such. The clear implication is that the such-and-such who does not comply is subject to exclusion. This implication raises further problems, but the immediate point is the assertion that "we do" certain things, and the question is whether or not alter will go along.

### Sanctions and Generalized Mechanisms of Control

According to the above paradigm, the deterrent use of force against the specific alter is an appropriate sanction in only one of the four major types of action oriented to control of an alter by an ego. That is to say, it is pre-eminently a means of coercion, through conditional threat and, at the extreme limit, of com-pulsion through the prevention of undesired action by alter. If, for the time being, we focus on coercion as a case that leaves a range of choices open to alter yet is but one of four ways of controlling him by manipulating contingent sanctions, what can we say about the place of force among the means of coercing compliance through the threat of negative sanctions and about the relation of a set of threat-sanctions to others that can conceivably control behavior?

First, a coercive threat can be that of *any* alteration in the situation in which alter acts that ego has the capacity to impose, depending on alter's compliance or noncompliance. If, however, we adhere strictly to the prime meaning of deterrence, it seems possible to designate one major dimension of variation in degrees of severity of contingent situational negative sanctions. This dimension is the *power* of alter effectively to carry out his intentions, regardless of ego's wishes—not necessarily against them, but *independently* of them. This power, which is, as we shall see, dependent on a number of other factors, is vulnerable to situational negative sanctions—which we interpret as counter-power—through the factors of capacity and opportunity for its exercise. Capacity in turn means essentially command of the facilities necessary for effective action, while opportunity is access to the support of those units that have somehow become or expect to become dependent on the output of the units in question.

Negative sanctions then, consist in the deterrent sense, of threatened deprivations of power, or the potential for effective action resulting from capacity, opportunity, or both. On this basis, it is possible to construct a scale of degrees of deprivation of effectiveness-potential. This step will necessitate, in turn, fitting a number of factors into an ordinal scale, which is too complex a problem to enter upon here. Suffice it to say that there seem to be two main sets that can be related in a tentative way. The criterion is the capacity of alter to affect adversely the interests of ego, in the simple sense of doing what ego does not want him to do, especially, we suggest, through enlisting the co-operation of third parties. One set of factors will comprise alter's resources without special constraints on how he shall use them. Thus monetary fines reduce his financial resources but do not impose limits on how he shall use those remaining to him. The other set comprises those special constraints.

Here the critical factor seems to be deprivation of liberty. Since in social conditions the most effective action is collective action, the most important liberty is liberty to co-operate with others, to participate in collective action. Furthermore, the most important single condition of effective co-operation is communication with others. The most important deprivations of liberty are therefore those that block communication, in order to limit or prevent altogether co-operation with others.

Physical force may be an important instrument in the enforcement of *any* deprivation. It is, however, intrinsic in the deprivation itself, particularly in deprivations of liberty. Although fines and taxation are backed by force, for example, the process of implementing such sanctions by taking over financial assets is ordinarily not a forcible one. If, however, an act of enforcement is challenged, the question of what to do in case of refusal to comply arises. This question can always lead to the problem of force, for resistance can be made effective by alter, through such physical means as leaving the field commanded by ego or removing assets from it. The ultimate preventive of such evasion is force. Hence in a very broad sense we conclude that force is an "end-of-the-line" conception of a type of negative sanction that can be effective—in the context of deterrence, please note— when milder measures fail.

From this argument it *must not* be inferred that what we are calling "power" is a simple linear function of the command of physical force. In the context of deterrence, we conceive force to be a residual means that, in a showdown, is more effective than any alternative. Power, on the other hand we conceive to be a *generalized medium* for controlling action—one among others—the effectiveness of which is dependent on a variety of factors of which control of force is only one, although a strategic one in *certain* contexts. To approach the problem of the relation between the two it is necessary to go back to the general paradigm of modes of social control.

We have held that coercion is one of a family of modes of controlling action in interunit relations, the others being inducement, persuasion, and activation of commitments. Similarly we hold that what we call "power" is one of a family of *generalized media* of the interaction process. The others are *money*, what, in a special sense, we call *influence*, and the special category of *commitments*. Because of its familiarity, it is best to begin the discussion with money.

Money is generally recognized to be a medium of exchange that is generalized in the sense that it is not simply another commodity but one that is acceptable in exchange for an indefinite range of different commodities and services. The latter category, as we shall argue, raises special problems. Money may be regarded from two points of view. On one hand, it is an institutionalized medium and measure, functioning in exchange transactions within a system. In this context, it is the medium to which units are expected to resort in securing access to resources through exchange and that they are obligated to accept in the case of *bona fide* offers—a binding obligation in areas where the concept of "legal tender" applies. On the other hand, from the point of view of the unit, it is a generalized *means* of securing what is wanted through the exchange process. But the reciprocal of using money to get what one wants is willingness to accept money in exchange for relinquishing rights in valued objects—accepting a valuation in money.

In common with both these levels is the fact that money is, in the first instance, a mechanism of communication; the monetary unit therefore is clearly a *symbol*. In a special prescriptive way—as categorized by Charles Morris—it symbolizes economic productivity. The prescription comes in its property of commanding a share of this productivity, specified as a particular commodity or service according to the wishes of the spender of money. Symbolization is, however, also involved in a second way, in that the concrete instrument—for example, a dollar bill—is a symbol to the unit and "in itself" is "worthless." It does not seem to be stretching matters too far to say that money is a highly specialized language, in which things "said" are not merely informative but also imperative. Money is a generalized symbolic medium of inducement, in that its offer in specific amounts is the offer of a conditional improvement of the advantageousness of alter's situation: The more money he has, the greater is his command of the immense range of utilities purchasable in the market system.

The question then arises: On what basis does the "value of money" rest? Clearly, if what is offered is a symbol, it cannot rest on the "intrinsic" worth of the object concretely offered—in the case of cash, the paper bills are virtually if not wholly worthless "in themselves." There are two directions in which this question can be followed. One is the suggestion that the symbolic object represents other concrete objects that themselves have this quality of value. This suggestion implies the continuum along which entries on certain account books, like the depositor's balance in his bank account, "represent" the cash to which he has a claim, so that he somehow "really" has not a generalized claim against the bank but instead "owns" particular dollars in cash, for which the bank acts as trustee. The cash then is also a symbol in a further series, in that it represents a "promise to pay," on the part of a bank of issue or of government, something of still more indubitable value—a certain amount of monetary metal. Along this line of symbolic relationships then, what a dollar on deposit "means" is that it is the equivalent first of cash, then of metal. The inference is clearly that the "real" basis of the value of any kind of money is the "intrinsic" (or as the economists say, "commodity") value of given quantities of the monetary metal, usually gold, and that somehow other components of alleged value are "fictitious."

It is by now a commonplace of economics—accepted even by tough businessmen—that this description does not tell quite the whole story. There are, to be sure, circumstances in which the holder of funds who is in a position to turn them into gold is in a more secure position than the one who is not. But they are not the "normal" circumstances of monetary transaction. First, nearly the last thing an ordinary party to such transactions thinks of is to demand gold for hoarding in place of the other forms of money. Second, and more important, if every holder of money assets did so, the whole monetary system would collapse and with it most of the economic process.

This statement is true, of course, because the monetary metal is not itself the primary form of money but only the base on which a complex structure of credit is erected. The focus of this structure is the banking function, by virtue of which dollars do double duty. That is, the bank simply does not have—at the cash level—enough dollars at any given time to meet its commitments to its depositors. If it did, it would simply be a storage vault, not a bank, and the increase of productivity facilitated by the creation of credit would be cut off. Yet, it must be noted, every depositor has the formal right to payment in full in cash on demand. If gold were the only "good" money, there would be an enormous constriction of the general flow of exchange transactions.

The other direction in which a series of symbolic references to the value of money can be followed involves, not the solidity of the base on which the structure is erected, but the nature of the structure itself and, in particular, the functions it performs. These functions are no more derivable from the properties of gold as a metal than are the functions of good nutrition for a population derivable from the properties of a particular category of soil.

This line of analysis leads to consideration of the conditions of productivity and hence the positive significance, not only of technological efficiency, but of the division of labor and exchange. In this context, money symbolizes, as suggested, not the base of ultimate security for the isolated individual holder of funds, but the potential of productivity achievable through a *system* of productive activity. In this context, the size of the pie to be cut is a function of the general utilizability of the products of production and therefore of the fluidity of resources available for allocation among many uses, which amounts to exchangeability.

The ultimate reference in this direction is not the intrinsic "worth" of a particularized base but the ordered reliability of an organized collective system of productive activities. The primary basis of the value of money is general confidence that expectations of the productivity of the system will be realized. If, however, such a productive system is to be ordered on a social basis, it must involve an institutionalized framework of expectations, notably though by no means exclusively expectations of the fulfillment of obligations in a contractual system. It is the stability of this system of expectations and therefore the belief that the acceptor of money will not lose because of any likelihood that the system will collapse that is the main basis for establishing money as a generalized medium of exchange.

From the limited point of view of a participating unit, such a system is a case of "operation bootstrap." The rational ground for confidence in money is that others have confidence in money and that this confidence is generally shared—which confidence for the "realist" seems to provide complete demonstration of the unreliability of all monetary systems except those restricted to solid gold. If such mutual confidence is in fact adequately institutionalized, however, it is the basis of a far higher potential of productivity than any conceivable "sound" money could be.

This argument is not merely a gratuitous digression into the commonplaces of economics. It is presented in order to demonstrate an exact parallel between money and power. The money held by a social unit is, we may say, the unit's capacity, through market channels under given rules of procedure, to command goods and services in exchange, which for its own reasons it desires. Correspondingly, the power of a unit is its capacity, through invoking binding obligations to contribute to collective goals, to bring about collective goal-outputs that the "constituents" of the processes of collective action in question desire. Unlike money, it may or may not operate through the market channel, through the offer of inducements. But once units are brought within the relevant context of collective organization, power is the medium of invoking their obligations to contribute to collective functioning. The implication of this argument is that failure to contribute as "asked" is subject to negative sanction in a sense parallel to that in which failure to accept an offer of inducement is subject to withdrawal of the offer and, potentially at least, to transfer of its benefits to a competitor.

The stability of monetary systems may be said to depend on their participants' continuing willingness to entrust their interests to a system, in the nature of which there can be no immediate, barter-like *quid pro quo* of value for every exchange. Indeed, the very meaning of money is that it is intrinsically valueless, so that there is a sense in which the acceptor of money gives up something valued for something worthless. We hold that the same principle applies to power systems. They depend on the continuing willingness of their members to entrust their stakes in and interpretations of the collective interest to an impersonal process in which binding decisions are made without the members' being in a position to control them. Giving a "mandate" to leadership is only one of a number of possibilities in this connection.

For participants in power systems, impairment of this willingness to entrust the collective interest to an institutionalized process may take the form of various levels of reservation—either of refusal to make commitments or withdrawal from the implementation of commitments already made. There is a continuum from full participation to total withdrawal, for example in resignation. But this continuum does not exhaust the matter. There is also the possibility of using positions *vis-à-vis* a collectivity—inside or outside it—to obstruct the process of collective goal-achievement.

Insofar as a member of a collectivity—or a unit in its environment—is in a position to exercise some degree of control over it, he may be motivated to withdraw resources on which it has counted or to take positive measures to obstruct its operations, a tendency that may be countered by attempts on the part of the "leadership" of the collectivity to maintain control over such resources. The meeting ground of these countertendencies seems to lie in the concept of coercion. To the extent that withdrawal of co-operation is oriented to deterrence of collective function and therefore serves as a threat of negative sanction, it is a way of coercing the collectivity—total noncontingent withdrawal through unannounced resignation is of course a case of compulsion. The strike is a clear case of coercion through contingent withdrawal. On the other side, deterrence by withdrawal may well call into play at least the contingency of coercive countermeasures, in that cooperation is obligatory in more than a "moral" sense and there are negative sanctions for failure to comply.

The attempt has been to formulate this complex in such a way that the distinction between the use of power as capacity to give binding assurances of the effectiveness of collective action, on the one hand, and the dependence on any one particular means of enforcement in case of noncompliance, on the other, stands out. Force in power systems is, we suggest, a particular means of enforcement. The question of whether it is or is not the "basis" of power is ambiguous in a sense exactly parallel to that of the question of "basing" the value of money on command of gold reserves. In the possible process of "deflationary" interaction between threats of withdrawal of contributory resources and tightening the conditions from which benefits of participation will be accorded, there is a general constriction, on the one hand, of the resources available for collective action and, on the other hand, of the degrees of freedom opened up by the availability of collective facilities of organization. Beyond this process, there is the interplay between attempts to disrupt collective operations and the attempt to forestall this disruption coercively. In this vicious circle, the threats on *both* sides readily reach the point where they become threats of force.

That is to say, in a vicious circle of threatening progressively more drastic coercive sanctions, the use of force is the end of the line. In this type of showdown, the commander of force can "protect his interests," that is he can win against those weaker in the command of force in the same sense that the controller of gold can keep his assets while those who somehow failed to secure gold lose out. Forcing the system to this point, however, means that the security of a minority is bought at the expense of a drastic deflation of the system's potential—for production in the economic case and for effective collective action in the political case. In this respect, the use of force occupies a place in power systems parallel to that of gold in monetary systems.*

### The Relations among Money, Power, and Influence

We have suggested a parallel between money as a generalized medium of inducement and power as a generalized medium of coercion. Since they belong in the still larger families of modes of social control and generalized media that operate in the process of control, we suggest that the process of persuasion also operates through a type of generalized medium—in systems of persuasive communication that have become sufficiently differentiated so that the "barter" stage has been transcended. This medium we shall call *influence* in a special technical sense. The activation of commitments should also be so characterized. Here we can speak of *real commitments*, using the term "real" as it is

---

* I am indebted to Professor Karl W. Deutsch (oral communication) for this insight.

used in economic theory as a contrast to "monetary." In this present paper, there will be less occasion to develop this last concept than the other three, so the reader will have to rest content with a rather truncated analysis.

The problem of influence can be better approached if a little more is said about the relations between the uses of power and of money. Money is a medium of exchange that operates precisely as a medium of social control when, with respect to the specific subject-matter at hand, the relations of ego are characterized neither by binding mutual obligations nor by a common solidarity. They are, very importantly, part of a wider system governed by a normative order and a set of values, but neither the rules nor any collective solidarity prescribe what ego and alter can expect of each other until they have entered into an agreement—the normative form par excellence being that of the contract.

The contract basically bridges the relation between inducement and coercion, and thus between money and power, in that contractual agreements, once entered into, become binding—in the extreme case, through the law of the state. Among the important types of contract is one that brings previously "free" resources within the control of a collectivity. For most purposes, these resources can be classified under three headings: physical resources, which, in an economic context, are called "commodities"; monetary resources, which include money or assets offering monetary liquidity; and human services, accessible, sociologically speaking, for performance in *roles*. Physical and monetary resources come to be merely "possessed" by a collectivity—the relevant institutional category is that of property—while human resources are "controlled" by authority on behalf of the collectivity, which has power over them in our strict technical sense. Collectivities can also contract to perform services, but, for the sake of simplicity, we shall confine the present discussion to the services of individuals.

The procedures by which a collectivity gains power over services or possession of property rights can vary over the whole range of the situational channel of social control as we have outlined it. At one pole is compulsion, which is typified by taxation, and among the means of compulsion may be force, although most generally it is held in reserve. At the other pole is "contribution" in the sense that resources are made available as a completely free gift—in the case of services, we say they are "voluntary." The most important middle cases are those of contract—in the physical and monetary instances, by "purchase" or loan; in that of services, by employment, which may or may not be called "purchase." Weber called this case "formally free labor," and it is, of course, the principal case in modern "bureaucratic" organization.

In the case of physical and financial possessions, a collectivity need not acquire power over them since they are not actors; there is no problem of whether or not they "comply" with ego's wishes. In the case of services, however, this aspect is crucial. The crucial factors in the exercise of power here are, on the one hand, the obligations assumed through the contract of employment and, on the other hand, the needs of the collectivity or organization as defined in terms of the exigencies for its effective operation in pursuit of the attainment of its goals.

We conceive of the transactions centering on the contract of employment as an *interchange* of power (and of economic utilities) between the performers of services and the organizations who, by employing them, utilize those services. The organization, through its executive officers, "spends" power in making commitments for the modes of utilization of the resources it controls, the implementation of which is to be carried out by employed persons. From the point of view of those persons, however, this arrangement constitutes a receipt of power. They receive "authorization" to operate *within* the organization effectively in making their "contribution" to its functioning. The input of power, which to some extent balances this output, is derived from the commitments of employed personnel to performance of services within the framework of roles in the organization. The power to operate thus acquired is then used in the framework of what we call the authority of office. When we speak of an approximate balancing of these elements, we mean it to apply to the aggregate inputs and outputs for the system of reference as a whole, not for any particular unit.

The other medium with which these interchanges are immediately articulated is that of money or resources controlled by money. In the external relations of an organization, monetary funds are the direct means of securing control over resources, both goods and services. Internally, the budget is the monetary aspect of control.*

The essential point to be made here is that money is the most general medium for the control of fluid resources, providing the potentiality of their acquisition through the market mechanism. Power then is the mechanism for their *mobilization* in the interest of effective collective action, which is what we mean by the process or organization of power. The bindingness of decisions, which is involved in the concept of power, and with it the involvement of negative sanctions—which must be threatened for noncompliance and actually implemented when noncompliance occurs—are conditions of effective organization.

The conditions on which these resources, particularly services, are made available to an organization must be distinguished analytically from the conditions of their utilization once committed to the organization. In the free market situation, to take an example of the first, money takes precedence over power, particularly because of an institutionalized insulation between the internal and the external contexts. The private organization— and some that are public—is forbidden to pre-empt resources from outside, either by compulsion or by coercive threats. Internally, however, power takes precedence over money. Budgetary resources are allocated rather than bargained for—in the ideal type, of course—and disposition of personnel at the higher levels is by assignment through executive decision, rather than by contract. This statement does not in the least mean that we accept without reservation the dominance of the concept of "line authority" in the functioning of organizations, but the use of authority does constitute a radical difference from the prototypical market—an organization that attempted to function internally on strictly market principles would not be very effective.

Here is a good opportunity to introduce another very important point about the relations between power and money, which

---

* This argument is an exceedingly condensed statement of a set of boundary-interchange relations, between economy and polity, as we conceive them. For a fuller discussion see "On the Concept of Political Power," Note 1 at the end of this chapter.

can be extended to those between positive and negative sanction systems generally. This point involves an essential *asymmetry*, which consists in the fact that the offer of a positive sanction commits the agent of the offer to implement his promise if alter complies with his wishes and accepts his offer. If it is a monetary offer, ego must pay if he is offered a commodity or service on the terms on which he and alter have agreed. In the case of negative sanctions, however, so far as they are contingent, compliance has the opposite effect. Ego is expected not to follow through with implementation of the sanction, which would indeed be a breach of faith, since the understanding was that if alter would comply, ego would refrain from imposing the threatened disadvantage on him.

There is a variety of implications of this asymmetry. One of the most important is that, when a system of normative order is functioning smoothly, the negative aspect of it is not highly visible because compliance is the rule rather than the exception. Negative sanctions therefore often remain, not only unimplemented, but only implicitly threatened. The positive sanction system, however, is highly visible, in that rewards are continually being given. The flow of monetary transactions that mean rewards may be very high, while that of the uses of power in a punitive sense may be low.

Above all, it should be remembered that, in our terms, the use of power is not to be equated with punishment, as we have defined it. The use of power is, in the unit-to-unit context, the control of alter's action through the invoking of binding obligations. If these obligations are fulfilled without resistance, there is no occasion for even threatening negative sanctions explicitly, to say nothing of actually implementing them—that is, punishing noncompliance. To speak of the holder of authority in these circumstances as not having or using power is, in our opinion, highly misleading. The question of his capacity to coerce or compel in case of noncompliance is an independent question that involves the question of handling unexpected and exceptional conditions for which the current power system may or may not be prepared. This question is parallel to that of a monetary system subjected to unusual pressures toward liquidity. Above all, the effectiveness of a power system should not be judged either by the degree to which it habitually resorts to the explicit threat of force or even by the aggregate amount of force at its disposal. The "need" for the latter may be highly variable in different power systems.

It has seemed best to deal with the case of power in a private organization first, rather than to adopt the customary focus on government, precisely because this perspective illuminates the relations between the power and the money media. Contrary to usual opinion, it may be argued that the case of government is analytically a special case. In government, the differentiation between the internal conditions of power precedence and the external conditions of market precedence is not allowed to proceed so far as in private organizations in a "liberal" society. Internally the power of government is generalized in the authority to pre-empt resources by compulsion, although it is a notable feature of such authority that in a liberal society it is normally confined to monetary resources (taxation) and physical resources (eminent domain). Only in emergencies is it extended to human services, the notable case being conscription for military service. That does not mean that market transactions are closed to government procurement in general. Employment of services plays a very big role, as do sale of commodities and of collective services to a lesser extent. The sale of financial assets in the form of government securities is, however, a major factor.

Externally, the essential point is that government maintains a particularly strict control over its own and its nationals' dealings with those of other societies through foreign trade, financial transactions, and the movement of persons. This control is, of course, an aspect of control over the territorial boundaries of a politically organized society. Again, the extensions of coercive authority and therefore the use of power by government in such connections should not be construed as definitive of such authority and power in an analytical sense, above all of the special part played by the use of force in such connections—internally in the form of police forces, externally in the form of military forces.

There is a second major area of the involvement of power besides the implementation of collective policies, as the one just discussed may be called. It is what in some political connections we have been calling the *support* system.[2] Its prototype is the democratic membership participation in the association, including the electoral aspect of governmental collectivities. Power here takes the output form of policy, distinguished from implementive—or administrative—agency, but remains within the context of membership and its responsibilities. The input of support for the executive elements is then political support, exercised, in the fully institutionalized instance, through the voting procedure, which confers the authority of office—which we construe as power—on a leadership element. The familiar complex of capacity to act through the mobilization of binding commitments applies here, as well as in the earlier context, and it applies in both directions. Thus the "verdict of the polls" is a binding decision by the electorate; even though each individual voter may have very little power, the aggregate of votes decides.

Here, however, power does not articulate through the medium of money but through influence, as we have defined it in our technical sense. The mode of control in this case is persuasion. We have defined "persuasion" as an offer of good reasons why alter should, in his own interest, act in accord with ego's wishes. The contingent positive sanction attached to persuasion is *acceptance*, which is an attitudinal as distinct from a situational sanction.

We may speak of influence then as generalized capacity to persuade through the offer of contingent acceptance. A person or collective unit with influence is one that has high generalized persuasive capacity in controlling the action of other units. As in the cases of money and power, it is important not to infer that "need for acceptance" is typically the dominating motive for alter to allow himself to be persuaded by ego. When we speak of acceptance as the relevant type of positive sanction, we imply that it operates in the context of "belongingness," that is that those who mutually accept each other come to be bound by ties of solidarity, so that to that extent they share membership in a collectivity. To persuade, in our technical sense, is then to give alter the status of shared membership, to treat him as "one of us." In using the term "acceptance" for the appropriate positive sanction for persuasion, we wish to distinguish it from "approval," reserving the latter term for the attitudinal sanction appropriate to the activation of commitments. "Approval" in this sense has a moral connotation that "acceptance" has not. Disapproval as the negative sanction threatened by ego is correlative with guilt as alter's internal or subjective negative sanction.

There will, of course, be various conditions on which acceptance is contingent—for example, acceptance by alter in turn of certain beliefs, collective goals, or what not. The contingent bases of acceptability may be summed up under the heading of conformity with the *norms* governing the operation of the collectivity of reference. Persuasion will involve a normative reference defining the sense in which the reasons offered are "good"; this reference may be called the *justification* of their acceptance by alter. The benefits alter then receives are those of acceptance and consequent freedom to act within the context of membership.

The use of influence as a medium operates in support systems in two ways. The first is in the assumption of leadership responsibility and therefore in the solicitation of support in order to assume authority and through it power. In highly developed democratic systems, this process is mediated through the party as a collectivity. Candidacy for high office and position of party leadership are identical. The candidate in soliciting commitment of votes is asking his constituents to "join with us." The justifications of the appeal then take the form of normative reasons why the policy of the party is superior to that of its rivals—including, of course, the imputed dangers of giving power to the latter. There is plenty of room for ideological selection and distortion in this process, but the basic reference seems to be clear.

To persons in a constituency, identification with a party—membership status need of course not always be formalized—may be regarded as an access of influence, however small in the individual case. It may also be regarded as involving expenditure of influence on the part of leadership. Conversely, constituents may be viewed as exercising their influence in attempting to persuade leadership to undertake the policies that they advocate. This process is most visible in the attempt to influence the leadership in power, but it also extends to that which may sometime come to power.

Influence may then be thought of as a medium that links the power aspect of social control with the structure of norms in the society. Group interests are most palpably implemented in terms first of power and then of money as modes of social control. In order for their interests to be so implemented, however, groups must not only have access to power, but their position must be "justified" to a greater or smaller extent within an institutionalized system of norms—for example (but not exclusively) at the legal level. In large-scale social systems, influence can only be exerted in major magnitudes if many join together to exert it—they must "organize." It is solidarity in this sense that we mean when we speak of an interest group. Moreover, any basis of solidarity becomes the basis for an interest group when it is considered in the context of influence, either to recruit members in the more usual mass-membership sense or to attempt to get potential leadership to "identify" with their interests—by acceptance of the reasons advanced for the action advocated as good, to act in a solidary way with those who have advanced them.

It is of critical significance that in "advanced" societies, in varying ways and to varying degrees, the social structure is pluralistic, both in the sense that there are many more or less independent groups and in the sense that the typical individual has plural memberships in such groups, often highly ramified. *One* major example of the exercise of influence is the attempt to secure transfer of allegiance or solidarity from one group to a competing group. This type of attempt is a highly conspicuous feature of party systems, since electoral rules do not allow voting for two or more party candidates for the same office. This zero-sum aspect of influence does not, however, hold true in all contexts of its use. New solidarities are continually being created, which although they modify do not necessarily eliminate the old. United States participation in the United Nations, for example, is not, as some of our nationalists would have it, bought at a simple zero-sum expense of national autonomy.

We have seen that money articulates with power in the command of resources for the implementive aspects of collective function. The significance of money in the social system is not, however, confined to this context. Indeed it is less familiar to the economist than that of the production of goods for consumption and the facilitation of consumption through the system of market exchange. Similarly, influence is, we hold, articulated with power in what we have called support systems. Its place in societies is, however, by no means confined to this role. We conceive of support systems as involved with the conditions of effective collective action. The other principal context in which influence is involved is that of the evaluation of interests and the allocation of loyalties among them. In this higher-order context of justification, reference is to the system of interests rather than to implementation of more particular interests.

We have spoken of two main contexts in which we hold that power is articulated with other generalized media: money in the implementive context, influence in the supportive. There is, finally, a third and somewhat different context that must be briefly mentioned, that of *legitimation*. In our terms, legitimation is an articulation of power with real commitments. It involves essentially a question of the standing of authority—as the frame of reference or "code" of power rather than the medium of control—in terms of the institutionalized values of the society. It is concerned with "rights" to exercise authority, at the level of both "constitutionality" and moral right. In normative terms, legitimation is the highest order of justification, but it seems best to use the term "legitimation" to distinguish it from the normative reference of persuasion. It is the highest normative defense against the breakdown of a system of societal order within which power can operate as a medium.

## The Monopoly of Force and the "Power Bank"

After this rather lengthy digression, we may now come back to certain questions of the relations between force and the power system. In the earlier part of this paper, we relied heavily on the parallel between money and power, and, in the present section, we propose to attempt to develop this parallel still further. It is a commonplace of political science that systems that are both stable and advanced—in the sense that they offer both high levels of differentiation and general political effectiveness for collective action—tend to enforce a relatively stringent monopoly of the control of organized and effective instrumentalities of force. This monopoly not only encourages the centralization of force but ensures that the constitutionally paramount organs of government are firmly in control of such force. We have here the doctrine of ultimate civilian control over the military, symbolized in the American system by the constitutional position of the president as commander in chief of all armed forces. There is perhaps no better criterion of a federal state, as distinct from a confederation, than the possession of paramount control of force by the central government.

The parallel in this case of course is the centralization of control over the monetary metal in economically advanced societies. Central banking systems, of which this control is an important aspect, have evolved late and often painfully, but they are a universal feature of advanced societies—and, of course, they are an integral part of socialist economies. Until recently—and still not unequivocally—there has been no formal prohibition against private agencies' holding gold, although an instance where such holdings were markedly superior to those of the government or central bank would certainly be considered anomalous and probably threatening and, if it tended to develop, would probably be stopped before it went much further. Such an instance would certainly, in a monetary system clearly dependent on gold to support a highly pyramidal credit system, carry with it a substantial potential for disruption, as the famous Black Friday makes clear.

Students of the subject are even more conscious that a major concentration of force in private hands has disruptive potentials because it can be used "against the public interest" or, with the opposite value-tag, as a revolutionary instrument against a decadent or iniquitous regime. The accent in this connection, however, has been on such force as a potential instrumentality of "seizing power." This potential is, of course, an important part of the picture but, as our discussion has indicated, only a part.

We have suggested that force plays a part in power systems parallel to that of gold in monetary systems. Only in one special instance is the commodity value of gold the "real basis" of the value of the dollar. Similarly, only in one special aspect is the command of physical force in a power system the "real basis" of the authority of government or the leadership of private collectivities, as the case may be. In the economic case, it is the credit system, built up primarily through the institution of banking but through several other types of mechanism, that "frees" monetary exchange from the limitations of metallic money. The "ultimate" basis of the value of its money then is the productivity of the economy.

We now suggest that there is a directly parallel set of phenomena in power systems. The primary functions of power are to facilitate the mobilization of instrumental resources like money and services and of support and the influence on which it partially depends. To repeat, this mobilization occurs through the promotion of binding obligations, the bindingness of which is symbolized by the willingness of those with power to resort to negative sanctions in case of noncompliance, sanctions that can be arranged in a rough order of severity from the threat of mild disadvantage to the drastic use of force. We have repeatedly insisted, however, that the problem of the motivation of compliance under normal conditions must not be confused with the problem of what sanctions will and will not be used in what order of severity and under what circumstances, when noncompliance occurs or is threatened. What motivation alter has for accepting or avoiding the sanctions is still a third question.

A particularly cogent set of reasons for making these distinctions lies in the existence and prominence in advanced political systems of a political analogy of the bank, which we may call, in appropriate quotation marks, the "power bank." The hallmark of the money bank is the fact that the dollars, as we noted, do double duty, remaining at the disposal of depositors while they are also at the disposal of borrowers. In the case of power, commitments to the performance of binding obligations are the analog of dollars and may be said to do double duty.

This point can be illustrated most clearly by the example of an electoral system, public or private. Members, in their capacity as voters, may be said to have entrusted power ("deposited" it) to elected leadership, power that they reserve the right to withdraw, if not on demand, at least at the next election. Some of this power is indeed immediately returned in the form of decisions that directly satisfy constituency interests. This return is reflected in party references to the record of benefits accruing to various categories of constituents during a term of office. In many political systems, private as well as public, however, this return does not exhaust the activities of leadership.

The leadership also "invests" a portion of its power in making commitments in what it conceives to be a larger collective interest, commitments that are in fact not in response to the immediate demands of constituent interest groups. Above all, these commitments tie up resources that in some sense "belong" to the constituency beyond the periods when the leadership is formally in control of them.

In the case of governments, the honoring of obligations assumed by opposing parties in previous administrations, frequently in foreign affairs but often domestically, is an indication of this phenomenon. For example, although the appropriations are made, for the most part, formally on an annual basis, money spent by the United States government in the fields of scientific research and training has in fact become, to a considerable extent, a permanent obligation, in spite of the legal authority of Congress to cut it off with a single vote. A good private example is the ploughing back of profits by corporations without detailed authorization by the stockholders, although the latter have the formal rights to stop it and take the money as dividends.

The essential point is that a "power bank," like a money bank, is, if it is functioning well, "insolvent" at any given moment with respect to its formal obligations, in the sense that it cannot fulfill all its legitimate obligations if there is insistence on their fulfillment too rapidly. Even relatively mild pressure to exceed the accustomed rate of fulfillment will force adoption of a rigid priority system and the rapid liquidation of some commitments that are otherwise highly desirable. Extreme pressure will tend to bring about a serious breakdown of the power system. When a vicious circle of "deflationary" pressure of this type gets under way, the tendency is to bring the role of negative sanctions increasingly to the fore and to resort to threats of sanctions of increasing severity. The "constitutional" powers can be quickly exhausted. At the end of the road lies the resort to force in the interest of what particular groups conceive to be their rights. The monopoly of force in the hands of government presents special problems that will be discussed presently.

This general set of considerations constitutes what we believe to be the basis of at least one of the most important objections to the very commonly held "zero-sum" conception of the nature of power. If power were equatable with physical force or even "based on" it in a sense other than the one we have discussed, it might be more plausible to hold that the power controlled by some units in the system was necessarily subtracted from a fixed total, the balance of which was controlled by the others.

That there is a distributive aspect of power is almost obvious and is clearly implied by our comparison with money. We wish, however, to extend the parallel to the point where we postulate a set of mechanisms of expansion and contraction of the total as a function of forces operating on the level of the system as a whole, which is parallel to the phenomenon of credit in the case of money. We think that these considerations are highly relevant to the problems of the place of force and constitute some of the reasons why the complexity of the relations between power and force that we have outlined is so important.

It should also be clear from this argument that we think that the basic phenomena of power systems are dependent on the institutionalization of what ordinarily is called authority. That is to say that, for cases of the exercise of authority—in which we include the vote—compliance is both legitimately and "normally" to be expected. It is, however, in the case of normatively regulated action that conformity with normative expectations sometimes, indeed often, fails. It is cases of this failure and the consequent possibilities of sequences of development that are the principal focus of interest for the remainder of this paper.


### Power and the Internal Use of Force

We have already laid stress on the tendency to develop a monopoly of the control of force in the hands of government. It is vital to our argument that this concentration cannot, except for a limiting type, be the case with power. A monopoly of the use of power in governmental hands would be a definition of the ideal type of a totalitarian regime. It has been one of our most important contentions that power should be regarded as a circulating medium that operates throughout the society wherever organizations in the sense of collectivities exist. Of course, in this

sense, the big organizations like governments, productive enterprises, and trade unions stand out conspicuously, but, in principle, families, even friendship cliques, and many other groups
also have some power. In the aggregate, the power of small units
may be very great, although, of course, the question of effective
organization always arises.

Among those societies with highly developed organization, the
modern Western, and rather particularly the American type, is
characterized by pluralism.[3] Although the scale of organization
is large, there are many, even among large organizations, that
are more or less independent of one another. It is important not
to make absolute independence in itself a criterion of pluralism.
There is, moreover, a shading from the very large through many
intermediate grades to the very small. Government is by no means
monolithic, splintered as it is by the separation of powers, fed-
eralism (in the United States), local independence, and the
internal complexity of such an immensely ramified organization
as the federal executive branch. The same is true, in varying
degrees, of many large private organizations.

In any complex society, more conspicuously in the more pluralistic ones, what may be called the "power structure" rests in a
state of more or less stable and probably significantly shifting
equilibrium. Processes of circulation operate continuously, through
exchanges of commitments of resources and of opportunities
for their utilization, through giving and withdrawing support
for various collective goals, and through the decisions that signify commitment—not only of mobile resources, but of organizations themselves.

There is, finally, the very important point that individual
persons have *plural* memberships in and commitments to collectivities. Although unevenly spread throughout a population,
this plurality increases with higher differentiation of the general
social structure. An increased spread of memberships implies, as
one price of enhanced effectiveness, an increased potential for
conflict among them or, put in obverse form, an increasingly
delicate equilibrium among such loyalties.

This equilibrium both among collectivities and among loyalties to memberships—which, it should be remembered, cut across
each other—is dependent on the maintenance of a level of "con-

fidence," a factor very similar to the confidence that operates in monetary systems. In the latter, it involves the expectation of probabilities, not only of the fulfillment of contractual obligations, but also of maintenance of given rates of entering into such obligations and of relinquishing them. In the political case, it is confidence in the probability of what we have called compliance. This confidence centers on the fulfillment of obligations already assumed through collectivity memberships, but in a parallel to the economic case, it extends also to rates of expected acceptance of new obligations—through entry of the younger generations into the labor force and hence into employment, for example.

Although this factor is only one among several that bear on the eruption of violence in internal situations, we would like to indicate a path leading in that direction that starts from the equilibrium of authority and power relations and the conditions of its maintenance. Disturbances of this equilibrium may originate in any of a number of places—specificity of origin is not an important consideration here. The question is whether or not the immediate consequence of a disturbance is "deflationary" in the sense of its effect on the system of expectations of which the power structure is made. One general condition favorable to such deflationary influence is, of course, an overextension of power commitments, analogous to inflation in the economic sense. This problem presents a very important field of inquiry that unfortunately cannot be followed up here; that such conditions exist will simply be taken as given.

In our present context, a deflationary influence is one that leads to a demand for a binding decision or exercise of power, to which the demander has some kind of right but which is out of line with the normal expectations of operation of the system. That some units will encounter emergency conditions, as some depositors unexpectedly must withdraw their balances, is to be taken for granted. Whether the rate of imposition of such demands is abnormal is a matter for statistical estimate, unless the individual case is of overwhelming quantitative magnitude in terms of claims either on resources or on support.

Any such disturbance may, of course, be met. On the other hand, if it is not met or if the difficulty of meeting it creates a question of the capacity of the system to meet its general obligations, it *may* (not necessarily must) motivate other units to present demands they would not otherwise have presented *at this time*.[4]

If such a process once gets under way, it may enter into a vicious-circle pattern. That is, each assertion of demands for collective decision, for satisfaction of interests that would not ordinarily have been presented, will stimulate other units to assert their demands. There can then develop a *cumulative* pressure on the relevant collectivities. The general type of response will then be twofold. First, an increasingly stringent scale of priorities of what can and cannot be done will be set up; second, increasingly severe negative sanctions for noncompliance with collective decisions will be imposed.

With respect to the first tendency, the most important point to note is the presumption that most if not all of the demands made on collective leadership are legitimate and that, in general, their presumptive legitimacy is not dependent on specific conditions of timing and other constraints—if the analogy to the bank depositors holds up. This circumstance, once "confidence" has been sufficiently impaired, is bound to increase the pressure, since there is no formal way to make newly imposed priorities seem legitimate other than the process of "legal" pronouncement, which may or may not match the normative "sentiments" of the important groups.

With respect to the second tendency, we have already asserted that increasing severity of sanctions leads in the direction of resort to force. If pressure to fulfill demands becomes sufficiently severe and the objective possibility of fulfilling them sufficiently low, then it seems inevitable that the most vociferous insisters, who at the same time are low on the priority scale, will have to be threatened with force to deter them. Here again it must be remembered that we are positing a situation where it is objectively impossible to fulfill all the legitimate demands within a short time but where, at the same time, this incapacity is also felt to be legitimate.

The most common responses to increasing severity of sanctions are two. One is to seek security through "digging in" in a protected position, the protection of which may involve independent command of force but may also take the form of command of other resources of the most various kinds. This reaction is the withdrawal from dependence on the ramified power system, which is analogous to economic withdrawal into gold or into "real" assets—a feature of economic deflation that, interestingly, is shared with inflationary situations. The other general response is the active, aggressive attempt to *enforce* demands against the inclinations of the collective leadership. This response clearly leads in the direction of seeking capacity to implement countersanctions of severity equal to or exceeding that of those commanded by the collective leadership. Force plays a central part in any such system of countersanctions, but it should be remembered that it does not stand alone. Financial assets may be very important and, above all, influence in the technical sense in which we have used the term.

Our general argument has been deliberately couched in terms that include all collective action, governmental or private. Government, however, occupies a very special position in any developed power system. First, it is the most comprehensive level of collective organization and hence in general commands considerably larger assets than any other "interest" at most levels and in most categories, although not necessarily in all. Second, government is in a very special position in relation to the command of force, usually that of monopoly.

In what we have called the vicious circle of coercive threats, which a power-deflation may well set in motion, there may, unlike the economic case, be an inherent tendency to set up a polarity between the elements in control of the machinery of government and those in opposition to that group. In more advanced constitutional regimes, this polarity usually takes the form of a two-party system. The way of securing fulfillment of demands not approved by the party in power is to seek electoral victory against it, which of course implies waiting, perhaps for a long period, for a favorable opportunity.

Essentially a constitutional regime is marked, on the one hand, by restraint in the expectation of fulfillment of various demands and, on the other, by restraint on the coercion of the opposition by those in power. In particular, the leadership refrain from abridging the freedom to displace the incumbents from power, not only by maintaining the electoral rules, but by upholding the other normal components of political freedom like freedoms of the press, of assembly, and so forth. The opposition must be free to influence the voters, although neither they nor the incumbents should coerce or bribe them.[5]

It is when, in the vicious circle of power deflation, these restraints are broken in the interaction between incumbents and opposition that the makings of a revolutionary situation are present. We have posited a situation in which it is objectively impossible for government to satisfy all the demands presented to it. We have, moreover, argued that, though by no means all such demands need be in any sense legitimate, the type of situation we are discussing always involves a major excess of legitimate (in a "formal" sense) demands over capacity to satisfy them. This excess means that, among the unsatisfied, to whatever forces of group interest in the more "material" sense exist there will be added a sense of normative, possibly moral, righteousness that will, as it becomes more intense, seem to justify increasing resort to more extreme measures.

At this point, certain well known generalizations about ideologies can be brought to bear. Ideologies combine an evaluative and an empirical element in the diagnosis of social situations. Because of evaluative pressures, they tend toward selectivity and sometimes toward outright distortion, both in stating the case of the proponents and attacking that of the opponents. It is typical that the former are pictured as actuated by the highest of idealistic motives, while the latter are guided by the grossest forms of self-interest. That is, ideological definition of the situation tends to get drawn into the general polarization.

A particularly important point is the question of the solidity or lack of it of the governmental monopoly of internal force. Most important, whatever the physical technology involved, a critical factor in socially effective force is always the social organization through which it is implemented. There is always some degree of dependence on the loyalties of the relevant personnel to the elements in the social structure ostensibly controlling them.

Up to a point, a pluralistic social structure can act as a very important preventive of the spread of the vicious circle of power-deflation, mainly by invoking solidarities at many points that cut across lines of incipient conflict.* The same type of analysis can, however, be applied at points where the vicious circle has begun to get out of control. Members of police and armed forces also have plural loyalties, among which those to their jobs do not stand alone nor necessarily predominate. Hence, even though at a given moment the sanctions against breaking away from these loyalties are very severe, there may be many critical points where mass breaking away can readily occur once a precarious equilibrium has been upset.

Connected with this point is the question of the plurality of factors in a power position, among which command of negative sanctions generally and force in particular comprise only one subset. From this point of view, a complex set of two-way forces operate around the threat and actual use of physical force. On the one hand, the use and threat of force have a set of symbolic meanings that define a penumbra of effect extending well beyond the direct effectiveness in the context of deterrence or compulsion. This statement is above all true of the meanings discussed briefly in relation to demonstration of capacity to act. On the one hand, exemplary uses and threats on the part of holders of force may be meant, not as specifically coercive deterrents, but merely as warnings. The same game may be played by outsiders, particularly minority opposition groups wishing to create an atmosphere of crisis. The general phenomenon of terrorism on both governmental and opposition sides seems to fit in this context.

On the other hand, a whole series of other factors are involved in willingness to resort to force and the probabilities of effectiveness once the plunge is made. In principle, all the major factors that operate on action within social systems are relevant to any such analysis. This point leads to a very important general conclusion. Social behavior in the application of physical force and in reaction to its threat or use is not subject to special "laws" of behavior. It should rather be approached by applying the generalized knowledge already available about the uniformities of such behavior to a special set of conditions, which necessitate

---

* I have called attention to this factor of stability in the paper on voting cited in Note 2 at the end of this chapter.

special exigencies of effectiveness on the one hand, special modes of reaction to threat and implementation on the other. In our opinion, understanding the use of internal as well as external force is as dependent on advancement of general theoretical knowledge of the operation of social systems as on specificities of the situations peculiar to the use of force, although of course both must be pursued and adequately combined.

### Conclusion

In this chapter, we have attempted an exceedingly sketchy review of a certain set of these general features of the functioning of social systems, insofar as they tend to connect with the significance of the use of force. We have viewed the problem in the general context of modes of social control and, within this context, in the light of coercion by threatening negative sanctions and of compulsion as a limiting type. In this connection, physical force appears as the ultimate instrument of coercion or compulsion, where the primary intention in its use or threat is deterrence. It also, we suggested, has the meanings of punishment and of demonstration and warning.

We then attempted to place physical force as sanction in the context, on the one hand, of a gradient of such sanctions that can be involved in the implementation of power positions and, on the other hand, of the place of coercion and power in a more comprehensive scheme of generalized media of social control. In the former context, force is the most severe in a continuum of potential deprivations of situational advantage imposed by an acting unit of reference—ego—on an alter that ego intends to control. In this context in most power systems, physical force is not the most important operative sanction but a "reserve" sanction available for emergencies. In particular, it is not likely to be resorted to internally or even directly threatened in a stable power system, except in minor instances like routine police functions in attempting to control ordinary criminals. In certain types of crisis situation, however, it may come to dominate the social scene.

We thus regard power as a generalized medium of social

control. Its properties have been analyzed above all in terms of a systematic comparison with those of money. It has in common with money that it is essentially a mode of prescriptive communication. Its effectiveness is not mainly dependent on any particular base but rather on confidence, which is itself dependent on many factors in the fulfillment of interactive expectations. There is, however, an ultimate symbolic basis of security of the value of the medium: In the case of money, it is the monetary metal; in that of power, physical force. Money and power viewed in this perspective should also be related to at least two other media of comparable importance, in particular the one we have called influence.

Against this background, it is possible to see that power systems involve a phenomenon analogous to credit creation in monetary systems. This analogy implies, on the one hand, a vast extension of the range of effective collective organization, compared with a system dependent either mainly on ascriptive obligations or on more primitive sanctions like force and summary dismissal. On the other hand, it implies vulnerability to certain types of disturbance parallel to inflation and deflation in the economic case. A highly developed power system cannot meet all of its presumptively legitimate obligations all at once.

It is this particular case that we chose to illustrate the relevance of this type of analysis to the problem of internal war. We suggest that the power systems we posit are vulnerable to vicious circles of power-deflation, a vulnerability that is accentuated by the general tendency of governmental systems to polarize. In such a vicious-circle process, there will be a tendency toward the use of force, in terms of both threat and counter-threat and in terms of warnings. (Space does not allow developing an empirical analysis very far, but other chapters in this volume, I am sure, contain ample material for its application.)

## Notes

1. Perhaps the most useful recent publications for this background purpose are, first, Part II of the "General Introduction" to *Theories of Society*, edited by Parsons, Shils, Naegele, and Pitts (New York: The Free Press of

Glencoe, 1961); second, Parsons's, *Structure and Process in Modern Societies* (New York: The Free Press of Glencoe, 1960); and, third, the paper on voting referred to below. See also two papers written subsequently to the present one: "On the Concept of Influence," *Public Opinion Quarterly*, May, 1963, and "On the Concept of Political Power," *Proceedings of the American Philosophical Society*, June, 1963.

2. Cf. Parsons, " 'Voting' and the Equilibrium of the American Political System" in Eugene Burdick and Arthur J. Brodbeck, eds., *American Voting Behavior* (New York: The Free Press of Glencoe, 1959).

3. For the concept of pluralism in the present sense, see William Kornhauser, *The Politics of Mass Society* (New York: The Free Press of Glencoe, 1959).

4. The most adequate generalized analysis, including much empirical material, of the conditions under which such crises of confidence are likely to occur and under which they may be checked is presented in Neil J. Smelser, *Theory of Collective Behavior* (New York: The Free Press of Glencoe, 1963).

5. The best analysis known to us of the institutionalization of the franchise bearing on these points is Stein Rokkan, "Mass Suffrage, Secret Voting and Political Participation," *European Journal of Sociology*, II (1961), 132-152.

## Thomas Perry Thornton

### TERROR AS A WEAPON

### OF POLITICAL AGITATION

Our consideration of terror will be confined within certain limits.
First of all, we shall deal with terror in the context of internal
war—that is, the use or threat of violence to effect a change
in the body politic. We shall thereby exclude manifestations of
terror in international warfare (like strategic bombing) and subviolent phenomena that are structurally related to terror (like nonviolent resistance and propaganda). Second, we shall treat terror
as a tool to be used rationally. Although we shall make reference
to irrational uses, we shall deal mainly with acts of terror instituted as parts of planned campaigns to achieve political objectives, thereby also excluding nonpolitical terror.

The word "terror" has two meanings. The basic one is an
induced state of fear or anxiety within an individual or group
of individuals. It is sometimes called "subjective terror." Derived from this meaning is the use of "terror" to describe the
tool that induces the state of being terrified. This tool is vari-
ously called "terror," "objective terror," and "terrorism." Although it would be convenient to distinguish simply between
terror (the psychic state) and terrorism (the tool), this distinction is not advisable, for frequently "terrorism" and "terror" are
used interchangeably to denote objective terror: Suffice it to say
that the subject of this study is the consideration of terror as a
tool; any discussion of the induced state is only secondary. Whenever we use the word "terror," it will be understood to refer

to the tool; in discussing the induced state, we shall use a different word.

This essay does not claim to present an operational study in counterterrorism nor, for that matter, guidelines for the aspiring terrorist. To be sure, operational information would be useful, but it is first of all necessary to achieve theoretical understanding of terror before one can project practical rules for producing it or coping with it effectively. We shall address ourselves to the theoretical problem.

Discussions of terror customarily include such events as the *Terreur* of the French Revolution; the suppression of the Paris Commune; the activities of the Russian *Narodniki*, Malayan Communists, and the Mau Mau; and the repressive techniques of the Hitler and Stalin regimes. Although all may well be called "terror," simply to lump them under one general heading is to fall victim to a semantic misapprehension and to make difficult any attempt to take the most elementary analytical step in the study of terror—the determination of the function or objective of the act.

I would distinguish two general types of terror. The first is, roughly, the activity of insurgents who wish to disrupt the existing order and achieve power; the second is the activity of the incumbents who wish to suppress a challenge to their authority. In general terms, this distinction was made, by Brian Crozier, between terrorism and counterterrorism.[1] It is, however, by no means inevitable that the insurgents will initiate terrorism; in some instances, they may be "counterterrorists" reacting to the terror of the incumbents. Although the literature of terror does occasionally present other examples of potentially useful differentiations among the basic types of terrorist activity, none offers the precision required for analytical work.[2] We must, regretfully, use new terms: *enforcement terror* to describe terror (or counterterror) launched by those in power and *agitational terror* to describe terroristic acts by those aspiring to power. The difference is between terror perpetrated by incumbents in power as an extreme means of enforcing their authority (thus the name "enforcement terror") and by insurgents out of power with a view to provoking certain reactions from the incumbents or an otherwise apathetic population.[3]

We are dealing, in a sense, with two continua of behavior— one of political agitation and the other of enforcement—which run parallel. At their lowest points, both represent minimum forms of enforcement and agitation (parking tickets and distribution of campaign leaflets, for example). Each then develops in intensity, reaching a maximum of wholesale murder and violence, and at some point on the scale (we shall attempt to specify this point later) the realm of "terror" is entered. Our attention here is to be devoted to the problem of agitational terror, with only marginal reference to enforcement terror. There is already an extensive literature on enforcement terror, called forth especially by the Soviet and German experiences.[4] The more immediate problem—and the one about which something presumably can be done—is the field of agitational terror.

### A Definition of "Terror"

It seems advisable to begin our consideration with a definition of the concept of terror as we shall use it, within the framework of the internal war situation.[5] The definition will serve a dual purpose, for, by discussing its component attributes, we can conveniently present our views on the nature of terror. Thus, in an internal war situation, *terror is a symbolic act designed to influence political behavior by extranormal means, entailing the use or threat of violence.* We shall discuss the terms individually.

"DESIGNED TO INFLUENCE POLITICAL BEHAVIOR." Under certain circumstances, the use of terror for other than political objectives is possible, but by terms of our preoccupation with internal war, such nonpolitical events are excluded by definition. Terrorism may gain political ends in one of two ways—either by mobilizing forces and reserves sympathetic to the cause of the insurgents or by immobilizing forces and reserves that would normally be available to the incumbents. A point of which insurgents are acutely aware—but which incumbents frequently overlook—is that, in the initial stages of internal war situations, the incumbents usually have an immense advantage with regard to the great uncommitted mass of citizens. For although this mass may be uncommitted in terms of the particular issue at stake, it is less likely to be uncommitted with regard to the incumbents as such.

The incumbents and the mass they dominate are part of a single social structure. The incumbents benefit from the natural state of inertia that prevails in the political relationship; the insurgents, on the other hand, represent an alienated factor, which the organism of the society will normally be predisposed to cast out. Among the various tasks of an insurgent group, the one that will interest us primarily is its need to disrupt the inertial relationship between incumbents and mass. In order to do this, the insurgents must break the tie that binds the mass to the incumbents within the society, and they must remove the structural supports that give the society its strength—or at least to make those supports seem irrelevant to the critical problems that the mass must face. This process is one of disorientation, the most characteristic use of terror, which will be discussed below in some detail.

Since terror is a weapon with political implications, it should be considered in its relationship to the entire spectrum of political agitation. Although we shall compare it with certain other political acts later, it may be noted here that the appropriateness of terror varies according to the degree of political support enjoyed by the insurgents. In view of its disorientation function, terror is only appropriate if the insurgents enjoy a low level of actual political support but have a high potential for such support. If their potential is low, terrorism is likely to be counterproductive. Even if the disorientation effect is achieved, the mass will look for other support structures than those offered by the terrorists. More likely than not their opposition to the terrorists will cause them to cling more closely to the already existing state structures. If the terrorists already enjoy a high level of active support, terror will not only be wasteful of energy and moral authority but may have a negative effect by endangering the orientation of those already included within the insurgents' structures.[6]

The political function of terror must also be emphasized, in contrast to the military role that is often ascribed to it. The military function of terror is negligible. It is a small-scale weapon and cannot *in itself* have any appreciable influence on the outcome of military action. Various sources suggest that it has been used as a means of recruiting troops, but this suggestion seems incredible and has never been documented. A man who is coerced into fighting will hardly make a very effective soldier and is likely to desert to the enemy at the first opportunity.[7] That is not to deny the importance that a well-planned terrorist campaign may have as a method of gaining short-term logistical support and, insofar as it contributes to the political strength of the insurgents, of lending valuable support to subsequent military action.

"ENTAILING THE USE OR THREAT OF VIOLENCE." In view of the high levels of alienation inherent in any insurgent group that feels impelled toward terrorism, it is inevitable that violence will play a characteristic role in terrorist activities. A nonviolent program could hardly qualify as terrorism. (If we seek an insurgent tactic that fulfills all the other criteria we shall postulate for terrorism, the Gandhian nonviolent movement against the British in India presents a model that shows almost identical structural features. Very few, however, would care to label Gandhi a terrorist.) Violence also is the ground for distinction between terror and propaganda, for both are tools for creating public support in the pursuit of political ends; indeed, an important function of terror is that of propagandizing for the insurgent movement.

There are, of course, as Hitler stated,[8] spiritual (nonviolent) as well as physical (violent) attributes of terror; in fact, terror operating solely on the physical plane would be obviously illogical. It is even theoretically conceivable that a victim could be terrorized without the threat of physical violence, but in the internal war context the possibility is so remote as to be nonexistent. Such an effect could at most be achieved on a few individuals at the hands of an exceptionally perceptive psychological manipulator with a thorough knowledge of the subconscious vulnerabilities of the victim.

"BY EXTRANORMAL MEANS." Terror occupies the upper reaches of the spectrum of political agitation, immediately above other types of political violence. Terror may be distinguished from these other types by its *extranormal* quality; that is, terror lies beyond the norms of violent political agitation that are accepted by a given society. If an agitator wishes to assault the structures of his society, he can best do so by engaging in extra-normal (and therefore disorienting) actions. The level of extranormality varies, of course, from society to society and from time to time.

The extranormality of terror can also be expressed as a function of the internal war situation. Internal war will not come about in a situation that permits the conflicting vital aspirations of the incumbents and the insurgents to be met by constitutional means—i.e., by "normal" means. If the contending sides can agree on formulae that permit the peaceful transfer of political power, any form of violence is anachronistic.

While in some cases the refusal of the incumbents to make constitutional provision for the transfer of power compels the insurgents to resort to extranormal means, at least equally often the insurgents utilize terror because they lack the political strength to make use of constitutional procedures that may be objectively adequate and just. They attempt to provoke the incumbents into repressive measures, in order then to claim that the incumbents have made the constitutional machinery unavailable. It therefore seems probable that, the longer the incumbents can delay opposing insurgent terror with extranormal means of repression, the more advantage they will have in belying insurgent propaganda.

In any case, the insurgent must attempt to communicate effectively to his audience the idea that terror is the only weapon appropriate to the situation. A basic requirement is formulation of the issues at stake in simple terms of black and white. Shades of grey are not conducive to terrorism, for the level of urgency falls off as the admixture of white increases. This black/white relationship is often established by pressing a serviceable ideology into use. As Hannah Arendt has pointed out, ideology is the precurser of totalitarianism, and totalitarianism breeds terror.[9]

Whatever justification the insurgents may attempt to create, the dysfunctional use of terror in terms of the political system must be considered immoral—and a sign of great political weakness and a dangerous extremist mentality on the part of those using it. The Russian *Narodnik* terrorists recognized this point in a comment upon the assassination of President Garfield: "In a country where freedom gives the people the possibility of an honorable contending of ideas; where a free peoples' will decides not only the laws but also the personnel of the government; in such a country, political murder as a means of struggle is a manifestation of the same spirit of despotism which we consider our task to eliminate in Russia."[10]

"A SYMBOLIC ACT." Definition of terror as a symbolic act does not mean that a person, say, is assassinated only symbolically and not in fact; rather, it means that the terroristic act is intended and perceived as a symbol. The observer realizes that the act implies a meaning broader than its own component parts.

The relatively high efficiency of terrorism derives from its symbolic nature. If the terrorist comprehends that he is seeking a demonstration effect, he will attack targets with a maximum symbolic value. The symbols of the state are particularly important, but perhaps even more so are those referring to the normative structures and relationships that constitute the supporting framework of the society. By showing the weakness of this framework, the insurgents demonstrate, not only their own strength and the weakness of the incumbents but also the inability of the society to provide support for its members in a time of crisis. The individuals and subgroups that comprise the structures tend to become atomized. If we envision each of these structures as dominated by a single symbol, in the sense that an arch is dominated by a keystone, destruction of the symbol results in fracture of the structure into its component parts in a most economical manner. It would obviously be impossible to terrorize a nation on an individual basis; furthermore, to the extent that terror destroys only the keystone-symbol, the individual components of the structure remain intact and available for restructuring along lines desired by the insurgents.

The symbolic concept of the terrorist act enables us to make two crucial distinctions: between terror and sabotage and between terror and assassination. Although sabotage is virtually always directed against objects rather than against people, while terrorism is generally directed against people, a distinction cannot be made solely along these lines—for terrorism is occasionally used against objects. The proper distinction—which coincides with the persons *vs.* objects distinction in most cases—is to be found in the psychological, rather than the physical objective of the act. If the objective is primarily the removal of a specific thing (or person) with a view towards depriving the enemy of its usefulness, then the act is one of sabotage. If, on the other hand, the objective is symbolic, we are dealing with terror.

In distinguishing between terror and assassination, the criterion again is the symbolic nature of the act. An assassination (or murder) may or may not be carried out publicly. If it is considered desirable merely to remove a certain public figure, a discreet poisoning will fulfill the requirement adequately, but it would not be terroristic. The elimination of a public figure may also be accomplished quite openly, with responsibility clearly fixed. If the cause is a personal grudge—as in the assassination of President Garfield by a disappointed office-seeker, for example—we are not dealing with terrorism. President Garfield's assassin was not interested in overthrowing the existing order— quite unlike Leon Czolgosz, the assassin of President McKinley, who was an anarchist and very interested in upsetting the established order. Czolgosz's was one of the rash of terroristic acts perpetrated by anarchists around the turn of the century, with the objective of attracting attention to the anarchist cause. McKinley's death was symbolic, thus an act of terrorism, especially when taken in context of anarchist doctrine and related to other assassinations of the time.[11]

As a general rule, assassination and sabotage are nonsymbolic acts directed against persons and things, respectively. Terror is a symbolic act that may be directed against things or people.

### Tactical Considerations

THE TARGETS OF TERRORISM. Who is the object of terrorism, and who are the actors in the terrorist drama? First, of course, in any act of terrorism, there is the person who commits the terrorist act—let us say the bomb thrower. Next, we have the person or object at which the bomb is aimed. The person who is struck by the bomb is clearly the *victim* of the act, and certain things happen to him. If not killed or incapacitated, he is at least frightened—perhaps to the extent of being neutralized for future action. This victim himself probably belongs to some *group that identifies* with him and will automatically feel itself exposed to danger—he is typically a policeman, perhaps a member of the governing élite, or a member of a rival insurgent organization. This group will probably be both "terrorized" and subjected to disorientation effects, but the former is likely to be the most important component. Finally, the terrorist act takes place in a social environment, all members of which will potentially take notice of it. For this *resonant mass*, the disorientation content is of vastly greater importance.[12]

The identification group and the resonant mass may in some instances be identical. In any case, a large-scale terror campaign is likely to involve a large number of subgroups of the society, so that the whole resonant mass will feel increasingly engaged.[13]

A terrorist act will usually also have a stimulating effect on the members of the terrorist organization and its immediate supporters. This function of terrorism is of a different nature and must be kept analytically separate, even though acts aimed at the hostiles and the neutrals will usually have this secondary effect.

Internal war situations involving colonial insurgency against the occupying power show radical differences when compared to the customary type of internal war, especially with regard to the resonant mass or target of intent of terrorist acts. Brian Crozier's study, *The Rebels*, deals almost exclusively with colonial "internal" wars and presents an excellent analysis of terrorism in these situations. Although the terrorists would probably like to terrorize the occupying forces and reduce their efficiency, Crozier points out that their principal task is to make repression so costly that the colonial government will prefer to withdraw rather than continue the struggle. The resonant mass is thus the government and population of the home country, completely removed from personal and direct involvement in the war.[14]

The principal lesson to be drawn from differentiation of victims and targets is that, in appraising a terroristic act, one must ask, not only "Who got hit by the bomb?" but also "What effects is this particular act likely to entail?" Since a terroristic act is public and thus meant to have a propaganda effect and since the victim is usually physically eliminated and therefore not in need of being propagandized, there is a *prima facie* requirement that the analyst of terrorism look for the real target of intent. When he locates this target, he will not only be better able to counter the propaganda effect of the act, but he also may be able to take measures to reduce the incident of terrorism by protecting targets that have high symbolic contents, rather than those that may be of purely utilitarian value. Lacking a knowledge of the target of intent, his chances for taking purposeful counteraction are extremely small.

RESPONSES INDUCED BY TERROR. Having discussed the various levels of target that may be affected by terror, we shall now summarize the responses that the terrorist may seek by his act. These responses can be classified for analytical purposes under three headings. The labels I shall give these groupings are to a considerable extent arbitrary.[15] I have chosen to assign names to them—rather than to use X, Y, and Z—but no more should be read into the names than is specified in the following definitions.[16]

The one positive response to be achieved is *enthusiasm* among the adherents of the insurgent movement. This response involves the purely morale-building function alluded to above and need not concern us further.

The lowest level of negative reaction is *fright*. The frightened person perceives a specific danger, which is not qualitatively different from other dangers with which he is personally or vicariously familiar. Since the perceived danger fits into the pattern of his previous experience, his response will be meaningful in terms of familiar norms of action; it will be both subjectively and objectively logical and reasonably predictable.

The middle level of response is *anxiety*, which is called forth by fear of the unknown and the unknowable. Traditional norms of behavior show no relevance to the new situation, and the victim becomes disoriented, casting about for guidance. The exact nature of response is unpredictable, but it is likely to lead to activity that is logical in terms of the new situation as perceived by the target.

The most extreme level of response is *despair*, an intensified form of anxiety. The victim perceives the threat to be so great and unavoidable that there is no course of action open to him that is likely to bring relief. As a result, the victim withdraws from the situation to the maximum possible extent.

DISCRIMINATION IN THE USE OF TERROR. Differentiations among targets and according to desired effects govern the degree of discrimination to be used in terrorism. Indiscrimination is often thought of as a necessary attribute of a terrorist campaign, and certain types of terror do give the appearance of being completely indiscriminate. Terror must always have at least some element of indiscrimination, else it becomes predictable, loses its broad character, and can no longer be legitimately designated as terror. Also, it becomes relatively easy to combat. Total indiscrimination, however, is not reasonable, unless one is a complete nihilist. Indiscrimination to the extent of a nihilist's bombing the nihilist party headquarters, for example, is an engaging but unlikely possibility, and short of this extreme, some discrimination must be practiced.

Discrimination plays an extremely important role in the creation of anxiety responses. Any element that tends to make terror more unknowable and therefore more disorienting contributes to the creation of anxiety.[17] The resonant mass and the identification group do not become anxious in the face of highly discriminate terrorism, but if they believe they are confronted with seemingly indiscriminate terror, they will experience the required sense of personal involvement. Again, however, total indiscrimination is not desirable, for the insurgents will wish to concentrate their attacks on specific targets of intent, social structures, and symbols, to achieve economy of effort and ensure the maintenance of those structures that are of potential value to them. They must therefore determine which structures are to be preserved, which structures are the most vulnerable to attack, and which are the most crucial in holding together the fabric of the society they wish to split. Certain compromises will inevitably have to be made, but the optimum targets are clearly those that show the highest symbolic value and are dominated by symbols that are most vulnerable to attack.

The terrorist must always have the distinction between *apparent* indiscrimination and *actual* indiscrimination clearly in mind, if he is to succeed. As a general rule, it may then be said that terror is most effective when it is indiscriminate in appearance but highly discriminate in fact.

### The Proximate Objectives of Terrorism

We have established that the ultimate objective of terror is the influencing of political behavior, and we have discussed three tactical considerations with which insurgent terrorists must contend. It is now in order to list the proximate objectives of terrorism in this context. Our inventory will perhaps not be exhaustive, although it claims to present all of the major categories of objectives to which insurgent terror may aspire. An economically-minded insurgent group will attempt to make each act effect as many objectives as possible, and, conversely, the analyst of an act of terrorism should not be misled into thinking that each act can have only one objective. We shall leave out of consideration the bonus-effects (like sabotage) that a terrorist act may have.

The first objective is *morale-building* within the terrorist movement itself, as well as in that element of the population that is already sympathetic to the insurgents. This objective is usually a side-effect of acts that have other primary purposes.

In terms of our tactical criteria, this objective would have the movement's sympathizers as its target, it would seek to call forth a response of enthusiasm, and discrimination would be irrelevant, except that the act should not adversely affect any of the target group.

Closely related, but of much more significance, is the objective of *advertising* the movement. Although not the most important objective of the terrorist, advertising is in some ways the most characteristic, for it is of the very essence of terror that it be noticed. Advertising not only calls attention to the existence of the insurgents but also serves as a reminder of their program and ideals. This thought is foremost in Kropotkin's mind in his description of terrorism—"the propaganda of the deed":

Indifference (following terrorist acts) is impossible. Those who originally did not even ask themselves what "those lunatics" were after, are forced to take notice of them, to discuss their ideas, and to take a stand for or against. Through the deeds which attract general attention, the new idea insinuates itself into peoples' heads and makes converts. Such an act does more propagandizing in a few days than do thousands of pamphlets.[18]

The advertising function differs from morale-building primarily in that it is directed toward a mass audience. The desired response can best be described as one of curiosity, and the level of discrimination indicated is extremely high, since the act must not only spare the insurgents and their sympathizers but also the mass audience they wish to captivate.[19]

*Disorientation* is the objective *par excellence* of the terrorist, removing the underpinnings of the order in which his targets live out their daily lives. The primary responsibility of any incumbent group is to guarantee order to its population, and the terrorist will attempt to disorient the population by demonstrating that the incumbents' structure cannot give adequate support.

This demonstration is, however, but one aspect of the disorientation process. On a much deeper level, the objective is the isolation of the individual from his social context. Edmond Taylor[20] described the German technique as aimed chiefly at the disruption of the socio-psychological ties among individuals that make them act as part of a group. The ultimate of the terrorization process, as Hannah Arendt conceives it, is the isolation of the individual, whereby he has only himself upon whom to rely and cannot draw strength from his customary social supports.[21] While this end can most readily be achieved by physically withdrawing the individual from his environment and isolating him (as in "brainwashing" techniques), the terrorist's most readily available substitute on a mass basis is the destruction of the social framework, so that the individual perceives himself to be alone in his anguish even though he may be physically undisturbed.

Disorientation occurs when the victim does not know what he fears, when the source of his fear lies outside his field of experience. Knowledge and understanding of the source of danger provide the victim with a framework within which he can classify it, relate it to his previous experience, and therefore take measures to counter it. If he is unable to do this on his own, he can draw strength by attaching himself to a leader who at least gives the appearance of wisdom. If, however, the leader

has been physically removed or has been demonstrated to be
incapable of dealing with the rapidly shifting patterns of order,
if existing organizational groups lose their apparent relevance,
then the individual can look only within himself for strength
and guidance.

Disorientation itself represents only a partial victory for the
terrorist, albeit a very useful one. By dissociating his victims
from structures associated with the incumbents, the insurgent
has removed the target from the ranks of the opposition. He has
little to fear, for terrorized victims are in a condition associated
with anxiety neurosis and are thus unlikely to do much except
look to their own security. In searching for safety and reassurance,
however, most will attempt to locate new structures of authority
that can alleviate their aloneness and give promise of being
capable of dealing with the changed situation.[22] The role of
agitational terror is now over; it now remains for the insurgents
to demonstrate that they are capable of infusing meaning into
the unstructured environment.[23]

Thus the target of the disorientation process is the mass, and
the desired response is anxiety. The level of discrimination should
appear to be low, almost nonexistent. Greatest anxiety will be
caused if terrorist attacks fall in an apparently random pattern,
are intense and unpredictable. The analogy to the Pavlov experiments is clear.

In view of the importance of disorientation effects, it is
worthwhile to consider briefly what types of society are most
likely to be vulnerable. It would be extremely difficult to induce
mass-disorientation in a society whose members feel a high degree of positive identification with the society and are firmly
committed to its values. The terrorist is probably always well
advised to inject himself into a situation that already shows a
high degree of disorientation. In a way, however, this consideration is minor, since it is precisely this sort of social situation that
evokes terror and internal war in the first place.

There are theoretical grounds for believing that a society
may be better equipped to withstand terrorist pressures when
it has passed the transitional phase from adherence to rigid traditional structures of long standing and has achieved a new
resolution, in which the individual draws support less from

family, clan, and small occupational units than from more diffused structures and, above all, from resources within himself.
The allegiance of man in a modern pluralistic society is generally
distributed over a much larger number of structures. To achieve
complete disorientation, the terrorizer would have therefore to
spread his attack much more widely. Above all, the individual
is supposed to gain strength by cutting himself loose from tradition, facing the existential problem, and establishing his source
of strength within himself, rather than seeking it outside himself.
David Riesman's analysis[24] tends to belie this concept, however,
and the course of contemporary history gives it still less support.
The strengths man finds within himself vary greatly from individual to individual, and the contemporary pattern seems to be
much more one of "other-direction" than of "autonomy" or
"inner-direction." It is precisely the "other-directed" man who
leans heavily upon the support of society, as did his "tradition-
directed" forefather. But even in the most advanced of societies,
he may not find adequate support, and thus prove a more vulnerable target than tradition-bound groups that have not yet begun
the transition to modernity.

Insofar as inner-direction is a transitional form between tradition-direction and other-direction, this period of transition
would appear paradoxically to be the most difficult for the terrorist to crack. There is no law that postulates this progression
of development, however, and it may be that, in our era at least,
inner-direction was a historical phenomenon peculiar to the industrializing ages of a few West European and North American
countries. The developing countries seem rather to be following
a path from tradition-direction to other-direction, or simple nondirection looking for a direction to take. Here we return to our
concept of disorientation, for nondirection is no more than
disorientation, whether developed historically or caused by destruction of the structures that give direction.

If simple other-direction provides a highly vulnerable target
for terrorism, then one might assume that a totalitarian society
—which is founded upon extremes of other-direction—would be
highly vulnerable to terroristic action. If the totalitarian structure
is shown to be incapable of fulfilling its self-proclaimed role, the
resultant shock is tremendous and the pliability of the masses

extreme—witness the psychological state of Germany and Japan after 1945. Parenthetically, it may also be noted that in a totalitarian state the symbols of authority are intimately connected with the actual locus of power and are thus especially tempting targets for terrorist action.[25]

The next general objective of agitational terror is the *elimination of opposing forces*, either physically or by neutralizing their effectiveness. In one sense, this is a by-product of terror, for the aim in itself is not symbolic; it could be accomplished by murder. Yet it is not feasible to remove, for example, the entire British police force on Cyprus, one by one. Nechayev's rather simplistic statement that "assassination will put fear in the hearts of the government" is valid only in a qualified sense. Like terrorism aimed at disorienting the social fabric, this more specific type also aims at achieving a demonstration effect. In fact, a considerable economy of effort may be achieved if acts aimed at disorientation utilize as their means the elimination of individuals who are in themselves harmful to the insurgent cause. From elimination of a harmful individual, not only will general disorientation be promoted, but a more specific fear will be instilled into the group to which the victim belongs ("Will I be next?" each will ask). This type of terrorism, directed as it is against an organized enemy who is a "legitimate" target of attack is quite similar to military operations. It represents the limiting case of terrorism in the direction of conventional military action.

The specific target in this case is the victim who is to be immobilized and his identification group; the level of discrimination must of course be very high so that the line is clearly drawn between those who are threatened and those who are not. The desired response is despair, total immobility that denies the incumbents the support of some of their most valuable forces and reserves.[26]

Another major use of agitational terror is the *provocation* of countermeasures by the incumbents. Faced with terroristic acts, the incumbents will find it necessary to suppress the terrorists. Ideally, suppression should be accomplished by routine methods of law enforcement, but if the terrorists are effective—and especially if the incumbents perceive themselves to be in a crisis situation—it is almost inevitable that extraordinary repressive measures will be taken. In combating an elusive terrorist, the incumbents will be forced to take measures that affect not only the terrorist but also his environment, the society as a whole. Although this result may be incidental to the aims of some terrorists, terroristic acts often are committed with the express purpose of provoking reprisals.

A much greater problem is whether or not repressive measures will actually have the desired effect. There is always the danger that the uncommitted will blame the terrorist for starting the whole chain of repression in the first place. Certainly a basic requirement of this sort of tactic is that the population not be actively committed against the terrorists. If the terrorists are opposed by the populace, provocation is very likely to be counterproductive. Even in the case of a populace that is sympathetic to the goals of the terrorists, much depends on the state of the popular mind.

Kropotkin believed that, while the government can normally stifle the opposition by repression, in times of popular upsurge (*époques d'effervescence*) the effect of repression will be to stimulate the insurgent movement, with corresponding divisions in the attitudes of the incumbents about the appropriate nature and degree of repression.[27] Che Guevara, on the other hand, appears most chary of utilizing terrorism, for fear that government repression will cost the insurgents more than they gain.[28] It is most difficult to find guidelines to specify when a population would react one way and when the other, and historical examples abound on both sides. A bonus effect of terror used successfully to provoke countermeasures is that these countermeasures themselves tend to be extraordinary and contribute to the general sense of insecurity and unrest that is the very objective of the terrorist, as well as to reduce the population's confidence in the incumbents.

In terms of tactical considerations, provocative terror must be highly discriminate in order to provoke the type of response desired. The target is not so much the victim (who will probably be killed and thus no longer be involved in the action) as his identification group—the incumbent élite—who will take the desired retaliatory action. The response to be achieved must be one of fear, so that the target will react and react specifically in a logical and predictable manner.[29]

### The Place of Terror in Internal War

As a weapon in the insurgent arsenal, terrorism has definite advantages and limitations that must be weighed against each other if terror is to be used effectively. Among its most prominent virtues is economy. It is a weapon that promises returns far out of proportion to the amount of time, energy, and materials the insurgents invest in it, enabling them to project an image many times larger than their actual strength. Terrorists also frequently argue that the economies of terror are very real in terms of human life. Trotsky proclaimed that simple reasoning showed terror to be essential for the saving of life, but only a few pages later he struck on the true economic value of terror by noting that "the revolution . . . kills individuals and intimidates thousands."[30]

The return on terror expenditures increases in direct but somewhat scaled-down proportion to the apparent indiscrimination of the terror employed. The psychological effect of indiscriminate terror is much greater, and it is extremely difficult for the incumbents to predict what the terrorist's target will be. Although no government would attempt to protect all potential targets, failure to protect any symbolically significant target can be used as a demonstration of incumbent weakness.

Most people would be willing to grant that terrorism, despite its economy, is not a desirable weapon to use. It is certainly undesirable from a moral point of view, and it is also generally recognized that terror by itself cannot be the final determinant of the outcome of an internal war. It can only be regarded as a means to an end, specifically, in our context, the end of political control. Its only effect upon the mass is to elicit an emotional response that results in no constructive activity. Having terrorized, the insurgents must then begin with the task of reforming the target into the desired patterns of activity.

The significance of this must be emphasized. If the insurgents

are in a position of political strength to begin with, it is unnecessary—and even wasteful—for them to initiate terrorism. They
lack, however, any less undesirable means of rendering the mass
mobilizable to their own symbols, and, by resorting to terrorism,
they tacitly admit their own political weakness. It is in this
sense that we must understand Brian Crozier's oft-repeated dictum that terrorism is the weapon of the weak.[31] Both Crozier
and Lucian Pye,[32] seem to envision this weakness in military
terms, but this reservation would only be valid in situations
where the insurgents are operating against a foreign colonial
power without the strength to engage in open warfare—or in any
situation where almost the entire population is actively opposed
to the government.

By presupposing a high degree of unanimity among the population, however, we exclude the most interesting cases of internal
war—in which the population is split. Even in such "colonial"
wars as those in Malaya or parts of Indochina, the real object
of the battle was control of the population. Only after the
insurgents had won this control could they move on to the stage
of directing their fire directly against the occupying power and
reach the position posited by Crozier. In fact, the Malayans never
reached this point. (Crozier, of course, recognizes this fact and
goes on to note that, if the support of the population is lacking,
terrorism may show great initial results but will ultimately become counterproductive.)

A crucial problem for all terrorists is that of timing. The
initial stage is the most important. If the terrorists can launch
a sudden massive campaign, they have the opportunity both to
create highly desirable psychological responses and perhaps even
temporarily to neutralize the incumbent forces. A movement
that could achieve such results, however, would probably be
politically so strong that it would not have to resort to terror.

For a number of reasons, agitational terror is not the sort
of activity that can be utilized effectively over a protracted period
of time. It tends to lose its effectiveness with familiarity; it is
perceived as an emergency weapon by most people; and it is not
appropriate to the legitimacy that an insurgent group must at
least claim to have. There are a number of interesting and sig-

nificant historical examples illustrating failure to realize weakness—particularly those of the right-wing Indonesians, the Burmese Communists, and the Malayan Communists.[33]

The reason for the importance of using extensive terror only in the initial stages of an insurgent movement, especially of not resorting to it after other means have failed, is obvious. The disorientation purpose of terror is followed by an attempt to supplant the demolished structures of authority by structures desired by the insurgents. To exploit the anguish of the disoriented mass, the insurgents must appear to be a pillar of strength, an infallible guide in a confusing world. This image will be somewhat tarnished, to say the least, if the insurgents have been proved incapable of overcoming the incumbents. Specific acts of terror, aimed primarily at intimidation, will be accepted by the population even in late stages of insurgency, especially if they are perceived as enforcement terror. The nature of these acts must be clear, however, for terror in late stages of an insurrectionary movement can look very much like (and frequently is) the irrational death throes of the movement. An attempt to begin a disorientation process *after* more direct methods have failed seems doomed to failure.[34]

On the basis of these considerations, we may discuss the possibilities of a model that would define the position of terror in an internal war. The most serviceable internal war model is that which Crozier presents, postulating terror as the first stage of a three-step development, which then progresses onward through guerrilla warfare to conventional warfare.[35] A more complicated model is given by Theodor Arnold, who distinguishes twelve phases of development in a "revolutionary war."[36] Arnold's model is too complicated for our purposes and devotes considerable attention to the previolent phase of internal war. He does agree with Crozier, however, in placing various forms of terrorism at the beginning of the violent phase.

With certain qualifications, we may take Crozier's model as our starting point. The first qualification is, of course, that not all of the three stages need be utilized. A movement with widespread popular support and at least a minimum military base can begin directly with guerrilla warfare operations.[37] More serious reservations involve the apparent time sequence that Crozier implies—that the terrorist phase terminates before the guerrilla phase begins and that guerrilla tactics are abandoned before conventional operations are undertaken. Certainly, combinations of guerrilla and conventional tactics are familiar enough in military history, nor is there any clear-cut dividing line between terrorism and guerrilla activity than can be deduced from experience.[38]

A revolutionary movement may also develop at varying speeds in different locations. A model could be constructed that would allow for these variations, but to do so would be to miss the point. Our criterion must again be whether or not the act is symbolic. Guerrilla warfare is, after all, only a variant form of conventional warfare, concerned like the latter with the physical destruction of the enemy by direct means. Terror is a psychological weapon that operates symbolically, that is, indirectly. In practice, we have little quarrel with Crozier's distinction of phases, except that it is more accurate to say that terror is *characteristic* of the first phase of revolutionary warfare and should not be characteristic of the later phases, which are properly dominated by guerrilla and conventional warfare.

Let us restate Crozier's phases in terms of two criteria: Are the implied actions symbolic, and are they conventional, in terms of traditional military doctrine?

| Terror | Symbolic | Unconventional |
|---|---|---|
| Guerrilla Warfare | Instrumental | Unconventional |
| Conventional Warfare | Instrumental | Conventional |

The logical grouping of terror and guerrilla warfare is more apparent than real, for it derives to a great extent from the discredited point of view that conventional warfare (whether internal or external) is a sort of God-given norm. There is somewhat more justification for a division that groups the three stages according to their symbolic content, but a rigid classification along these lines is also not valid, for, as we have seen, terror can extend throughout all three stages. It is better to consider the three stages as parts of a continuum, with significant elements of terror and guerrilla warfare continuing through to the

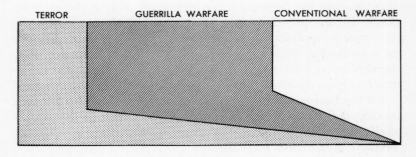

end. With this continuum in mind, we can construct our model on the basis of the three categories, expanded at either end.

| Phase | Characteristic |
|---|---|
| Preparatory | Previolent |
| Initial Violence | Terror |
| Expansion | Guerrilla Warfare |
| Victorious | Conventional Warfare |
| Consolidation | Postviolent |

In terms of incumbent *and* insurgent terror *appropriate* to given phases, the picture may be presented as follows:[39]

| Phase | INSURGENTS | | INCUMBENTS | | |
|---|---|---|---|---|---|
| | Agitational | Enforcement | Enforcement | Agitational | Totals |
| Preparatory | 0 | 0 | Low | 0 | Low |
| Initial Violence | High | Low | High | 0 | High |
| Expansion | Inter-mediate | Inter-mediate | Low | Low | High |
| Victorious | Low | High | 0 | Low | Inter-mediate |
| Consolidation | 0 | 0 | 0 | 0 | 0 |

Let us consider the problems in terms of the individual phases.

The *preparatory* phase represents the earliest period of nucleation of the insurgent movement. The insurgents are only beginning to organize their cadres and they enjoy the support of a minuscule part of the population. They hold no geographic area at all and have not yet openly proclaimed their movement.[40]

Their main concern is to remain unnoticed until they can get their forces adequately prepared. They therefore avoid acts of agitational terrorism that would invite the incumbents' attention, and they probably do not wish to utilize enforcement measures against any of their own members, except in the most pressing circumstances (imminent betrayal of the movement).

The incumbents do not know the movement is nucleating and therefore take no action in response to it. If, however, they should learn of the prospective insurgents and their objectives, this stage is the ideal time to crack down, with terror if appropriate. The incumbents should use as much enforcement terror as is required to do the job, but, given the weakness of the insurgents, it would probably not need to be a full-scale assault.

During the phase of *initial violence,* the movement is openly launched, begins to assume a characteristic form, and, after some time, gains strength in terms of a small geographic base and support of a small but significant portion of the population. The insurgents need to achieve maximum public attention and support for their struggle. If they are unable to achieve them by means of political tactics, they may choose terror for their weapon. This period is the classic one for the employment of agitational terror in all its functions—provocation, disorientation, elimination of rivals, and propaganda. The first signs of enforcement terror by insurgents also appear. They must enforce their mandate in whatever geographic area they may hold; they will also probably have enemies within the movement who must be neutralized. Some of these "neutralizations" may take place far behind the front, deep in incumbent territory. The insurgents will probably attempt to make their agitational terror look like enforcement, for, at this point, they will begin trying to establish a pretense of jurisdiction.

The incumbents, if they have not previously detected the insurgent movement, must now launch their maximum enforcement attack if they hope to stifle the movement. At this stage, therefore, both agitational and enforcement terrors will be at a maximum. It tends to be a time which tries men's souls.

The *expansion* phase covers the career of the insurgent movement from the end of its initial violence period to the point before the balance of power swings definitively in its direction.

In practice, this phase has many ups and downs and may last for a long time. The phase can be characterized by guerrilla warfare from a slowly expanding territorial base and gradually becoming more conventional as time goes on—as well as by an increase in support among the population in areas still under incumbent control. In the area controlled by the insurgents, a regular government will be established and assume appropriate functions. To this extent, the use of enforcement terror should at least be equal to agitational terror. The latter is still the appropriate tool in areas controlled by the incumbents, but it is not used in insurgent-controlled areas.

The incumbents may launch some agitational terror measures in the territory now controlled by the insurgents. They will be sorely tempted to counter the expanding insurgent influence—particularly as it is manifested in the extremely annoying tactics of guerrilla warfare—with terror. In all probability, however, this move will be a mistake, for they are more likely to alienate public support than to gain it. Their terror can no longer be directed primarily against the insurgents directly (as was the case in the earlier phases) but must compete with the insurgents for the acquiescence of the civilian population.

If the incumbents fail to perceive this need, and if their level of terror rises, they may have committed a fatal mistake. The level of insurgent terror must also decrease at this phase. If it does not, a decline, rather than an increase, in insurgent fortunes is indicated. This period is therefore critical in the development of terror on both sides.

In the *victorious* phase, the insurgents see the balance swinging in their favor, and they begin to consolidate their position militarily. They achieve jurisdiction over the entire country. Although there is no more organized resistance, the insurgents do not yet feel fully confident and will utilize a maximum level of enforcement terror as they weed out unwelcome remnants of the old regime and figures who are potentially dangerous. Considerable excesses are to be expected in view of the mixed atmosphere of elation and insecurity. The insurgents will also turn their attention to weeding out dissident or unreliable groups within their own movement. There is no scope for agitational terror.

The former incumbents now have no jurisdiction, but they may start thinking in terms of a comeback, and may initiate agitational acts against the new élite. More probably, they are thoroughly shattered and have no future beyond unsympathetic treatment in the insurgents' history books.

The final, or *consolidation*, phase finds the old incumbents completely destroyed, as the insurgents now take on the role of incumbents. The new incumbents should have no more need for enforcement terror and should be able to rely on routine law enforcement. They may, in fact, still have to use a considerable degree of enforcement terror to carry out their reforms in social and economic fields unconnected with the internal war situation.

It may not be too long before the entire process begins again, as new insurgent groups—arising either from the old incumbents or from new heresies—begin to seek the overthrow of the new incumbents. But that is another story.

## Notes

1. *The Rebels: A Study of Post-War Insurrections*, (London: Chatto and Windus, 1960), 159.

2. Friedrich Heer, *Sieben Kapitel aus der Geschichte des Schreckens* (Zürich: Max Niehans, undated (1957?)), p. 40, differentiates between "Red" terror, which manifests itself in murder and "strange forms of ritual ferocity" on the part of the rebelling (and temporarily successful) masses, as opposed to the "White" terror of the resurgent incumbents, which is characterized by institutionalized forms of punishment. Heer's distinction is not operationally useful, however, for insurgents are capable of being as cool and calculating as are the incumbents. Philip Selznick, *The Organizational Weapon: A Study of Bolshevik Strategy and Tactics*, (New York: The Free Press of Glencoe, 1960), p. 236, also stops short of an adequate differentiation. He lists such various tools of terror as assassination, "plus of course measures available to communist controlled governments." This distinction is implicitly the one we are making here. The definitions offered by Antoine Sotille in "Le Terrorisme International," *Académie de Droit International: Recueil des Cours*, III (Vol. LXV) 1938, 95ff., are concerned only with terrorism as a problem of international law.

3. The crucial difference between "in power" and "out of power" is that of jurisdiction, in the second Webster meaning "authority of a sovereign power to govern or legislate; right or power to exercise authority; control." No higher-level implications regarding the moral aspects of jurisdiction are implied.

4. On the Soviet Union see Carl Friedrich and Zbigniew Brzezinski, *Totalitarian Dictatorship and Autocracy* (Cambridge: Harvard University Press, 1957); Brzezinski, *The Permanent Purge; Politics in Soviet Totalitarianism* (Cambridge: Harvard University Press, 1956); and Barrington Moore, *Terror and Progress: USSR* (Cambridge: Harvard University Press, 1954); among many others. For Nazi Germany, interesting material is presented in Edmond Taylor, *The Strategy of Terror: Europe's Inner Front* (New York: Houghton Mifflin, 1940); Adolf Hitler, *Mein Kampf* (14th ed., Munich: Fritz Eher, 1932); Joseph Goebbels, *Kampf um Berlin* (Munich: Fritz Eher, 1934); and Bruno Bettelheim, *The Informed Heart* (New York: The Free Press of Glencoe, 1960). Generally valuable material can be found in Hannah Arendt, "Ideologie und Terror," *Offener Horizont: Festschrift für Karl Jaspers* (Munich: R. Piper, 1953); in Robert Payne, *Zero: The Story of Terrorism* (New York: John Day, 1950); and especially in Heer's *Sieben Kapitel* and Norman Cohn, *The Pursuit of the Millennium* (New York: Harper Torchbooks, 1961).

5. This definition is valid for both agitational and enforcement terror.

6. This danger could be reduced by increasing discrimination. See page 81.

7. See R. V. Burks, *The Dynamics of Communism in Eastern Europe* (Princeton: Princeton University Press, 1961), pp. 13-14. We can still read, however, in the United States State Department's blue book on the Viet Cong attacks that the Viet Cong is recruiting its forces by terroristic methods (*A Threat to Peace: North Viet-Nam's Effort to Conquer South Viet-Nam* (Washington, D.C.: 1961), Part I, p. 12). Conceivably, prospective recruits might be blackmailed into service and kept from deserting by threats against their families. Under such circumstances, however, one could hardly expect them to perform at the level the Viet Cong appears to be achieving.

8. *Mein Kampf*, pp. 45-46.

9. "Ideologie und Terror," p. 242. The ideology need not by any means be limited to Communism or Fascism.

10. *Narodnaya Volya*, Vol. II, No. 6 (October 23, 1961), reprinted in *Literatura Sotsial'no-Revolyutsionnoy Partii "Narodnoy Voli"* (1905), p. 401.

11. What if President Garfield's assassin had been advocating, not a more egocentric orientation of the spoils system, but the enactment of civil service legislation? It would be a limiting case certainly, and, although closely related to terrorism, would probably best be called something else. If, however, civil service enthusiasts throughout the country had at that time been urging the assassination of presidents to bring attention to their cause, we would have a clear case of terrorism and even a very effective one, since Garfield's death did promote civil service reform. On the other hand, if civil service reform had been the objective of the killing, his death would probably have retarded the reforms. Such is the dilemma of terrorism.

12. The term "resonant mass" is taken from the "Document on Terror," printed in *News from behind the Iron Curtain*, I (No. 3, March, 1952), 53.

13. Friedrich and Brzezinski, *Totalitarian Dictatorship*, p. 131, argue that in view of the manifold interrelationships among groups in society, the entire population will inevitably become affected by the terror.

14. Given this situation, it is highly questionable whether any such colonial war can be correctly classified as an internal war. Certainly the psychological relationships among the actors are very different from those

in a regular internal war situation, and the problems faced by both sides are of a different nature. Although we shall make certain observations about terrorist occurrences in colonial war situations, we shall exclude the colonial war as an analytical category of internal war in dealing with terrorism. Probably it should be completely excluded from the internal war inventory.

15. In fact, they are loosely derived from the terminology of scholastic philosophy, but no attempt has been made at exact accommodation to the scholastic framework.

16. It is not our purpose here to work out any detailed psychological background for the use of terror. Much work clearly needs to be done on the subject. There is interesting material in the volume *Identity and Anxiety*, Maurice R. Stein, et al., eds. (New York: The Free Press of Glencoe, 1960), especially Kurt Riezeler's article "The Social Psychology of Fear," reprinted from *American Journal of Sociology*, XLIX (1944), 489-498. Also important are the articles by Frieda Fromm-Reichmann, Franz L. Neumann, and Joost A. M. Meerloo. Reference should also be made to Bruno Bettelheim's *The Informed Heart* and to the experiments of John T. Lanzetta, et al., reported in the *Journal of Abnormal and Social Psychology*, XLIX (1954), 445-453, and in *Human Relations*, VII (No. 1, February, 1955), 29-52. Lanzetta's work with small groups is probably not directly applicable to genuine terror, since it is hardly possible to create artificially the conditions that would simulate the high levels of fear associated with terror. It does, however, raise the interesting question concerning the point at which external pressure begins to atomize individuals within a group rather than stimulating group cohesiveness.

17. Moore, *Terror and Progress*, pp. 169-170, considers that the Soviet terror appears capricious to the Russian people and thus undermines their "essential bases of social organization."

18. Pierre Kropotkin, *Paroles d'un Révolté* (Paris: C. Marpon et E. Flammarion, undated), p. 286.

19. A subcase of this objective is the attempt to polarize public opinion by means of terroristic acts. The insurgents' opponents (either incumbents or other insurgents) will respond strongly, perhaps with terror of their own, and neutrals will feel compelled to take sides. For a discussion of the activities of the French Secret Army in this context see Edmond Taylor, "The Ugly Trend," *The Reporter* (December 7, 1961), p. 26.

20. *The Strategy of Terror*, p. 183.

21. "Ideologie und Terror," pp. 239ff.

22. The Communists interviewed by Gabriel Almond for *The Appeals of Communism* (Princeton: Princeton University Press, 1954), showed, in many instances, a severe sense of isolation and rejection of stabilizing norms. Reminiscences of ex-Communists reinforce this impression to the extent that it becomes almost a stereotype.

23. Norman Cohn's description of the followers of mediaeval chiliastic movements bears striking similarities to the state of disorientation that we have assumed to be the objective of terror. Cohn conceives of this state as mass paranoia, which in more modern times has channeled itself into totalitarian movements. (*The Pursuit of the Millenium, passim*, especially the Conclusion.)

24. David Riesman, et al., *The Lonely Crowd* (New Haven: Yale University Press, 1950), *passim*.

25. The totalitarian state has, of course, a great advantage in the effi-

ciency of its repressive apparatus. In both Germany and the Soviet Union, this efficiency more than offset the vulnerabilities of the system.

26. In theory, the entire population, excluding the insurgents, could be the target. Once everybody else was immobilized, the insurgents would stand alone on the field. This effect may be possible in small-group situations, but it is rather unlikely in normal practice. In military terms, it is analogous to the physical elimination of the entire enemy population.

27. Kropotkin, *Paroles*, p. 287.

28. Guevara, *On Guerrilla Warfare* (New York: Frederick A. Praeger, 1961), pp. 56, 59.

29. There is an extensive and illuminating discussion of this technique in the "Document on Terror" (Note 12). The "Document" is worthy of intensive study, even though its source is at best questionable. Although no claims are made about its provenance, it is obviously intended to appear to be of Communist origin. This origin is highly doubtful on internal grounds, but no matter where or by whom it was written, the "Document" is of exceptional theoretical and operational interest. The German "original"—generously made available to me by the Free Europe Committee—contains important material not printed in the English-language version.

30. Leon Trotsky, *Terrorism and Communism: A Reply to Karl Kautsky* (Ann Arbor, Mich.: Ann Arbor Paperbacks, 1961), pp. 53, 58.

31. *The Rebels*, p. 191.

32. Pye, *Guerrilla Communism in Malaya* (Princeton: Princeton University Press, 1956), p. 95.

33. For Indonesia, see Crozier, *The Rebels*, p. 127. The Burmese case is explored by John H. Badgley in "Burma's Radical Left: A Study in Failure," *Problems of Communism*, X (No. 2, March-April, 1961), 52. On Malaya, see Pye, *Guerilla Communism*, p. 106, as well as Crozier, pp. 165-168, and J. H. Brimmel, *Communism in Southeast Asia* (London: Oxford University Press, 1959), pp. 327-8. The decree suspending large-scale terrorism in Malaya was reprinted in the London *Times* of December 1, 1952. It is an important example of problems encountered in gauging the proper degree of discrimination in a terrorist campaign.

34. This proposition holds true only if there is little or no time lapse between the two phases. There is no theoretical reason why a movement cannot fail, withdraw for a few years to regroup, and then begin a disorientation campaign as a fresh start.

35. Crozier, *The Rebels*, p. 163.

36. Theodor Arnold, *Der Revolutionäre Krieg* (Pfaffenhofen: Ilmgau Verlag, 1961).

37. The Chinese Communists are apparently an example of this method. Terrorism is not treated in the standard Maoist canon, nor does it seem to have played a significant role in the spread of the Chinese Communist movement. The extensive use of agitational terror by the Viet Cong is almost unique in Communist practice. George Modelski suggests that this may represent a significant V.C. weakness. ("The Viet Minh Complex" in *Communism and Revolution: The Strategic Uses of Political Violence*, ed. by C. E. Black and T. P. Thornton (Princeton: Princeton University Press, 1964), p. 210.

38. Crozier does not maintain that there is sharp distinction in time either, and, in fact, he implicitly recognizes the concurrence of guerrilla and terrorist tactics by distinguishing them according to their targets:

civilian targets for terror, military for guerrilla warfare. This distinction, however, is not valid, for terror can be directed against a military target (for example, bombings of officers' clubs in Saigon).

39. This model is specifically *not* concerned with colonial war situations. It postulates an internal war that develops steadily and shows no such complicating factors as racial antagonisms or foreign intervention. It is convenient to include material on enforcement terror for purposes of comparison. For the purposes of the model, it should be assumed that the incumbents *do not* represent a totalitarian system. Were they to do so, a number of complicating variants would have to be introduced.

40. Of course, the insurgents could represent a very old movement that embraces a large part of the population. It is improbable, however, for if they did have widespread bases of political strength, they would probably not embrace terrorism. We are, at any rate, concerned here only with the specifically violent aspect.

*Karl W. Deutsch*

## EXTERNAL INVOLVEMENT

## IN INTERNAL WAR

When we speak of "internal wars"—like civil wars, guerrilla wars, or revolutions—we usually take for granted the body politic to which they are "internal." We accept as unchanging the boundaries of the state, country, or political unit within which they are fought. Taking this unit as constant, we then observe the changes in the intensity and frequency of violence that lead from more or less uneasy civil peace to open civil war or back to a new state of peace brought on by victory or exhaustion.

### Spilling Across Boundaries: The Demonstration Effect

History shows many instances, however, where such revolutions, guerrilla wars, or civil wars spread across old boundaries. They may do so merely by the "demonstration effect" of their example upon neighboring populations, which are already attentive to such conflicts and favorably predisposed to engage in parallel attacks upon domestic foes in their own countries. Such was the case in the revolutions of 1848, which swept like wildfire over much of Europe.[1]

### Propaganda and Clandestine Intervention

In other cases, this "demonstration effect" may be strengthened by deliberate efforts at propaganda, aimed by one or both

[ 100 ]

parties in one territory at presumably receptive elements in the population of another. Such propagandizing has been the time-honored practice of revolutionists, from the efforts of the Continental Congress to subvert Canada against Britain to the all-out revolutionary and democratic propaganda of the French Legislative Assembly and National Convention in the 1790's—propaganda whose contemporary echoes and effects in many countries have recently been traced by Robert Palmer.[2] The practice has come down to our own century in the broadcasts of the Russian Bolsheviks in 1918 "to everybody" and in the sustained current propaganda efforts of the Communist regimes in Moscow and Peking.

Opponents of a revolutionary ideology have been equally willing to reach across the boundaries of states. While the French revolutionary governments flooded Europe with cheap translations of the works of Rousseau, Britain and other conservative powers soon saw to it that they were answered by cheap translations of the works of Edmund Burke and Joseph de Maistre. In our own time, the volume of international anti-Communist propaganda emanating from the United States and its allies has become impressive, and it is not unusual for domestic critics of United States foreign policy to demand that the United States output of international propaganda should match and even surpass that of the Communists, in both volume and intensity.

Mere propaganda is often supplemented by such drastic forms of intervention as the infiltration of individual agents, of larger numbers of guerrilla troops, or of technical specialists to make such troops more effective—sometimes together with considerable technical equipment like weapons, ammunition, or communications gear. The extreme cases are then the incursion of whole bodies of troops from the outside, as "volunteers," who may have been individually recruited through an organized campaign (the "Loyalist International Brigades" in the Spanish Civil War of 1936-1938) or who may have been sent in by governments as organized military troops (the Italian and German units on the Franco side in the same civil war or the massive forces of Chinese Communist "volunteers" who intervened in Korea in the fall of 1950). The unsuccessful invasion of Castro's Cuba in 1961 by anti-Castro volunteers with limited but highly visible

United States support is a more recent case in point. From such only nominally clandestine acts of intervention, it is only a small step to the overt intervention of foreign troops in domestic conflict—and only another small step to such open foreign intervention in countries where domestic conflict, although invoked as a pretext, is in fact insignificant or absent and the true aim is naked foreign conquest.

### Sovereignty and the Balance between Internal and External Elements

In most internal wars, elements of domestic strife and of external intervention are intermingled in varying proportions. If, on both sides of such a conflict, there is a clear quantitative preponderance of domestic motivations, recruitment, and resources, we may speak of an authentic internal war or revolution. If outside manpower, motives, money, and other resources appear to constitute the main capabilities committed to the struggle on both sides, then we are inclined to speak of a "war by proxy" —an international conflict between two foreign powers, fought out on the soil of a third country; disguised as conflict over an internal issue of that country; and using some or all of that country's manpower, resources, and territory as means for achieving preponderantly foreign goals and foreign strategies.

To be sure, these goals of foreign powers may appear wholly compatible with those of the two main domestic factions in the struggle. North Korean Communists in 1950, insofar as they were true believers in their ideology, may have viewed their interests as identical with those of Communist China and the Soviet Union; and South Korean anti-Communists may have felt a similar identity of their interests with those of the United States, and perhaps Canada and Britain. The fact remains, however, that only North and South Korean territory was devastated, while the territories and civilian populations of Red China, Russia, and the United States remained untouched. North and South Korea bore the major burden of military casualties, but substantial losses were also borne by the United States and China, while the Soviet Union suffered no appreciable losses, and Canada and other allies of the United States also remained substantially unscathed. An earlier example of a somewhat similar pattern may be found in the Thirty Years' War of 1618-1648, which assumed in some of its phases the function of a proxy war between France and Spain, with the latter supporting the Catholic faction, and the former the Protestant, in what began as a religious struggle within the Holy Roman Empire. In the outcome, the religious division of Germany and of Europe remained substantially unchanged. Germany was desolated and one-third of her population perished; Spain suffered a major political setback but remained undevastated; France emerged flourishing and her historians remember the seventeenth as "the great century"—*le grand siècle*—of French history.

In both 20th-century Korea and 17th-century Germany, major belief systems or ideologies have asserted the identity of interest between at least one local function and the great foreign power that protected it. If Communist Russia has claimed the role of the fatherland of all toilers, the United States has not less convincingly claimed that of the world-wide arsenal of democracy and citadel of freedom, while seventeenth-century Spain and Austria claimed the role of universal protectors of the Roman Catholic faith. Only France, under the leadership of the formidable Cardinal Richelieu, forsook such claims and resorted openly to power politics. The government of her *rex Christianissimus* paid subsidies to the Protestant king of Sweden in order to weaken the power of Catholic Austria and Spain—a successful maneuver that resulted in weakening the international power of European Catholicism and in strengthening the national power of France.

The Thirty Years' War thus contained an element of asymmetry; and much greater asymmetries in the extent of foreign intervention in internal wars have been frequent, for example in the case of the one-sided massive and bloody intervention of Soviet tanks and troops in the Hungarian rebellion of 1956 or that of the massive but bloodless intervention of the United States in the political crisis in Lebanon in 1958.

Soon after the beginning of an internal war, experienced observers may in many cases feel confident to judge the authenticity or artificiality of an internal war, the extent and significance of outside intervention on one or both sides, the larger relevance of this local conflict in the international arena, and the probable stability or instability of its outcome. They often arrive at these judgments, however, by means of criteria left implicit and unspecified, and when their judgments differ—as they often do —they may do so on matters not only of verifiable fact but also of semantic vagueness or misunderstanding.

How can judgment of the domestic or foreign-controlled character of an internal war be made more precise and more clearly comparable, by introducing some simple measurement of at least some of their relevant aspects?

### Some Quantitative Aspects of Internal Wars

The simplest quantitative aspect of an internal war seems to be its *duration*. How long did hostilities continue on a significant scale, and how much longer were special measures of suppression or "pacification" applied by the victor at a significant level of cost? In the twentieth century, substantial civil strife in China has lasted for at least forty years, in Mexico for almost twenty, in Colombia for more than ten, in Algeria for over seven, in Russia for almost four, in Greece, Spain, and Ireland for about three—the list could be continued down to the Austrian civil war of 1934, which lasted only a few days.

This concept of the duration of an internal war "on a significant scale" already implies a second aspect—its *extent*. How many people are actively involved? In how large a territory, with how large a population? Proportions may be more illuminating: What per cent of the population of the country is involved? What share of its territory? How did these proportions change in the course of the internal war?[3]

Behind these most primitive indicators of the size and duration of the conflict we can search for estimates or indicators of the *recruitment and attrition rates* of each of the contending forces. How many persons are added, on the average, to the fighters on one side? How many are lost to the same faction during the same period through casualties, surrenders, defection, or desertion? What are the corresponding rates for the opposing party? How are any of these rates changing over time?

If these rates can be computed or estimated, it should then be possible to set up a crude mathematical model of the war, perhaps in the form of differential equations similar to those proposed for another but formally similar problem by the Soviet mathematician Gause which were reported in a recent book by Anatol Rapoport. Even such a crude model could suggest answers to some interesting questions: What will be the relative strength of the two sides in a short war, and how will it tend to change as the war drags on? Can both parties maintain themselves indefinitely in the conflict, in a kind of "warlike coexistence," or is time working against one of them?

Gause's model, published in 1934, deals with the competitive coexistence of two species of beetles in a sack of flour. Its main variables for each species are rate of reproduction; the rate at which the increase in one species' numbers tends to inhibit increase among its competitor; and the rate at which its own increase tends to inhibit its own further reproduction. If we substitute the rates of recruitment of a guerrilla force and of the government forces opposing it, respectively, for the rates of increase of the two species of beetles and if we further substitute the relevant rates of attrition for the respective rates of inhibition, then Gause's model could be adapted, perhaps with some further modifications, to the problem of internal war. It is difficult to speculate about whether or not any thoughts of this kind may have occurred to Communist strategists. In any case, it seems noteworthy that rates of attrition and of recruitment appear to play a significant part in Mao Tse-tung's theory of guerrilla warfare.[4]

A well-known example of differential rates of recruitment is taken from the American War of Independence of 1775-1783. It has been estimated that roughly one-third of the Colonial population supported the Patriots in that conflict; another one-third sympathized with the Loyalists; and the last one-third was neutral. Although the two main factions were thus evenly matched, the Patriots produced 400,000 enlistments in the course of the conflict, while the Loyalists produced only 50,000 or one-eighth the rate of their opponents.

This example suggests that rates of recruitment and attrition may also serve as *indicators of the morale and the intensity of motivation of each side*. In this respect, they may be supplemented by other measurable indicators like the ratio of prisoners to casualties on each side. It has been reported that in the Austro-Hungarian army during World War I, the recruitment rate was far lower than that of Germany, while the attrition and defection rates among the non-German and non-Magyar subjects of the Habsburg monarchy were much higher. "Germany, France and Serbia ultimately placed 3.5 divisions in the field per every million of population, Turkey 2.5 divisions, and England 2 divisions, but Austria-Hungary only 1.5 division. This is to be explained solely by the *lack* of Austrian cadres which especially in the first year of the War were terribly attenuated. Austria sent at once into the War an army of 1,500,000, and by the close of 1914 reinforcements of a further 800,000 men. At the beginning of 1915 the Austrian strength was only 800,000 men, and only 516,000 rifles. The losses sustained in 1914 were officially acknowledged at 1,270,000 men. Of that number, 260,000 had been taken prisoner, and 210,000 were on the sick list. Among the sick, about half the number at least consisted of those who intended at all costs to avoid the duty of fighting for Austria. The Austrian army lost in the year 1914, through the passive resistance conducted by the downtrodden Slavonic and Latin nations, about 400,000 men, or approximately one-third of the original fighting force. The Germans, the English and the French had 2 killed for every 1 prisoner, whereas of the Austrians 5 were taken prisoner for every 2 killed."[5]

Even some qualitative aspects of the performance of the contending sides in an internal war can be gauged with the help of quantitative indicators. Such qualitative aspects include *coordination; style of behavior;* and the *presence or absence of certain themes, practices, symbols,* and *behavior patterns.* Coordination of behavior can be described in terms of its distribution in space and time, and the degree of coordination of expectations can be inferred from it to some extent.[6] Style of behavior and the presence, absence, or recurrence of relevant practices or symbols can also be described in terms of statistical distributions and recursion formulas—and thus in part by methods familiar from content analysis. Methods of this kind are quantitative and, in large part, impersonally reproducible, and they may thus serve as a relatively impersonal supplement to the expert's more personal judgment on the relevant area and history.

Once it is possible to derive such measurements for certain aspects of internal wars, it should also become practical to use them to estimate the extent and effects of foreign intervention in internal wars.

## Some Measurable Aspects of Outside Intervention

For purposes of comparison with the duration and extent of the internal war, the duration and extent of outside intervention on each side may be measured. *This measurement might be taken in terms of manpower, money, material, and specialized services.* A general estimate of the effect of outside intervention on the extent and duration of the internal war may then be attempted. Did intervention cut it short or confine it to a few holdout areas, by establishing or increasing the superiority of one of the contending parties? Or did intervention prolong the war or aid in its spread, by making the strength of the two parties more nearly equal?

More specifically, what were the effects of outside intervention on the rate of recruitment of the side on which it occurred? What did it do to the rate of recruitment of the enemy? What were the effects of whatever outside intervention occurred on the other side? And what were the effects of outside intervention on the rates of attrition on each side?

To estimate such effects, it may be necessary to estimate first what the rates of recruitment and attrition might have been, if there had been no outside intervention on either side, or on only one side. Such estimates could be made with the aid of data from earlier or later periods of the same conflict or from comparable conflicts elsewhere. In any case, it would be necessary to do explicitly what most of us in our thinking do by implication: to construct a set of expected performance data as a base line or null model in the background, against which the actually observed data are measured and found either "about as expected," "notably higher," or "lower." In this manner, "normal" or expected rates of recruitment or attrition may be confronted with actually observed ones, both in terms of absolute difference, $D = A - E$, and in terms of relative deviation, $R = \dfrac{A - E}{E}$.

The same general procedure can be followed in regard to the ratios of prisoners to casualties on each side. What, in the light of comparable data from other times and places, would be a reasonable estimate of expectable ratios on each side in the absence of outside intervention, and how much of the actual figures should be imputed to such intervention as has taken place?

Similar estimates may be made, finally, for the effects of outside intervention upon certain qualitative aspects of the performance of each side in the internal war: the degree of coordination in its action or the presence or absence of particular themes, symbols, or practices. The lack of any effective clandestine Soviet intervention on the side of the Mau Mau in Kenya could thus be inferred from the absence of guerrilla tactics that would have been technically rational and characteristic of Communist guerrillas (as well as of the West European resistance forces in World War II). Such rational tactics would have concentrated upon the sabotage and destruction of crucial material installations like telephone and power lines, water mains, gasoline depots, and all kinds of machinery. Such objects would have been very expensive either to guard or to replace, and sustained attacks upon them might have exacted a heavier price from the opposing side than did the gory but relatively ineffective tactics the Mau Mau actually adopted.

## Some Gains and Costs of Ruthlessness

The effectiveness or ineffectiveness of particularly ruthless or terrorizing tactics may also be studied in terms of their effects upon the recruitment and attrition rates of each contending party. It seems plausible that extremely ruthless tactics may serve as an additional amplifier of a substantial existing margin of superiority, but that they are likely to fail in its absence. In the first case, they may increase the enemy's attrition by frightening his troops, while only to a small degree increasing his rate of recruitment by provoking the anger of that part of the population on his side. There may also be a depressing effect on the ruthless party's own recruitment rate, due to the outraging of the cultural and moral standards of its own constituency, but this effect is unlikely to overcome an already existing strong margin of superiority.

Conversely, for either of two evenly matched factions, any recourse to extremely ruthless tactics seems unlikely to be profitable. The expectable decline in the ruthless party's own recruitment rate, together with the likely rise in the recruitment rate of his opponent, seems apt to shift the balance of forces further against the ruthless actor who lacks substantial superiority to start with. Finally, by the same reasoning, a substantially weaker side in an internal war is most likely to lose from a resort to ruthless tactics. Such tactics are likely to diminish its popular support, to increase the popularity and motivation of its enemies, and thus to hasten its downfall.

### Some Costs of Outside Intervention

In actual cases, the effects of outside intervention may be complex. It may help the faction on whose side it occurs, *if that faction already is more thoroughly alienated from its domestic adversary than from its outside ally.* If, however, the two contending factions still have much in common, which they do not share with the foreign power about to intervene, then such outside intervention may well damage the side it is supposed to aid. Indignation at this "betrayal" of the common homeland, tradition, or ideology may raise the recruitment and lower the attrition of the opposing faction, while having the opposite effect upon the faction that invoked foreign aid. Insufficient outside aid to a weak domestic faction may thus do more harm than good to the side that is intended to benefit from it; and outside aid to a faction still culturally or ideologically linked to its opponent may have a similar effect by damaging the motivations of its members. In 1793, for example, French aristocrats could perhaps accept foreign aid against the Jacobins more readily than could the Girondins; and in 1917 the Russian middle class parties and even the Mensheviks could accept Western aid against Lenin more easily than the adherents of Trotsky could accept aid against Stalin after 1924.

Even if victorious, outside intervention may exact its price.

If the domestic ally has become dwarfed in terms of autonomous capabilities by the preponderance of outside power, the outcome of the internal war-cum-intervention may be the loss of effective sovereignty and the emergence of another puppet or satellite regime.

If the domestic faction has not been thus reduced to a political appendage, however, then a crisis of sovereignty may follow upon victory. The victorious domestic faction now has the task of reasserting its sovereignty against its outside ally, and in the course of this process it may come to look upon its former ally as an enemy. Thus on the Catholic side in the Thirty Years' War, Bavaria became increasingly jealous of her independence from Austria after 1630, and for most of the period between 1630 and 1814 her rulers and people looked upon their Catholic neighbor and former ally, Austria, as a hereditary enemy.

### Notes

1. For a general discussion, cf. Priscilla Robertson, *Revolutions of 1848: A Social History* (Princeton: Princeton University Press, 1952).

2. Robert R. Palmer, *The Age of the Democratic Revolutions: A Political History of Europe and America 1760-1800* (Princeton: Princeton University Press, 1959).

3. For a striking, though slightly different, example of a change in the proportions of combat munitions output between the German-Italian-Japanese Axis and its enemies between 1938 and 1943, see Klaus Knorr, *The War Potential of Nations* (Princeton: Princeton University Press, 1956), pp. 34-35.

4. Anatol Rapoport, *Fights, Games, and Debates* (Ann Arbor: University of Michigan Press, 1960), pp. 76-82; G. F. Gause, *The Struggle for Existence* (Baltimore: Williams and Wilkins, 1934); Mao Tse Tung, *Selected Works* (London: Lawrence and Wishart, 1956), four volumes; Mao Tse Tung, *Selected Works* (Peking Foreign Language Press, 1961), Vol. IV.

5. Colonel Emanuel Moravec, *The Military Importance of Czechoslovakia in Europe* (Prague: "Orbis" Printing & Publishing Co., 1938), pp. 40-41.

6. On the importance of the coordination of expectations in mutinies, revolutions, and wars, see Thomas C. Schelling, *The Strategy of Conflict* (Cambridge: Harvard University Press, 1960), pp. 90-99, 146-147, 283-290, 294-295. For a critical discussion of Schelling's general approach, see also K. W. Deutsch, *The Nerves of Government: Models of Political Communication and Control* (New York: The Free Press of Glencoe, 1963), pp. 62-72.

*Arnold S. Feldman*

## VIOLENCE AND VOLATILITY:

## THE LIKELIHOOD OF REVOLUTION*

Social theory has remarkably little to say about the occurrence of large-scale violence.[1] Violence is almost never predicted and rarely measured accurately. The study of social violence is typically viewed as an area of social pathology, and the literature is quite often phrased in the language of the clinic.[2] In this sense, violence is conceived as being *incidental* to the basic character of social structures and processes. Indeed, the very conception of *social structure* ordinarily excludes the sources of structural destruction.

The temporary character of violence is, of course, attributed to its intimate relationship with social volatility. For large-scale violence is considered to be a correlate of social change. Thus, social science frequently uses the term "social instability" to connote either violence or volatility and often both, indiscriminately.

The intimate association between violence and social change at times results in a similarity in perception. All too often profound social change is viewed as if it too were incidental and intrusive, if not pathological.

This severely stylized, perhaps sterile, view of violence and volatility arises in part from the excessively stable image of social life that is projected by much of social science. The social systems portrayed by contemporary research are remarkably tame.

---

* Much of the content of this essay derives from work undertaken jointly with Professor Wilbert E. Moore on a book about the nature of industrial societies. Of course, this essay was written for the symposium, and only minimal revisions have been undertaken.

[ 111 ]

An extreme example of this domestication of the social world is the recent literature on the world of business, which increasingly describes a nice world wherein nice people nicely influence other nice people to buy nice things from nice stores. The occasional violence that intrudes upon this stately suburban world is quite incidental, like the unfortunate personal injuries that a few lady shoppers may experience during bargain days.[3]

It needs no great amount of perspicacity, however, to recognize that violence and volatility are neither rare nor incidental both within and between social systems. Why then does the world described by contemporary science seem so domesticated?

In much of systems theory, the relative lack of attention to violence and volatility is quite deliberate. During the past decade, the pre-eminent task of social theory has been the search for sources of order.[4] Given this program, the images of social life— the models of societies, constructed or projected—have, by choice, ignored or "held constant" the sources of profound discontinuities that I think all would agree are potential within societies. There is no denial in systems theory that achieving comprehension of violence and volatility is a most important task. Rather—and for heuristic reasons—this task has been assigned a relatively low priority.[5]

### Problem and Program

The main concern of this essay is with changes in the image of a social system that will provide a basis for incorporating violence and volatility. Of course the special concern is with that type of violence *cum* volatility that gives rise to revolutions.

Revolutions, however, are in a sense a special case of a more general class of profound social discontinuities. Put another way, revolutions are one kind of actualization of societal potentials for conflict and change. Thus, the potential for revolution is equally the potential for other kinds of social change. In sum, while this paper concentrates upon the likelihood of (the societal potential for) revolutions, it should be clear that such a potential or likelihood is capable of wider generalization and application.

More specifically, this essay will focus on [the relationship between change and conflict, as a "normal" property of social systems.] Thus, we shall be concerned with the manner in which volatility is generated within societies, as these societies experience profound social change.

In sum, the program for this essay consists of (1) The examination and listing of a set of assumptions that are sympathetic to the systematic inclusion of violence and volatility into the operating image of a social system. (2) The specification of the characteristics of such an image, that is, the description of some characteristics of social life that are *relatively* ignored in the typical view of social structures. (3) The beginning specification of some sources of strains that contribute to the likelihood of revolutions, especially as these sources of strain are generated through social change.

This program is obviously excessively ambitious, if not pretentious. There should be no doubt in the reader's mind that the exposition will fall short of achieving these goals. It may be possible, however, to provide some partial answers and to indicate the direction in which other answers can be found.

## Basic Assumptions and Conceptions

The manner in which revolutions are perceived in social science affords a convenient and relevant example of what is meant by the domestication of social life. For the tame image of social systems imparts to the view of revolution a particular form, in that it contains a number of assumptions about the nature of revolutions.

In brief, these assumptions include that of a series of relatively brief periods of time during which rates of violence and volatility experience sharp increases. These periods are assumed to be interspersed among a contrasting series of relatively durable social states during which rates of conflict and change are moderated. Thus, each "revolution" is preceded and followed by some kind of social hiatus wherein steps forward are consolidated and losses are made up.

This view of revolution might be termed the "theory of cor-

related moderates." For it assumes that societies are in stasis *only* when the different rates of change—political, economic, and social—enjoy some kind of equivalence at a moderate level. That is to say the conception of revolution is derivative from a conception of peaceful politics, and the conception of peaceful politics is derivative from that tame image of the social system.

The assumptions and conceptions of tame social systems and peaceful politics encompass a number of valuable and viable constructs for the study of order and change in social life. Rates of violence and volatility *do* vary quite widely both longitudinally and cross-sectionally. It is theoretically and empirically useful to describe conflict and change in terms of cycles, and the value of a "take-off" concept for certain kinds of analyses has been adequately demonstrated.

Thus, it is no doubt most convenient to contemplate revolutionary change as a sporadic phenomenon that permits societies periods of time during which expended energies may be renewed. One could then study conflict and change much as the popular military historian studies wars—as a series of pitched battles separated by periods for resting and regrouping forces.

Such assumptions and conceptions are, however, of dubious utility for other purposes, for they lead to the condition previously described: the inability to deal meaningfully with the sources of discordance and disequilibration that are ever-present in social systems.

## A Conception of Revolutionary Potential

Our conception of societal potential for revolution assumes, first, that the possibility of violent socio-political conflict is always present in every society. Of course, the magnitude of this potential varies quite widely. Nevertheless, the potential for revolution is a "normal" characteristic of societies. For conflict and potential violence are elementary properties both within and especially between a society's component social structures.

Each revolution is, of course, historically unique. The category of such events can, however, be studied, and the potential for revolution can be measured and related to various other social factors. From this point of view, revolutions represent the extreme manifestation of social and political strains and tensions that are always present in some degree. Any attempt to measure the likelihood of revolution should therefore encompass the social sources of strains and tensions present in the several societies and the social conditions that either encourage or balance extreme acts among the contending forces.

The previous sentence implies that the magnitude of the likelihood of revolutions is a function of both positive or conflict-generating factors and negative or conflict-controlling factors. The concept of society as a net balance between equilibrating and disequilibrating forces is, of course, quite ancient. Such a concept is an integral part of systems theory.[6] The emphasis on the over-all balance of the system, however, tends to make the over-all sum of opposing forces most salient, and, in that way, it downgrades the ubiquity of permanent sources of conflict. Thus, the conception of likelihood for revolution involves the notion that any net balance is likely to be quite fragile. In fact, the component forces themselves constitute the critical area for analysis. In any case, any attempt to estimate the degree of a society's revolutionary potential should include both classes of factors: those that generate, as well as those that manage, tensions.

Any society is simultaneously a host for tensions and a network of tension-management devices. It is important that sociological theory encompass both these aspects, rather than masking what I think is a highly dynamic relationship by attending only to the net balance. For at any one period of time, the chances are that these net balances will favor the tension-mangement arrangements—as, by the way, systems theory accurately perceives. Nevertheless, a society is as previously noted, considerably more subject to rapid and even radical alteration. The tensions may be managed, but they also endure unsolved.

A third aspect of revolutionary potential is its intimate relationship with social change. Social change and social conflict are highly correlated, not only by definition. Persistent social strains—the enduring tensions of societies—and the conflicts they engender present challenges to any given social system. Although social change in response to such challenges may reduce the strains and in that sense lead to more efficient tension-manage-

ment, it should also be noted that the optimistic solution will
not automatically occur. Changes that result from the presence
of persistent social strains are as likely as not to generate even
more tensions than they reduce.

As so many have noted before, the new social forms that
result from any given social change typically conflict with some
existing norms and typically affect adversely some existing interests. Of course, the same changes may support other previously
existing norms and interests. Any given social change may thus
simultaneously add to and subtract from the likelihood of revolution. Concepts and measurements should encompass the notion of a double-entry balance sheet.

In sum, the conception of a society's potential for revolution
emphasizes the following themes:

1. The potential for revolution is a function of basic social
structure and is in that sense a normal social property.

2. The potential for revolution is a function of the balance
between the conflict-generating and the conflict-controlling features of a society, *both of which are ubiquitous.*

3. The potential for revolution is a function of the degree
and kinds of social change experienced by societies.

This conception of revolutionary potential has been stated
somewhat categorically, with almost no explication of basic ra-
tionale. Just as the conception of "peaceful politics" is derivative
from a kind of image of the social system, however, so the conception of revolutionary potential is derived from a somewhat
different image of social life.

### Society as a Tension-Management System

The chief features of the model of society that most sociologists and anthropologists use is its emphasis on system and the
strict interrelations of social events. This functional approach
emphasizes the continuities, which are real and essential elements of social systems, and it provides a kind of checklist for
tracing the consequences of *given* changes Its chief flaws are,
as noted, that it tends to obscure tensions and strains and to
pay relatively minor attention to the variable probabilities of

change occurring within the system, especially the growing element of deliberate change in social systems.

While such an image is not to be discarded, clearly the analytical scheme must be supplemented. "Disequilibrating" variables must be included, or the scheme will demonstrate an ever-growing discordance with empirical reality. This analytical problem, I think, leads to a rather simple "tension" or "strain" conception of social systems and the manner in which they experience change. The theoretical posture may be briefly and summarily stated:

1. All social systems contain *persistent* social strains that generate social conflict and provoke social change.

2. All social systems also include persistent patterns of action that may change very slowly. Although these patterns may be viewed as containing and controlling strains between the part and the whole—the individual and the group, the subsystem and the supersystem—some of their functions of providing order may be viewed as preventing conflict.

3. The "order" characteristic of any social system consists both of regularized patterns of action *and of institutions that control, ameliorate, and canalize the conflicts produced by persistent social strains.* Thus, a society encompasses both conflict and its associated change, as well as a social order that comprises tension-preventing and tension-managing devices and systems.

4. Tension-management systems are inherently dynamic in that the persistent social strains that they manage offer most hospitable environments for social change within any society. Although profound social strains may never be completely resolved, they are also quite unlikely to endure unaltered.

5. Any given social change is potentially both conflict-producing and conflict-reducing. Revolutions result from unsuccessful tension-mangement; peaceful politics result from successful tension-management. In any case, revolutions and peaceful politics are two sides of the same coin.

As noted previously, the conception of a society's revolutionary potential is derived from the image of a social system described above. To the extent that strains are persistent and tension-management devices fragile, all societies are revolution prone.

## Sources of Revolutionary Potential

All of the preceding discussion has been on an exceedingly general, if not vague, level. In what follows, an attempt will be made to specify some of the factors that contribute to a society's revolutionary potential. Three *caveats* must be stated, however.

First, the connections between the general conceptions described above and the potential-creating factors described below are not as tight as one might wish or expect. The conception of revolutionary potential and the image of a persistently strained social system sensitize the observer to certain factors and mechanisms. Also, I think that it is possible to specify the relationship between general conception and specific factor much more precisely than is done in this essay. I have attempted here, rather, to cast the widest possible net in order to indicate, somewhat superficially, the range of factors that contribute to a society's revolutionary potential.

Second, what follows attends almost exclusively to [ potential-creating factors and relationships. It is asserted above that revolutionary potential is the sum of positive strains and negative tension-management. In what follows, however, the emphasis is on the positive or strain factors. The justification for this procedure is that sociological theory, in the main, attends to tension-management rather than to sources of tension. It is hoped therefore that attention to the discordant elements of social systems may balance this one-sided emphasis.

Third, not only will the following discussion lack precise connections with the general conceptions, it will fall short of systematic and rigorous analysis in its own right. The factors discussed are neither exhaustive of all potential-creating factors, nor have they been selected in a rigorous manner. Rigor has been sacrificed in order to obtain broad—if somewhat sloppy—coverage.

## Change and Revolutionary Potential

Throughout the preceding discussion, the intimate connection between social change and revolutionary potential has been repeatedly asserted. Most recent and quite worthy models of social change—for example, the conception of structural differentiation stated jointly and individually by Talcott Parsons and Neil Smelser—have emphasized, however, the manner in which change takes place as a response to strain or widespread and profound dissatisfactions; change is perceived as a set of processes leading to the reduction and elimination of strain.[7]

I have claimed that the partially disequilibrated image of a social system provides a basis for a somewhat different view of the consequences of social change. It is necessary at this point, therefore, to show how change contributes to revolutionary potential rather than eradicating dissatisfactions. Two aspects of social change comprised in industrialization will be analyzed, and, in both cases, an attempt to demonstrate the conflict-generating properties of change will be made.

### The Differentiation of Status Systems

Industrialization is typically perceived as a set of processes whereby a more or less tightly integrated and relatively undifferentiated social system is transformed gradually into a system that contains many separate and functionally specific subsystems. The differentiation of systems is but half the story. The other half, of course, consists of the manner in which the newly differentiated systems are recombined. The model of "structural differentiation" represents such recombination in terms of the functional equivalence of the new systems; the same general functions are performed, but by means of a more complex set of mechanisms.[8]

The assumption in such a conception of social change is that the total system enjoys consensus on values at a most basic level. Put another way, it is assumed that social change is partially intransitive, in that the newly differentiated subsystems do not necessarily affect over-all system goals and values.[9]

### The Fragmentation-Pervasion Hypothesis[10] – Why when are ?

If one assumes that the strains leading to change endure, it is possible to describe an alternative model of structural differentiation. The most popular example of structural differentiation is, of course, the separation of work from kinship, territorial, religious, and other relationships. The separation of work involves the creation of a new status system—a new basis for the allocation of rewards and punishments. In fact, a number of such systems are created, for the separation of work typically involves the growth of a labor market, the introduction of new occupations, and the restructuring of styles of life. Although, as I shall discuss below, there is no reason for all of these changes to proceed evenly and simultaneously, they are all involved. The point is that *a number of* new subsystems are created, each of which becomes a basis for the allocation of status within the society.

The newly articulated systems are functionally specific. In other words, the norms that constitute each of the new systems are more *internally consistent* and *externally discontinuous.* The newly differentiated systems are born out of strain and conflict and differentiation may separate conflicting norms like kinship obligations *vs.* market criteria for recruitment and evaluation of labor. To the extent that such separation creates statuses that are occupied by different people, interpersonal strain will be reduced. *The norms themselves remain in conflict,* however. Furthermore, the emergence of a system that is exclusively market-oriented means that the norms are in a sense purified or decontaminated. Thus, the newly emergent systems are "naturally" in conflict with each other. Indeed, the very fact of emergence may encourage the overt manifestation of such conflict, since the new systems themselves are no longer internally subject to ameliorating cross-pressures and considerations. The conflict becomes systemic rather than personal.

Put another way, an increase in the number of subsystems is likely to be accompanied by an increase in the *salience* of the particular social system to which a norm belongs. For once a subsystem emerges, it involves a primary status for people. In a sense, these people become a "party" and are devoted to fulfillment of the system's norms.

The preceding discussion identifies three interrelated processes that together constitute structural differentiation. They can now be stated in summary form. Differentiation (1) increases the number of social systems that constitute a society; (2) increases the salience of the particular system to which a norm belongs, which increases the salience of subsystem goals and values; (3) increases the discontinuity between subsystems as the normative content of each is purified and decontaminated.

Taken together, these subprocesses will be called "fragmentation." The differentiated or fragmented systems are oppositional. Thus, the over-all process of fragmentation contributes to a society's revolutionary potential. Nevertheless, societies do cohere and revolutions, although common, are hardly ubiquitous. The problem now is to discover how the recombination of a fragmented system takes place, given the conflict among subsystems as an enduring social property.

A society is viewed as the intersection of a variable number of conflicting social systems. Each of the subsystems forms a separate basis for status allocation, with a primary constituency. In other words, the new systems are the prime sources of status for different categories of men. Members of the same population, however, have secondary positions in many of the other systems. People simultaneously belong therefore to discontinuous status systems, although quite often status within a secondary system will be exceedingly marginal. Nevertheless, the differentiated systems do intersect and interpenetrate. In this way, the total position of any given member of a society is pervaded by elements of the secondary subsystems.

Pervasion as a recombination mechanism, may also contribute to discontinuity and thus to the revolutionary potential of a society. Since each total position is pervaded by several subsystems, status comparisons *within* any single system are possible. The accuracy with which total positions may be compared decreases, however, as fragmentation proceeds. The various combinations and permutations of rank in the several fragmented systems make the global comparison of positions increasingly difficult.

It follows that societies undergoing fragmentation are likely to be rife with status inconsistency among individuals and status ambiguity in comparisons of individuals and groups. Nor is there any reason to suppose that this situation is transitory or self-equilibrating. There may or may not be profound values that unite or manage the tensions that arise from fragmentation.

This question of values seems always to be problematic, however, and is not a part of the differentiation process by definition.

### Value Conflict and Revolutionary Potential

This conception of structural differentiation emphasizes the emergence of subsystems with conflicting goals. Of course, a society may also develop many different tension-management devices to handle such conflict. The source of the conflict, however, remains, since the subsystems are unalloyed and their pursuit of subsystem goals may be correspondingly more ruthless.

In other words, from this point of view, goal conflicts and the strains and tensions resulting from them are ubiquitous. In a sense, it may be incorrect to conceive of fragmentation as a process that introduces new goals into a social system, since the ultimate ends toward which each of the newly differentiated subsystems are dedicated were analytically present before fragmentation. This kind of formulation smacks of scholasticism, however.

Be that as it may, fragmentation does radically change the hierarchy of evaluation of existing goals. This kind of change is commonly referred to as "value change." The point is that the goals are in conflict with each other, and the unalloyed pursuit of separate goals by purified subsystems adds to the likelihood of revolution. In other words, fragmentation increases the salience of goal conflicts and provides new challenges for the tension-management features of the normative system.

It is then the "efficiency" with which the normative system can control, canalize, or resolve goal-generated conflicts that is most directly related to the likelihood of revolutions. Normative systems are constantly faced with the challenge of handling strains and tensions that result from conflicting goals, and, to repeat, the latter are socially ubiquitous. Any change in the goal system should therefore change, in one direction or the other, the severity of the challenge; changes in the goal system affect the responses of the normative system.

Two interrelated aspects of goal-system changes suggest themselves as especially relevant in this regard. The first is the extent to which goal systems change in a manner that might be broadly labeled "evolutionary." To the extent that the goal system either does not change or changes slowly and systematically in one or even several well known and recognized directions, the strain the changes place upon the value and norm systems is minor. A great deal of current social theory argues essentially that goal systems of established industrial societies generally rely on this mode of change—either change in basic goals is relatively absent or it constitutes a secular, evolutionary trend. If that is the case, then of course the revolutionary potential of such societies should be exceedingly low.

This mode of goal-system change is presumably related to the second aspect of goal systems, which is the extent to which peaceful solution of goal-generated strains and conflicts itself constitutes a high-priority goal for all segments of a society. When these two interrelated characteristics are present, the likelihood of revolution should be low, even though conflicting goals are being pursued by various segments of a society.

The point here is, of course, that when the two conditions described above obtain, the tension-management systems of societies can achieve relative durability and effectiveness. The range of value changes possible is drastically reduced since even multilinear goal evolution would not bring about radical changes in goal priorities. This conclusion also suggests that what violence does occur in such societies would be sporadic and of relatively short duration. In other words, the potential for political violence remains, but it is more easily or more effectively managed.

When these two conditions do not obtain—when goal changes are either relatively rapid or relatively unpredictable—the mode of resolving the resulting conflicts is "open," and revolutionary potential should be quite high. It should be clear that this situation is one in which goal priorities, rather than the goals themselves, are changing. It should also be noted that not only the rapidity of change, but also social discontinuity are involved—the suddenness of changing priorities and the extent of consensus on means to resolve conflicts generated by rapid and sudden changes in goal priorities.

## Forms of Change and Revolutionary Potential

The following discussion explores an additional set of relationships between social change and social strains. Again the argument will be made that change is strain-producing, and again the type of change examined will involve the processes that constitute industrialization.

FORMS OF SOCIAL CHANGE. By forms of change, I mean *sequence*, or the order in which different institutions change; *rate*, or the rapidity of change in one or several of the institutions experiencing industrialization; *timing*, or the intervals between component changes, especially the leads and lags that result from these intervals.

The effects of sequence, rates, and timing of change upon the trajectory of a society undergoing industrialization share some fundamental characteristics. That each of these forms of change is a potential source of strain and conflict, to the extent that it violates some "natural" trajectory toward industrialism, is the major underlying issue of this section of the essay. Is there some natural or optimal path that societies must follow if their efforts to industrialize are to be successful? If so, what are the presumed sources of this natural route and what are the consequences of its violation? If not, how do forms of change differ from, and in what ways are they related to, the regularities of social systems?

SEQUENCE AND INDUSTRIALIZATION. Various students have argued for the primacy of one or another institution in initiating a viable program of industrialization. What is most impressive about this literature is the extent to which all seem to be correct—and thus the extent to which the various primacies cancel each other. It is as easy to be persuaded that political stability is the crucial factor, as to believe that heavy industry or mass education or the recruitment of a managerial élite is the key element. A very good case can be made for each particular sequence—or at least for the fact that failure to adopt a particular sequence leads to profound strains.

Even more persuasive are those who argue, putting all of the single primacies together, that the viability of industrialization

demands a simultaneity of change; that each of the "core" institutions—political, economic, educational, and so forth—must, at
the same time and at much the same rate, change in the direction of industrialism. This position might be labeled "the all-or-
nothing" hypothesis.

At issue here is the basis upon which any particular sequence
is judged to be optimal. The crucial distinction is between those
sequences that are judged to be possible and those that, for one
or another reason, appear most efficient. Needless to say, the two
are not identical. They have often been confused, however, and
students frequently argue that the possible is most efficient or
*vice versa*.

It seems doubtful that there is a single sequence of changes
in the course of industrialization that is the only possible alternative. Indeed, it seems doubtful that there is a single sequential
arrangement. The trajectory of societies is somewhat more
complex.

To the extent that industrialization proceeds through fragmentation, each major institution (status system) will have its
own sequence. The sequences are likely to be competitive, for
they reflect allocations of priorities, conscious or not. Thus, any
sequence involves costs and will be disequilibrating.

In one sense, those who argue for simultaneity have the correct
premise and the wrong conclusion. It is true that anything short
of simultaneity will adversely affect some institutions, in that
their energy and resource allocations will be reduced. It is also
true that eventually the disparity between "leading" and "lagging"
sectors can seriously threaten an industrialization program. Nevertheless, it is exactly this sequential route that industrializing
societies will experience.

In other words, equivalence of change in major institutions is
impossible, but failure to achieve it introduces profound strains
and tensions, which *are* part of industrialization.

Industrialization may begin in any of the various spheres of a
society—work place, market, political structures, and so forth.
It will proceed through various leads and lags, but no single
sphere will lead throughout. Instead, the sequence will reflect
shifting leads, since continued advances in one sphere will require some equivalence in other spheres.

Questions of rate and timing essentially provide multipliers or divisors for the basic question of sequence. Sequence, as a matter of fact, is more often characterized by differential rates of change than by a single dynamic element and a residue of static ones.

### Some Concluding Remarks

I am painfully aware that, if all of the various *caveats* entered above were collected and arrayed consecutively, they would comprise a sizable essay in their own right. Nevertheless, it is necessary to add to these hedges.

First, and most obvious, the preceding discussion is quite incomplete in several ways. The principal problem that needs exploration is the heuristic utility of the conceptions developed here. Unanswered questions in this regard include: Toward what empirical relationships do these conceptions point? Is it possible to measure the revolutionary potentials of societies? What is the relationship between actual revolutions and the potentials for revolution?

Closely related to the problem of estimating revolutionary potential is the equally difficult problem of determining the validity of such estimations. In some ways, the problems of conducting research on the revolutionary potentials of societies are at least partially independent of the research problems involved in measuring the incidence of revolutions. There is nothing inevitable about the relationship between potential and actual, and even high-potential societies do not necessarily experience internal wars. In other words, societies can and often do exhibit large amounts of conflict, and they can contain profound social strains or "contradictions" without necessarily resorting to large-scale violence as the only means for resolving these strains. Indeed, it was precisely on this point that a great many of Marx's predictions floundered: He often correctly identified the contradictions within industrial societies, but he uniformly overestimated the extent to which such contradictions could only be resolved through revolution and counterrevolution.

It seems that the revolutionary potentials of societies are, in many ways, an analytically as well as empirically distinct research problem. First, these potentials are considered a "normal" aspect of *all* social systems. The incidence of internal wars is clearly not "normal," and such wars are not omnipresent in most societies.

Second, throughout the preceding sections on revolutionary potential, the principle focus was on those *processes* that influenced the size of the potential. When, however, attention shifts to actual incidence, the concern is with an outcome that is imperfectly related to the previously discussed set of processes.

Third, the categories of information employed in measuring potential are not those that will necessarily yield accurate predictions of occurrence and, more important, are not necessarily reflected in the kind of information about incidence that may be desirable. This point carries of course an additional implication of the differences between measuring processes and outcomes. In a sense, the over-all methodological approach to measuring outcomes is almost the reverse of that involved in measuring actual outcomes.

Estimations of potential pose methodological problems of the causal-assessment variety. The issues are those involved in assessing the contribution of a number of specific processes to a final outcome—*an over-all potential* for revolution. To repeat, this outcome *is not* the rate of incidence of revolution itself. In the measurement of revolutions, however, the concern is with the *distribution* of a universe of outcomes and perhaps with the comparison of variable characteristics, the *morphological analysis* of such outcomes.[11]

In sum, both the outcome and the methodological approaches are different when one shifts from research upon potential to research upon the incidence of revolutions. In the former case, the problem is to assess the contributions of processes to an over-all potential; in the latter, the problem is to measure the differential distribution of a universe of comparable events—revolutions—and to record information about the variable characteristics of such events, or their comparative anatomy.

Although the estimation of potential is but imperfectly correlated with the distribution of observable revolutions, the assessment of the size and characteristics of this correlation is of crucial importance for research upon potential. Even though a high potential is viewed as an outcome partially distinct from revolution itself as an outcome, the relationship between these two outcomes is not randomly variable. The expected relationship, put most simply, should be that high potential is a necessary but not a sufficient condition for revolution. A measure of the incidence of internal wars is therefore a crucial variable for any full analysis of revolutionary potential.

The imperfect correlation between actual and potential revolution leads us to a final *caveat*. This essay has ignored the role of tension-management devices, which are, of course, potential-reducing factors. It should be clear that estimates of revolutionary potential must include such factors. I think, however, that the conflict-creating factors represent the severest challenge to social research at this time.

### Notes

1. The reference here is to sociological theory. As Professor Eckstein points out in his introduction to this volume, violence is almost never a part of the conceptual paradigm employed by current theory.

2. The outstanding example of the use of the vocabulary of pathology is of course Crane Brinton, *The Anatomy of Revolution* (New York: Vintage Books, 1957).

3. The image invoked is often that of an affluent society whose consumers are incessantly stimulated by the opinion leaders.

4. As Talcott Parsons pointed out, the primary question for sociological theory was raised originally in its secular form by Hobbes. *The Structure of Social Action* (New York: McGraw-Hill, 1937), pp. 89-93.

5. See Parsons, *The Social System* (New York: The Free Press of Glencoe, 1951), p. 480.

6. A most precise statement of society as a net-balance between conflict-generations and conflict-ameliorations properties may be found in Robert K. Merton, *Social Theory and Social Structure*, rev. ed. (New York: The Free Press of Glencoe, 1957), pp. 40-41.

7. See T. Parsons and N. J. Smelser, *Economy and Society* (New York: The Free Press of Glencoe, 1956), Chap. V, and Smelser, *Social Change in the Industrial Revolution* (Chicago: The University of Chicago Press, 1959), Chaps. II and III.

8. Parsons and Smelser, *op. cit.*, pp. 255-256.

9. See the essay by Parsons in *Sociology Today*, R. K. Merton, L. Broom, and L. Cottrell, eds. (New York: Basic Books, 1959), pp. 3-38 and particularly p. 6-8.

10. This material was originally presented in an essay of mine, "The Interpenetration of Firm and Society," published in *The Social Implications of Technical Change*, G. Balandier, ed., UNESCO, Paris, 1961.

11. This tripartite distinction is taken from P. Lazarsfeld, "Sociological Reflections on Business," in Dahl, et al., eds., *Social Science Research On Business* (New York: Columbia University Press, 1959), pp. 99-158.

Andrew C. Janos

## AUTHORITY AND VIOLENCE:

## THE POLITICAL FRAMEWORK

## OF INTERNAL WAR

For purposes of systematic inquiry, internal war has been defined as a violent conflict between parties subject to a common authority and of such dimensions that its incidence will affect the exercise or structure of authority in society.[1] This definition, of course, is broad enough to include an inordinately diverse set of phenomena, ranging from small riots to civil wars in which millions participate actively. On the other hand, it is narrow enough to exclude all incidents of violence in society, such as crime and pathological manifestations of aggression that do not affect authority (unless they become so widespread as to menace stability, and even then only in an indirect manner), or sporadic individual attacks on representatives of authority in dimensions too small to alter the prevailing institutional arrangements and the exercise of authority.

If internal war is defined as a conflict between parties who, initially at least, are subject to a common authority, then it follows logically that the phenomenon is as old as organized communities or the institutionalization of authority. Since authority is the subject of political science, it is not at all surprising that interest in the systematic study of the phenomenon goes back to the very origins of that discipline.

Very frequently, however, legitimate doubt and concern have been expressed by political scientists about the proper framework for the study of violence in human affairs, and, at times, there has been considerable reluctance to treat violence as part of politics. Violence by the standards of western civilization is one of the unpleasant facts of human existence and, more frequently than not, it has been looked upon as a deviation from regular patterns, as a phenomenon outside the boundaries of normal social interaction. This view is best expressed by the dictum, "Where war starts politics end," reflecting the tenet of rationalist moral philosophy that power can and should, under all conditions, be dissolved into legal principles to regulate processes of interchange in the political arena. This dictum is diametrically opposed to the Clausewitzian concept of violence as the continuation of politics by different means.[2]

The theoretical framework in this paper follows from the latter perspective and addresses itself to internal war as a means in the struggle for authority. It is thus limited to the discussion of one particular type of internal war, leaving aside such others as internal wars waged to enforce (rather than challenge) authority and limited internal wars that occur in response to specific policy decisions rather than to the whole framework of authority within which decisions are being made.

## The Elements of Authority

In Lasswell's by now classic definition, politics is the study of who gets what, when, and how.[3] The ultimate concern of the political process is accordingly the distribution of social values: goods, services, amenities, health, esteem, deference, security, knowledge. While the distribution of these values may rest in part on agreement and common interest, the process of distribution also involves power, the ability to modify the conduct of others with respect to particular objectives. Power so defined may become an end in itself, but generally it serves as a means to achieve ends other than power. Since politics involves the distribution of social values, pursuit of such values most frequently involves a struggle for power. In different terms, therefore, politics can be defined as the "shaping, distribution and exercise of power."[4]

Authority is a special form of power. In the last analysis, it is, like other forms of power, an ability to evoke compliance, and it is meaningless unless viewed in the context of a particular set of objectives (authority to do what?). But authority, unlike other forms of power, refers to a "single set of levers of command sufficiently powerful to set the whole society in motion in a given direction."[5] Authority is the form of power underlying the process of decision-making about the distribution of the most fundamental social values.

Authority is related to two distinct elements: force and legitimacy. The two combine in specific institutional arrangements that define the relations between masses and élites and establish the scope and boundaries of political competition in society. The first element, force, implies a physical ability to compel someone. The instruments of force are more or less cohesive organizational structures with more or less specific functions. The efficiency (or "coercive potential") of the instruments of force varies with the specificity of their goal structures and their degrees of internal cohesion. These instruments may range from highly incohesive mobs with *ad hoc* goals and organizations that have been designed specifically for noncoercive purposes (political parties, trade unions) to paramilitary and military forces, highly integrated and specifically designed for coercion. Authority usually involves monopoly of the functionally specific instruments of force (armies, police) but not a complete monopoly of force. The latter is hardly conceivable, since even an unarmed aggregate of people represents a certain coercive potential, and so do functionally diffuse and relatively incohesive social organizations.

Legitimacy, the second element of authority, is the ability to evoke compliance short of coercion. It is a psychological relationship between masses and élites, involving acceptance by the mass of a claim by an élite to act in the name of the community. This claim is usually made in terms of principles representing "higher" truth or "inevitability." Insofar as the truth of these principles is accepted, legitimacy derives from compliance with certain processes—elections, hereditary succession—that are regarded as the right and morally just ways of determining who should make decisions for the community and in what manner. The perception of legitimacy evokes obedience in specific situations of interchange, and, as a recent analyst of revolutions phrased it, it is this "habit of obedience that makes it possible for the holders of power to delegate important functions"[6] and, in general, to exercise authority in relation to the everyday life of a community.

It follows from this definition of force and legitimacy that the two elements of authority are, at least to some extent, interchangeable. The more legitimate the position of an élite is, the less it has to rely on force or the threat of force; the less widespread are habits of obedience rooted in a basic conviction of justness, the greater will be the need for the use of force. The limits of interchangeability cannot be easily determined, but authority without the element of force is "power of low weight,"[7] and some principle of legitimating force must exist even in the most ruthless terroristic regimes. It is a commonplace to say that the position of an élite must be legitimate at least in the eyes of those who apply force. If legitimacy is questioned by those acting within the framework of organized force, then, sooner or later, the question of "who guards the guards" must be raised, with devastating implications to the authority of the élite.

## Patterns of Struggle

In terms of this framework, the struggle for authority involves a struggle for legitimacy and the instruments of force in society. The first aspect, the effort to win legitimacy, is a prime characteristic of internal conflicts, distinguishing them from international conflict situations. In the former, however severely circumscribed, there exists an institutionalized framework within which groups or individuals may compete for positions of authority. Compliance with rules confers legitimacy upon the participant, to the extent at least that the legitimacy of the élite is accepted in society, and legitimacy then gives access to the instruments of force. Other means of acquiring legitimacy are the manipulation of individuals or institutions, or coercing them to legitimate an illegal act. Legitimacy, outside the existing framework of authority, can be obtained by propaganda, but this kind of popular

acceptance, without accompanying force, will bring no authority
to its bearers. If the struggle for authority is primarily a struggle
for legitimacy, we might, again borrowing a term from Lasswell
and Kaplan, refer to "civic" means and a "civic" political arena[8]
and hypothesize that such an arena is characterized by a relatively low incidence of violence.

If the struggle for authority takes place mainly through a
struggle for the instruments of force, we may refer to a "military"
arena. We may also hypothesize that in that case the probability
of violence will be relatively high. The military arena, however,
does not exclude nonviolent techniques of struggle. The instruments of force may, for instance, be subverted or infiltrated and
used for alien ends. Subviolence may take the form of strikes,
provocation ("to bring the troops over to our side"), demonstrations or demonstrative barricade uprisings to exert psychological
pressures on the troops or other fighting forces. If the instruments
cannot be won over by nonviolent or subviolent means, then force
has to be met with force, and the opponent's coercive instruments
will be destroyed rather than "captured." As long as the insurgent
is weak this will be accomplished by techniques of terrorism—
the calculated use of relatively small force to produce extreme
anxieties—but, as the insurgent's strength increases, the methods
of struggle may be guerrilla warfare or "conventional" war, following the pattern of warfare among nations.

Whether an arena will be civic or military depends to some
extent on whether the struggle for authority takes place in the
existing framework—in which the insurgents try to seize the
instruments of force and the principles legitimating it—or involves the creation of a new system of authority based on rival
instruments of force and new claims for legitimacy. This distinction frequently depends in turn on the objectives in respect
to which authority is to be exercised. When and where old social
objectives are to be retained, the struggle for authority almost
invariably takes place in the old framework—usually the pattern
of traditional coups d'état and palace revolutions. Frequently,
however, the acceptance of the old framework of authority is only
for operational purposes. The struggle for authority may take
place within the old structure, but when authority is transferred,
it will be used to pursue new objectives. In this case, the authority

won by the rival group must be adjusted to the new objective, sometimes in the form of a war of enforcement or prolonged terror. "Revolutions by coups d'état" have recently taken place in many countries, especially in the Middle East. European history, too, abounds in examples. Both Hitler and Mussolini captured, rather than destroyed, the framework of authority, and a structure of new authority was built only after the subversion of the old. The armies of their respective countries were taken over by the insurgents unscathed, and the latter's claims to authority were based on pre-existing principles of legitimacy (respectively derived from parliamentary processes and royal sanction). Another, and probably the classic, example of the struggle for authority within an existing framework is the process leading to Napoleon's 18 *Brumaire*. Here again, the army (or initially its strategically located units) was won over by Bonaparte's prestige, and the elimination by force of a group within the élite was legitimated by the vote of a rump Assembly. Shortly thereafter, however, the boundaries of authority were changed to meet the objective of the new élite.

The struggle for authority in an existing framework gives certain opportunities to build up authority by civic means, through the manipulation of existing channels of political competition or recruitment or through the seizure of institutions that can legitimate illegal resort to force, as in the case of the military coercing an Assembly to sanction personnel change. Military means for the struggle will be limited and subviolent: the instruments of force will be won over instead of being destroyed. The methods of the "struggle for the troops" have been described in great detail by Marxist theorists. They include provocation, propaganda aimed at the ranks, and the infiltration of positions of control.

The struggle for authority usually takes place in the framework of two competing structures of authority when the conflict involves a new set of social objectives. The existence of two foci of authority, or at least the nuclei of their structures, sometimes dates back to a time preceding the beginning of the conflict. The authority of the southern political élites in the United States, for instance, had been granted by the federal Constitution and formed an operative political framework with some attributes of sovereignty. In other instances, no competing structures of authority exist prior to the conflict, but as the struggle proceeds, new structures of authority come into being, sometimes built on a territorial basis—to take the example of the Chinese civil war— or wedged into areas partially controlled by the incumbent élite —as was the case with both the *F.L.N.* and the *O.A.S.* in the urban areas of Algeria. What is outstanding in all of these instances is the absence of any pretext of operating within the existing framework or accepting its legitimacy. At one or another stage of the conflict, a countergovernment appears, sometimes abroad, sometimes underground. A counterforce comes into existence, and legitimacy is claimed in terms grossly different from those of the ruling élite. The pattern of the struggle will be predominantly miltary, involving the instruments of force and a high incidence of violence. The opponent's instruments of force are destroyed by terrorism, guerrilla warfare, or conventional war, and the pattern of conflict approximates the character of war between two communities.

A third pattern of struggle appears when, at some point in the process, a rival focus of authority emerges, but the two authorities temporarily coexist in what has been referred to as a "dual power" or "dual authority" arrangement. In such situations, the struggle for authority takes place in both civic and military arenas, although the fact of coexistence places certain limitations on the application of "military" means. Each party to the conflict claims legitimacy in terms of its own institutional framework, and frequently each has access to separate instruments of force recognized by the opponent. This framework circumscribed political struggle in the French Revolution, at least between 1789 and 1792, with the Assembly and the monarchy representing the two institutionalized foci of authority. The classic example of dual authority, however, was produced by the Russian Revolution of 1917, in the division between Workers' Soviets and the Provisional Government. From the first days of the Revolution, the Soviets had exercised authority over a wide area of public activities, and they also claimed control over matters concerning the armed forces and the conduct of the war. At a later stage of development, the Soviets in the capital cities organized their Workers' Guard, and in October, 1917, they also extended control over the garrison of Petrograd. Throughout the entire period, the boundaries of dual authority had never been clearly defined. The methods of struggle for the instruments of force were mainly subversion by propaganda and eventually political demonstrations. But the "umbilical cord of legality"[9]—to quote Trotsky on the subject—was not cut until the moment when one of the authorities themselves was already on the verge of collapse. The Provisional Government had little support for its claim of legitimacy, and its control over the army was at best nominal. The insurrection of October, 1917, only registered the transfer of authority with a minimum of violence.

### The Transfer of Authority

Political struggle frequently involves more than two competing élites, yet at any particular time and with respect to any specific issue, competing groups combine in coalitions or act as neutrals. To illustrate this point, one may use the example of a multiparty system. In the long run, there may be several competitors, but when it comes to alignment on specific issues, the votes are divided between ayes and nays. Similarly, in a multipolar military arena, conflict at any particular tactical phase concerns two parties or blocs, even though alignments may change from time to time. For the purposes of a model of the struggle for power, it is therefore possible to dichotomize the opponents and speak, as we have, of insurgents and incumbents.

The transfer of authority may be viewed as a process moving through a series of changes in the balance of power between insurgents and incumbents. Assuming a position of initial weakness on the part of the insurgents, we may distinguish analytically among at least three stages in the balance: a state of disequilibrium in the favor of the incumbent; a state of equilibrium; and finally a state of disequilibrium in favor of the insurgent.

Frequently the process, or major aspects of the process, are accidental: Planned action may have unanticipated consequences, and there may be outcomes beyond the control of the competitors for authority. The erosion of the power of Russian élites both in 1905 and 1917 was the consequence of military defeat;

the revolutions of 1848 have generally been attributed to the effects of a world economic crisis, which had not been planned either by those in positions of authority or by the competing revolutionary groups of the time. A similar impact of economic recessions is well known and documented in the context of institutionalized, democratic power processes. It is also well known how much Marxist theory stresses the importance of the role of the impersonal "forces" in creating power vacua into which a potential insurgent can move with relative ease.

The transfer of authority may take place by civic and military, as well as by mixed civic-military means. The character of the arena, however, may change in the course of the process, and as the character of an arena becomes increasingly military, the importance of civic instruments (parties, economic and professional organizations, pressure groups) and processes (lobbying, conspiracy, coalition formation, electioneering) gradually declines. It follows from the interrelation of the elements of authority, however, that a "military" objective can be pursued from a position attained by civic processes and vice versa.

Internal war is one of the means of transferring authority. Violence may dominate one or more phases of the process, and the problem of violence may also vary in physical intensity from subviolent to highly violent acts, from intimidation to total destruction.

The techniques of the struggle for authority and thus the techniques of violence involved change with the change in the balance of power. In the initial stages of the process, the capabilities of the insurgent are inferior, severely limiting the range of potential choices. The strategic objective is attrition in a military and mobilization in a civic arena. Patterns of violence appropriate to the first stage are terrorism, demonstrations, strikes, and other forms of subviolence. In the second phase, the equilibrium changes in favor of the insurgent, and struggle proceeds from attrition to annihilation in the military and from mobilization to decision in the civic arena. Techniques of violence appropriate to the advanced stages of the struggle for authority are guerrilla and civil wars, insurrections (the violent elimination of power holders), and *coups de force* to seize the institutional arrangements of legitimacy.

The resort to violence and its intensity is thus to some extent predictable in terms of power, but also in terms of the arena, that is, in terms of available alternatives that, everything else being equal, promise the same outcome at less cost. In a civic arena, violence is largely absent, and the fusion of military with civic elements limits techniques to subviolence. In a military arena, on the other hand, the use of force is restricted only by the lack of coercive capabilities.

### Techniques of the Transfer of Authority

| | | ARENA | |
|---|---|---|---|
| | Civic | Mixed | Military |
| Capabilities | paraviolence | paraviolence subviolence | subviolence violence |
| low | legal competition | subversion | terrorism |
| intermediate | conspiracy | strike, demonstration | guerrilla warfare |
| high | manipulation of elections, assemblies | insurrection | regular warfare |

### Some Further Questions

Once defined, the problem of internal war may be approached from a number of different perspectives. The first question that may be raised is *why* internal wars occur, a question that may be answered in causal or functional terms. The explanation may be linked to the operation of systems, to equilibrium models, or it may be formulated in terms of theories of frustration, aggression, anomie, or cultural-predispositional variables.

The next question that comes to mind is *how* internal wars will be fought, what patterns and variations are conceivable, and what factors can be linked with these variations? The answer to this question, whether formulated in the prescriptive terms of strategic analysis or in the factual terms of social theory, must be sought by analyzing actors, objectives, capabilities, and certain stable aspects of the environment that attend the application of capabilities.

The present theoretical framework follows from the second perspective and is concerned with the patterns rather than with the origins of violence. The framework is political because it focuses on the struggle for authority, of which violence is only one aspect. The model deals with *types* of conflict situations and techniques and analyzes violence in the light of strategic alternatives.

It should, however, be pointed out that the framework is far from being complete, whether from the perspective of the actor or from that of the observer. The first would further require an analysis of environmental conditions attending the application of means (and thus limiting the range of choice); the latter, an analysis of the costs and risks that actors are willing to take to attain their objectives. At this last point, a number of cultural-predispositional factors would have to be introduced in the analysis.

Above all, however, it should be emphasized that the generalizations presented here are descriptive and deal with the transfer of authority only from the point of view of the insurgent. They represent a preliminary statement on various forms of the struggle for authority and on the variations of internal war within the process. As such they are predictive only in the sense that they establish certain clusters of techniques and correlations that follow from the structure of force and legitimacy in society.

### Notes

1. Harry Eckstein, *Internal War: The Problem of Anticipation*, Report to the Smithsonian Institution (mimeo.), p. 1. This general line of investigation is taken by the Internal War Research Program of the Center of International Studies, Princeton University.

2. Carl von Clausewitz, *On War* (Washington, D.C.: Infantry Journal Press, 1950), p. 16. It has frequently been overlooked that this Clausewitzian formula is not so much the definition of war as a particular way to conceptualize power processes and the nature of force in inter- and intrasocietal contexts.

3. Harold D. Lasswell, *Politics, Who Gets What, When, How?* (New York: McGraw-Hill, 1936). Reprinted in *Political Writings of Harold D. Lasswell* (New York: The Free Press of Glencoe, 1951).

4. Lasswell and Abraham Kaplan, *Power and Society* (New Haven: Yale University Press, 1955), p. 75.

5. Barrington Moore, *Political Power and Social Theory* (Cambridge: Harvard University Press, 1958), p. 4.

6. Peter Amann, ["Revolution: A Redefinition,"] *Political Science Quarterly*, LXXVII (March, 1962), 38.

7. Lasswell and Kaplan, *Power*, p. 92.

8. *Power*, p. 252. Although Lasswell and Kaplan use the term in a slightly different meaning, it is hoped that no confusion will arise from the present usage, since its originators hypothesized that "an arena is military when the expectation of violence is high; civic when the expectation of violence is low."

9. Leon Trotsky, *The Russian Revolution* (New York: Doubleday, 1959), p. 423.

# William Kornhauser

## REBELLION AND

## POLITICAL DEVELOPMENT

### The Significance of Rebellion for Political Development

This paper is a preliminary attempt to examine the relationship between rebellions and the political structures within which they occur. The hallmark of rebellion is "open or determined defiance of, or resistance to, authority or controlling power" (*Oxford Universal Dictionary*). The following analysis is concerned primarily with rebellion against central political authority, as in revolutions, civil wars, military insurrections, *coups d'état*, colonial revolts, and riots and strikes against the state. Marginal cases include peasant uprisings and communal rioting in which central authority is not directly attacked unless or until it intervenes.

Rebellions are ways of making demands on authority, whether for the change of specific acts or rulers or of structures of authority. They are alternatives to established ways of making demands on authority in an orderly manner, whether through regulated political competition, judicial procedures, or other means. Rebellions therefore signify failures, small or large, of the political system. Nevertheless, rebellions may be a way of performing political functions in the absence of political structures capable of accommodating political demands. Rebellions also may help to create more effective political arrangements. A central interest of this paper is to distinguish rebellions that favor political development from those that act as alternatives or resistances to political development.

For this purpose, a very wide variety of rebellions in many different societies and historical periods are to be considered. If the objective were to seek a full causal explanation of rebellion, to describe the mechanisms of rebellion, or to analyze the multiple effects of rebellion, such an extensive treatment would not be feasible. But since this inquiry is restricted to quite limited aspects of rebellions, to examine a wide range of variation in these aspects is desirable. The cases selected for study are drawn for the most part from medieval and modern Europe and from countries in other parts of the world during the past century. Only a few are used as illustrations in this paper, but many others served as the basis for formulating propositions on the links between rebellion and political structure.

The direct links between rebellions and political structures are the features of authority that elicit or encourage defiance. These aspects of authority may be classified under four headings:

*Alien authority:* authority that is believed to be foreign rather than indigenous to the society, especially authority imposed from without and displaying symbols of an alien culture.

*Insufficient authority:* authority that is believed to be weak and ineffective, especially authority that is highly fragmented.

*Arbitrary authority:* authority that is believed to be capricious and irresponsible, especially authority that is highly repressive.

*Exclusive authority:* authority that is believed to be inaccessible to large sections of the population, especially authority that denies political rights to certain parties, classes, or ethnic groups.

Rebellions may be classified according to whether they are directed primarily against one or the other or a combination of these characteristics of authority. Rebellions also may be classified according to the kinds of political development they may facilitate or hinder. Rebellions may foster the development of political independence, centralization of authority, constitutionalism, or citizenship rights. Rebellion against alien authority, however, does not always encourage the development of a political community; it may seek instead only to escape from alien authority. Rebellion against insufficient authority may seek aggrandizement or autonomy at the expense of central government, rather than the development of a strong state. Rebellion against arbitrary authority may seek only the seizure of power or the redress of grievances rather than constitutional government. And rebellion against exclusive authority may seek the recognition of special corporate immunities or privileges rather than the extension of common political rights. (In a specific case, rebellion may oppose political development in certain aspects and advance it in others.)

The following pages explore some of the characteristics and conditions of rebellions that have favored or hindered political development.

### Rebellion and Independence

One aspect of modern political development is the formation of an independent national state. The common denominator of political independence is the freedom of a territorial group from alien authority, that is, from rulers who come from or represent another territorial group. The territorial group, however, need not exist prior to independence; rather, as in the case of Pakistan, it may be formed in the very process of seeking political independence for a religious, ethnic, or culture group. The territorial group, on the other hand, initially may be constituted by little else than the consciousness of a common territory but not by a common culture. In this situation, the territorial group is a creature of alien authority; thus colonial rule created many of the territorial groups that subsequently sought independence despite cultural, linguistic, ethnic, religious, and political differences.

Of major importance in the genesis of political independence is the emergence of a collective sense of belonging together against what comes to be perceived as alien authority. Since the desire to be rid of alien rule generally underlies the goal of independence, rebellion is a common means for its achievement. A majority of present-day national states became independent only after a period of rebellion, and many others gained independence when their foreign rulers withdrew in order to avoid rebellion.

But even successful rebellion against alien rulers does not guarantee the formation of an independent state. In addition, an indigenous government must be constituted. This requires not only the rejection of foreign rule but also the affirmation of a new political identity. Not all rebellions against alien authority are animated by a political identity, however. Many are traditionalist rather than nationalist movements.[1] Nationalist movements always contain traditionalist elements, but in addition they embrace aspirations for a new and broader political community—if only in embryonic form. Traditionalist movements generally are spontaneous expressions of resistance to alien rule and efforts to preserve or renew traditional authority. This kind of rebellion does not contain the germs of further political development. The Indian Mutiny of 1857 rejected foreign rule, along with all change, in an effort to return to the traditional order of princely power and privilege; but the anti-British activities of the Indian National Congress following World War I helped to create, as well as to express, aspirations for the development of an all-Indian political community to be realized through an independent government.[2]

Traditionalist resistance to alien authority generally precedes nationalist rebellion. The alien authority may itself unwittingly help to transform traditionalist resistance into nationalist rebellion: by undermining familial, tribal, religious, and other traditional authority; by uprooting and mixing people from different local groups; by introducing means of communication and uniform administrative practices into an area where no common life previously existed; by treating all people alike, especially as inferiors; by creating a new élite that does not have a place either in the traditional society or in the central administration. In these and other ways, alien rule facilitates the development of aspirations for a new political community, especially among the educated members of the society.

This pattern of development is most apparent in the new nations of Asia and Africa. The pattern, however, is not entirely new. Imperial rule in Western Europe in the early modern period and in Central and Eastern Europe in the nineteenth century helped pave the way for nationalist rebellions. Perhaps the earliest case occurred in the territory of the Netherlands inherited by Charles V at the beginning of the sixteenth century. During the reign of Charles V, many changes were made to facilitate the administration of a territory that included more than three hundred semi-autonomous cities and seventeen provinces: A uniform legal system was established where it did not conflict with city charters, the upper nobility was organized into an order, a supra-provincial council was formed, as was a States General. These innovations, made for the benefit of the crown, contributed to the unity of the northern provinces. This unity was strengthened and mobilized against foreign rule by the spread of Calvinism and Philip II's violent efforts to combat it. In the long struggle of the Netherlands for independence, a new political community began to take shape.

The very process of rebelling often contributes to the development of a new political identity. During the course of the struggle, rebels forge new bonds and symbols of unity. A famous example is the personal political path of Ferhat Abbas. In 1936 Ferhat Abbas said: "If I had discovered 'the Algerian nation,' I should have been a nationalist. . . . I did not find it. I consulted history, the living and the dead. . . . You cannot build on air." By 1943 he could write in the Algerian Manifesto, which he submitted in the name of the notables of Algeria, "The time has passed when an Algerian Muslim wanted to be anything but an Algerian Muslim." Shortly after the outbreak of armed rebellion in 1954, he joined the FLN and later became Premier of the Provisional Government of the Algerian Republic.[3]

Whether a rebellion seeks only to be rid of alien authority or also to build a new political community obviously has major consequences for the political order that follows independence: The smaller the role of traditionalist forces in the rebellion, the more likely that independence will lead to political development, especially the formation of a central government capable of attaining unity and stability.

### Rebellion and Centralization

A second aspect of modern political development is the creation of central authority capable of continuous and effective action. A society that lacks sufficient centralization of power is politically impotent. Political centralization requires the superiority of central authority over local authority. Effective centralization also requires strong links between the center and periphery of the country. Rebellions in outlying areas (cities or provinces, for example) indicate a low level of political development, specifically the failure to establish the hegemony of central authority. Rebellions for local autonomy, however, often have had the consequence of strengthening the hand of central authority—either by necessitating the mobilization of force to suppress them or by providing the occasion for intervention by the central authority to arbitrate the local conflict.[4]

In the early Middle Ages, the dominant type of rebellion —warfare among great nobles and monarchs for autonomy and aggrandizement—reflected the lack of political development. Central authority generally was too weak to suppress warfare, and warfare was a more or less accepted way of settling jurisdictional disputes and rivalries for power. Capture of control of the crown was often viewed as a means for enhancing feudal power, rather than as a basis for governing a whole country—since the idea of a unitary national state was hardly known. The result, for long periods of time, was a balance among the feudal powers at the expense of central authority.

In the later Middle Ages, "political authority, which up to that time was much subdivided, began everywhere to be concentrated in larger organisms."[5] The formation of nation-wide estates testified to the growing centralization of authority, as did the increasing frequency of rebellion of nation-wide groups. The monarchy on its side was able to mobilize sources of support that were independent of feudal and clerical control, notably the rising merchant classes and cities. The absolutism of the seventeenth and eighteenth centuries was the outcome of the struggle of royal authority against feudal authority. The central power gained considerable freedom from close and direct dependence on particularistic ties for the exercise of power. It came to rely increasingly on the creation of a permanent bureaucracy and military establishment.

During the early development of central authority in western European countries (notably France and England) rebellions generally sought to protect or enlarge autonomous jurisdictions. In contrast, during the past century rebellions increasingly have aimed at establishing strong central power. Frequently these rebellions have been precipitated by the failure of old rulers to prevail in the face of challenges from modern states. A notable case in point occurred in Japan following the failure of the shogunate to resist effectively the demands of Western states. The rebellion against the weak authority of the shogunate in 1867 sought to establish around the emperor a central government capable of strengthening the nation. The Chinese Revolution of 1911 overthrew the Manchu dynasty, which was not able to cope effectively with Western and Japanese encroachments, as well as with internal problems. When the Kuomintang sought to create an effective central government, however, it failed in the face of numerous rebellions of provincial war lords, Japanese attacks, and finally Communist revolution. Ataturk's revolution in Turkey, on the heels of the disintegration of the Ottoman Empire and the losses resulting from Turkey's participation in World War I, sought to modernize the nation on the basis of a strong central government. The military *coup d'état* in 1952, following Egypt's defeat by Israel, brought to power a group of young officers determined to build a strong state capable of defeating Israel, driving out the British, and overcoming internal stagnation. All these rebellions for strong central governments occurred in the face of threats to national power and independence from other states, and led to efforts to overcome internal weakness by means of modernization.

Insufficient authority also provided the target and the opportunity for the acquisition of power by Communists in Russia, Fascists in Italy, and Nazis in Germany. In each case, the rebellion was preceded by the disintegration of the capacity of the government to govern. A centralized structure of authority had been developed over a long period of time in Russia and during only some sixty years in Italy and Germany. Due to a different combination of circumstances in each case, the structure of authority broke down—first under Nicholas II and then under the Provisional Government in Russia during World War I; under the parliamentary system in Italy following World War I; and under the new and feeble Weimar Republic in Germany after great economic crises. In all three countries, the insurgents sought and achieved unprecedented concentrations of power. Yet, the fascist movements in Italy and Germany can hardly be said to have contributed to political development during or after their short and violent lives, since no stability was attained nor any institutional legacy passed on. The Bolshevik Revolution renewed and extended the historic pattern of Russian centralized power, but so far at the expense of constitutionalism.

## Rebellion and Constitutionalism

A third aspect of modern political development is the creation of constitutional regulation over the political action of both rulers and ruled. Constitutionalism is rule of law, power subject to general principles and controls. The opposite of constitutional regulation in modern society is arbitrary power, which in its extreme becomes tyranny. Arbitrary rule exists to the extent that power is not subject to regular limitations and restraints. Arbitrary rule breeds rebellion as a way of making claims for power and for the redress of grievances.

A stable system of authority requires rules for determining succession to positions of power. Where these rules are vague or conflicting or do not command respect, rebellion may become a substitute for institutionalized succession. That has been the case during long periods in the Middle East (notably in the Ottoman Empire) and in Latin America, and it continues to be a problem in many countries in these and other areas. Rebellions for succession also were frequent in medieval Europe, especially when the absence of an appropriate heir impaired the operation of dynastic succession.

Rebellion for succession may be merely a way of seeking to control and exploit the central authority, but it may also be a way of changing the direction of government policy. Frequent *coups d'état* to change policies as well as rulers may be viewed as "the nonconstitutional equivalent of periodic changes in party control through the electoral process."[6] Radical and conservative reforms have alternately been introduced in many Latin American countries in recent decades by means of *coups* rather than by elections. In Bolivia, for example, a conservative *coup* in 1946 was sandwiched between reform *coups* in 1943 and 1952.[7] Neither rebellions that merely change rulers nor rebellions that also change policies signify constitutional development, however, for they are not directed against arbitrary authority as such and are themselves attacks on institutional procedure.

In addition to institutions for seeking power, political order requires institutions for securing redress of grievances. Where channels for the registering of grievances are lacking, rebellion may serve this purpose. Like rebellions for succession, rebellions for redress may seek only satisfaction of limited interests, or they may seek political change. Examples of the former are periodic peasant rebellions against governmental demands for more than customary contributions or against governmental failure to perform expected services. Periodic uprisings of urban mobs are also ways of registering grievances in the absence of institutional outlets. In large pre-industrial cities like Naples, popular rioting was a well-established mechanism, accepted by rulers and populace alike, for registering protest against the ruler's failure to do his duty—to the point that the threat or onslaught of rioting often kept rulers ready to control prices, to distribute food or work, or to listen to their faithful commons on other matters.[8]

Rebellion for redress that becomes *generalized* resistance to arbitrary power but *not to the state itself* is a major source of constitutional development. Thus the Great Rebellion in seventeenth-century England sought lawful regulation of the state and not its destruction; whereas the rebellion of the *Fronde* in seventeenth-century France did not aim at a strong polity. "Unlike their English contemporaries, [the Frondeurs] did not accept this [centralized secular] state and [seek] to constitutionalize it; they rejected it in the name of a law of a bygone society, and refused to listen to the reason which would refashion the law to make it suit an emerging new society. . . . They enthroned absolutism by their failure to reform constitutionalism."[9]

Constitutional development, then, is more likely to occur where there is a strong state to be regulated and a variety of independent centers of power capable of restraining central authority without enfeebling it. Of course, the capacity for resistance to power is no substitute for its lawful regulation. Nevertheless, in the absence of a widely diffused capacity for rebellion against arbitrary rule, little constitutional development is likely to occur.

Since in new states neither central authority nor other centers

of power loyal to the state are well developed, the urge to constitutionalism tends to be feeble. Military officers often arrogate
to themselves the right to replace rulers whenever they appear to
be inept or corrupt or otherwise unsatisfactory. Tribal, religious,
ethnic, regional, and other communal groups frequently employ
violence against the state either to win autonomy or to gain
power. Against this background, all opposition parties may be interpreted by those in power as rebels against the state and therefore as targets of repression. As long as the dominant problem
in newly independent states is the development of political unity
and effective central authority, little constitutional development
is likely to occur. As the processes of urbanization and economic
development throw up new social groups adapted to a modern
polity, namely associational groups (like trade unions) rather
than communal groups (like ethnic communities), the capacity
to resist arbitrary authority without destroying the state may also
emerge—unless that capacity is forcibly suppressed by the central authority, as in totalitarian societies.

### Rebellion and Citizenship

A fourth aspect of modern political development is the
achievement of equal rights of membership, that is to say citizenship. Citizenship implies full status in the political community,
and it is therefore developed to the extent that all sections of
the population subject to common authority have certain political
rights in common, including the right to participate in political
life.
The rebellion of groups against subordinate status may or
may not signify the development of citizenship. Where a subordinate group rebels against its inferior position, it may seek or
accept corporate immunities or privileges. In such a case, the
principle of citizenship is not advanced, since no extension of
common membership in the political community has occurred.
Similarly, where a subordinate group succeeds in gaining dominance over its former masters and proceeds to deny them political
rights, common citizenship has not been advanced.
On the other hand, where rebellion against exclusion or

politically based privilege is also oriented toward incorporation
of new groups into the political community, then it is an expression of the struggle for full citizenship. The struggle may be only
for the extension of certain common protections or privileges
afforded by full citizenship. A stronger expression of the development of citizenship is to be found in efforts of subordinate groups
to acquire the dignity attached to equal opportunity of participating in the common life.

The struggle against exclusion from political life during the
Middle Ages centered in the city. If "the distinctive feature of
the communal oath . . . was that it united *equals*," then it was
in spirit and also often in fact rebellion against feudal authority.[10]
It was "personal membership, not that of kin groups or tribe,
in the local association of the city [that] supplied the guarantee
of the individual's personal legal position as a burgher."[11] Although
frequent rebellions of medieval cities against their overlords were
aimed at freedom from the restrictions of feudal domination,
this independence was founded on the local exclusiveness of the
city. The city fought for special immunities and privileges as a
corporate group, rather than for the extension of the principle
of citizenship beyond its own walls.

The struggle against exclusive authority *within* the medieval
city also was animated by a spirit of exclusive political rights.
Political authority typically was the monopoly of leading merchants. In those cities where the leading merchants successfully
established a closed oligarchy, rebellions against patrician rule
were frequent—notably in the large industrial towns of the Low
Countries, on the banks of the Rhine, and in Italy during the
second half of the thirteenth century and the fourteenth century.[12] These rebellions were mounted by craft guilds seeking a
voice in the governing councils of the town. Pirenne remarks
on the revolt of the crafts that "it is natural to compare these
conflicts with those which were provoked in the nineteenth century by the question of the parliamentary franchise."[13] But in
another place he observes that the crafts' horizons were "bounded
by the walls of the city and limited to the framework of their
corporation."[14] At Liège, for example, in 1384 the crafts drove
out the merchant oligarchy, only to restrict political rights to
those whose names were inscribed on their rolls.[15] Thus it was

that the principle of corporate privilege and exclusiveness generally restricted the concept of individual rights in the medieval city.

Rebellion of excluded classes for political rights has come to play an increasingly prominent role in modern societies. Now, however, the aim is incorporation into the national community rather than the local community, and the claim is for the extension of individual rights rather than corporate privileges. The Chartist Rebellion in England during the first half of the nineteenth century is an illuminating example because the central demand was for the further extension of the franchise beyond that granted in the Reform Act of 1832. The revolutions of 1848 also aimed at greater political equality, and one of the first acts of the Provisional Government after the February Revolution in Paris was to proclaim the right of universal suffrage. Where lower classes in modern nations still suffer from a sense of second-class citizenship, revolutionary movements have special appeal. Popular support for the Communist party in France and Italy derives in part from the resentment of many people who feel excluded from full membership in the polity. (Where the Communist party comes into power, however, enforced participation is instituted at the expense of civil liberties, and the party becomes a new basis of political privilege.)

There are instructive parallels between the struggles against exclusion of social classes and of minority groups. Ethnic and racial minorities also rebel for corporate immunities and privileges—like special status for their languages or religions or even for self-rule. Like social classes, minorities may seek domination rather than equality; but unlike social classes, minorities may go so far as to seek secession—to establish a separate state or to join another state. Finally, like social classes, minorities may seek assimilation into the political society. Rebellions against slavery, caste, or other forms of racial or ethnic discrimination may facilitate the extension of full citizenship rights to members of minority groups.[16]

Where western countries generally forged national identity, central authority, and constitutional rule over long periods of time and *prior* to the incorporation of all classes and minorities into political life, the new states often seek universal political participation from the beginning. Furthermore, they seek it in the absence of a strong group structure and cultural tradition capable of regulating popular participation. Under this condition, a premium is placed on the popular hero and political party that can mobilize a mass following. The ruler of a new state today is faced with the task of trying to build a *strong* modern state within a *weak* civil society. For this purpose, the ruler may attempt to create a large popular following and simultaneously forcibly to suppress opposition. Citizenship is enlarged in one sense, in that all sections of the population are activated on a more or less equal basis; but it is diminished in another sense, in that few civil rights or liberties are operative.

### Conclusion

The preceding analysis has tried to show that rebellions can be characterized by the structures of authority within which they arise and toward which they move. Four attributes of political authority have been considered: whether and to what extent authority is alien or indigenous, fragmented or centralized, arbitrary or responsible, and exclusive or open. Future investigation will seek to determine whether these attributes tend to become patterned in certain sequences or stages of political development, and if so whether or not there are corresponding sequences of rebellion. In Latin America, for example, the nationalist rebellions of the early nineteenth century mark the transition from colonial rule to independence; the civil wars and military *coups* during the century following independence mark the transition from the fragmented power of local *caudillos* to centralizing dictatorships; and revolutions in the twentieth century mark the transition from traditional dictatorship to a greater degree of constitutional rule and popular participation, as in the case of the Mexican Revolution. Political development in Latin America, then, has tended to move from the winning of independence to the centralization of authority to the strengthening of constitutionalism to the enlargement of citizenship. Strong countertendencies exist, however, and the political development of many Latin American countries has been very uneven. Nevertheless, the sequence of development may be fairly uniform in this region.[17] Different sequences undoubtedly are to be found in other areas.

Whether or not there are typical sequences, the development of modern political society shows a tendency toward the broadening of the basis for common goals and actions. The struggle against alien authority (imperialism) tends to change from the defensive reaction of local groups to a movement for the founding of a new political community. The struggle against insufficient authority (anarchy) tends to change from demands for autonomy to a movement for strong central administration. The struggle against arbitrary authority (tyranny) tends to change from claims for power or the redress of specific grievances to a movement for general restraints on power. The struggle against exclusive authority (privilege) tends to change from efforts to preserve or procure special privileges for particular groups to a movement for the extension of common rights of citizenship to all members of the society.

As societies reach high levels of political development, their capacities to define and achieve common goals are enlarged. One indication of this is the relative absence of rebellions in the highly developed political societies of northwest Europe and their overseas offshoots. Rebellion is also relatively rare in societies dominated by modern dictatorships and therefore without strong constitutional controls. Overt rebellion (if not rebellious impulses) can be forcibly suppressed for long periods of time. The absence of rebellion cannot, therefore, be taken by itself as a sign of political development, any more than the occurrence of rebellion by itself shows that political development is not occurring.

### Notes

1. James S. Coleman, "Nationalism in Tropical Africa," in John H. Kautsky, ed., *Political Change in Underdeveloped Countries* (New York: Wiley, 1962), pp. 169ff.

2. Rupert Emerson, *From Empire to Nation* (Cambridge: Harvard University Press, 1960), p. 204.

*William Kornhauser* [ 156 ]

3. Quoted in Immanuel Wallerstein, *Africa: The Politics of Independence* (New York: Vintage Books, 1961), p. 50; and Herbert Luethy, *France Against Herself* (New York: Meridian Books, 1957), pp. 243-47.

4. See, e.g., Henri Pirenne, *Medieval Cities* (Princeton: Princeton University Press, 1925), p. 186.

5. Marc Bloch, *Feudal Society* (London: Routledge, 1961), p. 421.

6. Samuel P. Huntington, "Patterns of Violence in World Politics," *Changing Patterns of Military Politics* (New York: The Free Press of Glencoe, 1962), p. 40.

7. *Ibid*, p. 36; see also Edwin Lieuwen, *Arms and Politics in Latin America* (New York: Praeger, 1961), pp. 78-80.

8. E. J. Hobsbawm, *Primitive Rebels* (Manchester: Manchester University Press, 1959), p. 116.

9. Carl J. Friedrich, *The Age of the Baroque, 1610-1660* (New York: Harper Torchbooks, 1962), p. 242.

10. Bloch, *op. cit.*, p. 355.

11. Max Weber, *The City* (New York: The Free Press of Glencoe, 1958), p. 102.

12. Henri Pirenne, *Economic and Social History of Medieval Europe* (New York: Harvest Books [1937]), p. 200.

13. Henri Pirenne, *A History of Europe* (New York: Anchor Books [1956]), II, 103.

14. Pirenne, *Economic and Social History*, p. 199.

15. *Ibid*, p. 201.

16. On types of minority movements, see Louis Wirth, "The Problem of Minority Groups," in Ralph Linton, editor, *The Science of Man in the World Crisis* (New York: Columbia University Press, 1945), pp. 347-72.

17. On stages of political development in Latin America, see Gino Germani and Kalman Silvert, "Politics, Social Structure and Military Intervention in Latin America," *Arch. Europ. Sociol.*, II (1961), 62-81

Lucian W. Pye

# THE ROOTS OF INSURGENCY

## AND THE COMMENCEMENT

## OF REBELLIONS

### On the Commencement of Rebellions and the Art of Controlling Rebels

In the normal course of events, there is little that is easier than looking over the shoulders of those in power and announcing to all the world how they might better manage their affairs. That is particularly true if the power holders are in distant lands that have strange customs and lack such commonplaces of modern governance as rational and honest bureaucracies, graduated income taxes, political parties that contend over principles in preference to personalities, and economies that can sustain their own growth. In such circumstances, the advice can take the ready-made form of suggesting that the governors of such unenlightened societies should, with all deliberate speed, change their peoples over into the image of the liberal, democratic, prosperous, and sober societies of the industrial West.

These disrespectful thoughts about the banalities and moralizations that are customarily offered as sage advice to the bedeviled governments of underdeveloped countries were provoked by the exasperating difficulty of arriving at any worthwhile principles for guiding governments faced with insurrections. How can one avoid sounding trite when discussing what fragile governments should do when, in moments of extremity, they find

themselves besieged by vigorous and irresponsibly ruthless insurrections? Certainly, there is no help in telling such a government
that it need not have happened if only the ruling group in the
threatened state had been more like us. Then what should the
advice be?

Our difficulty in confidently providing sound advice on how
to deal with rebels is directly related to the inadequacies of our
knowledge about the causes of insurrections and rebellions.

Significantly, the problem of coping with armed insurrection
has been largely ignored in the modern literature of both military
and political science. One must go back to the Renaissance and
the early formation of the Western nation-state system to find
writers on statecraft who are primarily concerned with the problem of creating republics in the face of insurrectionary attempts
by would-be tyrants. This problem was central for Machiavelli;
and it is interesting to note that his world was passing through
a phase of intellectual and social change similar in many respects
to the process of change now taking place in many underdeveloped countries. It does seem that there is a peculiarly close
connection between the prevalence of insurgency and the processes of nation-building, and we will have to examine in a moment why this should be the case. In the meantime, it is noteworthy that, once the nation-state became the accepted political
unit, Western political thinkers tended to pass over the problem
of internal disorders. Hence our continued ignorance about the
problem.

Whenever people lack empirically-based knowledge about
social and political phenomena, they tend to grope for certainty
by turning to moralistic explanations. Once history was largely
explained as the consequence of "good" and "bad" kings, and
now an equally unsophisticated approach relates insurrections to
the existence of "good" or "bad" governments. This moralistic
approach is particularly common among Americans; possibly
partly because we have had less experience with and understanding of insurrections, and partly because of our natural proclivity
to moralize about the big events of politics. The Civil War was
much too traumatic an experience to have given us an intellectual
understanding of the problem of managing threats to civic order.
Instead we are inclined to see the problem as one for foreign,

and of course less perfect, governments. Indeed, a fundamental article of faith in American political thinking is that any government with a rationally sound administration and morally correct policies will not be threatened with revolts. Also, of course, the general American sympathy for underdogs and the universal pleasure we derive in seeing any form of authority beset with frustrations have somehow made it seem unsporting to take too serious an interest in devising means for stamping out insurrections.

There is no question that our moralistic approach makes us deeply uneasy about being in any way identified with governments striving to suppress rebellions. We tend to suspect that any government confronted with a violent challenge to its authority is probably basically at fault and that a significant number of rebels can only be mobilized if a people has been grossly mistreated. Often we are inclined to see insurgency and juvenile delinquency in the same light, and we suspect that, as "there is no such thing as bad boys, only bad parents" so there are no bad peoples, only evil and corrupt governments. No doubt there is a fundamental connection between the basic American orientation toward the problem of insurgency and our deep-seated belief that good relations between the generations depend primarily upon the parent treating the child with scrupulous fairness and warm understanding. Possibly this belief is the source of our profound anxiety that those in authority can so easily compromise their position by not being precisely just and fair in all their dealings with inferiors.

Although we are not likely to advance far beyond our essentially moralistic understanding of insurgency without the assistance of more scientific knowledge, it may be helpful to observe that other peoples, proceeding also on the basis of relative ignorance, have seen the problem of insurgency in a slightly different light and have relied upon quite different assumptions about the causes of civic disorder.

The British, for example, throughout the colonial era had considerable experience with the problems of controlling rebels, and in the main the British authorities came to adopt the view that most civil disorders sprang from man's inherent and compulsively irrational urge to violence and mischief. If a people is not constantly controlled and restrained by the pressures of society, the dictates of firm government, and the general good sense and instincts of responsibility of men of authority, then it can be expected that there will be an inevitable movement toward disorder and insurgency. Instead of the analogy of bad parents producing delinquent children, the classic British view has paralleled the belief that schoolboys will always misbehave if not controlled by the schoolmaster. It is thus simply the inherent nature of man, in a sense the existence of the id, which is at the root of insurgency. The problem of counterinsurgency is merely that of strengthening social sanctions and developing the superego, which is likely to be particularly weak among less civilized and less technologically advanced peoples.[1]

The classic British view of the causes of insurgency had the effect of making counterinsurgency seem to be normal police work, rather than a moral crusade. There need be no feeling of malice toward rebels, and it is indeed truly remarkable how unemotional the British could be in seeking to stamp out civil disorders. Furthermore, the fact that a people might turn to violence did not, in the classic British view, suggest that an insurgency might represent a last resort and a response to an otherwise intolerable situation, as is so natural among Americans. To the British, it is quite easy to stir up a people's urge for violence, and therefore little political significance need be attached to the willingness of some people to risk their lives.

In rejecting the moralistic approach, which we have suggested is more common among Americans, the British also tended to discount the possibility that just and fair governmental policy might remove the causes of insurgency. On the contrary, the British have in the main held to the idea that the common run of people have little attraction to or basic appreciation for justice and fair government. It is a moral imperative to rule with justice, but no government should expect to be popular for seeing that fair play is upheld. The traditional British colonial position is that the moral imperative rule of justice has always created trouble because most subject peoples have little comprehension of justice. This position is, of course, in direct contrast to the moralistic expectation that fair and enlightened policies can eliminate the very sources of insurgency.

In the strict British colonial view, there is, in fact, some question as to whether or not it is appropriate to remove a people's source of discontent, even to eliminate the danger of insurgency. For example, at one point when Ghana was still the Gold Coast, local British officials became aware that a frustrated, Western-educated, young lawyer was turning to nationalist agitation because he had been unsuccessful in fulfilling his career ambitions. They requested permission of the colonial office to put aside certain formal regulations, in order to give a potential revolutionary a respectable job within the civil service. London denied the request on the grounds that no government has the right to deny men their inalienable right to express personal frustrations with political action.

Traditional Chinese governmental philosophy found the sources of insurgency partly in the moral realm, as do the Americans, and partly in the nature of man's spirit, as do the British, but primarily in the domain of the mind. The Chinese certainly recognized that the immoralities of government and the natural rascality of subjects might, in equal shares, contribute to the downfall of civic order. The basic Chinese suspicion, however, was that insurrections occurred when people got notions in their heads and became confused in their minds. The function of government, for the mandarin, was largely to keep people from endless scheming about life and calculations about how to improve one's lot. Good government should train people to keep to their stations and to accept the structure of society. In the Chinese view, the danger of insurgency was closely associated with excessive activity on the part of officials, for, once a government sought to do too much to change the state of affairs, ambitious people were likely to toy with the possibility of further changes. Chinese governmental reasoning, in grossly oversimplified form, held that innovation by government was invariably disruptive and confusing and that confusion about the stability of events was a certain cause for a revolution of rising expectations—which must always in time take on a direct political character. Governments thus invited their own downfalls by opening the eyes of their subjects to too many interesting possibilities of change. Again, here is a view that directly contradicts the assumptions behind the American moralistic approach to the roots of insurgency.

No doubt all of these approaches contain some elements of

truth, for each springs from an appreciation of one of the three basic dimensions of individual personality: man's moral sense or superego, man's spirited energy or id, and man's capacity to reason and to be excited by reasoning—the ego. A deeper under- standing of insurgency certainly calls for a much more profound analysis of the relationship between personality, politics, and violence than has been customary. The fundamentally shocking and disturbing character of insurgency has inhibited all societies from serious study of the problem. Americans are not the only ones to have had a traumatic experience: Most colonial govern- ments have been quick to put their experiences out of mind, and thus they have failed to acknowledge and codify their accumu- lative understanding of how to cope with insurrections. In any case, each outbreak of insurgency seems to call for relearning old lessons, for memories on this subject seem always to be peculiarly short. This propensity of governments to forget as quickly as possible all they may have learned about handling civil violence has been a major factor in inhibiting the develop- ment of knowledge and doctrine about insurgency.

There is another reason why a body of Western doctrine on fighting insurrections has not developed, which is comparable to the principles of war at the international level. The character of any insurrection is largely determined by the peculiar social structure and pattern of political relationships of the society in which it takes place. In contrast, in conventional wars between states that are geographical entities, there are more constant factors, like the fundamental character of armies and military establishments, levels of technology, and the more controlled range of situations that can arise when formally organized armies clash on fairly clearly defined fields of battle. The difficulty in generalizing about insurrections arises from the fact that strategies that may be highly successful in one situation may be completely irrelevant in another. As guerrillas must live by their wits, so governments fighting guerrillas must be quick-witted and un- encumbered by doctrines.

To some extent, the problem created by this diversity of in- surrectionary situations can be reduced by thinking in terms of some general categories of insurrections. Brian Crozier, in his survey of the anatomy of rebellion and the art of controlling rebels, employs a classificatory scheme that emphasizes the fundamental realities of postwar international politics.[2] Among anticolonial insurrections, he distinguishes between those directed against British and French rule and between those led by Communists and by non-Communists. He has a separate category for newly-independent governments combatting either Communist or non-Communist rebellions. Finally he has a category for non-Communist uprisings against Communist regimes, which, at the time of his writing, included only the tragic Hungarian uprising and not yet that in Tibet or the 196$ fiasco in Cuba.

For more strictly analytical purposes, particularly if we wish to classify insurrections in greater historical depth, it would probably be useful to establish a more generalized scheme. Such a scheme might be based on three considerations.

First, there is the matter of the organization of the general society in which the insurrection occurs, in particular the extent to which its political and social spheres are integrated. Second, the organizational form of the insurrectionary movement is a major factor that determines the pattern of the struggle. Third, there is the question of the characteristics of the government against which the insurrection is aimed.

Within highly complex industrial societies, it is almost impossible for political controversies to develop to the point of sustained and organized violence. In such societies, the political issues that may divide the population are less likely to follow lines that provide the necessary territorial basis for an insurrectionary movement. The possibility of an insurrectionary movement arising and then employing organized violence depends upon the existence of sharp divisions within the society created by regional, ethnic, linguistic, class, religious, or other communal differences that may provide the necessary social and geographic basis for supporting the movement; and a central authority that is unable to maintain uniform and consistent administrative controls over the entire country. Such situations are most likely to arise in essentially agrarian societies or in countries where there are extreme differences between the pattern of life of the urban and industrialized segment of the population and that of the rural elements.

The relative immunity to insurgency of highly complex indus-

trial societies, at the one extreme, and of homogeneously integrated traditional communities, at the other, points to the crucial
reason why the problem of insurgency is so closely related at this
time in history to the transitional and underdeveloped new nations of the world. The process of social and psychological disruption that accompanies the downfall of traditional societies
opens the way to a host of sharp cleavages within such societies.
A general sense of social insecurity may intensify the urge to
seek the sense of identity that comes from loyalty to ethnic,
regional, or other traditional and parochial associations. At the
same time, the process of cultural diffusion, which strikes a society at an uneven rate, can create new divisions between those
who are more modernized and those who cling to the old.

The fundamental difficulties of nation-building in transitional
societies also appear in the inherent weaknesses of most central
governments. The lack of basic consensus about the appropriate
ends and means of governmental action can raise widespread
doubts of the legitimacy of the formal government. The bureaucratic ineffectuality of most new governments also raises questions
about, not only their rights, but their inherent capacities to rule.
The environment is thus often peculiarly ripe for groups to try
their hand at creating a new state structure; quasi-states and
communities readily begin to arise within the state.

In the context of the second consideration, types of insurrectionary movements can best be distinguished by their goals, their
methods of recruitment and indoctrination, their organizational
characteristics, and their propensities in decision-making and action. Are the announced objectives of the movement limited
goals or total power? What is the relationship between the objectives of the movement and the basis of individual commitment
to it? Even though the professed objectives may be of a limited
nature, does involvement in the movement carry with it an
identification with a total way of life, which can be maintained
only by constant seizure of greater power? What are the considerations that guide the decisions of the leaders of the movement? What is their understanding of the workings of politics,
and what line of calculations do they follow in conducting the
struggle? From such questions as these, it is possible to distinguish
quite different types of insurrections. Thus, even though the

same fundamental social problems may be present in several situations, each particular insurrectionary movement is likely to have its own pattern of development based upon the manner in which discontent is mobilized and given new direction. This basis can be readily seen from the fact that, when the Communists exploit rural discontent, they produce a movement quite different from a traditional peasant revolt. The demands of peasants for justice and a better economic lot can usually be satisfied by means of administrative and legal measures, which have little effect on a Communist-organized movement.

In analyzing the character of an insurrectionary movement, it is particularly important to distinguish between the propaganda about objectives used by the movement and the actual appeals that attract its membership. Recruitment to violent and revolutionary movements is rarely based on the same considerations that dominate the announced political goals of such movements. This disjointed quality is particularly common in transitional societies, in which people are anxiously seeking a basis for association and personal security at a time when they are not yet prepared to treat political loyalty as a function of rational choice among alternative policies.

The third consideration, the character of the government against which the insurrection is aimed, determines both the range of effective counterpolicies and many of the advantages that the insurrectionary group may exploit. Governments with weak administrative organs cannot carry out many types of fundamental social and economic reform. On the other hand, it should be noted that high administrative standards, particularly with respect to law and order, may intensify and even prolong an insurrection. To a large extent, it was true in Malaya, where the British felt it appropriate to mobilize a heavy commitment of resources against an enemy that was at no time able to establish any degree of territorial control. In contrast, the governments of Burma and Indonesia have not felt it necessary to mobilize to the same degree against enemies who have consistently maintained territorial bases of operations. This distinction means only that, whenever a government is primarily an administrative operation, any threat to law and order is likely to be viewed as intolerable. On the other hand, a government with a more limited definition of its administrative responsibilities is likely to be less sensitive to localized disturbances and to react strongly only to insurgent movements that have developed enough strength to threaten its sovereign powers.

We could greatly increase our understanding of internal wars by isolating the critical considerations or variables under each of these three categories. By relating such variables to each other in terms of systematic hypotheses, we could arrive at a typology of insurrections. There is no doubt that the gradual accumulation of empirical knowledge about insurrections must depend upon some such systematic view of the total problem. Only as such studies are carried out can we reduce the webs of myth and fantasy that surround so much of the subject of insurgency.

The problem of understanding the causes of insurgency is not likely, however, to yield readily to such objective analysis, because, in the last analysis, the task of understanding causes is far too intimately connected with the task of designing policies to preserve the myth of government legitimacy. Any government faced with a violent challenge to its authority must provide a public interpretation of the causes of insurrection. The hypotheses about the causes of insurgency must not only be plausible, but they must leave the government in an effective position to carry on the struggle. Few governments can accept the view that it was their own policy deficiencies that drove people to violence. Governments more frequently prefer to picture insurrections as caused by misguided people lured on by some false prophet or evil conspiracy. Such a characterization has the virtue of making officials appear to be on the side of reason and their enemies essentially fools. The difficulty with the interpretation, however, is that it usually fails to explain how misguided people can behave with fanaticism.

Once we begin to relate the problem of explaining the causes of insurgency to the problem of governmental decision-making, we come to an extremely difficult area of analysis. In order to illustrate the profound complexities of coping with insurrections, it is appropriate to turn our attention at this point to only a limited aspect of the general problem of insurgency. Specifically, it may be useful to focus on the problems of the decisions that are likely to emerge at the commencement of an insurrection. As a result, we may be able to realize the dual objective of shedding more light on the causes of insurgency and providing some useful guidelines for public policy.

## The Initiation of Violence

The initial decisions of a government confronted with the threat of internal war are usually the most fateful and long-lasting of any it will be called upon to make throughout an insurrection. These decisions tend to have a binding effect, which, to an extreme degree, gives structure and form to the entire ensuing conflict. In a sense, the first acts of the government establish the crucial parameters of the conflict, because they generally define the issues at stake, the presumed character of the struggle, and the legitimate basis for any eventual termination of the struggle.

The enduring consequences of the initial decisions, both in law and in the administrative and political realms, are one of the important respects in which internal wars differ from international wars. In recent years, there has been considerable literature on how slippery war objectives can become in international conflicts. Governments may begin with limited objectives—to repel an invasion, to eliminate a dictatorship—but during the conflict, if all goes well, their sights are usually raised; the goals readily expand to take in total solutions—the reunification of a divided country, or the establishment of a new world order under the United Nations, for example. The dynamics of conflict tend to generate inconstancy of objectives, and the popular response to paying the price for victory is generally a demand for altering the *status quo.*

In contrast, in dealing with insurrections, governments must cling steadfastly to the single objective of maintaining the effectiveness of their claim to legitimacy. Governments cannot admit that their policies prior to the outbreak of violence were incorrect or unjust; even less can they suggest that they have changed their policies in the face of violence and illegal actions. No matter what changes may occur in practice, the formal positions of a government cannot change perceptibly during the course of the

conflict. For all the supposed virtues of flexibility in other realms
of public policy, it appears that people usually find it hard to
associate flexibility with the myths of legitimacy.

This view of the problem is, of course, that of the government.
Rebels, on the other hand, are not bound by the same restraints,
and their demands and objectives can therefore easily escalate, as
do war aims in international wars, if they seem to be succeeding
in the struggle. This difference between the necessarily more rigid
position of government and the shifting demands of rebels according to their fortunes is one of the most basic elements of
asymmetry in insurrections, an element that does not exist in
international conflicts. Indeed, this difference colors all stages
of an internal war and dominates all efforts at formal or even
tacit negotiations. Governments can usually allow themselves
very little elbow room for compromises.

It is customary to overestimate the extent to which insurgents
have the initiative in defining the issues at stake and in providing
the public with its understanding of the bases of the conflict. In
taking the first steps toward introducing violence, insurgents can
project the first propaganda claims and proclaim their version
of the causes of the conflict. In most insurrections, however, the
actions and pronouncements of governments are more significant
in determining the public's comprehension of the conflict. Government's behavior is usually the test people employ to judge
the credibility of insurgents' claims. The government can expect
to be judged according to its grasp of reality, its capability of
coping with the threat, its chances of controlling the future—
in sum, its ability to act as a sovereign authority should in pre-
serving its legitimacy. That is not to say that people readily
accept the views and announcements of a government in distress;
it is rather to stress that government is conspicuous and that
people tend to take their cues from government's own interpretations of its probable effectiveness and its basic capabilities. Rebels
claim all manner of injustices; it is the actions of government
that add or subtract plausibility to such claims.

One of the first tests of strength between government and
rebels is therefore to determine who will define the basic issues
of the conflict and what should constitute a solution. The manner in which the initial issues are first defined usually becomes

increasingly binding and generally determines much of the later strategy that each side follows throughout the conflict. Colonial governments have tended to place very rigorous definitions on such conflicts, because colonial authorities have had to demonstrate a monopoly of authority in the colonial societies and to suppress any appearances of an open political process at work. Thus the colonial authorities in most insurrections have posed the problem as one of threats to law and order and of a need to establish security as an absolute objective. This approach was particularly necessary because the main justification of colonial rule frequently was the argument that foreign control provided peace and security in otherwise disorderly societies. Even the lowest level of violence would thus appear as a threat to the legitimacy of colonial rule.

Newly-independent governments have usually tended to adopt far more tolerant standards toward violence within their societies. In part this tolerance arises because new governments have not tended to define the problems of government primarily in terms of administration. On the contrary, the leaders of new governments can see themselves as the political opponents of any potential insurgent group. Their need is only to remain dominant; they do not need to claim the same degree of monopoly of authority that their predecessors in colonial governments had to claim. In some of the new governments in Asia, the problem of insurgency has been handled largely by allowing insurgent groups a certain amount of freedom of action so long as they do not become a major challenge to the government. In Burma during the last decade, insurgency has become highly institutionalized in many areas, and the same is true in parts of Indonesia.

For both new governments and colonial authorities there is, however, a common problem of defining any conflict for the general public. Governments generally find it difficult to avoid giving a highly legalistic definition to most insurgency conflicts —primarily because one of the basic functions of government is to maintain the structure of the legal system, which is inevitably challenged by any insurgent movement. On the other hand, by characterizing the conflict as essentially a threat to law and order, governments often lose the basis for popular enthusiasm. Governments are expected to provide law and order for their communities, and their publics cannot reasonably be expected to become excited about helping the authorities in their basic tasks. What is more, the failure of a government to meet this basic function is often taken as an indication that the government has failed in other matters. That is one reason why some of the new governments in Asia, when confronted with threats of insurgency, have preferred to define the issue in other than legalistic terms. By accepting the conflict more openly as a political one, a government does not have to admit that the very existence of a conflict has brought its ability to rule into question. The fact that a particular political conflict has led to violence is a reflection only in part upon the ability of a government and can be accepted as a symptom of the weakness of a whole society. In this way, a government can reduce its own sense of responsibility for the evolving conflict.

The manner in which a conflict is defined in the beginning is also likely to affect the entire course of an insurrection, because it places certain definite limits upon the ways in which an insurrection can terminate. If the government characterizes the struggle as one of maintaining law and order, then it may have no other recourse but to push the conflict to a total solution and to insist that the insurgent organization be completely destroyed and all those who have violated any laws be punished. Thus, in order to convey the sense of seriousness of a budding insurrection, the government may establish objectives that will considerably prolong the conflict. On the other hand, governments that take a somewhat more tolerant view of insurgency are likely to define the conflict in terms that will permit earlier resolutions without forcing the issue to the point of a total solution.

The most fundamental way in which the government can define the conflict is in the way it chooses to characterize individual rebels. Are the rebels to be treated as criminals, and, when apprehended, must they be brought to trial? Or can they be treated as members of an opposing military organization and be handled as prisoners of war? The difference in these two approaches is fundamental and can shape the entire course of an insurrection. If the government is willing to treat those who have opposed it as misguided people who must be brought back into the society, it leaves itself the necessary opening to be able to treat captured insurgents in much the same way as prisoners are treated in international conflicts. If, on the other hand, the government chooses to characterize the conflict as a basic challenge to law and order, it must then treat each rebel as a member of an illegal organization who has committed crimes against the society. A difficult situation often evolves when, in the early stages of an insurrection, a government tends to take a very stiff view of the treatment of prisoners, while, as the conflict broadens, it may be forced to take a more lenient approach. The British in Malaya, for example, tried very hard at the beginning of the Communist-inspired emergency to characterize the struggle as entirely one of criminals challenging the legal order. They then had no alternative but to try all captured rebels. Very soon, however, it became apparent that this approach was impossible if there was to be, at the same time, any psychological warfare effort to induce people to surrender.

It is always tempting for governments to try to define conflict in terms that will be most meaningful if the enemy should be quickly suppressed. There is the tendency at the earliest stage for a government to characterize the rebels as an extremely minor and even insignificant group of people and to call for the heaviest penalties against those who have perpetrated crimes of violence. The government's need to redefine its conception of the enemy is often one of the first signs that a conflict is moving into a more prolonged and protracted stage.

DECISIONS IN A RELATIVE VACUUM. After emphasizing the crucial significance of the initial decisions in the face of an insurrection, we must unhappily now point to the fact that conditions at such a time are generally most inauspicious for making reasonable decisions. As we have suggested, the significance of such decisions is closely related to the long run; yet at the beginning of an internal war, the eyes of decision-makers must be more than usually fastened on immediate problems. The crisis of the moment is what impels the government to action, and it is almost impossible for officials to appreciate the extent to which their actions will have full meaning only at a later time.

In part, the difficulty lies in the government's tendency to have imperfect information about the intentions and capabilities of insurgent movements. There are the problems of penetrating the rebel movement to ascertain its intentions and of weighing the rebels' capabilities under conditions of open conflict. Can the insurgent leaders hold their following while exposing them to the constant threat of death? What potential do the insurgents have for recruiting replacements? In the insurgents' statements, how much is bluff and how much reflects commitment? As in any politics of challenge and confrontation, rebel leaders' statements must always exaggerate their case and their intentions. The government must therefore ignore almost completely the substance of rebel statements; it must analyze them only for indications of possible strategies. The need to clear up uncertainties is far more pressing than the need to deal with propaganda points.

Government decision-making is further complicated by the issue of whether it is best to over- or underreact to the threat of revolt.

Overreacting occurs when a government decides to mobilize more resources than it believes, on the basis of its most objective analysis of the situation, are necessary to deal with the situation. Underreacting occurs when a government decides not to apply immediately all the resources it believes would be necessary to crush the insurgents in a full test of strength. Governments tend, of course, to differ greatly in their standardized modes of reaction to threat and challenge. British colonial procedures have generally followed the pattern of sudden and dramatic overreaction to situations of potential insurrection, and they have tended to introduce countermeasures in quantum jumps, rather than by gradually phasing in new policies. By consciously overreacting to the initial challenge—for example, by declaring emergencies, abrogating constitutions, or employing preventive detention—British officials have been able to give themselves room to maneuver and to appear in a generous light if extensive measures turned out not to be actually needed. In direct contrast, the classic Chinese mandarin approach to the threat of rebellion was to underreact and to lie low initially while contriving and baiting various traps that might entice the rebels to show their hands prematurely. Within the margins of these different strategies there is still, however, a basic limit to over- and underreacting, which, if exceeded in either direction, will seriously—and possibly permanently—affect the government's claim to sovereignty and to legitimacy. The hope of gaining room for subsequent maneuvers by overreacting can easily be more than negated if the population reacts to these policies by assuming that the government is panicking and fears that it is losing control of the situation. On the other hand, the policy of underreacting involves the risk of suggesting to the people that the government is naïvely uninformed about the seriousness of the situation.

In the last analysis, decision-making at the beginning of an insurrection is complicated most by the fact that it must take place in a vacuum, in the sense that officials must accept an entirely new frame of reference for policy before they can appreciate the full facts of the situation. Without having experienced the realities of coping with rebellion, it is almost impossible for officials to visualize the complete significance of looming developments. Even worse, when faced with the prospect of widespread terror and violence, the human imagination is often a peculiarly unreliable guide to rational choice. Government officials in particular are likely to become unsettled when caught in a situation in which they can discern no reliable signposts to responsible and honorable actions. Men who have long been trained to aspire always to the sound and judicious act can become extremely disturbed when suddenly they can no longer determine what constitutes the sound act.

TENSION BETWEEN INNOVATION AND CONTINUITY. This point highlights the basic problem of determining how much innovation in policy is appropriate at the first signs of an insurrection. The instinctive reaction of a government is usually that a drastic situation calls for a drastic response. Every effort should therefore be made to put forward a new and dynamic front. On the other hand, there is the equally compelling need for the government to resist any action that might suggest panic. In deciding on how much change may be appropriate, acknowledgment must also be made of inertia, a powerful force in governmental organizations. Even the best trained and most highly educated governmental bureaucracies can have massive difficulties in trying to adopt new procedures and policies.

Hence the paradox that governments often find, at precisely the time when they are confronted with a radically new development, that they must fall back and rely more than ever upon unimaginative, routine, and essentially commonplace actions. Instead of trying to do too many new things at a time of crisis, a government may be better advised to try to do the old things well, for excessive novelty in internal governmental communications can be disastrous when there is equal novelty in developments in the society. That is to say, it is difficult enough for the organizers of government to adapt to a sudden change in their internal structure of organization and procedure. In a moment of crisis, it is essential to do the more instinctive thing, and for governments this usually means acting according to what appear to be the dictates of inertia. One of the problems in both Laos and South Vietnam during the last two years has been that government officials have been given so much advice about new and ingenious activities that they have had little time or inclination to concentrate on the elementary and prosaic functions that must be performed as prerequisite to any more elaborate policies.

RESPONDING TO REBEL DEMANDS AND PROPAGANDA. In internal conflicts there is a powerful temptation for governments to try to refute each and every propaganda point of the rebels. Immature governments in particular tend to be very uneasy about appearing in a bad light, and often officials in such governments are unnerved at the prospect of being described to the world as unjust, evil, and opposed to the flow of history. More experienced governments, and especially colonial ones, usually realize that in the voluminous flow of political verbiage before a crisis of violence very little is likely to stick, for very few people pay much attention to the specific sets of arguments advanced by rebel propagandists. For example, there are probably only a handful of specialists who are now aware of what the Huks, the Malayan Communist Party, or the Indonesian Communists were demanding in their propaganda at the outbreaks of their insurrections.

Inexperienced governments may also be tempted to blunt the vigor of a rebel cause by making concessions to its propaganda. The hope that some yielding will put off the test of strength is, of course, not unnatural, but historically it has rarely proved an advantageous maneuver. When, immediately after Burma gained its independence, the Communists began their insurrection, Prime Minister Nu publicly pleaded with the Communists, and assured them that his government would accede to all their policy demands. His behavior was understandable; but so was the Western reaction of horror and the Communists' reaction of redoubling their efforts at violence in the prospect of such an easy victory. The price Nu had to pay for learning and for demonstrating to others that the Communist insurgents sought far more than their propaganda objectives indicated was to appear a bit of a fool before his countrymen.

One of the most difficult decisions a government must make is that of judging when the time has been reached when it is no longer possible, through any act of public policy, to affect the decision of an insurgent group to turn to violence. Almost without exception, whenever rebellions occur, governments tend to lag behind events and to hope that it is still possible to divert by means of public policies the trend toward violence. In most circumstances, insurgent groups have had to make a firm commitment to employ violence before they have been able to show their strength. Once a revolutionary movement has committed itself to violence, it must carry out a large number of actions affecting its own internal organization, actions that cannot be readily reversed. Once these decisions have been made, the leaders must focus on mobilizing the strength of its membership, and they can be little fazed by developments external to the organization. Any movement that can be bought off at the last moment by changes in government policy probably does not have the sustaining drive and the organizational ability to mount a serious insurrection. The Malayan Communists, for example, made their decision to turn to violence six months before the emergency began, and during that six-month period no government activity shook its determination in the slightest.

Thus, when the public first becomes aware of an insurgent movement, certain irrevocable decisions have usually already been made. Outside critics, too, often become aware of a threatening situation only at a very late stage, and, in trying to acquaint themselves with the causes of the insurrection, they may assume that social reform policies at an earlier stage might have prevented the conflict. They often fail to appreciate that, after a certain point, such policies could no longer have altered the situation.

The fact that an insurgent movement makes its firm decisions at an early stage, combined with the fact that a government can never publicly convey all that it knows, creates a peculiar situation at the early stage of any insurrection. During this stage, it often appears that each antagonist is following a course of action that is very little affected by the behavior of the other. The issues the government chooses to discuss and the policies it chooses to advance often are irrelevant to the situation of the moment—and at a time when outside critics tend to place the greatest pressure upon the government to carry out policies that may be peculiarly irrelevant at a late hour.

There is thus, at a time of crisis, a tendency for politics to come to an end and for the possibility of negotiations to all but vanish. This peculiar phenomenon has often encouraged outsiders to think that a modicum of wisdom and sensitivity on the part of either side might have prevented the collision. Once violence has broken out, it is usually easy to argue that a little foresight and a little intelligence could have prevented the conflict. In a sense, the collision of government and insurgents is very much like the old story, which George F. Kennan recently repeated, of the two cross-eyed men who bumped into each other on a street in Philadelphia. The first said, "Why in hell don't you look where you're going?" To which the other replied, "Why in hell don't you go where you are looking?"[3]

THE APPEARANCE OF IGNORANCE AND THE NEED TO PROTECT INTELLIGENCE. Governments are expected to be well informed about all that transpires within their sovereignties; the capacity to rule is the capacity to be prepared for all eventualities. But when an insurrection erupts, it often appears to the public that the government must have been ill-informed and unready to cope with the exigencies. More often than not, however, before an insurrection breaks out and becomes a social phenomenon, governments are better informed than their critics are likely to credit them with being. Governments often appear to be ignorant of events, in part because the problem of dealing with the initial build-up of an insurgent movement and surveillance of rebel activities usually falls within the responsibilities of the police, and police are of course notoriously secretive. At this early stage, there is usually hope that policing procedures will prove adequate and that there will be no need to cause public concern.

Once violence has erupted, there are other compelling reasons for governments to withhold much of the information they have. As the emerging conflict becomes more sharply defined it becomes increasingly essential for the government to protect its sources of information and to withhold from the public much of what it knows about developments. The government is thus faced with conflicting demands. On one hand, it is anxious to convey the sense that it is still master of the situation and fully aware of all developments. On the other hand, it must be careful not to reveal all that it knows. It must, therefore, appear at times to have been ill-informed of the developments that it has not been able fully to control. This dilemma often makes a government appear extremely insensitive to reality. In spite of embarrassment to a government, the overriding concern must be the protection of sources of intelligence.

The very essence of counterinsurgency is the collection of intelligence for the government. The advantages guerrillas and terrorists may possess in opposing the far greater resources of the government can largely be countered if the government has adequate intelligence. At later stages in their insurrection, whatever advantages of mobility, surprise, and *esprit de corps* the guerrillas possess can usually be more than offset if the government has the crucial intelligence at the right moment. One of the earliest tests of the probable success of the government is its capacity to build up its intelligence and protect its sources of information, even at the risk of appearing to be extraordinarily poorly informed.

THE EXTRAORDINARY AND THE ORDINARY FUNCTIONS OF GOVERNMENT. One of the earliest problems with which a government facing an insurrection must deal is that of determining how much of its energies and activities will be devoted directly to the conflict and what functions will be guided by considerations irrelevant to the conflict. There is a strong temptation at the beginning of any rebellion to attempt to mobilize all the government's powers and to call upon all of its agencies to become engaged in the conflict. There is considerable danger though, if this temptation is followed, that the entire administrative apparatus of government will become politicized and most of its functions perverted.

Stronger and more experienced governments tend to make an early distinction between those resources that will be mobilized for fighting the insurgents and those reserved for normal activities. There is considerable danger of the government's conveying the impression that its entire administrative functions may be acting largely in response to enemy actions rather than according to its own internal impetus. For example, it is a sign of weakness if a government seems to be stepping up its social service functions solely in response to a challenge from the insurgents. The government should be able to convey the impression that it performs many of these functions according to criteria and standards that are not in the slightest affected by the demands of the insurgents.

Indeed, one of the most difficult problems facing a government in fighting a rebellion is the need to keep separate its ordinary functions and its extraordinary functions. A government has certain basic responsibilities to its society that must be maintained in spite of the threat of insurgency.

This dual responsibility of government to preserve domestic social order, while at the same time competing politically with insurgents, is very much analogous to the position the United States faces on the international scene when it tries to maintain international order and engages at the same time in competition in the Cold War. The genius of government, as well as that of international statecraft, is that of determining the appropriate allocations of effort to these two tasks at any particular moment of the conflict.

### Conclusion

From these observations about the host of problems that call for decision at the outbreak of violence, it is apparent that it is extremely difficult to provide governments with sound and useful devices on how to deal with a threat of insurgency. Our initial observations of the irrelevance of most such advice have been borne out by our subsequent analysis. It is certainly not enough merely to suggest more enlightened and liberal policies of social reform, although such policies clearly have a place in an over-all program of eliminating the threat of insurgency.

Nor is it possible simply to treat the problem of insurgency as essentially identical with that of good and effective government. The dynamics of insurgency have their distinctive qualities. It is only as we gain deeper understanding of how the various aspects of human behavior relate to the causes of insurgency that we can begin to arrive at a sound basis of knowledge for developing policies to cope with the threat of internal wars. In the meantime, however, we can begin to accumulate insights on the art of controlling rebels who would destroy the prospects of democratic development and establish the rule of tyrants.

### Notes

1. It is an interesting fact of history that British society overcame a fundamental problem of violence and aggression during the same period that British power was creating peace and order throughout so much of the world. In a very deep psychological sense, British national character seems to have been grappling with the problem of controlling the urge to individual violence just at the time when Englishmen were developing their basic concepts about the causes of civic disorder in colonial lands. For a revealing discussion of the prevalence of violence in eighteenth- and nineteenth-century England and the emergence of British feelings of anxiety over the dangers of not controlling one's emotions, see Geoffrey Gorer, *Exploring English Character: A Study of the Morals and Behavior of the English People* (New York: Criterion Books, 1955).

2. *The Rebels: A Study of Post-War Insurrections* (Boston: Beacon Press, 1960). Brian Crozier

3. Kennan, *Russia and the West Under Lenin and Stalin* (Boston: Little, Brown and Company, 1960), pp. 10-11.

*Alexander Gerschenkron*

## REFLECTIONS ON ECONOMIC ASPECTS

## OF REVOLUTIONS*

"Revolution" is a vague and equivocal term. In its common usage, it seems to hinge, in an uncertain and sometimes bewildering fashion, on certain modes of behavior—such as violence —and/or on certain elusive interpretative concepts—such as discontinuity. Through the use of assimilative imagery, the term has been extended to processes of change in various fields, yielding *inter alia* the kindred concepts of industrial, scientific, and technological revolutions. Similarly, the upward trend of commodity prices in the sixteenth century has been dramatized by describing it as a "price revolution." For present purposes, such extensions will be neglected, and the definitional difficulties inherent in the political mother concept will be circumvented by forcing an historical reference to events commonly recognized as revolutions to serve in lieu of a precise definition. Accordingly, the problems raised are those that have emerged from, or can be related to, actual historical experience, most notably in France and Russia.

To be manageable, the topic must be narrowed still further. There is no intention here to draw in the following what might be described as the "total economic balance of revolutions." The question whether revolutions "pay" must go unanswered. Still less should anything in this paper be regarded as an attempt at

---

* It is my pleasant duty to thank the members of my Seminar in Economic History at Harvard University for their helpfully ruthless onslaught upon an earlier draft of this paper.

appraising the social and political effects of revolutions, either in themselves or in their impact upon the economy. The purpose is more modest: to concentrate on the agrarian sectors of the economies of countries passing through revolutionary convulsions and to express some groping thoughts on the causes and particularly the long-run economic effects of developments within those sectors and of the policies that were pursued with regard to it in the course of the revolutionary period.

While the subject of this paper is thus restricted, it seems useful to reflect on those matters against the broad background of the Marxian view of revolutions. It is a peculiarity of that view that it attempts, on the one hand, to establish a bond between economic interests and ideology and to present the former as the "real" cause of revolution; on the other hand, ideology is treated as a program for the revolution and, by the same token, as predetermining the effects of a successful revolution. In the process of evolution from feudalism to capitalism and from capitalism to socialism, revolution occupies its pre-established place, once as a *bourgeois* revolution and then as a socialist one. It is, then, the function of political revolutions to mark the transition from one economic system to another, and as such to be an integral part of economic history. There is no need in this context to dwell on the admixture of teleological elements to what presents itself as a causally determined system. Nor is it relevant to point out that noneconomic causes of revolutions may be most plausibly considered along with—or even in precedence of—economic causes. Neither a "complete" explanation of revolutions nor the general adequacy of the materialistic conception of history is at issue here. The usability of Marxian concepts is to be discussed only in relation to the limited area of agriculture and, as far as possible, in the light of concrete historical experience.

It seems natural, therefore, to begin by looking at the agrarian conditions that prevailed on the eve of the French Revolution and at developments in agrarian policy that took place during its course. Those conditions were described by the men of the Revolution as "feudalism" and their own actions as abolition of the hated system. Those semantic preferences are readily understandable. When Emperor Joseph II of Austria, in 1781, abolished by a famous edict the existing restrictions on the personal freedom of the Austrian peasants, he did not hesitate to present his actions as *Aufhebung der Leibeigenschaft*. Since the Austrian peasant of the eighteenth century had not been *owned* by the seignior in any meaningful sense of the word, the phrase used was misleading and was aptly styled "a bit of Imperial propaganda." The use of the term "feudalism" in speeches and edicts in France, from Mirabeau to Napoleon, was open to similar objections. What was feudalism? Was it a totality of very complex, very subtle, and very inconsistent relationships, both harmonious and antagonistic, embracing widely disparate and incommensurate elements—in short, Marc Bloch's *Société Féodale?* But no one needed a revolution to melt away the snow of yester-ages. A system based on land grants for the consideration of homage and service, with provision for analogous sub-infeodations, of course, did not exist in eighteenth century France. Was feudalism a system of seignorial rights over the labor or the product of labor of enserfed peasantry? Such rights were more than a historical memory, but they had undergone a formidable transformation. The remnants of serfdom on the eve of the Revolution were small indeed. The *corvée* obligations had been greatly reduced. To an overwhelming extent, the demesne had been divided among the peasants, and the labor services performed on the demesne had been commuted into money payments—even though a variety of contingent obligations and monopolistic compulsions were preserved and regional variations were very great.[1] There is little doubt that the nature of those payments and other obligations was not entirely alien to normal economic rent. Indeed, the distinction between "feudal" rent and "economic" rent is not easy to grasp. Was the peculiarity of feudal rent that it was fixed once and for all, as the *cens* certainly was? That would imply, in concrete historical terms, that the *cens* was a feudal rent *because* its real value was being reduced over the centuries by the falling value of money, denoting an improvement in the position of the peasant—surely, a curious criterion.

Or were the payments "feudal" because in so many cases the peasants were the "actual" owners of the land for which the payments were made? This conclusion of Loutchisky's research[2] on the ownership rights of the French peasants is generally accepted today. As an "actual" owner, the French *censitaire* was a heriditary occupant of the land and was entitled to lease or sell it, even though such a transaction required payment of additional imposts to the seignior. Again, the argument is curiously paradoxical. It is apparently the very extent of the peasants' emancipation from the powers of the seigniors that defines the relationship as feudal. On the other hand, the degree to which a social phenomenon should be viewed in terms of its origins must depend on the extent of the change that has taken place in the interval. If the whole fief had been retained by the seignior as his demesne and the peasants converted into sharecroppers, the relation would not have been viewed as "feudal," even though the origin of the seigniors' rights in the land may have been—and in many cases certainly was—feudal in the unambiguous juridical sense of the word.

Leaving aside specific budgetary discriminations in favor of the nobility and neglecting marginal survivals, it is not easy to say precisely what was "feudal" in the economic structure of prerevolutionary France. Normally, though not very explicitly, the position is taken that the liberation of the peasant from his obligation toward the seignior must be regarded as abolition of feudalism because it implies the strengthening of the peasant economy and a strong and independent peasant farm was "unfeudal" by definition. There is every reason to remain aware of the difficulties inherent in such a definition. Assume, for instance, promulgation say in the 1770's of a legal act circumscribing the rights of the *censitaires* roughly within the then existing scope and describing those rights as statutory tenant protection thus limiting the seigniors' rights of ownership while leaving the determination of the rental payments to contractual agreements. Such an act would have placed the ownership rights of the seigniors on a new basis and, in addition, would have attached to them modern ideas of social legislation. From an economic point of view, it would be difficult to find anything "feudal" in this arrangement. It must be noted, however, that the rents agreed upon under such conditions most likely would have been greatly in excess of the "feudal payments." Such deterioration in the position of the peasants and the obverse improvement in that of the seigniors would have constituted the only economic change *vis-à-vis* the "feudal" situation. We obviously move on very uncertain ground. Nevertheless, let us, for the sake of the argument, accept the conventional way of equating creation of an independent peasantry with the abolition of feudalism. In fact, it is primarily this conception of the historical process that underlies the view that the French Revolution, a *bourgeois* revolution, stands as an historical landmark on the road from feudalism to capitalism.

Before we explore the further implications of this position, a few words may be said on the forces which must be held responsible for the agrarian antiseignorial policies. There is on record a long and persistent controversy about how far popular misery should be included among causes of the Revolution. As is true of most long-lived debates, the opposing views were in reality never mutually exclusive. It is true that the position of the French peasantry in the eighteenth century was much better than it had been in the preceding periods. It is also true that it was a good deal more favorable than the position of the peasantry in most, if not all, other countries on the European continent. On the other hand, however, the standards of living were low, and it was not very difficult for postrevolutionary historians like Taine to gather a sufficient number of illustrations, which in the minds of readers in the nineteenth century added up, somewhat unhistorically, to an impressive mosaic picture of abysmal misery.[3] More importantly, it is impossible to deny the findings of Labrousse that a general economic deterioration in the last prerevolutionary decade made the economy very vulnerable to the crisis, which began in the second half of 1788.[4] The so-called "feudal" or "seignorial" reaction, resulting *inter alia* from the revisions of the manor rolls (*terroirs*) and from attempted revivals of some claims that had fallen into desuetude, may have further contributed to the deterioration in not entirely negligible measure. De Tocqueville did not have the benefit of Labrousse's findings, and he did not attribute exaggerated importance to the restoration of hunting rights, the renewed insistence on observation of banality privileges, the *triage* or *cantonnement* encroachments upon the commons, and other developments of this kind. But he had a truly magnificent grasp of the mechanics of discontent. He understood that it was economic prosperity itself that hastened the advent of the Revolution. He knew that "it is not always by going from bad to worse that one tumbles into a revolution. It happens most often that a people after having suffered most oppressive laws, without complaint and perhaps even without awareness, turns vehemently against them once the pressure had begun to lighten."[5] This profound insight, which, incidentally, it is useful to keep in mind in judging many a situation of our own time, should have sufficed to explain the extent of the peasants' discontent on the eve of the Revolution— without any further reference to the subversive ideas of the age and the possible role of the country lawyer, let alone the village priest, in spreading them. But De Tocqueville's view is powerfully reinforced by modern research. Once the alienation of which he speaks had taken place and begun to generate discontent, any downward turn of the path of well-being was bound to exacerbate the feelings of ire and disaffection. It is therefore not at all surprising that in the streams of discontent whose cascading confluence brought the flood of revolution, the mass movements of the peasantry played a decisive role. As Georges Lefebvre has it, "the peasant uprising is one of the most distinctive features of the Revolution in France."[6] The attitude of the revolting peasants was an essential determinant of the dramatic events on the night of the Fourth of August, when the ideas of the Enlightenment provided as much illumination as the distant glare of the burning *chateaux*. It was their attitude that after August 10, 1792, and even more so, after June 2, 1793, led to abolition without compensation of all the seignorial rights that the contemporaries were pleased to describe as feudal.

Still, it is only one side of the picture. For the French Revolution is said to be a *bourgeois* rather than a "peasant" revolution. Much of the stress on the prosperity of the eighteenth century and the somewhat reduced emphasis on popular misery in the works of such historians as Jean Jaurès and Albert Mathiez comes precisely from viewing the Revolution as the triumphant advent to power of a rapidly rising and economically very successful class. There can be little doubt that the agrarian legislation of the French Revolution and the structure of agriculture that emerged from it differed in some respects from what they would have been if the peasants themselves, rather than the "friends of the people" in the Jacobin Club, had written the texts. It is true, as Jaurès says, that the urban leaders of the Revolution were at times afraid of peasant violence and sought to moderate and to restrain it.[7] But it was the town, rather than the country, that was responsible for some radical changes in the organization of agricultural production. For the bulk of the peasantry, while abolishing the privileges of the seigniors, would have preferred to preserve the manifold communal features and collective usages inherent in the prerevolutionary agrarian system. In a sense, then, some obstacles to the introduction of technological progress in agriculture were removed.

It is at least doubtful to what extent this outcome was produced by the economic interests of the *bourgeoisie*. Was the set of values that dictated the Jacobins' policies reducible to those interests? If so, it was certainly not in the direct manner in which the moral indignation of the peasants over seignorial encroachment was reducible to, or derivative from, *their* economic interests. The peasants' economic discontent and the economic discontent of the urban middle class do not seem to be elements of quite the same order. Obviously, many a knotty problem must be solved before concepts such as *bourgeois* ideology, economic interests of the *bourgeoisie*, Jacobin policies, and *bourgeois* revolution have been rendered operationally manageable and have been combined into a clearly articulated whole. For the limited purposes of this paper, it may suffice to have pointed to those difficulties and, for the rest, to accept the vague concepts of *bourgeois* revolution and *bourgeois* agrarian policies as we have accepted the uncertain and ambiguous concept of feudalism. The question then is to what extent the revolutionary policy of abolishing the feudal system—for which the peasants fought and which the *bourgeoisie* put on the statute book— was a favorable condition for the postrevolutionary development of French capitalism. It seems fair to say that there is a widespread readiness to answer the question in the affirmative—particularly in Marxian analyses of the period. In fact, the case of France is regarded as a paradigm, as a general model from which inferences for other countries can be drawn. The most impressive instance is the discussion of Italian economic development in the nineteenth century.

A few years ago an able Italian historian, Rosario Romeo, surveyed some recent contributions by Marxian scholars to the history of the Italian Risorgimento and its aftermath.[8] Romeo was struck by the virtual unanimity with which the relative weakness of capitalist development in nineteenth-century Italy was attributed to the failure of the left wing in the Risorgimento movement to emulate the Jacobin example—by abolishing large-scale agrarian ownership and establishing a strong land-owning peasant class that would have provided powerful popular support for the Italian *bourgeoisie.* It was claimed that the Italian *bourgeoisie's* coming to power (*andata al potere*) was not preceded or accompanied by recourse to the people (*andata al popolo*) in the form of a far-reaching agrarian reform. Accordingly, the *bourgeoisie* proved unable to create for the nation an efficient political structure, unencumbered by local particularism on the one hand and cosmopolitan catholicism on the other. Without such a framework, the economic growth of the country was slow and Italian capitalism fell far short of its potentialities. This thesis which goes back to the influential writings of Antonio Gramsci,[9] imputes far-reaching consequences to a specific difference between the French Revolution and the Italian Risorgimento, to wit, to the fact that the movement for national unification in Italy missed its opportunity to become a *bourgeois* revolution. A prerequisite for capitalist development failed to materialize. The Risorgimento, remained "une révolution manquée."

It is nothing if not amazing to observe the ease with which generalizations of this sort are accepted without much curiosity about how they can be tested, as well as about the probable results of such tests. In fact, the volume of empirical material that is ignored in such exercises in comparative history is considerable. Even with regard to seignorial rights before the French Revolution, one should not overlook the cases where the existence of such rights permitted a more efficient utilization of the available land resources. The cases of the seigniors' leasing timber-cutting rights in the forests or grazing rights in the commons to wealthy and enterprising tenants frequently brought about exploitation of forest and pasture lands that was more rational and more productive, even though it was introduced under the cover of "feudal" privileges.[10] Lefebvre was quite correct in stressing the "conservative" aspects of the agrarian revolution of 1789 in France. "The peasant destroyed the feudal regime, but he consolidated the agrarian structure of France."[11] He might well have added that in getting rid of the feudal regime the peasants *uno actu* got rid of economic phenomena that are usually described as capitalistic. The neat dichotomy of feudalism and capitalism is decidedly blurred when one descends from the heights of unduly dogmatic conceptualizations to the lower levels of abstraction.

There is no doubt that the picture of the French Revolution's introducing capitalism into France would be much more convincing if French economic development in the century following the revolution were characterized by brisk and steady growth. That, however, was not the case, particularly in the long interval between the end of the Napoleonic wars and the advent to power of Napoleon III.[12] With the reservation made in note 12, the period of both the Bourbon Restoration and the so-called Bourgeois Monarchy must be regarded as one of relative stagnation. The 1850's brought a spurt of rapid economic development, most notably in the fields of railroad-building and manufacturing; but the upsurge could not be sustained, and the French industrial economy continued at a rather slow pace until some acceleration occurred in the years immediately preceding the outbreak of war in 1914.

What are the causes of this unimpressive performance? Clearly, it is implausible to explain a complex phenomenon of retardation continuing over a very long period by reference to one or two decelerating factors. The range of such factors may well extend from the pattern of resource endowment to the scale of preferences of a housewife in Paris or Dijon. Still, in reviewing them it is impossible to overlook the conditions in French agriculture. There can be no doubt that the French family farm deserves a place of distinction in the array of hindrances and handicaps placed in the path of French economic development.

First of all, the French farms proved a very inadequate source of labor supply to the cities. The French farmer clung to his land. When torn away from it, he would move to the next local town, still eschewing a distant and irrevocable migration and always watching for opportunities for return to the land. It is not surprising that poetry in France has produced nothing comparable to Goldsmith's *Deserted Village* or to Verhaeren's melancholy vision of the dying countryside in Belgium ("la plaine est morne et morte et la ville la mange"). The French exodus from the land was very small throughout the whole first half of the nineteenth century. It did accelerate during the century's second half, but at no time did it become in the least comparable to the *Landflucht*, the rush from the large estates in East Elbia, of embittered landless laborers in search of better and fairer lives in the coal mines and the steel mills of the Ruhr Valley. At the same time, for a number of reasons closely connected with revolutionary and Napoleonic legislation, the desire to purchase additional land always seemed to rank highest in determining the economic decisions of the French peasantry. Thus its proverbial thrift meant abstention from buying additional consumers' goods; yet little of the savings was used for the acquisition of capital goods such as machinery and fertilizers in order to intensify the processes of agricultural production. As a result, the French peasantry not only failed to aid industrial development by providing it with cheap and disciplined labor (as did the Junker estates in Prussia); it also failed to act as a large and growing market for industrial products.

One must beware of attributing everything in the agricultural structure of nineteenth-century France to the French Revolution. It is certainly true, as we have intimated, that the French revolution in many respects simply marked the last stage of a development that had been continuing for centuries. But this point serves, if anything, to reinforce the inescapable conclusion: To further the cause of economic progress in France an entirely new direction in agrarian policies was needed. Hence, the positive economic effects of the Revolution must be sought outside the sphere of agrarian relations. Abolition of internal customs and other economic measures designed to produce the economic unification of the country are probably most relevant in this respect, even though there, too, the Revolution largely continued the policy of the absolute monarchy that it had overthrown, as Napoleon in his *Code Civil* continued the policy of the Revolution.[13]

It is much less certain how we should appraise the economic effects of the changed social and political position of the *bour-*

*geoisie*. It is easy to repeat a familiar sequence: *Bourgeoisie* is the class vitally interested in capitalist development; the Revolution increased the power of the *bourgeoisie* in France; ergo, the Revolution enhanced the prospects for capitalist development. However great the suggestive force of that syllogism, it appears to be a fact that the so-called Bourgeois Monarchy was characterized by a most narrow-minded economic policy. The *bourgeoisie* was in power or at least stood close enough to the seat of power, but it was perfectly content to perpetuate in France a hothouse atmosphere in which antiquated and inefficient enterprises were maintained at high cost, while new plants and enterprises lacked both the sting of competition and unobstructed connection with foreign countries for the importation of capital goods and know-how. Adam Smith knew well how short-sighted and detrimental the behavior of vested interests can be when they are using political power for economic purposes. He would not have been impressed by stolid syllogistic exercises, nor would he have been surprised by an historical experience that was clearly at variance with those exercises. If these connections are less clearly understood than they should be, the reason probably lies in the unwillingness to define "capitalism" in such a way as to make falsification of statements about it possible. If "capitalism" is defined as a system based on private ownership of capital goods and the existence of hired labor which is divorced from ownership of capital goods, then it is certain that all or nearly all industrial growth in nineteenth-century Europe was capitalist growth. It is then some quantitative yardstick be it growth of national income, or industrial output, or capital stock, over-all or *per capita*, or the numbers of gainfully employed—that must be taken as a measure of capitalist development. It is by a standard of this sort that the capitalist development in France appears to have been disappointingly slow.

It is precisely by quantifying his concepts that Rosario Romeo was able, in the study cited in note 8, to place the Gramsci thesis within an operational framework and to demonstrate that the failure to carry out an agrarian reform in Italy tended to aid rather than to obstruct the "capitalist" development in Italy, inasmuch as "unreformed" large-scale agriculture provided a basis for the creation of "social overhead capital" in the Italian economy to an extent that a "reformed" peasant economy never would have been able to match. The present writer feels that Rosario Romeo may have exaggerated the significance of the economic upswing that occurred in Italy after the unification.[14] By the same token, he may have exaggerated the extent of the contribution the large estate-owners made to the capital formation of the period. There can be no doubt, however, that Rosario Romeo was doubly correct in putting the problem into a form in which the arguments become refutable and in making very plausible, again in quantitative terms, what an agrarian reform would have meant for the economic development of Italy.[14]

It can be argued that this discussion applies at least to some aspects of the revolutions that occurred in Russia during this century. While abolishing personal subjection (serfdom or slavery) of the peasants and bestowing upon the peasantry ownership rights to part of the land that formerly belonged to the seigniors, the emancipation of the peasantry in 1861 preserved and, in fact, reinforced a number of archaic communal traits in Russian agricultural structure. In addition, land allotments were small, and the financial burdens placed upon the peasants very heavy. The subsequent increase in population inevitably led to further deteriorations. For about a quarter of a century after the Emancipation, Russia developed at a fairly slow rate, building its railroad network and expanding the scope of its industrial activities. Then, from the second half of the 1880's on, came a period of rapid industrial growth. Proceeding largely under the impulse and tutelage of the government, the great upsurge exerted a very considerable pressure upon the standard of living of the Russian peasantry and, to some extent, possibly even caused some depletion of agricultural capital. As the new century began, there was a body of large and rapidly growing discontent among the peasantry. The numerous local disorders culminated in the *general cataclysm* of the 1905 Revolution.

Again, we do not intend to ascribe that Revolution to economic causes alone. The points that must be stressed here involved the similarities and dissimilarities between the Russian and the French Revolutions. Peasant unrest, no doubt, constitutes a common element, but its causes appear to differ considerably. If the French peasant rebellions were the complex result of both the long-run progress and more short-run economic crises, the Russian peasantry suffered from the combined effect of the emancipation settlement and government policies designed to bring about the industrial growth of the country. Clearly, the relationship between peasant discontent and economic development was more intimate and complex in Russia than in France. In the long run, economic development in Russia could have been expected to lead to improvement in the position of the peasantry. But in the short run, it was precisely the economic development of the country that added so greatly to the burden of the peasantry. In France before 1789, the cessation of economic progress contributed to the growth of the peasants' discontent. It is true that the depression of 1900 cut short the great spurt of Russian industrialization in the 1890's. Yet the Revolution of 1905, to the extent that it was a peasant rebellion, was a protest, not against the depression, but against the prosperity that had preceded it. Whatever may have been the role of the weak and disorderly French budget, with its inequitable tax system, in bringing about the Revolution, the effect is hardly comparable with that of the Russian budget, which was neither weak nor disorderly at the turn of the century. But its pressure upon the income levels of the peasantry was formidable, and in its effects even assumed at times the nature of capital levies. Also in France, as in Russia, industry was favored by both sides of the budget, and, as a result some capital movements from agriculture into industry are said to have taken place before 1789. It would, however, be a gross exaggeration to depict French industrial progress in the eighteenth-century as proceeding at the expense of the French peasantry.

In this sense, the Russian peasantry's attitude toward economic development was a great deal more negative than that of the French. The latter was hurt by certain forms of large-scale exploitation in agriculture, but it could watch economic development outside agriculture with equanimity and, in fact, with satisfaction. The Russian peasant was grievously affected by the industrialization of the country, even though his hostility was directed against the traditional enemy—the landowning gentry—and expressed itself in a time-honored fashion by acts of arson, forest destruction, illegal grazings, and high-handed land seizures.

At the same time, to a much greater degree than had been the case in France, the vast majority of the Russian peasantry was anxious to preserve its communal organization of land tenure. That organization, with its periodic repartitions of land and underlying ideas of equality and collective ownership, was even more "unmodern" than had been the open-field farming in the manorial villages of medieval Europe, where rotation of strips among the village households was not practiced. It would seem, therefore, that, at least as far as the role of the peasantry goes, there is little justification for describing the 1905 Revolution as a "*bourgeois* revolution."

It is indubitably true that much of what happened during the upheavals of 1905-1906 can be meaningfully characterized as attempts by leaders of commercial and industrial groups to obtain for themselves a greater degree of influence upon governmental processes. The problem, however, is the use they would have made of their power with regard to the country's economic policy in general and agrarian policy in particular. In this context, it is quite significant that, after the revolution, steps designed to bring about the abolition of the Russian field commune were carried out by Stolypin. He was the man who had engineered a *coup d'état* in defiance of the constitution that the Emperor had granted at the height of the revolutionary cataclysm; it was his energy that stamped out the remnants of revolutionary fires, and it was he, more than anyone else, who was responsible for maintaining the system of absolutism under the new veneer of pseudo-constitutionalism. On the other hand, it was the representatives of Russian liberalism, in particular the leaders of the so-called "cadet" party, who fought Stolypin's measure, because it was designed to destroy the egalitarian character of Russian villages and to favor the economically strong elements among the peasantry at the expense of the weaker majority.[15] The French *bourgeoisie*, while liberating the peasantry from various burdens, could insist on abolition of communalism in agriculture. Such a course was not readily open to groups that can be fairly described as representing the Russian *bourgeoisie*. The reasons were partly ideological: Whatever economic interests may have been, they could not obliterate the strong feeling of compassion for the peasantry and the traditional respect for the principle of collectivity and egalitarianism. Furthermore, weighty practical reasons militated against such a policy, because no political party anxious to obtain popular support could possibly commit itself to a position against which the sentiment of the peasantry was so violently engaged.

The economic effects of the 1905 Revolution in the area under discussion were essentially twofold: A considerable alleviation in the financial position of the peasantry took place owing to the cancellation of land redemption payments, abolition of joint responsibility of the villages for tax obligations, and other measures. In fact, the removal of corporal punishment within the "peasant estate"—which followed an analogous measure for the "gentry estate" with a lag of about 150 years—must also be regarded, unironically, as a measure of fiscal policy. For that form of punishment and the threat thereof had been traditionally used to hurry tardy taxpayers. Thenceforth, it certainly was more difficult for the government to continue its policy of forced-draft industrialization based, as it was, on keeping the peasants under strong and steady pressure. On the other side of the ledger stood, first, the abolition of the various statutory discriminations against "the peasant estate" and, second, the acts directed against the field commune. Measures of this sort no doubt had a positive aspect as far as economic development was concerned. They tended to increase the supply of labor available to the growing industry and, in the long run, would have led to improvements in methods of cultivation and to increases in agricultural productivity. Even though the Revolution, in a very real and central sense, was a protest against previous industrial development, what happened in its course or as its consequence thus tended to favor to some extent subsequent industrial evolution.

It is far from easy, therefore, to draw a balance of the effects of the 1905 Revolution and to append to it a simple label like *"bourgeois* revolution." At least as far as Stolypin's reform was concerned, the Prince of Denmark had once more absented himself from *Hamlet:* as said before, the most radical *"bourgeois"* measure of doing away with archaic survivals in agriculture was adopted in the teeth of *"bourgeois"* disapproval. Nor is it without interest that a study of the motivations of the authors of the reform reveals with considerable clarity that the probable effect of the reform upon industrial development was the least important consideration in their minds. The measure was adopted for political purposes on the basis of a very disappointing political experience. The field commune had been considered by the government as the impregnable fortress of rural conservatism, a pillar of the throne. Yet during the revolution, the wildest excesses against gentry property occurred precisely in the areas where the field commune predominated. Stolypin understood the lesson. Like so many agrarian reforms in other countries, Stolypin's reform was carried out without any thought of its impact upon the country's industrial or "capitalist" development. The measure may qualify as a *"bourgeois"* measure, but it was dictated neither by the economic interests of the *bourgeoisie* nor by a desire on the part of the government to favor those interests.

Finally, another consideration may be in order. The years between 1906 and the outbreak of World War I were a period when—after the caesura of the revolution—the industrial growth of the country was resumed and proceeded at a fairly high rate. The government's contribution to the process was astonishingly small, particularly in comparison with its decisive role during the last decade of the nineteenth-century. But can this revival of industrial activities be regarded as a result of the revolution? This view seems very questionable indeed. Probably nothing was so important in causing the postrevolutionary economic upsurge in Russia as the legacy of the preceding upsurge, during which capital stock had been accumulated, labor skills acquired, and labor discipline "internalized," while the entrepreneurs learned to think in terms of higher time-horizons and to use rational and more complex cost calculations. No one can study the performance of the Russian economy in those two periods without feeling that between them there occurred something in the nature of a graduation, on the part of Russia's industrial economy, from the government-instituted—or at least government-supervised and government-subsidized—school of industrialization. By comparison, the favorable effects of the revolution appear to be of little weight, particularly if one sets off against them its negative effects. Among the latter, in addition to the previously mentioned reduction of the government's capability to tax the peasantry, one must mention the necessity to provide, in the postrevolutionary budgets, for a greatly increased service burden. For large loans had been contracted in order to cover the high cost of suppressing the revolutionary disorders. The result was the deflationary policy inaugurated after the revolution, which contrasted so strongly with the open-handed habits of expenditure in the 1890's.[16] We may say, therefore, that after the Revolution, the vastly decreased reliance of Russian industrial growth upon government aid and encouragement was, in part, a natural process; in part, however, it was the unintended consequence of revolutionary disturbances. To that extent, the revolutionary effects included a rate of industrial growth that was lower than could have, and probably would have, been the case in the absence of revolution. In the long run, it is true, Stolypin's reform could have been expected to help sustain Russia's economic growth and also to normalize further its character by strengthening the peasants' demand for industrial products. But the long run was cut short by the outbreak of World War I.

Within the area of problems with which this essay is concerned, the picture does not, therefore, favor any simple conceptual convention. Neither the agrarian policies of the French Revolution of 1789 nor those of the Russian Revolution of 1905 can be properly described as *"bourgeois"* revolutions directed against "feudalism" and carried out by the *bourgeoisie* in the interest of the *bourgeoisie* to further the development of capitalism. On the other hand, it is possible to suggest that in some respects at least the Russian Revolution of 1905 showed more pronounced positive tendencies for economic development than its great predecessor. The reason is likely to lie in the varying degrees of relative economic backwardness in the two countries at the times of the respective revolutions. This writer has ventured the proposition that the processes of modern industrialization are the richer and the more complex the higher the degree of backwardness in a given country on the eve of its great spurt of industrialization, which, if one wishes, may be called its industrial revolution. Arguing by unwonted reverse analogy from an economic to a political phenomenon, we may hazard a similar proposition about the economic attainments of political revolutions: The more backward a country, the more likely it is that a political revolution will carry out, or at least attempt to carry out, a larger program of economic measures. This expectation is partly the result of the fact that, in an advanced country with a rich pre-revolutionary history, a great many measures of modernization are adopted in the course of gradual evolution. In a more backward country, the poverty of the preceding history has left a legacy of *réformes manquées* for the revolution to put into effect.

This proposition is reinforced by the consideration that, in a backward country, successful execution of industrialization policies requires more than simply introducing the institutional framework that suffices for the purposes of industrialization in an advanced country. It would be attractive, though in the nature of an excursus, to illustrate this relationship by a somewhat indirect personal comparison of two historical figures placed in a similar position *vis-à-vis* the approaching revolutionary storm: Turgot and Witte. It must suffice here to indicate the main points of such a comparison. The personal differences between the two men need not be overlooked. Voltaire would not have called Witte—as he called Turgot—the most learned man of his age. For Witte's original contribution to economic doctrines was nil, while Turgot's doctrinal influence extended far into the nineteenth-century. But there is also an impressive set of similarities. Both statesmen towered high above their contemporaries in vision, resolution, and resourcefulness. They both tried to meet the threats of revolution. Each failed and was eliminated from the scene by a weak and incompetent monarch about the same number of years before the fall of the dynasty provided belated justification of his foresight and his warnings.

And yet, one must still discern the vast difference in the magnitude and complexity of the respective tasks: We may assume that Turgot's six edits of 1776 would have gone far toward reducing discontent. A further arrangement concerning partial redemption of seignorial rights probably would have greatly diminished the likelihood of a successful revolution. A merely negative policy of abolition might well have sufficed. By contrast, Witte, in his economic policy, had to do a great deal more than simply remove obstructions from the path of economic progress. We may say that, in a general political situation resembling Turgot's he had to pursue policies strongly reminiscent of Colbert's. Those policies are costly, and their fruits ripen slowly.

It is not only that, in trying to forestall the revolution in the long run, one increases its danger in the short run. In order to carry out positive policies of this type, certain negative measures, most desirable in themselves, must be postponed.

Witte's attitude toward the *obshchina*—the field commune—is a case in point. In his *Memoirs*, he explains at some length his changing views on the subject. Originally, he says, he was favorably disposed toward the institution because he regarded it as an ancient product of the Russian or Slavic genius. He goes on to say that Bunge, his predecessor—one step removed—in the Ministry of Finance, explained to him the economic drawbacks of the field commune and caused him to change his mind on the subject. Yet he did nothing to reduce the scope of the institution. On the contrary, he supported, in the middle 1890's, a measure designed to stop up a loophole and prevent peasants of certain description from leaving the field commune. In fact, he went so far as to persuade the very reluctant Emperor of the usefulness of the measure.[17] Witte himself tends to explain his actions as the result of inexperience. It is, however, much more plausible to assume that the Minister of Finance could not dare abolish the field commune precisely because of his ambitious budgetary policy. The commune was in fact a fiscal agent of the government and played an important part in the processes of tax collection. In a backward country with an inefficient bureaucracy, a considerable lapse of time was required before a modern tax collecting mechanism could be built up. In addition, the change presupposed a protracted struggle between the Ministry of Finance and the Ministry of Interior, whose police force was in charge of collecting taxes from the communes.[18] We must once more conclude that economic development in a very backward country is a most complex matter. To expect political revolutions in such countries to exercise simple and straightforward economic effects is even more unrealistic than are similar expectations for more advanced countries—in which the economies are so much more complicated, but the problems of policy *per contra* so much simpler.

We must still say a few words on the Russian Revolution of 1917 and its economic aftermath. In every real sense, the overthrow of the Imperial regime and the subsequent establishment

of the Soviet dictatorship were the results of the war. As Witte—
and probably Stolypin—understood so clearly, one thing that the
Russian government as it emerged from the Revolution of 1905
could *not* afford was to engage in major military conflicts. It is
true that, after 1905-06, the process of Russian westernization
in the economic field proceeded continuously and smoothly as
never before. Still, a number of years of a steady rate of growth
was needed to raise the population's income above levels conducive to passive resignation or violent protest—and to continue the
gradual process of transferring the gentry's lands to peasant hands
before the *muzhiks'* craving for more land would cease to result
in periodic riots and rebellions. For the time being, the tensions,
while diminishing, remained great. In addition, the political structure was extremely shaky. There is little doubt that the question
of widening the rights of the Duma at the expense of the monarch would soon have become acute and that it would have
required an enormous application of skill and wisdom to solve
the problem without skidding into another revolutionary crisis.
Under the circumstances, it was utter folly and incredible short-
sightedness to view the war in the light of the brief outburst of
patriotic sentiments that marked its beginning; yet we may assume that this view played a large part in the minds of the Emperor and of those in his immediate environment.[19] The illusion
persisted despite the lessons of the Russo-Japanese War.[20]

The Revolution of 1917 in St. Petersburg in its first moments
resembled *la guerre des farines* of Turgot's times. But once started,
all the disappointments and grievances, all the resentment and
discontent broke into the open and with them appeared all the
problems that, in peacetime, were susceptible of gradual solutions
but now demanded immediate and radical settlement. This reaction was particularly true of the land question. It was not the land
hunger of the peasants that had caused the revolution, but once
the old powers had fallen, the land problem overshadowed everything else and, in particular, rendered impractical the continuation of the war. If the war was to continue, immediate action by
the Provisional Government would be necessary to nationalize
all gentry lands and keep them in an undivided fund until after
the end of the war, when an orderly division could take place.
This solution, which is so readily suggested by easy hindsight,

would have presented the administration of the fund with problems of economic exploitation of the gentry estates that probably were insoluble or nearly insoluble in terms of the practical possibilities of the moment. At any rate, no such dams were erected by the Provisional Government, and the seizure of gentry lands by the peasants—as well as mass desertions from the army by peasants who were eager to take part in that seizure—proceeded with an elemental force. This violent appropriation must be regarded as by far the most important economic consequence of the 1917 Revolution. It was its approval and encouragement of this process that carried the Bolshevik Party to power in the fall of 1917.

What kind of revolution then occurred in Russia in 1917? Was it a *bourgeois* revolution? Or was it a socialist revolution? We can suggest that the radical change in the land-labor ratio in the peasant economy was bound to retard for a number of years, if not stop altogether, the flow of labor to nonagricultural employment. Strengthening the peasant economy was bound to affect the composition of the country's industrial output in favor of goods that may be described as "peasant harvest goods" and would have consisted primarily of mass consumers' goods and cheap farm implements. We might also describe such goods as "low investment goods." The long-run effect, once the ravages of war and revolution were repaired, would have been to produce a perhaps steady, but fairly low, rate of economic development. In other words, in its very essence the revolutionary movements of 1917 deserve to be described neither as a *bourgeois* nor a socialist revolution, but a peasant revolution, even though the concept does not readily fit into the conventional conceptual schemata. That is not to forget either the advent to power in November, 1917, of a political party that regarded itself as a socialist party or the fact that, under the pressure of circumstances, that party proceeded to nationalize most of Russia's industrial and financial enterprises. Neither of those events would have justified regarding them as emanations of a "socialist revolution." The Bolshevik government throughout the 1920's can reasonably be considered a vicegerent tolerated by the mass of the peasantry. The ownership conditions outside agriculture remained subject to change as the Bolshevik government—in a historical rather than constitutional sense—remained subject to recall.

It is only when Stalin successfully launched his policy of collectivization and superindustrialization that the historical period initiated in 1917 reached its termination. Rilke's prophecy with regard to the Russian peasantry—"Weit schreiten werden welche lange sassen in ihrer tiefen Daemmerung"—remained unfulfilled. For the march of the peasantry was stopped, and the effects of the peasant revolution of 1917 were undone by what Stalin himself once called "a revolution from above" and what to all intents and purposes amounted to a counterrevolution. One is free, if one desires, to describe that counterrevolution as a "socialist revolution." Yet before doing so, it may be useful to consider first that the house that Stalin built and that, despite some alterations, the Soviet dictatorship still inhabits has little in common, in its architecture and interior decoration, with the traditional concept of socialism as it was developed in the course of the nineteenth-century. No less important is that, in carrying out his counterrevolution and embarking upon a policy of a high rate of investment, sustained far beyond what may have been justified by military threats from Germany, Stalin and his government were primarily moved by the mechanics of dictatorial power.

There is no doubt that Stalin's dictatorial counterrevolution resulted in a rate of industrial growth in Russia that was unprecedented in the country. And this is perhaps the note on which these reflections can be suitably ended. For it seems to reinforce the conclusions that have forced themselves upon us throughout these pages: The economic meaning of such terms as *"bourgeois"* or *"socialist"* revolution and of their respective relationships with the subsequent course of economic change are most elusive. On the other hand, there is nothing ambiguous or elusive in description of the French and Russian Revolutions as "agrarian." In both countries, the peasants formed the mass of the population. May one not assume that in those conditions any popular movement against the established regimes was bound to fail, unless it not only enjoyed the support of the peasants, but to a very large extent *was* a peasant movement? Assumptions of this kind may be accepted or rejected. However plausible, they are not part of the historical record. But it is a matter of historical record, that the French and Russian Revolutions went far toward satisfying the desires of the peasantry and that in so doing they placed serious obstacles in the path of subsequent industrial development. This conclusion appears to be valid whether that development is described as *"bourgeois"* or *"non-bourgeois,"* as "capitalist" or "socialist." Historical processes are complex, and attempts to integrate the story of economic development with that of political revolutions are likely to fail, as soon as one moves from the realm of easy abstractions to more concrete levels.

The foregoing remarks have been confined primarily to French and Russian illustrations with a side glance at Italy. It would be illuminating to evaluate the French and Russian experience against the background of economic development of those countries where, in the nineteenth century, agrarian policies were much better adjusted to the needs of industrialization. In particular, contrasting comparisons with England and (for a limited period) Germany would offer additional confirmation of the views expressed here. This task, however, must be reserved for another paper.

## Notes

1. In general, as was clearly observed by Turgot, the peasants' burdens seemed to grow with the distance from Paris. Cf. Otto Fengler, *Die Wirtschaftspolitik Turgots und seiner Zeitgenossen im Lichte der Wirtschaft des Ancien Régime* (Lucka: 1912), p. 13, and *Oeuvres de Turgot*, E. Daize and H. Dussard, eds., II (Paris: 1844), 68-69.
2. J. Loutchisky, *L'État des classes agricoles en France sur la veille de la Révolution* (Paris: 1911).
3. H. Taine, *Les origines de la France contemporaine*, Vol. II, "L'Ancien Régime" (Paris: 1910), Book V, Chapters I and II.
4. C. E. Labrousse, *La Crise de l'économie française à la fin de l'ancien régime et au debut de la Révolution*, I (Paris: 1943), xxxix-xl.
5. *L'Ancien régime et la Révolution*, Édition Annotée par E. Pognon et J. Dumont (Paris: n. d.), p. 238.
6. *The Coming of the French Revolution* (New York: 1960), p. 113.
7. *Anthologie de Jean Jaurès*, Louis Levy, ed. (London: 1947), p. 114.
8. *Risorgimento e Capitalismo* (Bari: 1959).
9. *Il Risorgimento* (Turin: 1949).

10. Georges Lefebvre, "La Révolution française et les paysans," *Études sur la Révolution française* (Paris: 1954), p. 256.

11. *Ibid.*, p. 257.

12. It should be noted that a recent study by Jan Marczewski ("Some Aspects of the Economic Growth of France, 1660-1958," *Economic Development and Cultural Change,* IX: 3, April 1961, 369-386) casts a different light on the course of French economic development, suggesting in particular a relatively high rate of growth between 1825 and 1844. This result must cause surprise, as it is at variance with much of the quantitative and qualitative information that has been available thus far. As long as the raw materials underlying the calculations and the calculations themselves, including the derivations of the weights used, have not been published, one must confine oneself to a reference to Dr. Marczewski's study. Nevertheless, it may be in order to add that, even if one were to accept his data as impeccably correct, the rates of growth communicated would still be below those reached for comparable periods either in England or Germany.

13. It is interesting that Engels draws a sharp contrast between the French Revolution and the English Revolution of 1688. The latter, he says, resulted in a compromise between the landed interests and the capitalists. It preserved the continuity of the common law. In France, he goes on, the battle was fought to the bitter end; the last vestiges of feudalism were swept away, the break with tradition was complete, and a masterly adaptation of the legal framework to modern capitalist conditions was created through the *Code Napoléon* (Friedrich Engels, *Die Entwicklung des Sozialismus von der Utopie zur Wissenschaft* (Berlin: 1951), pp. 25-26). It is difficult to interpret the postrevolutionary economic histories of the two countries in the light of that contrast. While France gloried in the proper prerequisites for economic development, England excelled in the thing itself. In one of his recent novels, Italo Calvino speaks of "un paese dove si verificano sempre le cause e non gli effetti." France seems indeed to have been a country well endowed with causes but sadly lacking in effects. There was, of course, a dialectical loophole kept open: "The roots which the small scale farm had struck into the French soil deprived feudalism of all nutritional supplies. . . ." "But in the course of the 19th century . . ." a change took place. The young and vigorous peasant farm *("die jugendfrische Parzelle")* turned into the old and decrepit peasant farm *("die ueberlebte Parzelle")*, an easy prey for the capitalist usurer (Karl Marx, *Der achtzehnte Brumaire des Louis Bonaparte* (Stuttgart: 1914), pp. 105-108). Peasantry was seen as having assured the predominance of capitalism, only to be subjugated and swept away by the latter. "*Code Napoléon* has become a code of distraint and foreclosure" (*Ibid.*). But the French peasantry refused to accept the dialectical solution. It remained on the stage, thus forcing the Marxian interpretation to shift its ground rather unmetaphorically. For if one looks at modern Marxian literature, on the subject it appears that, rather than to abandon a good hypothesis because of obdurate facts, it has become customary simply to abstract from the English Channel and to regard the French Revolution as a natural political counterpart of the Industrial Revolution in England. In this way, one could, in good conscience, forget the negative effects of the French Revolution upon France's economic development.

14. Alexander Gerschenkron, "Rosario Romeo e l'accumulazione primitiva del capitale," *Rivista Storica Italiana,* LXXII:1 (1960).

15. See the speeches on the subject by P. N. Miliukov, which he made in the Third Duma. *Gosudarstvennaya Duma*, Treti sozyv, Stenograficheskiye otchety (The Third State Duma, Stenographic Records), 1907-1908, First Session, Part One (St. Petersburg: 1908), November 16, 1907, p. 301; and *Ibid.*, Third Session, Part One, October 10, 1909 (St. Petersburg: 1910), p. 22.

16. It was the policy of what V. N. Kokovtsev called "budgetary modesty . . . the only correct policy for a country living beyond its means." *Gosudarstvennaya Duma*, Trety sozyv, Stenograficheskiye otchety (The Third State Duma, Stenographic Records), 1907-08; Third Session, Part I (St. Petersburg: 1908), November 27, 1907, p. 611. Kokovtsev, at that time Stolypin's Minister of Finance, became in 1911 his successor as Premier.

17. Graf S. Yu. Witte, *Vospominaniya*, I (Leningrad: 1924), 446, 455-458.

18. It was only toward the end of his service as Minister of Finance that Witte stated that the apparatus of his Ministry was able to collect the taxes from the rural population without having to rely on the help of the communes and the institution of joint responsibility. It is also of interest that despite Witte's conversion and his many statements on the economic importance of individualism, his criticism of Stolypin's legislation in the State Council was severe. In his memoirs, he predicted that "much innocent blood will be shed" in consequence of that legislation. *Vospominaniya*, II, 343.

19. It is revealing indeed to recall Nicholas II's words to one of his provincial governors at the beginning of the Russo-Japanese War: "Now you will find your work to be much easier." He went on to explain to the governor, who did not at once grasp the Emperor's meaning, that subversive tendencies were bound to be choked in the resurgence of patriotism. S. D. Urusov, *Zapiski Gubernatora* (A Governor's Notes) *Kishinev 1903-1904* (Berlin: n.d.), p. 210.

20. How much of an illusion it was has been vividly recalled very recently by General Spiridovich, a police officer who, in 1914 and thereafter, was in immediate charge of the Emperor's personal security. The patriotic wave in 1914 never seemed to climb higher than it did in August, 1914, when the Imperial family, following the tradition for declarations of war, went to Moscow and participated in a number of ceremonies. Even at that solemn moment, Spiridovich's agents, spread through the dense crowds, brought to him a considerable number of "terse but expressive" popular sayings on the subject of the Imperial family, particularly in relation to the ominous figure of Grigori Rasputin. General A. I. Spiridovich, *Velikava Voyna i Fevral'skaya Revolyutsiya, 1914-1917 gg* (The Great War and the February Revolution) (New York: 1960), I, 16-18.

## Sidney Verba and
## Gabriel A. Almond

## NATIONAL REVOLUTIONS

## AND POLITICAL COMMITMENT

Internal war inevitably focuses attention on popular attitudes toward government and politics. Most theories of the causes of internal war deal at some point with concepts like disaffection and alienation—either as the major determinants of the breakdown of peaceful political activity or as the intervening step in the translation of other social processes into political violence. The relationship between political attitudes and political violence does not, however, end with the impact of these attitudes upon the outbreak of violence. Attitudes are affected in turn by internal wars. More than most other political events—more than wars with other nations, more than economic crises—one would expect internal warfare to play a major role in shaping the attitudes of individuals toward politics, their nation, and their fellow citizens. Internal wars lay bare the authority structures of political systems—structures that otherwise may remain implicit and unrecognized. Furthermore, internal violence makes strong demands upon ordinary citizens for commitment to politics. One goal of those who engage in internal warfare is usually to mobilize the uncommitted. One of the most important topics in the study of internal warfare, therefore, is the consequences of internal war experiences for political attitudes.

The ways in which experiences with violence mold political attitudes is of crucial importance in the modern world. Throughout the world, nations are being created in violence. This creation involves more than a change in formal political structures—the overthrow of traditional political structures through violence or the achievement of national independence through violent conflict with a colonial power. The very sense of national identity and membership in a state is often the by-product of these violent conflicts. It is within the framework of these conflicts that individuals often first become aware that they are members of a nation. It is furthermore within the framework of conflict that individuals whose major orientation has been to traditional structures—family, village, tribe—become involved in politics in the broader sense.

This latter phenomenon, the induction of people into politics through experience with violent revolution, is widespread and deserves close attention. In the nations that have achieved stable democratic political systems, the process by which new people have been inducted into political roles is long and gradual. The political history of Britain in the nineteenth century could be written around the problem of the gradual expansion of the franchise and the development of political parties in which individuals could participate. Other nations have also manifested this gradual pattern of expansion of access to politics. But politics in the twentieth century is characterized by two new factors. In the first place, the demand to participate in politics has become almost universal. Even within those new nations where the effective participation of all citizens is not allowed, the belief that such participation is legitimate and necessary is widespread. The belief that politics is the legitimate concern of the ordinary members of society—that they ought to be informed, that they ought to be mobilized, that they ought to take part—is found in most of the new nations. Political leaders talk to the masses; they cannot ignore them. This does not necessarily mean that there are effective means whereby ordinary individuals can participate in political decisions, but it does mean that they must be reckoned with.

The second major characteristic of participation in the twentieth century is the suddenness with which the demands for participation spread. There has been little gradual expansion of political involvement and participation from the center of society to the periphery, from one social stratum to another. Rather, all levels of society demand entrance into the system at the same time. The modern world is thus faced with a "participation explosion." People are inducted into politics suddenly— not through gradual involvement in political matters or through experience with political activity, but through participation in some violent political upheaval. What sorts of political attitudes are thus created? What kind of citizen is the citizen whose political loyalties are thus formed?

This paper will explore the nature of the political attitudes and political loyalties that are likely to grow out of experience with political violence and sudden induction into the political system. It will do so by concentrating essentially on one nation in which entrance into political participation took this violent form—Mexico. Mexico is a good case to use in studying the nature of the political attitudes likely to be created out of political violence. One cannot be sure, of course, that one can generalize to other nations from the experience of one nation, but Mexico is similar in many respects to many of the new nations that have had their origins in violent struggle. The modern Mexican nation was to a large extent formed out of a major violent upheaval, the Mexican Revolution of 1910-1920, which, at least until the post-World War II period stands with the Russian Revolution as the major social upheaval of this century. The Mexican Revolution, furthermore, was in many ways similar to many of the anticolonial revolutions that have led to the formation of new nations in the postwar era. It was an antitraditional revolution, in which social ruling classes and religious authorities were displaced. It brought into politics a wide range of people who had previously been apolitical. Though it was not an anticolonial revolution, it did have strong nationalistic overtones, especially in its attitudes toward the United States. Finally, the revolution has remained a major political symbol in Mexican politics.

A study of the relationship between political violence and political attitudes in Mexico is useful for several other reasons. Mexico has had forty years since the Revolution, in which it has been relatively free from external intervention or conflicts and could build a political culture out of the revolutionary experience. We can therefore observe what we cannot yet observe in the new revolutionary nations: what the long-term consequences of political revolution on political attitudes are likely to be. Finally, data is available on Mexican attitudes that is generally unavailable for other nations. There is much general speculation upon the nature of postrevolutionary attitudes but little empirical data on the subject. Furthermore, the data presented here on Mexican political attitudes is especially useful, for it derives from a larger, cross-national study of political attitudes, and the existence of comparable data from other nations allows useful comparison of Mexican political attitudes with those of nations that do not have a similar revolutionary history. In particular, we shall concentrate on some contrasts between Mexico and Italy. The use of these data is only suggestive, however, for they were not gathered for the purposes of analyzing the impact of violence on political attitudes. Nevertheless, they do have some relevance to this topic.[1]

The contrast between political attitudes in a nation like Italy and those in Mexico is especially instructive for understanding the impact of a violent nationalistic revolution upon political attitudes. In certain significant respects—respects that have important implications for political attitudes—Mexico and Italy are similar. Neither could be described either as fully industrialized and modernized or as underdeveloped. Each has a mixture of both elements, with some areas of the country highly urbanized and others quite backward and poor. Both nations have high levels of poverty, especially outside certain prosperous urban areas (Mexico City and the northern industrial cities of Italy) but in the urban areas as well. Both are Roman Catholic nations in which the Church and attitudes toward the Church have played major political roles. Both are nations in which a widespread sense of national identity is fairly new: in Mexico due partially to physical isolation and the existence of tribal loyalties, in Italy to late unification and the persistence of local loyalties and attachments.

These similarities are important for our purposes, but, of course, they ought not to be overemphasized. In numerous ways, the two nations differ significantly. It would be convenient if they differed only in the nature of the revolutionary experience—

Mexico having had a nationalist revolution, Italy having had none —for that would simplify the task of analyzing the revolutionary impact on Mexican political attitudes. But of course such clear-cut experimental situations are rare in the social sciences, especially when one is comparing two nations.

The Mexican Revolution occurred in a country of mixed Spanish and Indian culture. Its economy, prior to the Revolution, was primarily rural and agricultural. Its social structure was traditional and feudal. Government and public administration were largely extractive, exploitative structures. Mexican modernization is almost entirely postrevolutionary. Industrialization, urbanization, the penetration of government and bureaucracy into the countryside, the attainment of literacy, the trend toward amalgamation of European and Indian culture are all matters of the last few decades. And they are all unfinished business.

Italy, on the other hand, though a nation for less than a century, is an integral part of Europe's culture, even though the specifically modern developments of industrialization, secularization, and democratization have deeply affected only the northern and central regions. Though its national unification is less than a century old, its former kingdoms and principalities had functioning administrative structures that were assimilated into the governmental organization of the Italian nation and have persisted into the present. The Italian state has never acquired full legitimacy. It was first boycotted by the Church and the clerical-traditional right wing. Then, after the synthetic legitimacy of the Fascist interval, the Italian state was boycotted by the left. Even those elements that support today the governing Christian Democratic Party cannot be viewed as unambiguously in support of the Italian state. They consist in large part of Church-dominated women and men whose votes are cast as acts of faith, rather than as secular political choices.[2]

The Italian and Mexican attitude patterns reported here are therefore the consequences, not only of their revolutionary tendencies or experiences, but of these other characteristics as well. In analysis of the data, we will constantly be confronted with the problem of distinguishing the impact of the revolutionary variable from those of other cultural and social differences.

There are many contrasts between the political attitudes

found in Mexico and in Italy. We shall concentrate on attitudes toward the structures of politics and the individual's role in relation to these structures, rather than on attitudes toward specific governmental policies. Broad orientations toward the political system are a useful focus, for they are heavily influenced by the great crises of a nation's history—like wars and revolutions—and in turn play a major role in determining the types of political roles individuals will play or aspire to play.

In analyzing attitudes toward the structures of politics, we employ a threefold classification: parochial, subject, and participant. A parochial political orientation is characterized by the absence of orientation to the specialized structures of the political system. The parochial individual is oriented in his local units, family, kinship group, village; but he has little awareness and, what may be more important, little expectation of change from the specialized structures of government.

The subject is oriented to the larger political system but in a predominantly passive or "output" sense. That is, he has knowledge of government, as well as feelings toward it. But he perceives and experiences government as a source of actions that affect him and his surroundings. He does not perceive himself as being obliged or able to exercise any influence over decisions about what the government does. Participants, on the other hand, are related to the political system in an active sense. They perceive themselves as involved in the process by which government decisions are made. They have information about political affairs, make positive and negative political judgments, and attempt to affect the course of governmental action—if only by using their votes.[3]

This threefold classification allows us to isolate some basic political orientations. Much of the history of recent political development has to do with the transformation of parochials into subjects and participants. The process by which subject and participant orientations are added to parochial orientations—whether through the gradual induction of groups into the political process, as happened in many nations of the West, or through the sudden upheavals of the twentieth-century nationalist revolutions—has a major effect on the way in which the three types of orientation mix with each other.

This classification of political orientations is cumulative rather than discrete. The subject of an authoritarian system does not necessarily cease being oriented to primary and intimate groups. He adds subject orientation to the central governmental institutions to his diffuse primary orientation to tribe, religious community, and village. Similarly, the participant orientation to politics does not necessarily supplant the subject and parochial orientations. It supplements them, so that the citizen is still oriented as subject to governmental authority, as well as being a member of primary groups. He has added an input dimension to his output dimension and his basic primary orientations.

But this threefold scheme is not enough. We must also introduce into our analysis concepts that will enable us to diagnose the symptoms of instability, transition, and change. We cannot assume that the patterns of political orientation in any country are necessarily consistent with the institutions of its political system. We therefore need another classification to discriminate patterns of change or transition. Another threefold classification will serve our purpose here, one which distinguishes relatively stable orientations from relatively unstable ones. When a participant, subject, or parochial finds his political system appropriate or satisfactory, we shall refer to his orientations as "allegiant." When a participant, subject, or parochial rejects his political system, we call it "alienation." The "alienate" is the individual who is negatively oriented toward his political system.

Finally, we can speak of an "aspirational orientation," characteristic of transitional systems. Here we are dealing with political cultures that are changing and in which large proportions of the population are learning the knowledge, feelings, values, and skills that the emerging political system requires. It is a type of orientation that is high in feeling but low in knowledge and competence. It is characteristic of the tribesman and villager suddenly caught up in a nationalist movement, the shouter of freedom and independence in the new African nations. Or it may be the mood of the rebelling subject, the revolutionary democrat, the man who seeks to make government the people's instrument but has not acquired the civic expertise and know-how of the citizen in a stable democratic polity with a well established political infrastructure.

These categories allow us to distinguish political attitudes in Italy from those in Mexico.

### Attitudes toward Governmental Output

We may begin with attitudes toward governmental performance. Respondents were asked how much effect they thought the activities of the government had on their daily lives.

In Mexico, respondents are much more likely than in Italy to report that the government has no impact. Sixty-six per cent of our national sample in Mexico attributed no effect to their national government. Among Italians, 54 per cent attribute some or great importance to national government, and a little less than half attribute no importance to the national government or state that they do not know what importance the national government has for them.[4] The pattern is almost the same in response to a question on local government. In Italy and Mexico, then, and particularly in the latter, many respondents are unaware of the impact of government—or are aware of it but reject it as having no significance for them.

We are also in a position to determine whether or not the impact of government is viewed as valuable, in other words whether individuals are satisfied by governmental output. A follow-up question was asked, "On the whole, do the activities of the national government tend to improve conditions in this country, or would we be better off without them?" A majority in Italy and Mexico who attribute significance in their daily lives to the national government also view this impact as tending to improve conditions. Sixty-six per cent of those who attribute significance to the national government in Italy answer the question positively, compared to 58 per cent in Mexico. The Mexicans in this group show a higher proportion (19 per cent) who believe they would be better off without the activities of the national government. (In Italy, 5 per cent of the sample give this negative reply.) The same pattern appears in the follow-up question on the impact of the local government.[5]

If we compare Italian and Mexican respondents in terms of their awareness and evaluation of government impact, we find a much greater frequency of alienative or parochial responses in Mexico than in Italy. Almost two-thirds of the Mexican respondents say that the activities of the government have no effect on their lives. Even among the relatively small group of Mexican respondents that reports awareness of governmental impact, a substantial proportion reports that it would be better off without the activities of the government. Thus, though both Mexico and Italy differ in the same direction from the other three nations we studied, in terms of the frequency with which respondents report that government has either no impact or negative impact, there are sharp differences between Mexico and Italy. The frequency of alienation or parochialism toward either national or local government appears higher in the former.

In each of our countries, we reinterviewed about 125 of our respondents, repeating some of the same questions but probing more deeply and recording their responses verbatim. These interviews allow us to fill in some of the meanings of the quantitative data cited above. What we discovered in this fuller material is that, among the respondents in Mexico and Italy who attribute no impact to the government, are both "parochials" and "alienates"—respondents relatively unaware of the impact of government and respondents aware of but unsatisfied with the impact. A Mexican house servant who lives with her family in her mistress's house in Mexico City, when asked whether or not government is necessary, replied, "I won't answer this as I don't know what to say." She attributes no significance to government for her and her family's lives. Asked what taxes are used for, she replied, "What are they? I don't know." She can neither read nor write and has never voted. A Mexican housewife in San Luis Potosi replied to the question on government's effects by saying, "Its activities have no effect on me, as I have nothing to do with the government." She reported that she has too many children to be able to think about anything else. Insofar as the parochial is aware of government, he tends to see it in relation to family interests. A poor Mexican tailor in Oaxaca said about the government, "It has no effect. I have no family or job connections with the government."

An elderly Italian widow living in Milan not only displayed parochialism but seemed to argue that the poor should be content with their parochial lot. When questioned on the effect national government has on people like her she remarked, "It has no effect. Madame Gronchi (The President's wife) has become a lady, and I am poor, but perhaps I am better off than she is. She has satisfactions in her life. She has been presented to queens. But I don't envy her. She wasn't born a lady, and, when she makes a 'gaffe' everybody laughs." An Italian tilemaker in Cremo replied that he has no interest in government and politics and that he has no idea what effect the national and local government have on him and his family. Like other Italian workmen among our respondents, his picture of government is extremely vague and colored both by diffuse anxiety and discontent.

Much more frequent among the Mexican and Italian cases are explicitly alienated respondents. Most are "output" alienates, people who believe that government should do things for themselves and for people like them but that it is indifferent to the interests of poor people or it is corrupt and only responsive to bribes or family connections.

Here are a few Mexican examples:

*A housewife on the effect of local government on her life*
"It has an effect for them. They take all the money."

*A secretary on what taxes are used for*
"Public officials say they are for improvements for the town, which seems incredible, since each new governor increases taxes and does nothing for the town, only for his pockets."

*A shoemaker on the chances for government reform*
"If they wanted to they could improve things. They could do it by keeping the money from the hands of unscrupulous people who take the funds that belong to the people."

*A housewife on the effect of national government*
"There is much poverty, now everything is expensive, they don't try to lower prices. They don't think about us, the poor people."

*A woman white-collar worker on the effect of local government*
"They have neglected the food shops and the markets where the merchandise is not of good quality and expensive. Vegetables are sometimes rotten but are sold just the same and this causes sickness among the people."

The same themes of corruption and neglect appear among the Italian respondents. A cab driver in Bari replied impatiently to the question on the effect of the national government on people like himself, "Of course it has an influence, but we don't have any influence. The government officials have influence to fill up their own pockets. What effect can they have? There is nothing that one can do. My family keeps its place and is not interested." Questioned further about the local government, he replied, "All local activities are for interested parties. They make a lot of propaganda; they promise many things, but nobody does anything for the people. How can I approach the mayor or join a party if nobody thinks about us?"

A dressmaker in Tolmezzo commented, "They (the local government) are quite inefficient. I don't think they are able to have any effect on the people of Tolmezzo." A young woman teacher in the Campania, when asked if taxes can be put to better use, replied hopelessly, "They could be put to better use, but what is the point of expressing one's own ideas, when the pattern is set, and one has to follow it." A young housewife in Calabria replied to the question on the effect of the national government by saying, "I don't believe that in Rome they realize what the life of the citizen is like. When they think about sending money, only a fourth of it gets here. They don't visit the country and don't know the situation."

These negative attitudes toward governmental output are apparent throughout our interviews in Mexico and Italy, but they are especially prevalent in Mexico. It is interesting, further, that awareness of the significance of government impact varies sharply with level of education in both nations. Among Italian and Mexican respondents with no formal schooling (9 per cent of our sample in Italy, 20 per cent in Mexico), the incidence of awareness is quite low—24 per cent for Italy and 25 per cent for Mexico; the figures for those with no more than primary education being 48 per cent for Italy, 30 per cent for Mexico. Italians with secondary-school educations have an incidence of awareness of 72 per cent, those with university educations of 85 per cent. What is striking about the results for Mexico is that even those with secondary-school and university educations showed a relatively low incidence of awareness of the significance of government: only 35 per cent of the secondary-school Mexicans, and 57 per cent of the Mexicans with university education report that the government has an impact. In Mexico, then, the alienative and parochial orientation to governmental output extends even into the more highly educated groups.[6]

### Treatment by Bureaucracy

The extent to which individuals are satisfied with the actual performance of their political system can also be measured in terms of their expectations of treatment from government bureaucracy. Respondents in Mexico and Italy were asked a series of questions designed to find out what expectations they had about the treatment they would receive in a governmental office or from the police. We confronted our respondents with two hypothetical situations. In the first, they were asked to imagine themselves in a government office with a problem that called for official action. How did they think they would be treated? Would they be treated equally with everyone else? We then asked them to imagine that they were explaining a point of view to the official or officials. Did they expect that they would be heard attentively and considerately? In the second situation, they were asked to imagine themselves having some minor trouble with the police. Did they expect to be treated equally and considerately by the police? In relation both to the expected equality of treatment and the expectations of consideration, the Mexican and Italian response patterns both indicate a higher level of alienation than do the responses in Britain, the United States, or Germany, but for our purposes, the interesting difference is between Italy and Mexico. In Mexico, respondents are much more likely than Italian respondents to expect inequitable treatment in a government office or from the police, and they are also more likely to expect their points of view to be ignored in administrative situations. Fifty-seven per cent of the Mexican respondents, for instance, expect inequitable treatment from the police, in contrast to only 10 per cent of the Italian respondents (though many Italian respondents are uncertain about what treatment to expect).[7] As with their views of the impact of government, Mexican respondents are more likely to have an "alienative" orientation.

Furthermore, the distribution of expectations of fair treatment and consideration among various educational groups again suggests that alienation *vis-à-vis* the bureaucracy varies sharply with the level of education in both nations. In Italy, 27 per cent of those with no formal education expect to be treated equally by the police, compared to 74 per cent of those with some university education. In Mexico, only 19 per cent of those with no education expect equal treatment by government compared to 68 per cent of the university-educated. The difference among educational groups in expectations of equal treatment by the police is similarly high in both countries. There is somewhat less variation among educational levels in the frequency of expectation of consideration in government offices and from the police, but in general, those with higher educations are more likely to expect consideration for their points of view. Of particular interest is the fact that the expressed dissatisfaction of the Mexican respondents with the treatment they expect in administrative situations extends into all educational levels. Even on the university level, hardly more than one in five Mexicans expects consideration for his point of view, while more than half the Italian respondents on this educational level expect consideration.

The data on attitudes toward governmental output and bureaucracy suggest a rather high level of alienation toward the actual operation of the government in both Italy and Mexico, but a substantially higher level in Mexico. This Mexican rejection of the actual working of the political system is found throughout our interview data. When asked, for instance, whether any groups had so much power over the government that the interests of the people were ignored, 49 per cent of the Mexican respondents replied that politicians and political parties were too powerful. (In Italy, though, many also feel that there were such harmful groups. The most frequently named are big business, the rich, and the Church.) Mexican attitudes toward government operations are negative and cynical.

### Exposure to Politics

If we switch our perspective from the expectations individuals have about the output of government to their more general attitudes toward politics, we find that the quite dim view Mexican respondents take toward output is not matched by their general attitudes. On the basis of the earlier comparisons between Italian and Mexican responses, we might expect Mexican respondents to be less interested in politics than the Italians and to reject their political system in general. That, however, does not appear to be the case. When we ask questions about general interest in what goes on in politics or general evaluations of the system as a whole—rather than about specific performance—we find that Mexican respondents are more positively oriented than the Italians.

Italian respondents are more likely than Mexican respondents to say that the activities of the government have an impact on them and, if there is an impact, that it is likely to be beneficial. But Mexican respondents more frequently report that they follow political affairs and that they pay attention to political campaigns. Less than a majority of Italian respondents reports that it follows government and political affairs (37 per cent) and that it pays attention to political campaigns (42 per cent). More Mexicans report some political exposure (the respective percentages in Mexico are 55 and 53). Thus the majority of Italians attributes personal significance to national and local governments, but less than a majority follow government affairs or pay attention to politics. Only a small minority of Mexicans, on the other hand, attributes personal significance to national and local government, but a modest majority follows governmental and political affairs and pays attention to political campaigns.

The difference between the Mexican and Italian patterns is illustrated in Table 1. In this table, respondents are grouped according to their level of exposure to politics, and the levels are related to respondents' perceptions of the impact of the government. As we would expect, in Italy (and in the other three nations we studied, as well), higher levels of exposure to political communications are associated with higher frequencies of awareness of the impact of government. In Mexico, on the other hand, there is relatively little relationship between exposure to politics and awareness of the impact of government. In fact, among those who are highly exposed to politics, 56 per cent report that neither the local nor the national government has an impact on their lives. In contrast, only 8 per cent of those with high political exposure in Italy report no governmental impact.[8]

**Table 1.  Awareness of the Impact of Government by Level of Exposure to Politics***

| Percentage of Respondents Who Report that | ITALY Exposure Level | | | MEXICO Exposure Level | | |
|---|---|---|---|---|---|---|
| | Low | Medium | High | Low | Medium | High |
| *Both* national and local government affect them | 33% | 62% | 69% | 14% | 29% | 27% |
| *Either* national or local government affect them | 23 | 28 | 19 | 18 | 19 | 17 |
| *Neither* national nor local government affect them | 19 | 6 | 8 | 64 | 49 | 56 |
| Don't know and other | 23 | 3 | 3 | 3 | 3 | — |
| Total | 98% | 99% | 99% | 99% | 100% | 100% |
| Number of cases | 672 | 173 | 150 | 584 | 257 | 167 |

* Low exposure to politics involves negative responses to both the question on following political and governmental affairs and that on paying attention to campaigns; medium exposure involves positive response to one question and negative to the other; low exposure involves two negative responses.

The frequent expression of belief in the inadequacy of governmental performance in Mexico is thus not accompanied by indifference to politics. Indifference to politics (as indicated by reported exposure to political communications) is more frequently found in Italy, although Italian respondents less frequently report that the government has no significance in their lives.

This difference between Italy and Mexico is also reflected in responses to a series of questions on the respondents' feelings about elections. Italian respondents are more likely than Mexican respondents to report little emotion in connection with election campaigns—that they never find them enjoyable, that they never get angry during campaigns, that they never find them silly and ridiculous. In general, the picture is one of widespread apathy to political campaigning. In Mexico, on the other hand, respondents more frequently report that they find elections "silly or ridiculous"—as could be expected from the high levels of alienation in Mexico from the operation of the political system—but Mexicans also are more likely than Italians to find campaigns enjoyable or to get angry at campaigns. Mexican respondents apparently have not turned their backs on politics, even though they are unimpressed with the operations of the government.

The Mexican responses present, at first glance, a curious paradox. On one hand, respondents report that the government has little impact or a negative impact on them, and, on the other, they report that they follow, are interested in, and are more often aroused by political campaigns than are Italian respondents. Furthermore, more than half of the very respondents who are most exposed to political communications report that neither the national nor the local government affects their lives. If the government's activities have little meaning for an individual's life, why does he follow politics and become aroused by electoral campaigns? One possible explanation is that this paradox is a manifestation of what we have called the "politics of aspiration" in Mexico. Although current government output is considered inadequate, there are possibilities for the future. This interpretation cannot be confirmed by our data on exposure to politics, but it is suggested by the responses to one question in our follow-up interview about the reasons why individuals are or are not interested in politics. In many of the Mexican interviews, respondents express little faith in the present government but speak of their interest in what may happen in the future. A Mexican truck driver, when asked if he was interested in political and governmental affairs, replied, "Very much, because the government can help the general conditions of life of all the Mexicans. At least this is what I wish." When asked when he first became interested in politics, he said, "About ten years ago when I began to realize that our governors tend to benefit themselves economically without considering the needs of the other citizens." A Mexican shoemaker replied to the same question, "Yes, I like politics. I am very interested in it, because I want to see a betterment of my people and also because I want to see that everything goes well, because many political leaders, rather than helping the worker, hurt him." A stenographer commented, "I have an interest in my town that is neglected by its governor. I have compared it with other cities that were at the same level as Pueblo, and now they have gone way ahead in culture and beauty." She first became interested in politics when she visited

Guadalajara "and saw how it had improved. I remember that last year Pueblo had second place in the republic for its beauty and now she had lost it because her governors have neglected her." The actual government seems to operate badly, but these respondents aspire to better things.

In Italy, on the other hand, the most typical reply stresses the danger and futility of interesting oneself in politics.

*A retired worker on his interest in politics*
"Reading the paper is the most that I do, and when I read it, I read it very slowly. It takes me a whole day to read it. I don't like to take part in discussions. As I told you before, they are very lively and at times even dangerous."

*A mechanic on "Who is interested in politics."*
"The fanatics that believe in what they are doing and in their aspirations, or the ignorant people who are behind and pushed by the first."

*A housewife who waits on customers in the family grocery store*
"None! I have an aversion for it, because I feel nothing is just."

### Pride in Nation

The existence of a "politics of aspiration" in Mexico, in contrast with Italy, is suggested more strongly if we turn from the levels of political exposure and interest in the two nations to more general attitudes toward the political system expressed by our respondents. So far, in dealing with the extent to which individuals report satisfaction with politics, we have discussed only satisfaction with the output of their political systems. As we suggested earlier, however, what may be more crucial, in terms of a political system's potentialities for stability, is the more generalized attitude of attachment to the political system. Quite early in our interview, we asked our respondents, "Speaking generally, what are the things about this country that you are most proud of?" In replying to this question, the respondents were not in any way directed to select political characteristics. When they give political responses, we may assume that expression of pride in the political system is spontaneous. Table 2 summarizes the results. The contrast between the two nations is sharp. In Mexico, 30 per cent of the respondents express pride in some political aspect of their nation—ten times the proportion of respondents in Italy, where only 3 per cent expressed such political pride. A large proportion in Mexico also expresses pride in its economic system—in particular, they talk of economic potential and growth. In contrast, few Italians express pride either in the political aspects of their nation or in the economic system. Italian respondents are likely to report that they are proud of Italy's contributions to the arts or of its physical attributes. Furthermore, 8 per cent of the Italian respondents indicate that they are proud of nothing about their nation, while only 3 per cent of the Mexican respondents are alienated in this way. The responses to the question on pride in nation, therefore, form a sharp contrast to the pattern of responses in connection with governmental output. While few Mexicans have favorable views of government output, they are quite likely to express pride in their political system.

**Table 2. Aspects of Nation in Which Respondents Report Pride**

| Percentage Who Say They Are Proud of: | Italy | Mexico |
|---|---|---|
| Governmental, political institutions | 3% | 30% |
| Social legislation | 1 | 2 |
| Position in international affairs | 2 | 3 |
| Economic system | 3 | 24 |
| Characteristics of people | 11 | 15 |
| Spiritual virtues and religion | 6 | 8 |
| Contributions to the arts | 16 | 9 |
| Contributions to science | 3 | 1 |
| Physical attributes of country | 25 | 22 |
| Nothing | 8 | 3 |
| Don't know | 19 | 12 |
| Other | 21 | 14 |
| Total Responses* | 118% | 143% |
| Total Respondents | 100% | 100% |
| Number of cases | 995 | 1007 |

* Percentages do not add up to 100 because of multiple responses.

Furthermore, there is an interesting difference between the two nations in the distribution of pride in the political system within Italy and Mexico. In connection with the output of government and the treatment respondents expect in a government office, we pointed out that the frequency of alienation was both higher in Mexico and more widespread—that is, that respondents from all educational levels are likely to express negative views about the government. In Italy, on the other hand, there is a strong tendency for those higher on the educational ladder to express more positive views of the operation of the government. In connection with the more general system affect as it is reflected in the frequency of expressed pride in the political system, an opposite pattern is apparent. In Mexico, those with higher education are somewhat more likely to express pride in the political system, while in Italy, the lack of pride is spread throughout all educational levels. Mexican alienation from the operation of the government seems to run through the whole society; Italian alienation from the political system on the symbolic level appears to run through the whole society.

The aspects of the political system in which the Mexican respondents express pride are, in most cases, not very precisely defined, but here are some responses to this question:

*A bricklayer*
"Of the President Lopez Mateos, as he does what is necessary for the nation, we lack nothing . . . we are in a free country, and we have no war difficulty."

*A teacher*
"The laws of the constitution that rule us, as they protect and help us."

*A truck driver*
"Of the laws of our country, the law of the Reform."

*A telephone repairman*
"The actual government—the President of the Republic is bettering the whole nation."

*A housewife*
"That the government is working hard for the progress of Mexico."

Especially when compared with the responses to the question on the impact of the national government, this set of responses indicates that, in Mexico, there is indeed a "politics of aspiration" —rejection of the actual government; strong attachment to the symbolic and potential government.[9] Although Mexican respondents reject their real government—real bureaucrats, real governmental output—they are positively oriented to their political system on the symbolic, national level. Italian alienation from politics, though not as striking as the Mexican alienation in relation to the actual operation of the government, is more pervasive, since it extends to the political system as a whole.

### Competence and Allegiance

The contrast between the patterns of attitudes in Italy and Mexico can be further illuminated by examining the relationship between the individual's perception of his ability to participate in the political system and his satisfaction with that system. In general, we expect the individual who thinks of himself as a participant in decisions made within a system to be more attached to that system and to be more satisfied with the output of that system.[10] It is often alleged, at least, to be one of the advantages of democracy that it leads to greater loyalty to the system. A comparison of the data for Italy and Mexico suggests that the impact of an individual's sense of participation in a system on his sense of attachment to that system may take several forms.

The respondents in our study were asked a series of questions about the degree of influence they think they have or could have over governmental decisions. The responses to five of these questions were combined to form a scale of "subjective competence."[11] Respondents were grouped into three categories of subjective competence—high, medium, and low—depending on their scale scores. The question was then raised: What effect does an individual's sense of subjective competence have upon his satisfaction with his government?

Table 3 compares the individual's sense of competence with his evaluation of the output of the local government.[12] The results indicate another interesting contrast between Italy and Mexico. In Italy, the individual who believes he can participate in the decisions of the local government is also more likely to believe that the output of that government will be beneficial. Seventy-five per cent of the Italian respondents high on our subjective competence scale report a belief that the activities of the local government are beneficial for their area, in contrast with 63 per cent of respondents low in subjective competence. (The relationship, however, is not as strong as that found in the other three nations we studied.) This pattern is repeated, even when the level of education is controlled. On the other hand, in Mexico, the sense of ability to participate appears to have no effect upon the individual's belief in the beneficial effects of local government activity. As Table 3 indicates, there is little difference among those high, medium, or low on the subjective competence scale in the frequency with which they believe that the government's activities are beneficial.

**Table 3.** **Subjective Competence and Belief in the Beneficial Effects of Local Government Activities—by Nation and Education (among those respondents who report that the local government has an impact)**

| | ITALY | | | | | |
|---|---|---|---|---|---|---|
| | LEVEL OF SUBJECTIVE COMPETENCE | | | | | |
| | *High* | | *Medium* | | *Low* | |
| Total | 75%* | (175)† | 69% | (155) | 63% | (240) |
| Primary education or less | 72% | (99) | 67% | (90) | 62% | (173) |
| Secondary education or more | 79% | (75) | 72% | (64) | 66% | (67) |
| | MEXICO | | | | | |
| | LEVEL OF SUBJECTIVE COMPETENCE | | | | | |
| | *High* | | *Medium* | | *Low* | |
| Total | 46% | (79) | 52% | (109) | 44% | (122) |
| Primary education or less | 38% | (61) | 45% | (91) | 41% | (112) |
| Secondary education or more | 71% | (17) | 79% | (18) | [71% | (10)] |

\* I.e., 75 per cent of Italian respondents "high" in subjective competence believe the government has a beneficial impact.

† Numbers in parentheses refer to the bases upon which percentages were calculated.

The data reported in Table 4 offer a sharp contrast to the data in Table 3. In Table 4, we compare respondents on various levels of subjective competence in terms of the frequency with which they express more general attachments to their political system—measured by whether or not they express pride in political aspects of their nations. In connection with what we have called "system affect," we find that, in Mexico, those respondents who consider themselves more able to participate in their political system are more likely to express pride in the political aspects of their nation. Thirty-eight per cent of the respondents high in sense of ability to participate express pride in some political aspect of their nation, in contrast to 26 per cent of those low in subjective competence. This contrast is also seen on both educational levels. Furthermore, as we go up the scale of subjective competence, we find that respondents are less likely to express

**Table 4. Subjective Competence and Pride in Nation— by Nation and Education**

| | TOTAL | | | | | |
|---|---|---|---|---|---|---|
| | *Italy* | | | *Mexico* | | |
| | | *Subj. Comp.* | | | *Subj. Comp.* | |
| *Respondents Are Proud of:* | High | Medium | Low | High | Medium | Low |
| Governmental and political system | 3% | 8% | 2% | 38% | 31% | 26% |
| Other aspects* | 80% | 76% | 61% | 60% | 60% | 48% |
| Nothing | 8% | 4% | 11% | 0% | 2% | 5% |
| Don't know | 9% | 12% | 26% | 2% | 7% | 21% |
| | 100% | 100% | 100% | 100% | 100% | 100% |
| Number of Cases | 243 | 234 | 514 | 201 | 332 | 474 |

| | LEVEL OF EDUCATION | | | | | |
|---|---|---|---|---|---|---|
| | PRIMARY OR LESS | | | | | |
| | *Italy* | | | *Mexico* | | |
| | | *Subj. Comp.* | | | *Subj. Comp.* | |
| *Respondents Are Proud of:* | High | Medium | Low | High | Medium | Low |
| Governmental and political system | 3% | 4% | 2% | 35% | 30% | 25% |
| Other aspects* | 77% | 72% | 56% | 63% | 60% | 48% |
| Nothing | 10% | 5% | 11% | 0 | 3% | 4% |
| Don't know | 10% | 19% | 31% | 2% | 8% | 23% |
| | 100% | 100% | 100% | 100% | 101% | 100% |
| Number of Cases | 149 | 138 | 402 | 153 | 287 | 436 |

| | SECONDARY OR ABOVE | | | | | |
|---|---|---|---|---|---|---|
| | *Italy* | | | *Mexico* | | |
| | | *Subj. Comp.* | | | *Subj. Comp.* | |
| *Respondents Are Proud of:* | High | Medium | Low | High | Medium | Low |
| Governmental and political system | 3% | 12% | 2% | 49% | 38% | 37% |
| Other aspects* | 85% | 83% | 80% | 51% | 59% | 50% |
| Nothing | 4% | 2% | 8% | 0 | 1% | 5% |
| Don't know | 8% | 3% | 10% | 0 | 1% | 8% |
| | 100% | 100% | 100% | 100% | 99% | 100% |
| Number of Cases | 93 | 94 | 111 | 47 | 45 | 35 |

* "Other aspects" refers to those respondents who are proud of other aspects than the political system. Respondents who report pride in the political system, in addition to other aspects, are in the top row.

the distinctly alienative pride in nothing or to say that they don't know. In contrast to the results in Mexico, the results in Italy suggest little relationship between sense of political competence and more general attachment to the political system. Those high in subjective competence are not more likely to be proud of some political aspect of their nation. Furthermore, although those respondents are less likely to say that they do not know what they are proud of as Italians, they are as likely as respondents with little sense of ability to participate to say that they are proud of nothing.

The relationship between pride in nation and sense of participation suggests the depth of political alienation in Italy. Given recent Italian history, it is, of course, not surprising that so few Italians express pride in their political system. Absolute frequency of expressed pride in the political system aside, however, it is interesting that even those Italians who think of themselves as able to participate in political decisions are no more likely than those low on subjective competence to express pride in the political aspects of Italy and are as likely to say that, as Italians, they are proud of nothing. Sense of participation in Italy does not appear to be translated into general system affect, as it is in Mexico.[13]

In Mexico, on the other hand, although system affect increases with participation, satisfaction with the output of government does not. This combination suggests that participation in politics in Mexico is, indeed, on a symbolic or aspirational level. The Mexican with a high sense of ability to participate may still take a dim view of the operation of the government. His participation is, however, related to a closer attachment to the symbols of Mexico.

The general patterns of attitudes that one finds in the two nations, then, suggest that Mexico has a political culture of aspiration, Italy one of alienation. In both countries, large proportions of the respondents reply negatively when asked about the actual performance of the political system. The level of alienation from governmental output is somewhat higher in Mexico than in Italy, however. Nevertheless, Mexican respondents are in many ways more involved in their political system— they at least have some pride in it and some hope for the future.

Italian involvement in politics tends to be more pragmatic and perhaps more cynical. Furthermore, Mexican respondents are more likely than Italians to report themselves emotionally involved in election campaigns, capable of influencing the government, and having some obligation to participate in politics. These attitudes are not matched by actual performance. Mexicans are not more politically active than Italians and are somewhat less informed about politics. The interesting combination of low performance and expectation about actual political performance coupled with high aspiration for future performance is highlighted by the fact that, though more Italians than Mexicans are informed about political events, a much higher proportion of Mexicans are ready and willing to offer opinions on a wide range of political and ideological questions.

### Some Implications of the Italian-Mexican Comparison

The data presented on the patterns of political attitudes in Italy and Mexico strongly suggest that we are dealing, in both nations, with alienation from politics but that the alienation is of quite different kinds. In Mexico, the alienation from the "real" world of politics is coupled with a high level of aspirational attachment to the "symbolic" world of politics—to Mexico as a nation and to the hopes engendered by the Mexican Revolution.

This difference has important implications for the study of internal war in one of its most important aspects—the problem of the implications of experience with internal violence for the political attitudes of a citizenry. The Mexican pattern of "aspirational" politics, as we have suggested, may be typical of postrevolutionary societies in which awareness of national politics comes suddenly through involvement in a highly emotional struggle and in which the symbols of nationalism and social change play an important role. The man we have called a "parochial" becomes involved in politics, not through "bread and butter" contacts with government activities but through his attachment to this revolution with its symbols of nationalism and change. The Mexican Revolution was such a revolution—antitraditional, nationalistic, violent, and of profound symbolic meaning in Mexican political history.

It is of course impossible to trace the set of attitudes we ascribe to Mexico directly to the Mexican Revolution. Such a pattern of attitudes probably has many roots. There is some evidence, however, that the continuing impact of the Revolution explains part of the attachment to their political system that Mexican respondents manifest. Respondents in Mexico were asked if they could name some of the ideals and goals of the Mexican Revolution. Thirty-five per cent could name none, while the remaining 65 per cent listed democracy, political liberty and equality, economic welfare, agrarian reform, social equality, and national freedom. What is of interest here is that 34 per cent of those respondents who could name some of the goals were proud of some political aspect of their nation, in contrast to only 19 per cent of those who could not name any goals. More interesting in this connection are the responses to a follow-up question. Those respondents who mentioned goals of the Revolution were then asked if they thought those goals had been realized, had been forgotten, or were still actively being sought. Twenty-five per cent of the 614 respondents in this category think the goals have been realized, 61 per cent think that they are still being sought, and only 14 per cent think they have been forgotten. As we would expect, those respondents who think the goals of the Revolution have been forgotten are the least likely of these three groups to express pride in their political system. Thirty-one per cent of the eighty-four respondents in this group say they are proud of the Mexican political system. In connection with our hypothesis about the continuing effects of the Mexican Revolution, it is significant that those respondents who believe the Revolution's goals are still being sought most frequently express pride in the political system—39 per cent of 379 respondents, in comparison to 34 per cent of 151 respondents believe the Revolution's goals have already been achieved. Mexican pride in nation does thus seem to depend, to a significant extent, on continuing symbolic identification with the Mexican Revolution.

Though the form of political attachment that derives from this revolutionary involvement may be somewhat unrealistic in that it is not based on attachment to the "real" government, it does imply a deep and rather stable attachment to the political system—an attachment perhaps more lasting than one dependent solely on the specific performance of the political system. A revolutionary experience may thus have certain eufunctional effects 'on political stability.

In Italy, in contrast, we find no such attachment to the state as symbol. Countries of this sort, characterized by the politics of alienation with no major unifying symbol, face enormous problems before their governments can attain legitimacy. If our data on Italy are applicable, it is unlikely that small increments of improvement in the economic and social situation of the population will significantly increase the legitimacy of social and political systems. What sharply differentiates Mexico from Italy is the promise of the Revolution. The legitimacy of the Mexican political system seems to be based on these hopes and aspirations. We are not suggesting that only revolution. can transform Italian political culture in this direction. There will have to be a functional equivalent of such a revolution that can narrow the gap between people and politics and transform distrust and despair into confidence and hope.

A revolutionary experience does have mixed consequences. In Mexico, there is also political vulnerabilty, although it is of a different order. The Mexican people have accepted the promissory note of a revolution. They accord legitimacy to their political system because of their faith in the promise of the Revolution and not because of satisfaction with present benefits or performance. Indeed their rejection of the present quantity and quality of government output seems almost complete. The continued legitimacy of such a system depends upon an increasing scale of delivery in all areas. The danger in Mexico is that aspiration will be frustrated and loyalty betrayed.

In this sense, the Mexican politics of aspiration throws light on the opportunities and vulnerabilities of many of the emerging nations that have attained independence through resolute and enthusiastic movements and are ruled by democratically inclined modernizing élites. Their peoples, too, accord legitimacy to their governments and political élites because of promises to introduce the values of the modern, secular, industrial world. They, too, are political systems based on hope, and they will survive as long as hope remains alive.

## Notes

1. The material for this paper is based on approximately 1000 interviews in each country, using a national multistage probability sample, plus approximately 125 follow-up interviews among the respondents. This paper is part of a comparative study of attitudes toward politics and citizenship in the United States, Great Britain, Germany, Italy, and Mexico that is being carried on under the direction of the authors. The study is sponsored by the Center of International Studies at Princeton University and is supported by a grant from the Carnegie Corporation of New York. Further material on the study is reported in Gabriel A. Almond and Sidney Verba, *The Civic Culture: Political Attitudes and Democracy in Five Nations* (Princeton: Princeton University Press, 1963).

2. On this point, see Almond and Verba, *Civic Culture*, Chapter 5.

3. For a further elaboration of this scheme, see *Ibid.*, Chapter 1.

4. The number of cases on which the percentages are based are 1007 for Mexico and 995 for Italy.

5. In the United States, Britain, and Germany, there was more frequent attribution of impact to the government than in either Italy or Mexico—and less frequent assertion that the activities of the government have a negative impact.

6. The number of cases on the various educational levels were:

*Italy*. No education, 88; some primary, 604; some secondary, 245; some university, 54.

*Mexico*. No education, 221; some primary, 656; some secondary, 103; some university, 24.

7. Our Mexican respondents' expectations of treatment form an even sharper contrast with expectations in some other nations. For instance, only one out of three Mexican respondents expects equitable treatment from the police, in contrast to nine out of ten British respondents.

8. The Mexican pattern also contrasts with those in the other three nations. In those nations, the proportion of respondents with high political exposure but low perceived impact of government is, as in Italy, low: 3 per cent in the United States, 6 per cent in Germany, and 6 per cent in Britain.

9. One may similarly contrast the negative attitudes expressed toward politicians (reflected in the data reported on p. 217, showing that 49 per cent of the Mexican respondents believe that politicians and political parties have too much power over the government) with the fact that 34 per cent of the Mexican respondents, when asked to name an individual whom they admire very much, name someone from the realm of government or politics. This compares with 15 per cent of the Italian respondents who mention a political figure. In most cases, the political figures mentioned by the Mexicans

are the great national heroes of the Revolution or Presidents of the Republic.

10. There is a large literature on the "participation hypothesis," which cannot be summarized here.

11. The responses formed an acceptable Guttman scale in each nation. For further details on this scale and on the other indicators used in this study, see *The Civic Culture*, Chapter 9.

12. Evaluation of the output of the local government is used because the questions that make up the scale of subjective competence were asked about the local government.

13. It is interesting to note that the relationship between subjective competence and pride in the political aspects of one's nation, apparent in Mexico, also appears in the data for Britain and the United States but *not* in the data for Germany.

*Marion J. Levy, Jr.*

## A REVISION OF THE GEMEINSCHAFT-

## GESELLSCHAFT CATEGORIES AND SOME

## ASPECTS OF THE INTERDEPENDENCIES OF

## MINORITY AND HOST SYSTEMS*

*Introduction*

It is, perhaps, the prejudice from which one speaks that defines the times in which we find ourselves as "parlous." The majority of citizens in the "authoritarian" nations might take the negative point of view and describe the times as turbulent but not parlous. Citizens of what we generally call the "democratic" nations would insist that these are, indeed, parlous times in the extreme. Whatever controversy might be stirred up on these grounds, it is reasonably safe to say that all who observe the trends in today's world would readily assent to the proposition that enormous social changes are afoot.

These changes have been brought into dramatic focus by the rapid rise of the "authoritarian powers," or, conversely, by the failure of the "democratic" countries to retain supremacy in the world without partially or completely abandoning their liberal tenets. For the social scientist, this failure raises the question of the strategically necessary but insufficient cause

* I am indebted to the National Science Foundation for time to complete this paper. I am also indebted to David E. Apter, Harry H. Eckstein, Alden D. Grimshaw, William Kornhauser, Edward A. Tiryakian, Sidney Verba, and Maurice Zeitlin for criticisms of this manuscript, though its vagaries are entirely my own.

[ 233 ]

or causes for the continued existence of such liberal *laissez-faire* societies as England, France, and the United States. This question is not an impractical one. An answer to it is the necessary minimum for any policy program that has as its object the preservation of that type of society, which has been so much under fire of late. Any program that works will have, of necessity, hit upon such an answer, either explicitly or implicitly. There is therefore good reason for making explicit efforts in this direction, in the interests of such a program. For the purist, however, it is fortunate that the same problems are of quite general structural interest—taking us to the heart of some of the hoariest distinctions in the social sciences.

In the parlance of sociology, the type of modern society that laymen call "democratic" has been referred to generally as a *"Gesellschaft* system." This term has been lifted from the famous dichotomy of Ferdinand Tönnies. I do not believe that this use of the term does violence to Tönnies's intent, since the empirical examples on which he based his concept were, for the most part, modern West European (including the United States) social systems.[1] It is contrasted by Tönnies and by other sociologists who have followed in his wake with the *Gemeinschaft* social system. The dichotomy has gained wide acceptance since its publication by Tönnies more than seventy-five years ago.[2] In a sense, it bestrides much of modern sociology.

In its original formulation by Tönnies and certainly in its use and formulation by those who followed Tönnies, the dichotomy has severe limitations. This paper has three objects: A brief discussion of the dichotomy and its shortcomings, an attempted revision of the dichotomy in order to salvage the fruitful core of insight that I think it contains, and a study of some theoretical implications of this revised formulation for what may be arbitrarily defined as one element in "democratic" social systems—the treatment of real or imagined dissension among the members.

### Shortcomings in Tönnies's Theory

Tönnies's book is almost incredibly diffuse. There is little semblance of ordered analysis in the work. It might better have been titled *Bemerkungen zur Gemeinschaft und Gesellschaft*. It is a truly impressionistic work. In the entire volume there is no precise definition of the two central terms. In a sense, it is nothing but an attempt at definition of the two terms. It adds little to our understanding to define *"Gemeinschaft"* as "community" and *"Gesellschaft"* as "society," particularly since the term "society" is commonly used with a vastly different set of denotations and connotations from those of the term *"Gesellschaft."* In order to understand Tönnies's view of these terms, one must rely on some of his more compact passages:

> The relationship itself, and also the resulting association is conceived of either as real and organic life—this is the essential characteristic of the Geimeinschaft (community)—or as imaginary and mechanical structure—this is the concept of Gesellschaft (society). . . .
> All intimate, private, and exclusive living together, so we discover, is understood as life in Gemeinschaft (community). Gesellschaft (society) is public life—it is the world itself. In Gemeinschaft (community) with one's family, one lives from birth on bound to it in weal and woe. One goes into Gesellschaft (society) as one goes into a strange country. A young man is warned against bad Gesellschaft (society), but the expression bad Gemeinschaft (community) violates the meaning of the word . . . the domestic Gemeinschaft (community) or home life with its immeasurable influence upon the human soul has been felt by everyone who ever shared it. Likewise, each member of a bridal couple knows that he or she goes into marriage as a complete Gemeinschaft (community) of life. . . . A Gesellschaft (society) of life would be a contradiction in and of itself. . . . One becomes part of a religious Gemeinschaft (community); religious Gesellschaften (associations, or societies) like any other groups formed for given purposes, exist only in so far as they, viewed from without, take their places among the institutions of a political body or as they represent conceptual elements of a theory; they do not touch upon the religious Gemeinschaft as such. There exists a Gemeinschaft (community) of language, of folkways, or mores, or of belief; but, by way of contrast, Gesellschaft (society or company) exists in the realm of business, travel or sciences. So of special importance are the commercial Gesellschaften (societies or companies), whereas, even though a certain familiarity and Gemeinschaft (community) may exist among business partners, one could indeed hardly speak of commercial Gemeinschaft (community). To make the word combination, "joint-stock Gemeinschaft," would be abominable. On the other hand, there exists a Gemeinschaft (community) of ownership in fields, forests, and pasture. The Gemeinschaft (community) of property between man and wife cannot be called Gesellschaft (society) of property. Thus many differences become apparent.[3]

The theory of the Gesellschaft deals with the artificial construction of an aggregate of human beings which superficially resembles the Gemeinschaft in so far as the individuals peacefully live and dwell together. However, in the Gemeinschaft they remain essentially united in spite of all separating factors, whereas in the Gesellschaft they are essentially separated in spite of all uniting factors. In the Gesellschaft, as contrasted with the Gemeinschaft, we find no actions that can be derived from an a priori and necessarily existing unity; no actions, therefore, which manifest the will and the spirit of the unity even if performed by the individual; no actions which, in so far as they are performed by the individual, take place on behalf of those united with him. In the Gesellschaft such actions do not exist. On the contrary, here everybody is by himself and isolated, and there exists a condition of tension against all others. Their spheres of activity and power are sharply separated, so that everybody refuses to everyone else contacts with and admittance to his sphere. . . . Such a negative attitude toward one another becomes the normal and always underlying relation of these power-endowed individuals, and it characterizes the Gesellschaft in the condition of rest; nobody wants to grant and produce anything for another individual . . . if it be not in exchange for a gift or labor equivalent that he considers at least equal to what he has given.[4]

Gesellschaft, an aggregate by convention[5] and law of nature, is to be understood as a multitude of natural and artificial individuals, the wills and spheres of whom are in many relations with and to one another, and remain nevertheless independent of one another and devoid of mutual familiar relationships. This gives us the general description of "bourgeois society" or "exchange Gesellschaft," the nature and movements of which legislative economy attempts to understand; a condition in which, according to the expression of Adam Smith, "Every man . . . becomes in some measure a merchant."[6]

These quotations should suffice to indicate the diffuseness of this pioneer work. Many subsequent commentators have given more succinct versions of the terms,[7] but none has eliminated the lack of precision in the concepts or the admixture of evaluations, metaphysics, and so forth. Subsequent writers have also been at pains to comb out the variables associated with the two branches of Tönnies's dichotomy. In Tönnies's book, analytically distinguished aspects of behavior are to be found thoroughly mixed with concrete phenomena associated with the concepts. For example, self-interestedness, rationality, and manufacturing companies are all common to *Gesellschaft*; disinterestedness, traditionalism, and the family are all common to *Gemeinschaft*.

Tönnies is, at best, open to the charge of confusion for failing to differentiate clearly between the analytic structures and the concrete structures to be found in his two types.

Tönnies's work is in one respect much like that of William G. Sumner. That is, each had in his work a core of fruitful insight, but each obscured it, sometimes by lack of rigor and sometimes by passages altogether out of the realm of empirical science. On almost any page of Tönnies, one can find examples of nonscientific analysis. He frequently falls into the animism that has so dogged the social sciences and that continues to hide under the "natural-artificial" distinction. The use of spatial symbolism for pejorative rather than for scientific purposes appears in his work. He violates the rules of consistency, which are so essential to science. For example, we find the dichotomy used as a set of ideal types, as groups of variables, and as concrete types without adequate distinctions. In one instance, social systems seem to be identified with one or the other polar concept, in another they may be mixtures, in another they are always mixtures, and so forth. Precise definitions and consistent use of such definitions seem to have been completely foreign to his nature.

There is another difficulty with Tönnies's system, if it may be called a system. As noted, the two categories contain many different variables. Whether Tönnies viewed his dichotomy as a clear-cut difference in kind or simply as polar terms with an infinite number of possible gradations between them, there seems to be no room for doubt that he viewed any departure in any respect from *Gemeinschaft* as tending in the direction of *Gesellschaft*. A shift toward rationality implies for Tönnies a shift toward functional specificity and self-interestedness. This proposition is clearly invalid, unless Tönnies is able to demonstrate the impossibility of independent variation among these elements —which he has not done. On the other hand, Talcott Parsons has pointed out that the medical profession, because of its institutionalized attitude of "disinterestedness" rather than "self-interestedness," differs radically from the typical business vocation —though it is identical in four other institutionalized attitudinal aspects (universalism, rationality, functional specificity, nonaffectivity). He has further observed that the medical profession is in no sense a variation on the scale in the direction of the typical *Gemeinschaft* relation—that the difference in the institutionalization of "disinterestedness" does not tend to make the medical profession more traditional, more particularistic, more functionally diffuse, or more subject to affectivity than business.[8] The medical profession is not a type of social phenomenon intermediate between modern business and the family, as Tönnies would have to argue. His concepts must be revised to eliminate this difficulty, if they are to be used.

One other difficulty of the Tönnies system must be mentioned, since it is the central point of departure for the revision that is to follow. It is not clear whether Tönnies regards the difference between the concrete embodiments of *Gemeinschaft* and *Gesellschaft* as a difference of degree or of kind. A case can be made for characterizing the difference as one of kind, if one adheres to the early editions of the *Gemeinschaft und Gesellschaft* essay, though even here there are passages that make the difference seem one of degree.[9] What is important, however, is that sociologists in general have conceived of the difference as one of kind and have almost universally referred to societies and relations as *Gemeinschaft* or *Gesellschaft* relations and almost never as *predominantly Gemeinschaft* or *predominantly Gesellschaft*. It is commonplace for sociologists to say that the family is *Gemeinschaft* and that the business world is *Gesellschaft*, that rural communities are *Gemeinschaft* and urban communities are *Gesellschaft*, that modern West European society is *Gesellschaft* and medieval West European society is *Gemeinschaft*, and so forth.[10] This usage is not the result of a misunderstanding by subsequent sociologists. In a book of 238 pages, there is only one two-page section devoted explicitly to mixed or complex forms;[11] only one concrete structure of a mixed type is discussed —the cooperative.[12] It is therefore not difficult to understand why the usual interpretation has been that of a difference in kind, while at the same time many of the interpreters, if questioned closely, would assert that there are *Gemeinschaft* elements in predominantly *Gesellschaft* phenomena.

Not the least of the elements contributing to interpretation of the difference as one of kind are some of the dichotomous branches Tönnies designates *Gemeinschaft* or *Gesellschaft*. For example, the female is *Gemeinschaft*, the male *Gesellschaft*; the vegetable is *Gemeinschaft*, the animal *Gesellschaft* (this whole animal-vegetable discussion is more like romantic pantheistic metaphysics than science); the natural is *Gemeinschaft*, the rational *Gesellschaft*. Even here, however, Tönnies inserts an occasional phrase about the development from *Gemeinschaft*,[13] so that it is impossible to maintain that he was unaware of the fact that concrete phenomena are likely to mix the two concepts. Tönnies sacrificed consistency rather than leave out empirical facts that he observed, for he was a keen observer with acute insight. His inability to carry his system to a generalized level with the consequent need to alter his theoretical structure, forced him to leave it a welter of confusion—since his powers of observation and insight were too keen to allow him to omit mention of phenomena inconsistent with some of his formulations.

The confusion on the difference between *Gemeinschaft* and *Gesellschaft* is increased by two other factors. First, Tönnies did not publish his clearest formulations of the difference as one of degree until some time after the first editions of the work were widely known.[14] Second, there are two different levels on which this mixture of the two elements may take place. The mixed form may be like the "cooperative" in which the difference is along the scale between the polar terms at which the concrete phenomena are located. A cooperative is not, Tönnies feels, like an ordinary business firm, yet it does not exemplify a *Gemeinschaft* relation either. It varies from the latter in the direction of commercializing the property involved and from the former in other ways (for example, it is less rationally self-interested than the typical business firm). The other level of mixture involves a concrete phenomenon made up of structures, some of which may be of the *Gemeinschaft* type and others of the *Gesellschaft* type. In modern society, which Tönnies terms *Gesellschaft*, there are many structures that even he would not term *Gesellschaft* (the family, for instance). If closely questioned, Tönnies would probably have agreed that there were all sorts of *Gemeinschaft* elements even in metropolitan life, and most subsequent sociologists using these concepts would also agree. The revision of these concepts that will be attempted here takes its point of departure from the mixture of Tönnies's elements in the concrete case and tries to define them analytically in order to preserve Tönnies's core of insight.[15]

### Revisions of the Theory

The important point about the concept of *Gemeinschaft* from the point of view of this paper is not that its referent is "natural" or that it arises from the "forces of consanguinity." From a scientific perspective, these statements are generally either meaningless or false. There is no scientific evidence on which to base the statement that there are instinctively stronger relationships among blood relations than among others. This illusion arises from the universality of kinship structures. In every known society, there is an institutionalized kinship structure, centering to some degree around the facts of biological relatedness. Children are reared in some sort of intimate connection with this structure, which is to some degree oriented to biological heredity. Although children may be turned over to the wife's brother, there is typically some blood connection between them and the adults who rear them in all societies. Very strong sentiments, what Tönnies calls *"Gemeinschaft* relations," develop. Such relations, however, have never been shown to be the result of the blood ties themselves. There is a wealth of material to show that equally strong relations develop if the children are of no blood relation to the adults. There are very strong *Gemeinschaft* relations of the type to which Tönnies refers between adopted children and the adults who rear them, even when both are aware of the lack of consanguinity—perhaps, in some cases, because of it. Even if a disposition to solidarity between biological mother and child were highly probable, no one has ever proved that family devotion in general is biologically determined.

What is important for this paper is that facet of the concept of *Gemeinschaft* that refers to its existence in any given instance as an expression of the "community will," of the basic value orientations of the group. I shall, then, define *Gemeinschaft* as pertaining to the basic value orientations characteristic of a society.[16] There are, then, *Gemeinschaft* aspects of any relationship, and those aspects hinge on the relevance for the relationship of the basic value orientations of its members. *"Gesellschaft,"* will not be defined as a concept on the same level, but polar to, the concept of *Gemeinschaft*. It will be used to denote a special set of *Gemeinschaft* elements, which exist either ideally or actually. See pp. 244-251.

It is a functional requisite of social systems that there be a more or less well integrated and clearly defined set of *Gemeinschaft* elements. (It is not necessary to go into the functional necessity of the *Gemeinschaft* element or basic value orientation in the social system. Scholars in the field are almost unanimous in affirming this point, whatever their differences on other scores may be.) Now from one point of view, systems containing *Gemeinschaft* elements may be of two sorts. They may be social systems with a *stable Gemeinschaft* set or social systems with an *unstable Gemeinschaft* set. A *stable* set of *Gemeinschaft* elements may be defined as a set that institutionalizes the means of dealing positively with what members of the system regard as threats to the existence of the system. In a social system with a stable *Gemeinschaft* set, it is to be expected that any recognized attempt to alter the *Gemeinschaft* set will be met positively, and, if necessary, force will be invoked to dissuade, neutralize, or eliminate the dissenters. A *system with a stable Gemeinschaft set is by no means necessarily stable in the sense that it cannot be defeated or altered*. A stable *Gemeinschaft* set may, of course, be overthrown by members of the society concerned or by members of some other society. Members of the society may exercise the institutionalized force at their disposal ineffectively, and so their society may change. They may even fail, on occasion, to act in terms of their institutionalized patterns at all. The important point is that "stability" lies in an institutionalized form of self-preservation that is at least not inherently defective.

An *unstable Gemeinschaft* set is defined here as a set in which there is either a positive injunction to tolerance* or effec-

---

* "Tolerance," as used in this paper, denotes the absence of coercion and compulsion as methods of social control. In this sense, an area of tolerance in a social system is an area of action in which there is no resort to the use of force in the last extremity to obtain from dissenters conformity to the social norms.

tive tolerance due to the lack of institutionalized means of self-preservation. This injunction to tolerance or absence of the means of self-preservation need not cover the entire *Gemeinschaft* set for the system to be unstable. The *Gemeinschaft* set may be *more or less unstable,* to the degree that the various *Gemeinschaft* elements in the set are or are not provided with protection. A social system with provision for the imprisonment of felons may still possess a *Gemeinschaft* set that is unstable in other respects. The concepts of stable and unstable *Gemeinschaft* sets must not be confused with the question of the more general stability of the system. *Stability of the Gemeinschaft set is not a sufficient condition for stability of the system, and instability of the Gemeinschaft set is not a sufficient condition for instability of the system.* Nevertheless, both concepts are relevant to many questions of social structure. It is quite easy to conceive of social systems with unstable *Gemeinschaft* sets existing over long periods of time. It is only in the face of resistance in the area in which tolerance exists, whether the resistance is from members or non-members, that the instability of the *Gemeinschaft* set becomes relevant to general social stability. Any set of individuals willing, as a last resort, to use force to gain their ends will force a change in the *Gemeinschaft* set. That is, of course, unless there is a *deus ex machina* or an internal failure of the threatening set itself, which serves to eliminate the members of the set as a threat. The change in the set occurs through one of two channels. The *Gemeinschaft* set may be altered to institutionalize the use of force in the area concerned, in which case, though the total *Gemeinschaft* set has been altered in the direction of stability, the rest of its elements may be preserved. This is not to say that it "will be." The successful answer to threats is by no means necessarily found in the institutionalized ability to exert force. Such institutionalization can be very rapid indeed. The relatively short period of time in which areas of wide freedom of speech have been drastically narrowed in many societies is an example. It seems to indicate that there is nothing inherently requiring a great lapse of time in the process of institutionalization or in the process of habituating members of a society to the invocation of institutions not generally in force (strong press censorship in war periods, for example.)

On the other hand, if no such change is made and if the threatening set of individuals is willing to exert force, then the latter will carry out their ends and impose their will on the system—unless otherwise deterred by a *deus ex machina* or internal failure—and will alter the *Gemeinschaft* set.

The *limiting type* of unstable *Gemeinschaft* set is that in which there is an injunction to complete tolerance throughout the system, no institutionalized means of exerting force, or a combination of both. The only conceivable complex of conditions in which such a social system could be stable would be one in which every member was perfectly integrated, no possible contingencies could arise to confute the system of basic value orientations, all problems would be soluble by peaceful tolerant means (and were in fact so solved), the values and institutions themselves formed a perfectly defined and integrated set, and no disrupting external forces were operable. These conditions would amount to perfect integration in a perfectly tolerant system. It does not seem that a system based solely on interlocking interests is a possible alternative. Such a system is only social in an equivocal sense and is not conceivable without some social origin. Where would the interests to be interlocked have their origin?

So far as I know, no such thoroughgoing tolerance has characterized any social system. There have, however, been numerous examples of social systems characterized by extremely wide margins of tolerance. Some may have failed because of an inability of the members to abandon this tolerance. There often are cases of tolerance through lack of institutionalized means to deal with certain sorts of defiance of the *Gemeinschaft* set. B. Malinowski cites a particularly striking case of this sort.[17] In this case, a young native broke the rule of kinship exogamy with the daughter of his mother's sister. The matter was well known by the members of the society. It was not approved. It is important to note that the taboo violated was a basic one, the incest taboo. The members of the society took no coercive action. In the end, the youth committed suicide after being publicly accused of incest by a rival. The point of interest is that other members of the society did not have what they regarded as legitimate physical sanctions to use against the culprit. In the face of a minority of individuals willing to break the rules of exogamy and not moved to suicide by their departure from the mores, the members of that society would have to institutionalize a method of dealing with this situation or abandon the strict exogamy rule.

Less extreme cases of instability than the limiting case or the one exemplified by the young native constitute a central modern problem of "democracy." Modern moves to limit the activities of minorities regarded as subversive of democratic government are well known. There are signs on every side that people fear that our tolerance in matters of speech, assembly, press, and action, is too great and that its limitation is imperative—lest freedom be used by minorities who are in fundamental disagreement with the *status quo* to move for changes in our way of life, with force if necessary. Steps have been taken in several directions to forestall this possiblity. Some of these steps have been taken through institutionalized channels, and some have been taken spontaneously by groups of morally indignant citizens. The crucial consideration here is that, in the face of a threat to the *Gemeinschaft* set, changes have been made in the area of tolerance, which we shall discuss later.

There is one type of unstable *Gemeinschaft* set that is of special interest here. It contains, either ideally or actually, both the norms of tolerance and rationality in the same area. When these two norms are present in an area, the resultant relations may be termed *contractual* or *Gesellschaft* relations. The aspect of action that is peculiarly susceptible to this combination is that concerned in the allocation of goods and services, the realm of economics. It is not difficult to see why that should be so. The areas in which the norm of rationality is applicable at all are restricted to the intermediate means-end schema for obvious reasons. Of the various possible divisions of the intermediate means-end schema—economic, political, and technological—only the economic seems able to combine both norms. The technological realm cannot, because it does not involve the tolerance co-ordinate at all; tolerance does not enter into an inanimate engineering problem. The political realm cannot very well combine the two norms, since the solution to a political problem must involve some unequal allocation of power. If there is such an allocation of power, some intolerance is present. Complete tolerance would result in capricious changes in the solution to the power problem. In a limited but important sense, tolerance and rationality vary inversely in the solution to a power problem. Intolerance may enter an irrational solution of the power problem too. It would not therefore, be strictly speaking correct to say that they always vary inversely. There are also other complicating factors which need not detain us here. Tolerance is by definition a renunciation of the use of the final bulwark of power.

In the realm of the economic aspects of action it is possible to combine the two normative elements of rationality and tolerance. The contract relationship, as the term is used here, is implicit in the combination of these two norms. A contractual relationship may be defined as one in which two or more parties voluntarily and in the absence of intent to defraud bind themselves to specific commitments in return for specific considerations.[18] The norms of tolerance and rationality cannot be maintained short of some such arrangement. If the relationship is not functionally specific, sooner or later the norm of rationality will be undermined. A member of a functionally diffuse relationship may be presented with all sorts of unpredictable obligations by the other party. The crucial point here is that his choice of alternatives is limited by factors that may well forestall rational conclusions. Given a functionally specific relationship, such factors can be eliminated, at least in theory. For any type of relationship, choice of a rational course of action is hindered by the categories of error and/or inadequate knowledge, but, for the functionally diffuse relationship, there is an additional obstacle in that considerations other than rationality *necessarily* enter into the choice of means to ends. In the long run, therefore, any departure from functional specificity indicates a departure from the norm of rationality.

On the other hand, *adherence solely to the requirement* of functional specificity will conflict with the norms of tolerance because of the high efficiency of the use of force for limited purposes. The absence of intent to defraud is a functional requisite of voluntary, functionally specific relations, since the confidence necessary to maintain a system of such relationships could not be mustered if the use of fraud were unrestricted. No contract system could be maintained at all unless the vast majority of contracts was entered into in good faith by all the parties concerned and fulfilled without recourse to court action. It seems that contractualism is an inevitable concomitant of the institutionalization of rationality and tolerance in the intermediate means-end chain.

This paper will use the term, *Gesellschaft*, to mean contractual, in the specific sense given above. A *Gesellschaft relationship* is defined as a contractual relationship. A predominantly *Gesellschaft* society is defined as a society characterized by a set of *Gemeinschaft* elements that is not only unstable but also explicitly includes the norms of both tolerance and rationality in the economic aspects of behavior. It is important to note here that, while the *Gesellschaft* relationship is theoretically inherent in a social system with a *Gemeinschaft* set containing the norms of tolerance and rationality ideally speaking, it *may also appear* in many other social systems. When it appears in any stable form of society, the elements of tolerance and rationality are present, but *they need not be institutionalized*. There may be, and in fact there seem to be in all societies, whether the *Gemeinschaft* set is stable or not, some *Gesellschaft* phenomena. *In a society with a stable Gemeinschaft set, however, Gesellschaft phenomena are subject to elimination without involving a change in the basic value orientations of the members of the society.* So far as *Gesellschaft* phenomena exist in such societies, they are confined to those residual areas of activity concerned with allocation, to which it has not been deemed practical or necessary to extend the authoritarian mechanism or the priority of nonrational considerations. In these areas, individuals do not act tolerantly and rationally because such behavior is part of the *Gemeinschaft* set covering this portion of activity, but because such areas of social action have been overlooked or present no problem—that is they are not dysfunctional from the conscious point of view of other actors in the system. In the event that these social actions do come to the attention of the "authorities" (or of other actors who are members of the system) and are deemed to present a problem, there is a positive sanction for the invocation of intolerance if lesser methods of persuasion are unavailing or, perhaps, regardless of whether or not such methods are unavailing. For example, there are undoubtedly instances in recent and current totalitarian societies in which such relations can be found. Although such areas may exist, it is highly doubtful that any moral indignation would greet the abridgement of these ranges of "tolerance by default" except from disaffected individuals already held in abeyance by coercion. It is within the sphere of legitimate expectations of all the relatively well integrated members of totalitarian systems, that these areas be invaded by the "powers that be" when and if the "powers" deem it necessary. This difference may be put succinctly in the statement that relative to a society with a stable *Gemeinschaft* set, if interference with *Gesellschaft* relations can be questioned at all, the person challenging the interference must show reason why the relationship should not be disturbed; while relative to a predominantly *Gesellschaft* society, he must show that the reason for disturbing the relation is to preserve the norm of tolerance itself. The question of *Gesellschaft* phenomena in a social system with an unstable *Gemeinschaft* set that does not give rise to a predominantly *Gesellschaft* system (i.e., not characterized by the institutionalization of both tolerance and rationality in the allocative sphere) has not been discussed here. The purpose here is to show that *Gesellschaft* phenomena can arise even in a social system with a stable *Gemeinschaft* set—where they would seem least likely to occur (there being in such a society neither a specific injunction to tolerance nor tolerance as a residuum of the absence of institutionalized methods of exerting force). It goes without saying that *Gesellschaft* phenomena also can and do occur in social systems with unstable *Gemeinschaft* sets that do not give rise to predominantly *Gesellschaft* societies. In such cases, the reasons for noninstitutionalization of the *Gesellschaft* phenomena may spring from one of two sources or from both. First, the area of tolerance need not be the allocative area; second, there need be no institutionalization of rationality in this area.

*Two aspects* of predominantly *Gesellschaft* societies may be noted here: the delicacy of the *Gesellschaft* equilibrium with the accompanying necessity for providing complex safeguards for its maintenance and the inherent spread. of tolerance past the sphere of economic aspects of behavior in terms of predominantly *Gesellschaft* societies. As far as the first is concerned, it is obvious that, short of perfect integration of all members of the society, some forms of restraint are imperative. Current cynicism about contracts and their uses has some basis in the spectacular nature of the frequent cases that threaten to upset the equilibrium. It is not the norm of rationality that is in need of safeguards if it is to be stable. The level of rationality can be maintained, it seems without legislation against stupidity or indifference to the results of rational procedures. Not so with the elements of tolerance! Constant vigilance and restraining laws are necessary to prevent the influx of force and fraud. The degrees to which such measures are necessary and/or present determine the degree to which a society is predominantly *Gesellschaft*. The limiting case is, of course, that of perfect integration, when no such measures are either necessary or present. The system of pure and perfect competition envisaged by the classical economists is such a system. The only empirical examples of predominantly *Gesellschaft* types fall considerably short of this limiting case, but they are characterized by the norms of tolerance and rationality in the economic aspects of action to a significant degree. It is, however, clear that the presence of tolerance assures an element of instability, and, in all empirically known cases, there have been important pressures driving or keeping the system away from the limiting type of predominantly *Gesellschaft* system.

More important perhaps is the fact that the institutionalization of tolerance cannot be strictly confined to the economic aspects of the intermediate means-end sector of action, because the spread of the area of tolerance is accompanied by spread in the area of instability—not only to the political aspects of the means-end sector but into the area of the ultimate ends themselves. The area of tolerance within these other spheres may be large or small, but the spread must be present. The simple and most obvious reason is that the individual actor has roles in more than one sphere. Furthermore, the spheres themselves are not disparate. For example, the exercise of restraint is a politically oriented act, which, as has been shown, is imperative to the maintenance of the institutionalized area of tolerance in the economic sphere. When there is machinery to enforce the conditions for voluntary, predominantly economically oriented relations, this machinery also limits the area in which political power can be used—since exercises of power by members of governments or others constitute an obvious avenue for interference with voluntary predominantly economic relations. Furthermore, in those societies characterized by predominantly *Gesellschaft* relationships, influence on economic aspects has to some extent, though never completely, gone hand in hand with influence on political aspects, either legitimately or illegitimately in the form of graft and corruption. This connection is necessary, unless it can be shown that materialistic orientations are irrelevant to social action, which is certainly not true for any substantial portion of the membership of any known society. It is further obvious that, for any sort of tolerance to exist, it must be reflected in the *Gemeinschaft* set itself. It must be reflected by positive institutionalization or by lack of positive institutionalization to the contrary—or by members of the society ignoring, for a time at least, elements of the *Gemeinschaft* set. The last two possibilities constitute *Gemeinschaft* elements by default.

What does this reformulation of the *Gemeinschaft-Gesellschaft* concepts mean? In the first place, there are both *Gemeinschaft* and *Gesellschaft* elements in all societies. The question of the quantitative appearance of these two types of relations in a given society is not considered here. Such calculations, even if they were possible, would be of no significance in terms of the system of analysis employed here. These two types of element are not, as they were for Tönnies, of the same order in a closed specific set of relationships, so that an increase of one means a decrease of the other. In this revision, *Gemeinschaft* elements are as much present and as important in predominantly *Gesellschaft* societies as in societies with stable *Gemeinschaft* sets. The emphasis is on the differing manners in which the two elements enter the structure of relationships, rather than the degrees of their presence or absence. The difference between societies with stable *Gemeinschaft* sets and predominantly *Gesellschaft* societies lies in the difference between their respective *Gemeinschaft* sets. Furthermore, this revision distinguishes societies with stable *Gemeinschaft* sets and those with unstable

*Gemeinschaft* sets. Those with unstable *Gemeinschaft* sets have been divided into two groups, predominantly *Gesellschaft* societies and a residual category. These various concepts have been defined and elaborated to a degree. The three types of society distinguished here (those characterized by stable *Gemeinschaft* sets, predominantly *Gesellschaft* societies, and those that are not predominantly *Gesellschaft* societies but that are characterized by unstable *Gemeinschaft* sets) make up a classification among whose categories there are differences of kind rather than of degree. There are very important differences of both degree and kind within each category, but the categories themselves do not blend by imperceptible degrees into one another—though they may be transformed from one to another. They do not comprise polar types with an intermediate type, despite the fact that, from the sole point of view of stability, the society with stable *Gemeinschaft* sets is the opposite of the two with unstable *Gemeinschaft* sets. A society may be characterized by a more or less unstable *Gemeinschaft* set, depending on the area of tolerance, but the difference between such a society and one characterized by a stable *Gemeinschaft* set remains one of kind. A society may be more or less predominantly *Gesellschaft*, but the differences between it and societies characterized by stable *Gemeinschaft* sets or by other types of unstable *Gemeinschaft* sets remain differences of kind. The *Gemeinschaft* sets of societies are either stable or more or less unstable. There may be, and in fact there often is, great variation in the substantive content of stable *Gemeinschaft* sets, and, of course, stable *Gemeinschaft* sets may be changed into unstable ones and *vice versa*. The substantive contents of the *Gemeinschaft* sets of any of these three types of society can and do range widely and change often. Limiting cases of these various types of society can be erected. The stable *Gemeinschaft* set is a limiting case in itself. The limiting cases of societies with unstable *Gemeinschaft* sets have already been mentioned on pages 243 and 248.

Finally, one more general and fundamental difference between this revision and the original scheme is apparent. Tönnies's theoretical structure focuses attention on the specific contents of his categories rather than on their structures. For him, the *Gemeinschaft* is traditionalistic, diffuse, disinterested, and so forth. On this level of generalization, Tönnies gets no further than indication that *Gemeinschaft* consists of those things he has mentioned and things like them.[19] The same is true for *Gesellschaft*. It has been pointed out that, in centering his attention on content, Tönnies has given examples on several different levels; this diversity does not, however, alter the center of his attention. This paper focuses on the structure of societies and thus of social relationships in one respect, the basic value element, and has confined its interest to the most generalized level of consideration of this problem. Only two elements of content have appeared in the revision, that of tolerance and that of rationality. They have been introduced because they are of direct structural significance on the most general level of consideration within the category of all societies and therefore of all social relationships.

### Some Theoretical Implications

This revision is quite limited in scope, yet it is sufficient to serve as a background for certain structural features of the interdependencies among *minority social systems* (shortened hereafter to *minority systems*) and the societies in which they exist.[20] The phenomena that will be under discussion here are well known. One of the interests of this line of thought is the light it may throw on the vexatious and elusive phenomenon of "democracy." Discussion will include restrictions of the activities of "real" or "imagined" members of "real" or "imagined" minority systems. The importance of these topics for the problem of "democracy" is plain. At least one element of a democratic society is the relatively wide area in which dissenting opinions about the society or its subsystems can be held and expressed by members or even resident nonmembers of the society with a high degree of safety and even protection.

A minority system is defined here as any subsystem of another social system that differs in one or more matters of normative content from its parent social system. This definition raises the question of the level of generalization on which a problem is considered. For a society to be stable at all, there must be some general agreement among its members on basic value orientations. The most generalized minority systems are those whose members differ from the general membership of this society on the *Gemeinschaft* set of the society as a whole. It is also conceivable that any social system involving more than two members has a minority system in one sense. In this paper, the focus of attention is on the most general level—that of minority systems within a given society. In this sense, a particular family system is not necessarily a minority system, despite the fact that numerically its membership is only a small fraction of that of the total society. On the other hand, in a monogamous society, a single family whose members practice polygyny is a minority system. At any level of generalization, it must be kept in mind that, while all minority systems are subsystems of a "'host'" system, it does not follow at all that all subsystems are minority systems. The test is the attitude of the members of the subsystem toward the institutionalized basic value orientations of the host system. Despite the fact that a university system is a peculiar kind of subsystem within American society, it is not necessarily a minority system— indeed it is usually not one.

The membership of a minority system may vary from two or more people whose only common bond is a single common value to a large number of people involved in a highly complex organization. A *significant minority system* is one in which the values conflict with the set of basic values of the host social system or are deemed to be in conflict by members of the larger system. The degree of significance varies according to two important factors: the extent to which the values characteristic of the minority system are (or are deemed to be) in conflict with the basic value system of the host system of which it is (or is deemed to be) a subsystem—and the effectiveness with which the members of the minority system can (or are deemed able to) take or threaten to take control of the host system. The limiting case of high significance involves conflict with members of the host system over the total *Gemeinschaft* set—when that set includes an injunction to complete tolerance, and the members of the minority system are willing to use force to gain their ends. The limiting case in the other direction is trivial. It consists of the minimal divergence "real" or "imagined," from the *Gemein-*

*schaft* set necessary to distinguish a minority system from the host system—plus complete ineffectiveness, for whatever reasons, of the members of the minority system in trying to spread their influence.

It is also useful to differentiate the significance of a minority system from the point of view of a member of the host system and from that of a hypothetical, omniscient, objective scientific observer. In the first case, the significance will be called *subjective*; in the second, *objective*. In addition to basing classification of the significance of minority systems on the objective-subjective distinction, it must be noted, classification of a subsystem as a minority system, whether significant or not, may be based on the same distinction. A given subsystem will be called an *objective minority system* if it is in fact a minority system, as that term has been defined here, from the point of view of a hypothetical, omniscient, objective, scientific observer. A given subsystem will be called a *subjective minority system* if it is a minority system, as that term has been defined here, from the point of view of members of the host system. Thus a given minority system may be an objective and/or a subjective one. A minority system may be subjective in varying degrees, depending on the proportion of the members of the host system who perceive it as a minority system and the intensity of their perceptions. Mistaken identification by members of the host system would mean a minority system, from the point of view of the host system member(s) but not from that of an objective observer—a subjective minority system that is not an objective minority system.

The classification could be pushed much further from this point in various directions. For example one might ask what sorts of emotional attitudes accompanied the subjective classification of subsystems as minority systems, i.e., how do members of the host system *feel* about those whom they perceive as members of a specific minority system. One might also raise the question of the perception of members of subsystems of themselves as members of minority systems or not. There is not space or need here to push the taxonomy further. See, however, also notes 20 and 21.

If the objective and subjective significances coincide, the significance will be called *logical,* and the minority system will be termed *logically significant.* If they do not, it is *nonlogical.* If it can be verified empirically that the subjective significance is attributed on invalid grounds, then the significance is an *illogical* one.[21]

The distinction between objective and subjective significance of minority systems and the distinction between logical-non-logical categories and sub categories that supplement it are important in differentiating minority systems. The most important distinction is that between the minority systems that are logically significant and those that are illogically or alogically significant. In the first instance, the members of the minority system represent a genuine threat to the host system. It is a sign of malintegration if the members of the host system do not respond to actions of the members of the minority system with outraged moral feelings and forcible action—at least, when the norm of tolerance does not forbid it (in societies characterized by stable *Gemeinschaft* sets or sets unstable only by virtue of lack of positive specification for the use of force under such circumstances). On the other hand, illogical or alogical significance is itself usually a sign of malintegration and frustration among members of the host system. Its typical form is to single out a set of individuals with certain striking and peculiar features and to identify them as members of a minority system.[22] These peculiar features may become foci around which unattached feelings of aggression may be discharged. If these feelings are the result of malintegration and frustration among members of the host system, then a few observations can be made. It may be observed that persecution of the members of the minority system in question (such a minority system would be an illogically or alogically significant, objective and/or subjective, minority system) does not put a stop to the supposed menace, since it does not remedy the source of social disruption. The persecutions serve only as means of discharging constantly generated feelings of aggression. This function is of no small importance, however. In lieu of eliminating the source of malintegration and frustration, the absence of a means for performing this vital discharge function might result in the disruption of the total social system. Alogically or illogically significant minority systems may serve as safety valves through

which certain disruptive forces may be eliminated by action ranging from the expression of moral indignation to the harshest of
persecutions. Unless alternative discharge or remedy of the source
of aggression is available, it is conceivable that a convincing
and successful *exposé* of the alogicality or illogicality of the significance of the minority system would lead directly to a quite
far-reaching disruption of the host social system, perhaps even
to a state of anomie.

If the *Gemeinschaft* set of the host system is a stable one, the
members of any subjectively significant minority system may and
probably will be persecuted, that is, will be held in check forcibly
if necessary. As already pointed out, social systems with stable
*Gemeinschaft* sets are not necessarily invulnerable to members
of minority systems. Minority systems may develop, and their
members may conquer those of the host system. History offers
many instances of the most "intolerant" social systems falling before the onslaught of minority-system members in *coups*, ranging
from palace revolutions to the triumphs of members of religious
sects. The essential point of interest is that dealing with the
members of such a minority system does not necessarily entail
alteration in the *Gemeinschaft* set of the host system. Members
of the host system may persecute the members of the minority
system without institutional let. They may do so ineffectively,
in which case the members of the objectively significant minority
system can triumph.

The opposite case, that of the social system with a completely
unstable *Gemeinschaft* set, is equally clear. In this case, if the
minority system is objectively significant some change in the
*Gemeinschaft* set is inevitable, to the degree that the members
of the minority system spread their influence or use force. When
the members of a minority system triumph, the rapidity and
extent of the changes depend on the rapidity and extent of the
spread or the use of force by the members of the minority system and the degree of contradiction in the value systems involved.
The change may take another direction, however. The members
of the host system may alter its *Gemeinschaft* set to meet the
situation, and they may then determine to use what force
or other forms of coercion are deemed necessary to stop the
threat. Needless to say, this change may or may not be successful.

In either case, barring the elimination of the significance of a minority system by fortuitous circumstances—circumstances external to the members of the host system—or internal dissension among the members of the minority system, the *Gemeinschaft* set of the host system will be changed. If the members of the minority system triumph, they will modify the host system to some extent by replacing at least some of its values with theirs. If the members of the host system efficiently employ such force as might be necessary to protect their system, it will survive, but its *Gemeinschaft* set will have been altered to the extent of permitting the use of such force. If the minority system were subjectively and illogically or alogically significant, an alteration in the *Gemeinschaft* set might take place only through the members of the host system's abandoning tolerance from fear of the members of the minority system.

The class of social systems with unstable (though not completely unstable) *Gemeinschaft* sets, is the great area of intermediate cases. For present purposes, both predominantly *Gesellschaft systems* and other social systems with unstable *Gemeinschaft* sets may be lumped together, since the element of tolerance, rather than the combination of rationality and tolerance, is crucial here. In such social systems there is room for considerable variation in the minority system problems that the *Gemeinschaft* set enables members of the host system to handle. In the United States, for example, there is not a moment's hesitation in deciding on the proper solution to a band of kidnappers; it is forcible restraint to whatever degree is necessary. On the other hand, there is much more hesitation about the proper treatment of persons holding what have been called "nondemocratic" or even "un-American" political ideologies. Members of other systems characterized by unstable *Gemeinschaft* sets might hesitate to use force on kidnappers or might not hesitate to use force on political dissenters.

The following generalizations may be laid down for social systems characterized by unstable *Gemeinschaft* sets:

To the degree that there exist subjectively significant minority systems in which the area of value conflict is in the stable area or areas of the unstable *Gemeinschaft* set, the real or imagined members of these minority systems will be subjected to the use of force or other forms of coercion.

To the degree that there exist subjectively significant minority systems thought to contain values in conflict with those of the host system in the unstable areas or areas of tolerance, the real or imagined members of the minority system may or may not be subjected to the use of force or other forms of coercion.

If the minority system is objectively significant in an unstable area, some change in the *Gemeinschaft* set must ensue. (Tolerance must be at least temporarily abandoned in the unstable area, or the members of the minority system, unless stopped fortuitously or by external or internal forces or by some combination of the three, will enforce their will in the area.) If tolerance is abandoned by the members of the host system, there is a change in the *Gemeinschaft* set; if the members of the minority system prevail, they substitute to some extent their values in this area for former ones.

If the minority system is subjectively and illogically or alogically significant, a change may be wrought, but it must be a change by the members of the host system themselves.

In summary the following may be said:

Relative to all social systems, the appearance of a logically significant minority system is always followed by applications of force or other forms of coercion and/or change in the *Gemein-schaft* set of the host system. Which accompanies the appearance of a subjectively or logically significant minority system depends primarily on the stability or degree of instability of the *Gemein-schaft* set.

Depending most generally on the nature of the *Gemeinschaft* set of the host system, the appearance of a subjectively but illogi-cally or alogically significant minority system may or may not be met by applications of force or other forms of coercion and by change in the *Gemeinschaft* set of the host system.

1. If the *Gemeinschaft* set is stable, there will be an institutional-ized use of force or other form of coercion by members of the host system.

2. If the *Gemeinschaft* set is unstable, the possibilities are (a) use of force or other form of coercion by members of the host system in spheres where tolerance is not institutionalized; (b) change by mem-bers of the host system of the *Gemeinschaft* set and the use of force or other forms of coercion if tolerance is institutionalized in the relevant sphere, or (c) no use of force and no change in the *Gemein-schaft* set if the minority system is illogically or alogically significant and the members of the host system do nothing despite the subjective

Marion J. Levy, Jr.                                   [ 258 ]

(but illogical or alogical) significance of the minority system. The last of these possibilities is highly improbable. Unless the source of the subjective but illogical or alogical significance is somehow removed, even though the minority system is not objectively significant and tolerance is institutionalized in the area concerned, the members of the host system are not likely to maintain the norm of tolerance in the face of either constantly or increasingly generated anxiety about the minority system concerned. Despite alternative logical possibilities, we may generalize empirically that the appearance of a subjectively *or* of a logically significant minority system is always followed by applications of force or other forms of coercion—and/or change in the *Gemeinschaft* set of the host system.

Of course, minority systems may be objectively but not subjectively significant, in which case, no matter what the *Gemeinschaft* set, the members of the minority system will triumph and change the *Gemeinschaft* set, again barring fortuitous, external (to the host system), or internal (to the minority system) circumstances.

This discussion has certain implications for "democratic" social systems. For the purposes of this paper, no attempt has been made to give a "complete" definition of "democratic systems." Since this paper focuses on a specific area, it is sufficient to state the criterion, for present purposes, of "democratic" social systems in this area. "Democratic" social systems are characterized by unstable *Gemeinschaft* sets, usually because of a positive injunction to tolerance over part of the *Gemeinschaft* area. The most striking cases of modern societies generally referred to as "democracies" have been cases of predominantly *Gesellschaft* societies, as that term is defined here. While definitions are, of course, arbitrary, this criterion does not seem by any means out of keeping with either the popular or general social-science use of "democracy." The implications should be clear. Members of "democratic" social systems are faced by an insoluble problem, once subjectively and/or logically significant minority systems appear in the area of institutionalized tolerance. Once they appear, the "democratic" system is changed either by its own members or by triumphant members of the minority system. It appears that, if there is a solution to this problem, it lies in the existence in "democratic" social systems of tolerant but effective patterns such that actions in terms of these patterns prevent minority systems from becoming significant ones or even prevent altogether the development of such minority systems.[23] Logically speaking, the appearance of subjectively, but alogically or illogically, significant minority systems need not force a change in democratic social systems, since it is conceivable that the members of the host system may think them significant yet do nothing about them. In this case, if the minority system is not objectively significant, nothing need happen except an increase of tensions borne by members of the host system. Given the extreme improbability, however, of this specific combination of variables being present in any concrete case of complexity comparable to that of most social systems with unstable *Gemeinschaft* sets, I do not think it worth while to pursue the implications of this logical possibility for "democratic" social systems.

In the past, solution of this "democratic" problem seems to have been a function of what has generally been called a "frontier." A *frontier* is any area of social activity, in terms of which the energies of dissenting individuals may be so absorbed or integrated as to prevent their coming into significant conflict with the members of the host system and/or in terms of which the energies of members of the host system may be so absorbed or integrated as to obviate the illogical or alogical apprehension of significance in objectively insignificant or nonexistent minority systems. Land frontiers are the classic instance—not the land itself, of course, but the social activities located there and the fact that those activities were to a large extent "out of touch" with the general action of the general membership of the societies concerned. The concept of frontier, as used here, has a long and respectable history. My only departure, if any, lies in the details of the specific definition given here.

Typical frontiers associated with Western "democracies" seem to have been the unsettled lands of the western hemisphere, intercontinental "imperialistic" expansion, and the building of new industries. The last has been a particularly well-suited frontier for these social systems. The social systems concerned have been typically capitalistic, and since the building of new industries is eufunctional for such systems from many points of view, this form of frontier not only serves as a safety valve but also is conducive to increased integration of the members of these systems on other counts as well. Such activities are simultaneously eufunctional as an elimination of some of the sources of aggression that may find release in "scapegoating" activity.

The frontier is, however, essentially a negative check on the development of significant minority systems. The frontier activities drain energies away from such developments. If the frontier is removed or voided, the very individuals it once kept from becoming members of significant minority systems may become members of such systems. If it is removed, so is its effect in damping down the factors leading to the development of illogically or alogically significant subjective minority systems. There is a "positive" mechanism too, however—that portion of socialization called "value education." It is the process by which new individuals are imbued with the basic value complex of the social system. This value education is a functional requisite for the continued existence of any social system. To the degree that it is efficiently performed, it will prevent the rise of objectively significant or subjectively, but illogically or alogically, significant minority systems. It is important to note that this value education must itself lie within the limits of the area of tolerance of the host system. Otherwise, it would be self-defeating, since one of the functions of this value education is the preservation of the social system with its area of tolerance intact. This process has one signal advantage over the frontier: After a certain point, depending on its efficiency, an individual's value education may be stopped without his becoming subsequently a member or nonlogical perceiver of significant minority systems. Efficient value education cuts off the development at its source, whereas a frontier prevents development without necessarily affecting the source at all.

Perhaps a word about the position of modern Western "democracies" is in order, taking the United States as an example. The typical frontiers have been the lands to the West and the building of new industries involving continuous capital formation. Value education has proceeded mainly in terms of the family and the school system, aided and abetted by the informal controls and pressures exerted on individuals by social contacts. At present, there may be a question whether or not objectively significant minority systems already exist. It is certainly true that, in the eyes of large segments of the membership of the host system, there are already subjectively significant minority systems. The lands to the West are gone. The degree of efficiency of value education in United States society has never been objectively and accurately determined, but there is a great deal of criticism of this efficiency, and large sections of the populace at least hold vehement opinions that it is by no means efficient enough. It appears, therefore, that some combination of new activities associated with rapid capital formation, other frontiers, or increased efficiency of value education without diminution in tolerance represents our only hope for preservation of at least one of the *sine qua non* criteria of "democracy." If that is true of United States society, it is probably true of any highly modernized "democratic" society. If it is true of any highly modernized, "democratic" society, it also has implications for highly modernized, "nondemocratic" ones. If it has implications for all of those, it probably then also has implications for those societies in process of modernization.

## Notes

1. See Tönnies's *Gemeinschaft und Gesellschaft*, which, together with a late essay of the same title by Tönnies, has been translated under the title, *Fundamental Concepts of Sociology*, by Professor C. P. Loomis (New York: American Book Co., 1940). All references in this paper to Tönnies's work, unless otherwise specified, are to this translation. Tönnies states specifically, "This new phenomenon, the capitalistic society, increases in power and gradually attains the ascendency. Tending as it does to be cosmopolitan and unlimited in size, it is the most distinct form of the many phenomena represented by the sociological concept of the Gesellschaft" (p. 28), and "Gemeinschaft (community) is old; Gesellschaft (society) is a new name as well as a phenomenon. This has been recognized by an author who otherwise taught political science in all its aspects without penetrating to its fundamentals. 'The entire concept of Gesellschaft (society) in a social and political sense,' says Bluntschli (Staatsworterbuch IV), 'finds its natural foundation in the folkways, mores, and ideas of the third estate. It is not really a concept of the people (Volks-Begriff) but the concept of the third estate. . . . Its Gesellschaft has become the origin and expression of common opinions and tendencies. . . . Wherever urban culture blossoms and bears fruit, Gesellschaft appears as its indispensable organ. The rural people know little of it.' On the other hand, all praise of rural life has pointed out that the Gemeinschaft (community) among people is

stronger and more alive. . . . In contrast to Gemeinschaft, Gesellschaft is transitory and superficial" (p. 39). See also Tönnies's definitions quoted in "Shortcomings in Tönnies's Theory," beginning on page 234.

2. It first appeared in 1887. It is to be noted, however, as Professor Pitirim Sorokin observes in his foreword to the Loomis translation, that this dichotomy "like many fundamental categories of social thought . . . is in a sense perennial, appeared long before Tönnies, and is reiterated after Tönnies." (p. v)

3. *Fundamental Concepts*, pp. 37-38.

4. *Ibid.*, p. 74.

5. By "convention" Tönnies means "what springs from tradition and custom or the folkways and mores . . . only in so far as it is wanted and maintained for its general use, and in so far as the general use is maintained by the individual for his use. Convention is not, as in the case of tradition, kept as sacred inheritance of the ancestors." *Ibid.*, p. 87.

6. *Ibid.*

7. P. A. Sorokin, *Contemporary Sociological Theories* (New York: Harper & Bros., 1928), p. 491.

8. Unpublished lectures on the professions. These lectures, of course, long antedate the current formulation of Parsons's "pattern variables."

9. See for example Tönnies, *op. cit., supra*, pp. 142-143 where there is a discussion of some "mixed or complex forms of rational will which contain the elements of natural will . . ."

10. In some cases, both in Tönnies's work and in that of later men, some caution has been observed. Professor F. N. House in his *Development of Social Theory* (p. 195) observes, "By community he means the type of *group exemplified in a relatively pure form by a simple* rural community." Unfortunately, this rigor is by no means maintained with any consistency, even by those who adopt it at all, and, in Professor House's next sentence, one reads, "Society is a term used to refer to the life of commercial towns and cities." [Italics are mine.]

11. *Fundamental Concepts*, pp. 142-44.

12. *Ibid.*, pp. 227-28. It is important to note that this passage did not appear in the book until the 1912 edition.

13. *Ibid.*, p. 186.

14. The section on the cooperatives referred to in Note 12 above was not inserted until 1912, although the original edition appeared in 1887. While Tönnies seems to have been clearly aware of the difference in degree in the essay published as an introductory article in the Loomis translation, this essay did not appear until 1931. "I call all kinds of association in which natural will predominates Gemeinschaft, all those which are formed and fundamentally conditioned by rational will, Gesellschaft. Thus these concepts signify the model qualities of the essence and tendencies of being bound together. Thus both names are in the present context stripped of their connotation as designating social entities or groups or even collective or artificial persons; the essence of both Gemeinschaft and Gesellschaft is found in all kinds of associations, as will be shown." *Fundamental Concepts*, pp. 17-18.

15. In this connection, the distinction between Tönnies and Emile Durkheim is most instructive. Durkheim invented a dichotomy almost precisely analogous to that of *Gemeinschaft* and *Gesellschaft* in his work, *The Division of Labor*. Midway in that work, however, Durkheim turned his

attention to the nature and importance of the "non-contractual elements in contract," destroying in the course of this discussion the basis for setting up "mechanical" and "organic" societies as different in kind. In little of his further work, if any, does the dichotomy play a major role. It is one of the ironies of the teaching of the history of sociology that the distinction between "mechanical" and "organic" societies is always cited as one of Durkheim's theoretical contributions. Actually, his contribution lay in the fact that, unlike many others who used such a distinction, he saw through it, salvaged what was useful to his work and abandoned the original naïve dichotomy.

16. All terms, like "society," "social system," "social," which are not defined here are used as I defined them in *The Structure of Society* (Princeton: Princeton University Press, 1952).

17. See B. Malinowski, *The Sexual Life of Savages* (New York: Halcyon House, 1929), p. 565 ff., and *Crime and Custom in Savage Society* (London: Routledge and Kegan Paul Ltd., 1926), p. 77 ff.

18. Feudalism suggests some interesting points that may be mentioned in passing. At present there is a strong academic reaction against the picture of medieval days as a dark, unthinking, hidebound period. This revolt has emphasized the "contractual relations" among members of various social systems of that period. There is certainly a great deal to be said for this emphasis, though it seems to have gone too far. The so-called "contractualism" of that period was not the same as that of modern capitalism, but there are certain similarities. The interesting aspect for this paper is that the feudal contractual element focused on settlement of the power problem. It was, however, a feature of feudal society that solutions to the power problem and the economic problem overlapped to a larger degree than in modern capitalism. A feudal contract between lord and vassal settled at one stroke both the political and economic aspects of the relations between the two parties. The feudal contract was not a contract as the term is defined here. Although. the elements entering into the present definition entered the feudal contract to a considerable degree, the feudal contract was not functionally specific and was not necessarily voluntary. It is an intriguing coincidence that the general social solution to the power problem that comes nearest in its approach to the modern contract phenomenon is characteristic of a social system in which the more general solutions to the political and economic problems were always made together. In modern capitalistic society, there does not seem to be a phenomenon in the political sphere that even approaches contractualism.

19. That seems to be what Tönnies means at such points as the one in which, after giving a long list of examples of both categories, he adds, "Thus many differences become apparent." *Fundamental Concepts,* p. 38.

20. Certain distinctions should be made clear. The most important is that between "social systems," "social organizations," "societies," and similar concepts on the one hand, and "groups," "aggregates," or "sets of individual actors," on the other. The first type I conceive to be examples of "social systems." I follow Parsons's early lead and define a "social system" as any "system of social action involving a plurality of interacting individuals."*Essays in Sociological Theory Pure and Applied* (New York: The Free Press of Glencoe, 1949), p. 6. I define a "system" as any patterned collection of elements in *The Structure of Society,* pp. 19-20. I define "social" as referring to any variation that cannot be adequately explained in terms of the heredity of the species concerned and the nonspecies environment. Ibid., Chapter I. Although "social system" is defined here as "involving a plurality of inter-

acting individuals," the essence of the definition is that a social system *is not defined as a plurality of individuals* but rather as a system of action. I have always considered Parsons's early insistence that social systems must be identified as sets of patterns, in terms of which action takes place, rather than as sets of individuals, to be perhaps the most highly generalized conceptual contribution of his work. It is confusing, therefore, to find in his current work and that of his followers special cases of social systems, the family, for example, treated sometimes as systems of action and sometimes as sets of individual actors—or even defined as sets of specific individuals.

There are three quite important reasons for keeping the two approaches distinct. Clarity is the first and the humblest of these three. It is quite easy to give examples of "groups" (i.e., sets of individuals), the constituents of which do not act in terms of any common social system, in the sense defined here on the level under consideration. It is also quite possible to specify social systems of which the detailed membership is by no means precisely tied down. To use an example, which will be germane below, one may speak of the Jews who are members of modern U.S. society as a "minority group." From the point of view of certain individuals it may be alleged that all Jews belong to a common social system. Empirically it is not true, however, that all people who meet the definition of the term "Jew" in fact participate in a single common social system on that level of consideration.

In the second place, failure either consciously or unconsciously to keep the two distinct ties the level of generalization possible with the concept concerned to the specific membership of the group. Thus, if the family is defined as a unit consisting of father, mother, and nonadult children, then any addition or subtraction to that set of individual actors by birth or by death or by any other means makes it a "nonfamily" or a new and different family. If one asks anyone using the concept of a "social system" as identical with that of "group" (regardless of whether he does so explicitly or implicitly) why he continues to refer to the "same social system" despite additions or subtractions from the membership, inevitably the answer is given in terms of the fact that the patterns of action on the level under consideration have not been changed despite the fact that there have been additions to or subtractions from the set of individual actors who constitute the membership. Of course, if one goes to sufficiently descriptive levels, it is true that any addition to or subtraction from the membership of a given organization to some extent changes the patterns which in the view taken here constitute the "social system." On the other hand, very rarely is the focus of interest of the analyst on nearly so descriptive a level of generalization as that. The focus of interest of the analyst is almost inevitably on some level of generalization such that many concrete changes in membership do not affect the system of action (that is to say the set of patterns in terms of which actions by the members take place) that the term "social system" or "group" is in fact being used to refer to. In other words, the actual referent of these concepts is most often the set of patterns in terms of which action by the members takes place and not the set of individual actors who are in fact involved in the action. But concepts referring to a wide variety of "sets," "aggregates," or "groups" of individual actors are also very important for social analysis. After all, some sets of individuals are involved in a common system of action (i.e., are members of the same social system), some are not but are thought to be by others, some are sets of actors only by spatial definition, etc. One of the most important distinctions among such sets is the variations in the relationships among the constituents of such sets in terms of social systems or the relative lack of social systems. It is therefore of the essence of concept formation in this field that there be clearcut concepts of both sorts without confusion, and without ignoring empirical distinctions and variations of great relevance for social analysis, and with the possibility of developing the implications of various referents of these concepts for one another.

The allegation of the importance of having the two sets of concepts without confusing them leads directly to the third major reason for keeping the two distinct. The distinction is important for fruitful theory formation which is after all the first concern of science. If one keeps the concepts distinct, as I would urge here, there is the possibility of a set of theorems which refer to social systems in general (or to any specific set of social systems); there is the possibility of a set of theorems which refers to any and all sets of individual actors (or any specific set of individual actors); and finally there is the possibility of a set of theorems which refers to any and all combinations of the two (or any specific combination of the two). There are, therefore, no clearcut theorems which can be formed by leaving these two concepts muddled which cannot be formed if they are clarified, and there are a great many which can be formed if they are kept distinct which cannot be formed, even potentially, if they are left muddled.

If one is to define a social system as a set of patterns involving a plurality of individuals, one must be careful to use the concept as defined. Whatever the usage of laymen may be, the social scientist must carefully avoid the pathetic fallacy in social analysis. This consists above all in the attribution of the qualities of an individual actor to organizations or social systems. Organizations or social systems in the sense of the term used here do not *do* anything. They constitute certain patterns of action in terms of which things are done by individual actors. In this sense "governments" do not do anything. Individuals do things in terms of governments. Perhaps the most important example of general confusion of this sort is the dual use of the term "actor." Here again I would consider one of Parsons's most important contributions the explicit attention he called to the concept of "actors" in social phenomena. This was reflected not only in his early insistence on what he referred to as "an actor-situation" frame of reference but also in a set of essays and observations which still constitute some of the most sophisticated efforts to interrelate the findings of the general field of psychoanalysis and the elaboration of general views of social structure. Nevertheless what is involved in the actor-situation distinction is radically obscured if the term "actor" is to be used as the action referent of the biological individual and hence closely associated with the concept of individual personality and for any system of action which "acts" only in the sense that a set of individual actors "act" in terms of it. If one wishes to consider social systems or organizations as "actors," one must sharply differentiate between the meaning of the concept in this context and its meaning when it refers to individual actors. I suppose one could, if one chose, set up the concept as a general one and then distinguish between "organizational actors" and "individual actors," but I suspect this would continue to involve one in the pathetic fallacy and in the begging of very important questions. In the first place, every such alleged case of an organization as "actor" refers to individual actors in a dual sense. All such instances of "action" by "acting organizations" involve individual actors as such and in their special roles as members or representatives of the organization referred to. No matter how separate, ideally speaking, the roles an individual may have outside such an organization may be from those in terms of which he acts as a member of the organization, actually speaking, such distinctions may not be carefully maintained. Every sophisticated social analyst knows this full well. It is one thing for the layman who is not interested in many of the details of analysis of what goes on to refer to the "action" of the United States government, it is quite another thing for a social scientist to refer to the "actions" of the United States gevernment and the "action" of, say President Kennedy as though these "actions" on some general level were identical. The use of the term "actor" to refer to both social systems and individual actors is in the first place confusing. In the second place, it obscures an understanding of the roles of individual members in such organizations. In the third place, it is a special form of thinking in terms of the organismic analogy in general and of anthropomorphism in particular. I have no doubt that social organizations are "man made," but that does not mean that they are "man like." It may be extremely cumbersome to refer to the members of an organization doing things in terms of the patterns which comprise that organization rather than to refer to the organization as "doing something," but I believe that until conceptual advance enables us to simplify the language used we are very much better off being cumbersome and at radical odds with the layman in our discussions of these matters than we are being confused in ways about which we neither know nor care. On the other hand, if the professional social scientist is limited in the sophistication of his analysis to what is implied by the layman when he refers to governments as "acting," the concern expressed here is probably an example of being queasy about concepts beyond the call of intellectual development.

21. One may establish further categories of nonlogicality, apart from illogicality. This discussion is, of course, an application of an adaptation that I have made from Vilfredo Pareto's very fruitful positions on these matters. Further elaboration may be found in *The Structures of Society*, pp. 240-248.

These classifications are additional to the classification of subsystems as minority systems. Subjective or objective minority systems may be *logically, nonlogically, alogically,* or *illogically perceived* minority systems.

Finally, it might also be useful to extend these distinctions still further by reference to the significance or existence of a minority system from the point of view of its own members.

22. It is very important to note that such a set of individuals may or may not in fact be members of a common subsystem of action. For example, "Negroes," "Jews," or "foreigners" may constitute a set of individuals with certain striking and peculiar features, subjectively and/or objectively—without all or a majority or even a large number of the members of any of those sets sharing membership in any single minority system or even in any single subsystem. For this reason, it is important not to confuse "minority system," with "minority group." See Note 20.

23. From the point of view of social change in the forms of social reform or social improvement, it is important, however, that minority systems develop in some cases. It is further important to realize that, although the development of significant minority systems under the circumstances discussed here means change in the *Gemeinschaft set,* whether these changes are "desirable" or "undesirable" is a matter of evaluation, which is not broached here. This discussion is concerned exclusively with the structural implications—not with whether those implications are "good," "bad," or "indifferent" in ethical terms.

*Seymour Martin Lipset*

## DEMOCRACY AND THE

## SOCIAL SYSTEM[1]

There have been many different approaches to the study of the functional requirements of political democracy. Among them have been analyses of the relationships between stages or degrees of economic development and political forms, studies of the processes through which the varying structures of the polity itself have affected the stability of these systems, and investigations of the ways in which variations in the number and type of secondary organizations mediate between the population and the state and thus affect the conditions for democracy.[2] In this paper, I propose to approach the problem from yet a fourth perspective, by treating the basic values of societies as the foci of analysis.[3] As Talcott Parsons, perhaps the foremost contemporary sociological exponent of the importance of value systems as key causal elements, has put it,

That a system of value-orientations held in common by the members of a social system can serve as the main point of reference for analyzing structure and process in the social system itself may be regarded as a major tenet of modern sociological theory. Values in this sense are the commitments of individual persons to pursue and support certain *directions* or types of action for the collectivity as a system and hence derivatively for their own roles in the collectivity. Values are, for sociological purposes, deliberately defined at a level of generality higher than that of goals—they are *directions* of action rather than specific objectives, the latter depending on the particular character of the situation in which the system is placed as well as on its values and its structure as a system.[4]

This emphasis on values is not intended to negate other approaches but is rather intended to illustrate how values may be usefully considered in specifying the sources of variation in the stability of different democratic systems. I shall ignore the many other determining variables, which are of obvious importance to the functioning of the political system, some of which I have discussed elsewhere. This strategy is common in social science; perhaps the most important example is Max Weber's analysis of the rise of capitalism, in which, without denying the arguments of economic determinists that capitalism arose after certain economic preconditions had developed, Weber sought to prove that a given value system, such as that subsumed in the Protestant Ethic, was exceptionally encouraging for the emergence of a fully developed capitalist economic system. Parsons has provided a *caveat* for the assumption that emphasis on values implies a monistic approach to social analysis:

It should be clear that using values as the initial point of reference for the structural analysis of social systems does not imply that they are the sole or even the most important *determinants* of particular structures and processes in such systems. I do not think it is useful to postulate a deep dichotomy between theories which give importance to beliefs and values on the one hand, to allegedly "realistic" interests, e.g. economic, on the other. Beliefs and values are actualized, partially and imperfectly, in realistic situations of social interaction, and the outcomes are *always* co-determined by the values and the realistic exigencies; conversely what on concrete levels are called "interests" are by no means independent of the values which have been institutionalized in the relevant groups.[5]

The value orientations of different societies, social groupings and subsystems will be characterized in this paper by a number of pattern variables. These were originally developed by Parsons as an extension of the classic differentiation of societies between those which emphasized *Gemeinschaft* (primary, small, traditional, integrated community) values and those which stressed *Gesellschaft* (impersonal, secondary, large, socially differentiated, society) values.[6]

The Parsonian pattern-variables which will be used in this paper are achievement-ascription, universalism-particularism, and specificity-diffuseness. According to the achievement-ascription distinction, a society's value system may emphasize ascribed or inherited qualities (such as race or high birth) in judging individuals and placing them in various roles, or it may emphasize individual ability and performance. According to the universalism-particularism distinction, it may emphasize that all people should be treated according to the same standard (e.g., equality before the law), or that individuals should be treated differently according to their personal qualities or their particular membership in a class or group. Specificity-diffuseness refers to the difference between treating individuals in terms of the specific positions which they happen to occupy, rather than diffusely as total individuals.[7]

To these variables I add the equalitarian-elitist distinction. According to this distinction a society's values may stress that all persons must be given respect simply because they are human beings, or it may stress the general superiority of those who hold elite positions. That is, in an equalitarian society, the differences between low-status and high-status people are thought to reflect accidental and perhaps temporary variations in position, differences that should not be stressed in social relationships and that do not convey to the high-status person a general claim to social deference. In contrast, in an elitist society, those who hold high positions in any structure—business, intellectual activities, or government—are thought to deserve and are actually given general respect and deference.[8] This distinction is not intended to introduce a new and logically independent pattern-variable since it overlaps considerably with ascription-achievement. All ascriptively oriented societies are necessarily also elitist in this use of the term. On the other hand, achievement orientation and egalitarianism are not necessarily highly correlated since a stress on achievement is not incompatible with giving generalized deference to all in elite positions whether they have inherited or achieved them. To a considerable degree societies in the process of changing from a stress on ascription to one on achievement seem disposed, as we shall see later, to retain their elitist orientations and institutions when contrasted with social systems in which ascriptive values never had a pre-eminent role.

In actual fact, *no society is ever fully explicable by these analytic concepts, nor does the theory even contemplate the possible existence of such a society.*[9] Every society incorporates some aspect of each polarity. We may, however, differentiate among social structures by the extent to which they emphasize one or another of these polarities.[10]

### Value Patterns and the Conditions of a Democratic Polity

I have chosen to discuss the United States, Great Britain, Canada, Australia, France, and Germany in my attempt to illustrate the relationship between societal values and the stability of democratic political systems.[11] These nations are all relatively industrialized, all have capitalist or mixed economies, and the religious traditions of all are traceable to the same Hebraic-Christian source. They all have democratic political systems. Yet they differ in one important respect—the United States, Britain, Canada, and Australia have stable democratic systems, while France and Germany have (or have had) unstable democratic polities. The prime empirical focus in this paper is on the four most populous countries; the two overseas dominions of the British Crown are discussed toward the end in a separate section designed to illustrate the way in which the same theoretical approach may analytically differentiate extremely similar countries.[12]

Since I have attempted to elaborate on a sociologically meaningful definition of a democratic system elsewhere, I do not want to repeat those discussions here.[13] Essentially, I have urged the view "that the distinctive and most valuable element of democracy [in complex societies] is the formation of a political elite in the competitive struggle for the votes of a mainly passive electorate."[14] This definition is premised on the common assumption that "democracy" means a system in which those outside the formal authority-structure are able to influence significantly the basic direction of policy. If the citizenry as a whole is to have *access* to decisions, there must be a meaningful competitive struggle within the political elite which leads factions within this elite to look for generalized as well as specific support. The political elite can only be leaders and *representatives* if there are mechanisms within the culture that foster the kinds of personal motivations that lead men to perceive and strongly support their own interests within a political system which has relatively well-defined rules. Mechanisms that undermine the democratic rules or inhibit institutionalized conflict are destructive of democracy, that is of the general population's access to or power over key societal decisions. It is necessary, therefore, to look for factors both that sustain the separation of the political system from excesses that may be inherent in the populist assumptions of democracy—for example, the belief that majority will is always sovereign—and protect it from vulnerability to the day-to-day fluctuations of mass opinion *and* that encourage participation in organizations in conflict with one another and with state agencies involved in directing public policy on all major issues.

THE UNITED STATES AND GREAT BRITAIN. The connections between differences in values and differences in political stability are not simple nor the same for all countries. The United States and Great Britain, although they are similar in being heavily urbanized, industrialized, and politically stable, are actually integrated around different sets of values and class relations. The two best known nineteenth-century analyses of the bases of these societies, Alexis de Tocqueville's *Democracy in America* and Walter Bagehot's *The English Constitution* accurately identified very different organizing principles for each. According to Tocqueville, American democratic society was equalitarian and competitive (achievement-oriented); according to Bagehot, Britain was deferential (elitist) and ascriptive. These differences are partly to be explained by the degree to which each broke from its traditional past—the break was much more pronounced in America than it was in Britain. As both Tocqueville and Bagehot indicated, a society in which the historic ties of traditional legitimacy had been forcibly broken could only sustain a stable democratic polity if it emphasized equality and if it contained strong, independent, and competitive institutions. Conversely, if its privileged classes persisted and continued to expect ascriptive (aristocratic) and elitist rights, the society could only have a stable democratic system if the lower classes accepted the status system. These differences will be explored in more detail later. It is enough to emphasize here that a stable democracy is made possible by different combinations of pattern-variables.

The United States, probably more than any other modern, non-Communist industrial nation, can be characterized as emphasizing achievement, equalitarianism, universalism, and specificity.[15] These categories of the pattern-variables tend to be mutually supportive. That is, each may be perceived as functionally interrelated with any other given variable stressed in the American typology. This supportive relationship does not, of course, mean that other stable combinations are not possible or that the "American" combination does not exhibit tensions. It may be argued that any achievement system has a tendency to undermine equality, stress elitism, and even eventually to sustain ascription. Successful achievers seek generalized elite status to sustain their sense of importance and to reduce tenure insecurity (witness the complaints of American intellectuals or Australian businessmen that they are not respected outside their immediate circles). Also, the strong affective values inherent in all family systems impel the successful to find ways to pass on to their kin, especially to their offspring, any advantages they have gained.

From the perspective of the polity, however, this combination of variables seems to be highly functional for a stable democracy. The normative system allows or encourages the upper classes to accept improvements in the status and power of the lower strata *without feeling morally offended.* Since all men and groups are expected to try to improve their position *vis à vis* others, success by a previously deprived group is not resented so deeply as in countries whose values stress the moral worth of ascription. Like all comparative generalizations, this statement is relative rather than absolute. It is obvious that in the United States, as in other countries, those with higher status dislike any challenge to their privileged positions and resist and resent new claimants to higher status. The common resistance to the claims for status equality of upwardly mobile ethnic groups like the Jews, the Irish, and the Italians illustrates this point. Status resentments against rising groups have been a frequent source of social tension throughout American history. The relative emphasis on equalitarianism, universalism, and specificity in American society means that men can expect and, within limits, can receive fair treatment according to abilities or merits. Lower-class individuals and groups that desire to change their social position *need not be revolutionary.* The dominant values of the society legitimize their aspirations. Consequently, their political goals and methods are relatively moderate and even conservative. They attempt to make changes by playing according to the rules of the game. There is a low level of class consciousness, since class consciousness is partly an adaptation to the behavior of the upper class in societies characterized by ascription, elitism, particularism, and diffuseness. These values imply that men must stay in their class position and that they will be treated by others and will treat each other diffusely in terms of class status. In fact, American values reject treating an individual in terms of a diffuse status but treat him in terms of his role as worker in one situation, as suburban dweller in another, as a member of the American Legion in a third, and so forth.

It must be stressed again, of course, that the above comments are based on abstracting ideal-typical elements of American society. In fact, there are ascriptive, elitist, particularistic, and diffuse culture traits in the society. They are not completely dysfunctional, as will be shown. They do create frictions (see the analyses of McCarthyism as a reaction to "status-panic"),[16] but, in general, with the major exception of race and ethnic relations, they have not affected the basic stability of the polity.

The American South, which has stressed ascriptive-elitist-particularistic-diffuse values in race relations and even to some extent in its total social system, has constituted one major source of instability in the American polity. In a real sense it was kept in the nation by force, and to this day it does not have a stable or a democratic polity. To the extent that its citizens have felt the pull of the dominant value system, the South has always found it difficult to build even an integrated regional social order on its own terms.[17]

Unlike America, where achievement and equalitarianism have gone hand in hand, Britain has come to accept the value of achievement in its economic and educational system and to some extent in its political system, but it retains the assumptions inherent in elitism (that those who hold high position should be given generalized deference) and in ascription (that those born to high places should retain them).[18] In a sense this is the meaning of Tocqueville's suggestion that Britain has an "open aristocracy," which can be entered by achievement or by merit and which then conveys to new entrants many of the diffuse perquisites of rank enjoyed by those whose membership stems from social background.[19] Tocqueville's phrase "open aristocracy" may easily be converted into a value-pattern type, the combination of ascription and universalism, which in turn implies elitism and diffuseness.

Britain clearly differs from the United States in having hierarchical orders that emphasize different values. It entered the modern era (the nineteenth century) with a strong emphasis on ascriptive, elitist, particularistic, and diffuse values. Its business classes arose with economic and social needs that challenged the traditional pre-industrial value integration. For reasons to be discussed later, the British upper class (compared to Continental aristocracies) did not resist strongly the claims of the new business classes and later those of the workers to take part in politics. The leaders of the old land-based aristocracy recognized that they could retain what they seemingly valued most—ascriptive rights to diffuse elite status—if the new classes were granted access to the economic and political systems. Since preservation of ascriptive status implies elitism, the new elites of business and politics have been allowed to enter at least the outer limits of The Establishment, of the self-conscious, mutually supportive elite, all of whom command deference from the non-elite. The crucial areas of economy and polity are therefore characterized by achievement-elitism-universalism-diffuseness. The social-class system is characterized by ascription-elitism-particularism-diffuseness. This difference means that the traditional upper classes and their institutions—the public schools, the ancient universities, and the titled aristocracy—retain their positions at the summit of the social structure.[20] At the same time, achievers in the occupational sphere (job and school) are not barred from securing very gratifying diffuse elite status, and the lower classes feel that the political institutions operate for their benefit. Like the liberal bourgeoisie before them, the British workers, unions, and Labour Party have never seriously aimed at eliminating the old privileged classes, either socially or economically.[21] Having been allowed into the political club almost from the start of their organized political consciousness, the leaders of British labor have supported the rules of the parliamentary game. Unlike many early continental socialist parties, they were willing, while still a small minority party, to cooperate with one of the older parties. They remain the only socialist party whose policies "sustain" the legitimacy of aristocracy; their leaders, like other members of the Establishment, willingly accept aristocratic titles and other honors from the Crown.[22]

Two comparative analyses of American and British society have clearly emphasized the distinctions between the two great English-speaking nations—one by Edward Shils in the sphere of the polity, the other by Ralph Turner in education. Shils seeks to account for the great emphasis on publicity concerning political matters in the United States—Congressional investigations, for example—contrasted with the stress on privacy and secrecy in Britain. As he points out:

> The United States has been committed to the principle of publicity since its origin. The atmosphere of distrust of aristocracy and of pretensions to aristocracy in which the American Republic spent its formative years has persisted in many forms. Repugnance for governmental secretiveness was an offspring of the distrust of aristocracy. In the United States, the political elite could never claim the immunities and privileges of the rulers of an aristocratic society. . . .
>
> American culture is a populistic culture. As such, it seeks publicity as a good in itself. Extremely suspicious of anything which smacks of "holding back," it appreciates publicity, not merely as a curb on the arrogance of rulers but as a condition in which the members of society are brought into a maximum of contact with each other. . . .
>
> Great Britain is a modern, large-scale society with a politicized population, a tradition of institutionalized pluralism, a system of representative institutions and great freedom of enquiry, discussion, and reporting. . . . British political life is strikingly quiet and confined. Modern publicity is hemmed about by a generally well-respected privacy. . . .
>
> Although democratic and pluralistic, British society is not populist. Great Britain is a hierarchical country. Even when it is distrusted, the Government, instead of being looked down upon, as it often is in the United States, is, as such, the object of deference because the Government is still diffused with the symbolism of a monarchical and aristocratic society. The British Government, of course, is no longer aristocratic . . . [But it] enjoys the deference which is aroused in the breast of Englishmen by the symbols of hierarchy which find their highest expression in the Monarchy. . . .
>
> The acceptance of hierarchy in British society permits the Government to retain its secrets, with little challenge or resentment. . . . The deferential attitude of the working and middle classes is matched by the uncommunicativeness of the upper-middle classes and of those who govern. . . . The traditional sense of the privacy of executive de-

liberations characteristic of the ruling classes of Great Britain has imposed itself on the rest of the society and has established a barrier beyond which publicity may not justifiably penetrate.[23]

The protection from populist criticism that an elitist system gives to all who possess the diffuse status of "leaders" extends not only to the political and intellectual elites but to school teachers and the school system as well:

> Conservative, Labour, and Liberal parties alike have consistently held to the view that the content of education and methods of instruction are not matters for popular debate and decision, but should be left in the hands of teachers themselves and of other professional educators. This being so, individuals or groups seeking to "use" the schools for their own purposes are confronted, not by the hastily constructed defenses of the teacher or of a single school or school board, as in America, but by the massive disregard of experienced politicians and administrators. This willing delegation of educational issues to educators is possible because the latter form a coherent and predictable element in the authority structure that moulds English society. . . .
> The relation between the school and the family also differs in the two countries. In America, for the most part, the parents hand over their child to the school system, but maintain a continuous scrutiny over his progress. In England, "interference" by the parents in the school is resisted both by teachers and by educational administrators. Parents' associations and parent-teacher associations are becoming increasingly common, but they limit their activities to social functions and to meetings at which school policy is explained but not debated.[24]

Ralph Turner also shows how variations in the basic values of the two societies, which he calls the "organizing norms," impinge on their educational systems.[25]

American education reflects the norms of *contest mobility*, "a system in which elite status is the prize in an open contest and is taken by the aspirants' own efforts. . . . Since the 'prize' of successful upward mobility is not in the hands of the established elite to give out, the latter are not in a position to determine who shall attain it and who shall not." Conversely, Turner suggests that British education is determined by the norms of *sponsored mobility*, in which "elite recruits are chosen by the established elite or their agents, and elite status is *given* on the basis of some criterion of supposed merit and cannot be *taken* by any amount of effort or strategy. Upward mobility is like entry into a private club, where each candidate must be 'sponsored' by one or more of the members."

The American system, with its emphasis on the common school and extensive opportunities for further education at every level, encourages all to try to advance themselves through their own efforts. "Every individual is encouraged to think of himself as competing for an elite position, so that in preparation he cultivates loyalty to the system and conventional attitudes."[26] Conversely, the British system has always operated to select the minority who will go ahead in the educational system at a relatively early age and to give those not chosen for such advancement an education designed to fit them for their appropriate (lower) station. Those not selected, the large bulk of the population, are taught to "regard themselves as relatively incompetent to manage society, by restricting access to the skills and manners of the elite, and by cultivating belief in the superior competence of the elite. The earlier that selection of the elite recruits can be made, the sooner the masses can be taught to accept their inferiority and to make 'realistic' rather than phantasy plans."[27] Those selected for the elite, on the other hand, are removed from competition and admitted to a school situation, either in the public or grammar schools, in which there is great emphasis on absorbing the elite aesthetic culture, manners, and sense of superiority and paternalism toward the nonelite. Unlike America, where, in the absence of a sense of a special elite culture, the masses retain their right and ability to determine taste, society in England operates on the assumption that only the elite may determine what is high or low quality.[28]

In his discussion of the sources of stability of English democracy, which he relates primarily to "the congruence of social authority patterns in all its aspects and degrees," Harry Eckstein observes with insight that these patterns vary among the classes—authoritarian social relations increase as one moves down the social ladder—as well as within the different strata. He relates these differences to the British elitist governmental pattern. Specifically, he suggests that within the British elite, social relations "tend to be quite surprisingly democratic, or at least consultative and comradely; here . . . we might note the ubiquity of committees at every conceivable level in the higher civil service, the unusual use of staff committees in the military services, and the easy relations among officers of all ranks in military regiments, especially in elitist regiments like the Guards . . . while behavior among pupils [in upper-class public schools] is modeled to a remarkable extent on the political system." That is, within the elite there is diffuse respect for all. Conversely, where hierarchical relations are involved as "between members of the Administrative Class [of the Civil Service] and their underlings, officers and their men, managers and their help, relations are highly non-consultative and certainly not comradely. . . ."[29] Presumably Eckstein would relate the stabilty of American populist democracy to the congruence between egalitarian social relations at all levels in diverse nongovernmental institutions and the pattern of American political life.

The United States and Great Britain, which exemplify how two large industrialized societies may institutionalize a democratic polity around different value-patterns, differ, of course, not only in the patterns but in the extent to which the same value orientations dominate the key hierarchical subsystems of the society (particularly, as has been noted, the status, economic, and political subsystems). American society has greater homogeneity of values in these dimensions than does British society. On the other hand, the particular distribution of different value orientations in Britain also seems to be congruent with the stability of an industrialized democracy, since it legitimates open participation by all groups in the economy and politics, while the diffuse elitism stemming from the combination of ascription-universalism in the status order rewards all with a claim to high position. All elite positions are thus mutually supportive. The latter consequence reduces the possibilities for such populist aggressions against any section of the elite as anti-intellectualism, McCarthyite attacks on the civil service, and challenges to the patriotism of the left or the moral integrity of the right.

FRANCE AND GERMANY. The two nations that best illustrate political instability, France and Germany, bear strong resemblances in parts of their values to the United States and Britain. France, through her Great Revolution of 1789, sought to deal with the needs of a modern society by adopting the same syndrome of values that the United States developed, achievement-equalitarianism-universalism-specificity. The Declaration of the Rights of Man, like the Declaration of Independence, proclaims doctrines that are subsumed by these concepts. Germany, on the other hand, has resembled Britain in that the pressures stemming from economic change and the rise of new social groupings in the late eighteenth and the nineteenth centuries did not result in a successful political revolution proclaiming a new value ethos. Rather, Germany seemingly sought to adapt or modify existing institutions and values in terms very similar to those which developed in Britain. The French failure stems from the fact that, in contrast to American experience, the forces underlying revolutionary change were not strong enough to sustain value-sharing or consensus among the key social groupings; the German failure is related to the fact that, while Germany resembled Britain in seeking to adapt through diverse value-patterns in different hierarchical subsystems, its combinations were basically incompatible with the requirements for a stable *nonauthoritarian* political system.

French society, as many commentators have noted, is difficult to classify in terms of basic or overriding values. Its internal political tensions flow in large measure from the fact that major sectors of the nation adhere to largely incompatible value systems. The French sociologist François Bourricaud has pointed this out.

It is . . . difficult to seize upon and isolate the unconscious or semiconscious motivations [basic values] which give French institutions their tone and their specific color. They are more apparent in some groups than in others. Certain themes of French culture are more clearly discernible, more sharply outlined, among the bourgeois than among the workers. All research of this nature begins by determining what social groups are culturally dominant. America, for example, has developed a culture of the middle classes. But in France a group can be culturally dominant in one area and not at all present in another. . . . For example, the tradition of the noble life continues without doubt to be very influential in French society even though the nobility as a social group does not amount to much. . . . In brief, cultural themes are very far from being unified even within the society, both by reason of the diversity of the groups which make up this society and the diversity of activities by which this culture is expressed.[30]

These internal cleavages result from the fact that the French Revolution succeeded in eliminating neither the old set of ascriptive-particularistic values nor some of their key institutional supports, particularly the Roman Catholic Church. A large part of the French *bourgeoisie*, the class whose status and economic objectives sustained the Great Revolution, either never completely rejected the traditional value system, particularly the Church that continued to foster it, or was led, by reidentification with the Church or the old bases for hierarchical status, to re-accept the values of the traditional aristocratic and clerical elites as models to be followed. As François Goguel points out, this value system was directly hostile to democracy.

A pessimistic idea of human nature—an idea of Catholic origin, and directly opposed to the optimism of J. J. Rousseau—is at the basis of this conviction; man, being naturally evil, must have teachers, or guides, to direct him toward good. These guides are the traditional institutions, the social authorities. The first is the authority of monarchy, temporarily the highest, and then the First Families, predestined by birth and wealth to a leading role. Finally, above all, there is the Catholic Church, charged with shaping conscience and soul and conditioning them toward the social order and eternal salvation. These theocratic ideas, expounded by Bonald at the time of the Restoration, survived much longer than one would have thought possible. . . .[31]

The economic behavior of many French small businessmen, as many economists have noted, follows the logic of precapitalist society by emphasizing the maintenance of the family fortune and status. They refuse to take economic risks or to enter into serious competition designed to eliminate others in similar activities.[32] The politics of the petty *bourgeoisie* has been oriented toward maintaining the stability of existing business, even though this has limited the expansion potential of individual businesses and of the country.[33] More than any other industrial nation, France has maintained particularistic values in industry. This particularism has been one of the sources of tension, because French employers, especially in the many relatively small plants, have expected particularistic loyalties from their employees.[34] All through its history, French industry has attempted to deny representation rights to trade unions and, when forced to grant them as the result of strikes or political changes, has undermined these concessions as soon as possible. To permit unions rights of representation, to acknowledge universalistic norms, is morally offensive to the particularistic values of the businessmen. The behavior of the French businessman is, of course, even more complicated than this brief analysis suggests, since the requirements of a capitalist or commercial economic system inherently dictate a considerable degree of universalism.[35] As Bourricaud has pointed out, "Between the 'bourgeois' money criterion and more aristocratic criteria—antiquity of family and connection—the bourgeois hesitates. This ambiguity explains in part, perhaps, why his relations with the workers have been so difficult."[36]

The French working class, on the other hand, has largely supported in ideology if not always in behavior, the revolutionary values of achievement-equalitarianism-universalism. It has, however, been faced with a situation in which, as contrasted with American workers, it finds mechanisms for individual or collective mobility are morally disapproved by the more privileged orders—although, of course, as in other industrial societies, considerable individual mobility occurs.[37] The French workers' efforts to improve their lot through collective action are bitterly resisted by the *bourgeoisie* as illegitimate, and the cultural emphasis on local particularism inhibits their efforts to form strong nation-wide organizations, especially trade unions.[38] There is perhaps no more impressive evidence of the deep-felt moral hostility of many French employers toward yielding rights to unions than the systematic effort to demolish all union rights during the period of the so-called "phony" war from September 1939 to May 1940. Both employers and their representatives in the government apparently put "teaching the workers and unions a lesson" ahead of national unity and, in the last analysis, national survival.[39]

The effort to sustain traditionalist preindustrial norms within a growing economy has systematically inhibited the creation of a democratic parliamentary system based on achievement and universalistic values. Every French republic has sought to apply these values to the polity and has admitted the lower classes to equal rights of access to government. Such rights and norms applied to the polity meant in most other countries a tempering of aggressive lower-class ideologies; in France, however, it meant an intensification of such sentiments. The norms of the polity as expressed by its representatives have systematically pointed up the contradiction between equalitarian goals based on revolutionary values and the deferential requirements of industry. The contradictory values of industry and polity adversely affect the stability of each.

The strongest moral strain in French culture has been the cleavage between the emphasis on pre-industrial values which have continued to affect the economic sector and the competing legitimacy of the revolutionary tradition, which has formally dominated the political structure. The ascriptive, elitist, and particularistic aspects in French values facilitated the emergence of politics along class-conscious lines—while the emphasis on equalitarianism, universalism, and achievement has encouraged the less privileged strata to resent their positions sharply. Tocqueville pointed to this problem in an exaggerated form when he suggested, "To conceive of men remaining forever unequal upon a single point, yet equal on all others, is impossible; they must come in the end to be equal upon all."[40] (Equality in this sense does not mean equality of condition but rather universalistic treatment in all sectors.)

The retention of pre-industrial values within French capitalism did not mean, of course, that all of French industry adhered to them. Within large-scale industry as within government, the corollaries of bureaucratization and rationalization emerged: stable definition of rights and duties, systematic universalistic ordering of authority relationships, publicity of decisions, the appearance of personnel experts or specialists in labor relations as a consequence of the division of labor.

The picture of a relatively stagnant France with "stalemate" politics, a reluctance to take advantage of economic opportunities, and a low birth rate, which was accurate enough before World War II, has changed drastically since then. The European economic miracle—great and rapid economic growth and a sharp increase in the consumption of mass-produced items—has affected France as much as any country. The net reproduction birth rate, which stood below 100 (the rate at which a population reproduces itself) all during the interwar years, has

hovered around 125 since 1946.[41] A number of observers of the
French scene have argued that "the combination of the 'new
men and new attitudes' inherited from the war period has made
French society much less different from the societies of other
industrial nations."

In the civil service, in business, in professional organizations, even
in the military forces, new groups of "technocrats" appear—men who
specialize in the management of a highly industrialized and bureaucratic society, men who earn high incomes without necessarily own-
ing much capital. . . .
Within the business world, a kind of managerial revolution has
led to a new conception of profits, in which management and ownership are less tightly fused and in which the firm's power counts more
than the owner's fortune.[42]

The emergence of a "modern" France would seem to be
negated by the continued strength of the Communists as a party
and union movement (CGT) among the industrial workers,
and the highly unstable political system. It may be argued,
however, that the current instabilities of the political system now
reflect the tensions of rapid change superimposed on a polity
whose political leadership has a traditional bent toward uncom-
promising rhetoric. The Communists have retained most of the
electoral strength which they secured in the late 1930's and mid-
1940's. They have not gained new votes—in fact, they have lost
a large proportion of their party and trade-union membership.
But if the majority of French workers still vote Communist,
various opinion and factory studies suggest a relatively low level
of class alienation among the workers. On the "right," the principal version of anti-democratic extremism—the Poujadist movement—secured almost all of its backing from the declining
middle-class strata, often in regions that were being economically
impoverished. That is, those who found their relative or absolute
economic and social position worsening as a result of changes
in French society were attracted to a politics that was "against
the system." The tensions over the Algerian War similarly
involved efforts to resist inherent "modernizing" tendencies. In
a real sense, the Gaullist fifth republic is engaged in an effort
to bring France's polity and values into line with the changing
reality of its class and economic structures. But political and

organizational loyalties do not disappear quickly, and consequently the political system, in which conflicts over these values are acted out, seems much more resistant to change than are other institutions.

The way in which historic tensions are maintained may be seen most clearly by examining the sources of the perpetuation of value differences between those white-collar workers who are employed in the bureaucracy of industry and those employed by government. In France, it has not been possible to speak of the "white-collar worker" as such; rather, there are the sharply differing backgrounds of the *employé* (private employee) and the *fonctionnaire* (civil servant). As the French sociologist Michel Crozier has described the situation in his country.

> We meet two opposite types of participation and integration in society: one type which can be described as paternalistic and which is present among traditional white-collar workers (bank employees, insurance employees, and those employed in industry), and an egalitarian type, present in the world of the lower civil servants. . . . The same basic psychological situation has produced two role types, and with these two roles, two different concepts of society, two sets of religious attitudes, two approaches to politics. These differences have tended to decline since the second World War, but there are still two different worlds which are determined in one case by channels of social mobility through the lay and anti-clerical sector of the society, and in the other through paternalistic and even confessional methods of entrance.[43]

These two non-manual strata are recruited from different sectors of French society. Private industry tends to secure its employees from the graduates of the Catholic schools, often on the basis of personal recommendations and "many private firms examine carefully the family origins . . . of prospective employees." The Civil Service on the other hand is recruited almost exclusively from state schools whose faculties are overwhelmingly on the left politically. Its recruitment procedures and operation emphasize rigorous selection criteria, particularly formal academic achievement. These differences in the operation and recruitment of the principal employers of non-manual labor deeply affect French trade-union and political life, since the Catholic trade-union federation (CFTC) and the liberal Catholic party (MRP) have their principal base of support in the white-collar workers employed in private industry, while the socialist influenced union federation (*Force Ouvrière*) and the Socialist party (SFIO) have their strongest support among the lower echelons of civil-service workers.

The political consequences of these differences are known: the inability of the parties of the Center, of the Third Force, to overcome their differences and to form any permanent unity. These differences support and are in turn nourished by the opposition of the socialist FO and the Catholic CFTC unions, a conflict based in the last analysis on the essential incompatibility between the religious mentality of the old Federation of White-Collar workers, the base of the CFTC, and the lay mentality of the federations of Civil Servants in the FO.[44]

Thus France remains unstable politically. It may currently be in the final process of cultural "modernization," but historic institutional commitments still prevent the emergence of a fully modern domestic politics, one in which the basic internal issues revolve around an interest struggle for the division of national income within a welfare state. Rather, issues concerning the legitimacy of various institutions, the role of the religious and the secular school, and the structure of authority still divide the nation. Historically, the resistance of the French ascriptive and particularistic "right" to accepting changes in power relations within industry, to the enactment of social legislation and especially to legitimating (i.e., morally accepting) unions was in large measure responsible for the fact that the French workers, though possessors of equal suffrage before workers elsewhere in Europe, remain alienated from the polity.[45] Conversely, to the extent that the workers have supported extremist movements, anarcho-syndicalism and Communism, the conservative strata have been enabled to feel morally justified in their refusal to share power. To break through this vicious cycle of extremism and counter-extremism is not an easy task, even though the cleavages in basic values may be ending.

The difficulties of the German polity stem from sources different from those of the French. While France has encouraged participation by the lower classes in the political arena but denied them rights in industry, the German system sought to resolve the problem of the incorporation of the working-class into the larger society by giving them rights and protection within industry but limiting their access to the polity. Until 1918 at least, the German aristocratic classes successfully maintained ascriptive and particularistic values in the noneconomic areas of life, while modifying values and behavior in the direction of achievement and universalism—but not equalitarianism—in the economic order. That is, the upper classes permitted and sometimes even encouraged the working class to improve its economic position through higher wages, social legislation, and trade unions. They were not willing, however, to accede to achievement criteria in the status and political orders. Men and organizations were still judged and rejected according to their social origins. In this ascriptively oriented status system, therefore, political movements emerged on the basis of distinct status or class lines buttressed by class organization in industry. These political groupings, however, could never gain a secure foothold in the political system.

Concretely, the Prussian aristocracy and the Wilhelmine monarchy, while sympathetic to the objectives of the unions in industry, first attempted to suppress the Socialists as a party between 1878 and 1890 and refused to accept a democratic electoral system in Prussia, the main state of the Reich, until the overthrow of the monarchy in 1918. This refusal to allow the workers' political representatives a share in political power forced the socialist movement to maintain a revolutionary ideological posture which was at complete variance with its social position and aspirations. The workers' movement wanted not to destroy the state, but to be admitted to it, to become part of the apparatus of support. In southern Germany, where ascriptive status lines were much less rigid than in Prussia and where the conservative classes admitted the workers' political movements into the body politic, the socialist parties quickly developed a moderate, reformist, and pragmatic ideology. In these states, the revisionist doctrines of Eduard Bernstein had their earliest and strongest supporters; in some states, the Social Democrats supported cooperation with nonsocialist parties, thereby reducing the emphasis on class warfare.[46] In Weimar Germany, the Social Democratic Party developed into an extremely moderate organization and, until the outbreak of the Great Depression and the rise of Nazism absorbed most of the old left socialist and Communist electoral strength.

Many conservative groups, particularly those which had been especially involved in the status system of the old empire— such groups as the landed aristocracy, the teachers, the professional officers, and much of the civil service—never accepted the Weimar Republic and its universalistic norms.[47] The middle classes seem to have wavered between an initial enthusiasm at the proclamation of a political system incorporating the universalistic values that they had long supported and a reaction against the challenge to the privileges, and the deference they received from lower strata. The support that both the old and new middle classes gave to Nazism in the early 1930's may be linked, as it has been by many observers, to the strong emphasis in German values on ascription and elitism. Faced with a dire economic threat to their status (the Depression affected Germany more severely than any other industrial nation), the middle classes turned to the Nazis, who promised a National Socialism which would restore prosperity and preserve the values of the *Stande-Staat* (strong respect for hierarchical rankings).

In distinguishing between the operation of the pattern-variables in the economic, political, and social orders, I have assumed that the economic order is more likely than the others, in the context of industrialization, to require the application of universalistic, specific, and achievement criteria. Employers are forced to deal with workers in terms of these values, and workers, in turn, are constrained to secure a stable, universalistic definition of their rights in industry. The demand for universalistic behavior in the factory is a prime demand of workers in modern society. The demand for universalistic treatment in the political sphere occurs often as part of the struggle in the economic order. Consequently, it may be suggested that satisfaction or dissatisfaction with rights in the economic order is more important for workers than access to the political order. On the other hand, the middle and upper classes tend to be more oriented toward maintaining their status, toward seeking their privileged position in status rather than in economic terms, that is, toward enforcing the norms inherent in elitism. Hence, a working class which has made gains in the economic order is likely to be relatively satisfied, while middle and upper classes which feel threatened in their status position are more prone to react aggressively. It may be argued that in Weimar Germany the majority of the workers were relatively moderate politically because they had secured access to the economic and political orders, while traditional conservative groupings and the middle classes were disposed to accept militant politics in a crisis because their value orientations of elitism and ascription led them to perceive such gains on the part of the workers as a threat to their over-all status position and to their sense of "the way things ought to be."

Harry Eckstein argues that the instability of the Weimar Republic was a result of the strains between the authoritarian norms that characterized all nongovernmental institutions and the democratic patterns of the political system.

> The German governmental pattern was . . . one-sidedly democratic, at any rate if we confine analysis to the level of parliamentary representation and decision-making. . . . On the other hand, social life, including life in parties and political interest groups, was highly authoritarian. . . . Not only were society and polity to some degree incongruent; they existed in unprecedented contradiction with one another. . . .
>
> This unalleviated democracy (pure proportional representation, strong detailed bill of rights) was superimposed upon a society pervaded by authoritarian relationships and obsessed with authoritarianism. . . . German family life, German schools, and German business firms were all exceedingly authoritarian. German families were dominated, more often than not, by tyrannical husbands and fathers, German schools by tyrannical teachers, German firms by tyrannical bosses.[48]

Eckstein does not contend that the Germans as individuals always preferred authoritarian politics. Rather, he points to the fact that from the first universal suffrage elections in pre-World War I Imperial Germany down to 1928, liberal, center, and socialist parties secured between 80 and 90 per cent of the vote, and that antidemocratic pre-Nazi parties were always in a small minority. He seems to suggest that a more authoritarian "democratic" system, like that of Imperial Germany "which the great majority did not seem to want" consciously, would have provided a "proper base" for a stable regime. It might be argued, in line with the reasoning behind both my own and Eckstein's analyses, that Germany could have best evolved into a stable constitutional democracy through the gradual growth of a system that retained elitist and monarchical forms and strong executive power in the hands of a powerful Chancellor. The symbolic retention of legitimate power in the hands of a Kaiser conceivably might have preserved the allegiance of the middle and upper classes to a democratic political system.

Such arguments are impossible to prove, but it may be suggested that the political history of Sweden illustrates "what might have been" in Germany. In many ways, pre-World War I Swedish social structure resembled that of Germany. The Swedish privileged classes strongly resisted giving universal suffrage, and adult suffrage was only adopted in 1909 for the lower house and in 1921 for the upper one.[49] Swedish social life contained many of the same authoritarian patterns that characterized Germany, and Sweden as a nation strongly looked to Germany for intellectual and cultural leadership. But Sweden was both small and geographically isolated from European wars; it escaped the tensions resulting from the overthrow of a monarchy after military defeat. Its radical Socialist Party became moderate and its extreme conservatives and upper class came to accept the right of the workers to participate in, and ultimately even to dominate, the polity. But even today, the values of the Swedish status system contain strong elements of ascription-elitism, particularism, and diffuseness.

Much of the elitist quality of Swedish life has gradually declined under the impact of thirty years of Socialist government. The phenomenon of political rule by a party, many of whose leaders began life as workers, which has successfully countered the dire predictions of the inability of a workers' party to govern, has undoubtedly weakened the value orientations which sustained elitism. In many ways, Sweden has moved towards egalitarianism, although various manifestations of elitism remain. Swedish politics remain highly particularistic, and the syndrome of particularism and diffuseness remains important in other spheres. For example, Swedish telephone books still list individuals alphabetically *within* occupational groups. So to look up a Swede in the phone book, you must know his occupation. He is still a doctor, printer, or carpenter before he is a person.

To a considerable extent the egalitarian changes reflect conscious efforts on the part of the governing Socialists. The Swedish educational system has been changing from one similar to that of Britain and other parts of Europe, with their class-stratified divisions of secondary schools—modern, technical, and grammar— to "single-type comprehensive schools, into which all the existing schools are to be incorporated. . . . The eventual aim is a 9 year school, with differentiation beginning in a very mild form in the 6th year, and only taking shape in 3 different 9th classes [at age 16] (preparation for higher education; general finishing class with mainly theoretical bent; and preparatory vocational training with some theoretical courses)."[50]

C. A. R. Crosland, who sees class values in his own England as little changed in spite of the great structural reforms introduced by the Labour government of 1945-51, twenty years of full employment, and the welfare state, has pointed to at least one of the major conditions required for a political impact on class values in a democracy:

Political power can also have an influence on class attitudes, but in a democracy only, I think, *if one party remains in office for a long time.* . . .
Thus in Britain, before the war, when Conservative Governments seemed the natural thing, collective feelings of superiority and inferiority were intensified by the belief that political power was an additional, semi-permanent attribute of a class which already appeared to possess all the other attributes of a ruling class. Conversely in Sweden, the fact that a Socialist Government now seems the natural order of things has a profound effect in weakening collective class feelings, since at least the attribute of political power is differently located from the other attributes of the "upper class."
It creates, in other words, a definite "scatter," and prevents a concentration of "top-class attributes." . . . Thus political power counterbalances the influence of other class determinants, and hence diminishes the likelihood of strong, coagulated class feelings. But this will occur only if the period of one-party rule is sufficiently prolonged to cause a definite adjustment in psychological attitudes.[51]

Evidence from a Swedish survey study suggests that long tenure in office by a workers' party may modify the traditional assumptions concerning the inter-relationship of different indicators of high position in the manner suggested by Crosland. Those interviewed were asked, "Which class do you think is the most influential in our society today?" The responses indicate that Swedes who perceive their status as "working class" are more likely to believe that their class is the most influential one than "middle-class" individuals believe is the case with the middle class. And to explain this phenomenon of consensus concerning the greater power of the working class, Torgny Segerstedt comments: "Perhaps I ought to remind you that we have had a Labour government in office in Sweden for more than 20 years."[52]

To return to Germany briefly, it would appear that major changes in its value system have been occurring since the end of the last war, changes that are weakening ascriptive values. In part, these may result from the fact that two of the major bulwarks of ascriptive and particularistic values in the society no longer exist or have been weakened: the army and the Prussian aristocracy. The major regions of Germany previously dominated by these values (most of old Prussia) are now either part of Russia, Poland or Communist East Germany. What is now West Germany is largely composed of areas which even before World War I were willing to admit the working-class as a *Stand* or status group into the political club. In addition, the upheavals of Nazism and World War II have upset the old German class structure and have reduced the significance of ascriptive elements.

It should be noted, however, that ascriptive and, even more significantly, elitist values in Germany are far from dead. To some extent, the society still emphasizes social origins as a crucial determinant of status, and clearly men are still viewed diffusely in terms of status position, that is, professors, engineers, industrialists and so forth are members of the elite. However, similar treatment for all groups (universalism) is now much more dominant, and, while workers remain an inferior status-group, they are part of the body politic and no longer outside it. The workers have achieved their long-term objective of being able to take part as a class in the political structure of Germany. They have, however, not secured an end to diffuse emphasis on class (elitism) and ascription. On the level of formal system analysis, the current West German system seems to approximate that of Great Britain or Sweden. There is also much more authoritarianism or perhaps, more accurately, executive power

in Bonn than there was in the Weimar Republic. Chancellor
Adenauer plays a role much more comparable to that of Bismarck
in the Imperial system than to any of the Weimar Chancellors,
and elections have been fought to a considerable degree as con-
tests for the Chancellorship.[53] Whether Germany actually maintains itself as a stable democracy, only time will tell. Particularly
crucial will be the resolution of the challenge to the values of
the privileged classes when the working-class-based Social Democrats actually move toward national office.[54]

This effort to relate value-patterns to the conditions of the
polity would seem to indicate that the requisites for a stable
democracy are well met where achievement-universalism are
dominant values in both the political and economic subsystem.
These values are congruent with the requirements of consensual
decision-making in complex pluralistic societies and with the requirements of dynamic industrial economy. (Pluralism and industrialism are seen as endemic aspects of modern democratic
political systems.) A democratic polity and industrial economy
marked by these values is characterized by conflict among class-
determined solidary groupings, but such conflict both in polity
and economy will largely involve "collective-bargaining" issues,
questions of the relative distribution of national income, and
ways of using resources to maximize return. Intense ideological
issues and severe class-conflict will be de-emphasized.

Where the achievement-universalism pattern is absent in the
political or economic spheres of modern industrial society, sharp
ideological conflict occurs and the polity is unstable. The existence of a democratic political system in which diverse political
groupings have access to political decisions does not seem to
reduce this tension; rather it contributes to it. The application of
the universalistic norms inherent in modern industry to labor-
mangement relations, without their application to the political
system, does not make for greater stability.

### Equalitarianism-Elitism in the Status Hierarchy

While the stability of a democracy demands that universalism
and achievement values be dominant in both the economic and

political spheres, it does not require them to be dominant in the status hierarchies. That is, the status hierarchy may be elitist, as it is in Britain, or equalitarian, as it is in the United States. Both of these nations are stable democracies nevertheless.

These differences do have their effects, however, on the functioning of the political system, particularly in the viability of the "rules of the game," and in such matters as the tolerance of opposition and of nonconformity, and in respect for the due process procedures of the law.

Although popular agreement about the importance of such rules would seem an important requisite for their effectiveness, the empirical data do not clearly sustain this expectation. The less educated and the lower strata in most countries do not accept the need for tolerance of what they consider to be "error" or "wickedness"—opposition to what is "clearly right."[55] Conversely, the "rules of the game" are most respected where they are most significant—among the various politically relevant and involved elites. Perhaps the highest degree of tolerance for political deviance is found, therefore, in democratic systems that are most strongly characterized by the values of elitism and diffuseness. Diffuse elitism of the variety that exists in most of the democratic monarchies of Europe tends to place a buffer between the elites and the population. The generalized deference the latter give to the former means that even if the bulk of the electorate do not understand or support the "rules," they accept the leadership of those who do. It is deferential respect for the elite rather than tolerant popular opinion that underlies the vaunted freedom of dissent in countries like Britain and Sweden. The ability of countries to operate with an unwritten constitution, which places no formal restrictions on parliamentary violations of civil liberties, is in considerable measure made possible by the emphasis on diffuseness and elitism in the system.[56] In these societies, the elites, whether those of the intellect, of business, of politics, or of mass organizations, are both protected and controlled by their membership in the "club."

The seemingly lesser respect for civil liberties and minority rights in more equalitarian democracies such as the United States and Australia may be viewed as the consequence of a social system in which elite status is more specific, so that contending elites do not receive diffuse respect and have less sense of the need to conform to an appropriate set of rules in conflicts with each other. They do not see themselves as part of the same club, as within an Establishment. Hence disagreement about the *rules*, as well as over policies, are thrown to the broader public for settlement. This system entails appealing in some degree to a mass electorate to shape or adhere to rules whose utility, in large part, they cannot be expected to understand; appreciation of the necessity for such rules often involves a long-term socialization to the nature of the political and juridical process, which is secured primarily through education or participation. To attempt to redefine or ignore the rules of the democratic game is an appropriate tactic for counter-elites who regard these rules as illegitimate and perhaps are expressly concerned with undermining them.

Thus, though civil liberties will be stronger in elitist democracies than in equalitarian ones, the latter may be regarded as more "democratic" in the sense that the electorate has more access to power over the elite.

Elitism in the status hierarchy has its dysfunctions as well as its functions, however.[57] Such disintegrative elements derive from the assumption that a system of differential status rankings requires a large proportion of the population to accept a negative conception of its own worth compared to those in more privileged positions. To be socially defined as being low, according to a system of values which one respects must mean that, to some degree, low status is experienced as "punishment" in a psychological sense. This sense of deprivation or punishment is often manifested by "self-hatred," a phenomenon which has often been deplored when perceived as characteristic of inferior ascriptive racial or ethnic status. The principal content of ethnic "self-hatred" occurs among lower status majority group members as well: rejection of behavior patterns associated with one's own group as uncouth, negative judgments of the value of occupational roles characteristic of the group, and the desire to leave one's group and "pass" into a dominant group. It is universally recognized that such feelings on the part of a Negro or a Jew are indicators of psychic self-punishment, yet the same reactions among the lower class are often not perceived in the same way. To a considerable degree, the social mechanisms which operate to legitimate an existing distribution of status inequality succeed in repressing such discontent, sometimes by structuring perceptions so that individuals may view themselves as higher and therefore "better" than others or by creating bonds of vicarious identification with those in higher positions. The latter mechanism is particularly prevalent in systems that emphasize ascriptive and elitist values. It is doubtful, however, that such mechanisms alone are a sufficient solution to the problem of social rejection and psychological self-punishment inherent in low status.

There are different adaptive mechanisms which have emerged among various strata and individuals to reconcile low status individuals to their position and thus contribute to the stability and legitimacy of the larger system. The three most common, which may be adduced from analyses of the subject, are:

*Religion*—Belief in a religion with a transvaluational theology, one which emphasizes the possibility or even the probability that the poor on earth will enjoy higher status in heaven or in a reincarnation, operates to adjust them to their station and motivates those in low positions to carry out their role requirements. Religious movements may constitute a major element in secular political protest, as is true today among American Negroes. Lower-class churches and their ministers may directly or indirectly help form class-based political movements. Of course, sectarian groupings have often expressed the hostility of the depressed strata to the privileged order and its religion. Such forms of institutionalized protest, like radical political movements, themselves serve as means of defining lower status in forms that are palatable to those in low positions.

*Social Mobility*—The belief that achievement is possible and that virtue will be rewarded by success for one's self or one's children serves stabilizing functions comparable to those of religion.

*Political Action*—Participation in or support for political movements that aim to raise the position of depressed groups and which contain in their ideologies transvaluational elements— the assumption that the lower strata are morally better than the upper classes—also helps to adjust the deprived groups to their situation.

Since the first three mechanisms may be regarded as functional alternatives, that is, as satisfying similar needs, it may be posited that where one or more is weak, one or both of the others will be strong. Specifically, where belief in religion or achievement is weak, the lower strata should be especially receptive to radical transvaluational political or economic appeals.[58] Social systems undergoing major institutional changes that weaken faith in traditional religion—and do not replace this lost faith with the value system of an open, achievement-oriented society— have experienced major extremist political movements. It has been argued by some that one of the factors sustaining the bases for Communist and anarchist movements in countries like Spain, France, and Italy has been the perpetuation of strong ascriptive and elitist value elements in the context of a "dechristianized" lower stratum.[59]

A strong societal emphasis on achievement and equalitarianism (which may be partially perceived as a secular transvaluational ideology), combined with strong religious belief, particularly among the lower strata, should maximize the legitimacy of the existing distribution of privilege and thus minimize the conditions for extremist protest. That is, of course, the situation in the United States. The strong emphasis in American culture on the need to "get ahead," to be successful, seems to be accompanied by powerful transvaluational religions among those who have the least access to the approved means of success.[60]

### Social Change

The relationship of value-patterns to political systems has largely been discussed here in a static framework, but implied in much of the discussion is the assumption that changes in the economy and the ways in which different societies react to these changes, play a major role in determining the interaction between values and polity.[61] While a detailed discussion of the conditions affecting the emergence of particular value-patterns is beyond the scope of this paper, some illustrative analysis seems to be in order, if only to prevent the oft-made criticism that an emphasis on the causal effects of values inherently inhibits or even prevents a concern for the analysis of social change.

THE RESPONSES TO NEW ELITES.  One problem faced by all
societies entering the stage of a modern economy is that the
legitimacy of the existing distribution of resources and privileges,
and of the political decision-making process itself, comes under
severe tension, because new criteria for high position are emerging.
A new economic class achieves high position using methods that
have been traditionally defined by the elite and the value system
as inappropriate or illegitimate. The social system, in turn, may
adjust by incorporating those fulfilling the new achievement
criteria into the ascriptive elites or by attempting to insulate
the old ascriptive elites from the new ones (e.g., by reserving
for the old elite certain privileged positions, often in government, the military, religion, and education). The first course
maintains the integrity (unity) of high status strata, and aug-
ments the tendency of the lowly to accept the existing structure
of authority as legitimate. The "insulative" course precipitates
a reactionary-radical polarization, thereby inhibiting integration,
especially as this approach is more readily rationalized in un-
compromisable, absolute value terms—such as the "natural" superiority of the nobility, or the "natural" enmity of capitalist
and worker—rather than in more relativistic and issue-oriented
terms, such as how the pie shall be divided.

The "incorporative" response and its effects are demonstrated
by the bulk of British parliamentary history. The articulate leadership of the *bourgeoisie*, and later of labor, were given access
to political decision-making and were then incorporated into the
ranks of the Whig party and the Liberal and Labour parties
respectively. Not only did the old ascriptive elites admit individuals of achieved position into the formal institutional structure, but they acculturated the newcomers to many of the old
ascriptive orientations. Hence the House of Lords has been
able to withstand the influx of *bourgeoisie* and labor into the
political process, and one is presented with the interesting phenomenon of the Labour Peer.

France provides an example of the "insulative" response
and its effects. The *ancien régime* provided virtually no institutional access for the rising bourgeoisie to political decision-
making, much less incorporation into the ranks of the decision-makers. A potent, hostile counter-elite was thus formed

which, in collusion with disaffected elements of the nobility, provided the leadership for the Revolution of 1789. This carnage did not, however, mark the end of the insulative response. Rather, the antagonistic role into which the aristocracy was cast produced a lasting counter-elite of the right. Moreover, the bourgeoisie themselves adopted an insulative attitude toward aspiring labor elites. There were strong disintegrative results because of this double insulative response. Largely, this was due to its having occurred in a context of early industrialization (not, of course, an historical accident, both bourgeoisie and labor being part of the industrialization process). The achievement values had begun to corrode the ascriptive ones without the material benefits of mature industrialization to cushion the impact. In such an historical pattern, the rising bourgeoisie, by virtue of its exclusion, did not absorb the *noblesse oblige* ethic of the traditional aristocracies. It was thus prone not to feel responsible for the welfare of the lower orders—just at a time when those orders were undergoing severe material deprivation and social dislocation; no particularistic protection was provided, but particularistic loyalty was demanded. The lower class counter-elites were thus provided with followers who were increasingly alienated from the system. In this manner, France arrived at the difficult position of having counter-elites of both the left and the right, each with a considerable following in the electorate and neither according legitimacy to the political process as such.

The German case offers a different variant of the failure to develop an "integrated" response and is both similar to and different from Britain and France. A strong business class arose, but it was unable to reach the pinnacle of a society in which the monarchy and nobility continued to hold power and resisted accepting it as a partner in government or as an equal in status. As Roy Lewis and Rosemary Stewart described the situation:

The growth of capitalism in Germany was affected, to a far greater extent than in Britain or France, by a rigid structure of class and status. . . .
Capitalism, technology and business came to Germany in various ways. But the structure of a society based on status—and still divided

between Catholic and Protestant states—was so strong that it had to shape itself largely to the form of the society. . . .

Bismarck made the mold into which German business was poured in the last half of the nineteenth century. He broke the out-of-date medievalism of the *Junker* (land-owning) squires, but maintained the autocracy of their king (and later, emperor). . . . However, top businessmen did not find themselves, as in England, at the apex of society. Status remained decisive, and the army retained its caste privileges. The successful businessman might in time be allowed to put "von" in front of his name, but he could not aspire to become a full part of the nobility; and the purchase of a great estate did not (as, again, it did in England) provide his children with a springboard into the ruling circles.[62]

The German upper class, as represented by Bismarck and the Kaiser, sought to make the workers as a class loyal to the polity by "protecting" them against the *bourgeoisie* through a variety of social welfare legislation. The aristocracy, in fact, saw the workers as potential allies against the power and status claims of the "vulgar" business classes and perceived its actions on behalf of the workers as reflecting the morality of *noblesse oblige*, of the responsibility of those born to rule to protect their inferiors. In a real sense, Bismarck and Disraeli reflected similar reactions by political spokesmen of comparable strata. The Germans differed from the British, however, and resembled the French in that they refused to "incorporate" the leaders of the new classes, in particular the workers, into the consensual process. As indicated earlier, they gave the workers social legislation and even permitted them trade unions; they attempted to deny them the legal right to their own party (the anti-Socialist laws) and manhood suffrage (the three-chamber system of Prussia). The middle classes, too, were barred from equal participation in the polity, particularly in policy positions.

To account adequately for the differing ways in which the various nations with ascriptive traditions met the tensions of entering a commercial and industrial society would require reference to many unique historical factors.[63] Much of the difference between northern and southern Europe is related to the success or failure of the Protestant Reformation. Britain's position as an island was important because, among other things, it eased the problem of national unification and national defense and reduced the role of the military as a major factor in its economic and political development. The historic timing with which different nations entered the industrial age or unified politically also cannot be ignored. On the level of the specific variables with which this paper has been concerned, however, one factor would seem to stand out, and that is the cluster of variables which produced "open" or "closed" aristocracies. In seeking to account for the differences in the political adaptation of Britain and France to the tensions occasioned by modernization, Tocqueville found the key precisely in the variations between British and continental upper classes. As he put it:

> I have always been surprised that a circumstance that renders England so different from all other modern nations and which alone explains the peculiarities of her laws, history, and traditions has not received more attention. . . .
> England was the only country in which the caste system had been totally abolished, not merely modified. Nobility and commoners joined forces in business enterprises, entered the same professions, and —what is still more significant—intermarried. The daughter of the greatest lord in the land could marry a "new" man without the least compunction. . . .
> The reason why the English middle class, far from being actively hostile to the aristocracy, inclined to fraternize with it was not so much that the aristocracy kept open house as that its barriers were ill defined; not so much that entrance into it was easy as that you never knew when you had got there. The result was that everyone who hovered on its outskirts nursed the agreeable illusion that he belonged to it and joined forces with it in the hope of acquiring prestige or some practical advantage under its aegis.[64]

The British aristocracy obviously was not inherently more sophisticated than the French or German, but its *structural position* made it more adaptive to a changing class structure, to the creation of new elite positions.[65] This process has been well summarized by Robert Ulich in a discussion of Britain as she entered the modern age:

> Despite terrific social contrasts between the upper and middle classes on the one hand and the poor on the other, there was no exclusive ruling caste as in France up to 1789 and again in the latter periods of reaction, and as in Germany up to the twentieth century. Greater mobility . . . was secured by the English custom of succession, or primogeniture, according to which the title of the parent is trans-

mitted only to the oldest son of a noble family, while the other children become commoners. In contrast, in France and Germany every descendant of a nobleman, whether male or female, inherits the title. Until the modern democratic revolutions the mere name made the bearer a privileged person. Intermarriage with commoners meant degradation; even scholarship could only be a hobby. Only through some middleman could the nobleman go into business . . . this aloofness from modern occupations involved a kind of glorified poverty. There remained nothing but to fight desperately for the monopoly of officers' positions in the army and the higher offices of the civil and diplomatic service. . . .[66]

The fact that most of those who had a claim to aristocratic position were secure in their status, while in France and Germany many were relatively impoverished, meant that in Britain the aristocrats were relatively uninhibited about associating with "commoners." In contrast, the French and German aristocrats sought to protect what was their sole claim to high position, namely their aristocratic title, by refusing to admit achievers, "new men," to any semblance of equality. Those with claims to ancient titles insisted on their status prerogatives against new titles. In England, the aristocracy "without condescension laid value on the friendship of great men of whatever social origin.[67]

Unencumbered by a title and seeking ways to regain a firm claim to high status, the "younger sons" of British aristocracy entered the new occupations and married with the new families much more rapidly than their continental brothers. Since many of the "new men" and their families often had family connections with the aristocracy, the problem of "integrating" the new and old elites was nowhere near as difficult as in countries where the aristocracy sought to differentiate itself as much as possible from corrupting contact with the "vulgar" money-makers.

Nor was it [in England], in contrast to Germany, considered a sort of high treason—at least after the middle of the nineteenth century— if a member of the privileged group joined the masses in their struggle for better conditions. Leftists have come from all groups of English society including graduates from Eton; they have provided an organic exchange of ideas, however controversial; and they have supplied labor with men whose background and experience gave them that sense of social security, grace, and freedom that political leaders in other countries, having come from the working class, so often lacked.[68]

As Robert Michels once pointed out, the presence of upper-class leaders in a working-class party serves to reduce the moral hostility to it among the conservative groups. To the extent that the social system permits a left party to recruit leaders from the existing elite, to that extent is the task of its becoming an accepted part of the polity eased. It is noteworthy that, unlike the British Labour Party, the German Socialists recruited few, if any, leaders from the old upper classes.

EFFECTIVENESS AS THE BASIS OF LEGITIMACY. The discussion on change and stability has, up to now, focused on the way in which ascriptive values have been handled in establishing who should have the right to rule in a political democracy. There is, however, an alternative basis for gaining support for a new system: effectiveness, or demonstrated and successful achievement. As a sole foundation for legitimacy, it is rather tenuous; it may almost be said to be untenable. Any system of government is likely to become involved in crises; major groupings will become alienated because of opposition to specific policies. Consequently, any government which persists for any reasonable length of time must have or develop ascriptive grounds for support, that is, a sense of traditional legitimacy. Where a polity does not have such legitimacy, as in the case of new states or post-revolutionary governments, it is inherently unstable. If the basic value pattern of the society includes a strong emphasis on ascription, the government will find it difficult to rule by any means except force. Where the value pattern stresses achievement, however, the political system, like other institutions, will be in a better position. The success of the American republic in establishing a post-revolutionary democratic legitimacy may be related to the strength of achievement values in the society.

These analyses suggest that the persistence of ascriptive-particularistic norms is only compatible with democracy in societies that have retained ascriptive legitimacy for their polity—in monarchies, for example.[69] Where such traditional supports are missing, the only way to create a legitimate regime is through long-term effectiveness, that is, achievement. This is a difficult method at best. To succeed, it requires rapid change in fundamental values. A look at societies which have attempted to achieve political legitimacy while retaining strong ascriptive elements in their value systems indicates how difficult it is. (Such nations include most of Latin America, Spain, Germany, Italy, France, Turkey, and many others.)

A genuine problem for achievement or effectiveness as a basis for legitimacy arises in the contemporary "new states," almost all of which, like the Latin American republics in the early nineteenth century, lack traditional legitimacy. The problem of ascriptive and particularistic values apart, the need for effectiveness poses a real dilemma, because in contemporary times effectiveness is apt to consist of a demand for the equitable distribution of a rapidly increasing social product. The utility of effectiveness as a foundation for legitimacy may vary directly with the size of the gross national income and disparities in visible distribution of status symbols.

In the developing areas there are formidable obstacles to effectiveness as a source of legitimacy for democratic regimes: the economy is primitive and unbalanced, the bulk of the population is impoverished, capital is lacking, political experience and skills are rare, and much of the available store of political and entrepreneurial experience is distributed among individuals associated with the former colonial masters. As Weber, among many others, has pointed out, periods of rapid economic growth often engender violent class and political conflict, rather than faith in the social system.[70] To the extent, therefore, that democratic rulers who lack legitimacy are responsible for a rapid increase in the pace of economic transformation, to that extent they may also serve to undermine the capacity of the system to receive generalized support. By fostering rapid transformation, the political system sustains dislocations in such basic social relationships as the extended kinship system, mutual aid within small preindustrial communities, and traditional orientations to work and time. The problem posed for the political system, therefore, is to move toward a developed economy with its need for a greater emphasis on universalistic-achievement values, without seriously undermining the conditions for a stable and ultimately democratic polity. Facing this dilemma, which he portrayed as "rapid industrialization and Stalinism," led the Indian socialist, Jayaprakash Narayan, to urge a policy of moderate economic development and a concentration on improving social and economic conditions on the land and in the villages.

In applying these considerations to the prospects for political and economic development, in the "new" or "underdeveloped" states, it is important to recognize that the now economically developed, stable democracies were able to develop either in societies which for the most part possessed traditional legitimacy or in achievement-oriented societies like the United States—which also had widespread and relatively equitable distribution of land ownership for much of its early history. In addition, these societies did not have to counter a partly artificially (that is, politically) stimulated rising "level of expectation" that was beyond the capacity of the economy or polity. As it is clearly difficult to generate support in the new states on grounds of either ascription or achievement, the chances for stable democracy in the Western sense are slim. Communism and other forms of totalitarian rule apart, the general alternatives available are either representative charismatic domination by party or leader—pursued in countries like Mexico, Ghana, or Tunisia—or particularistic appeals to the existing ascriptive solidarities—family, village, tribe, religion, linguistic unit, or caste—an approach that is obviously dysfunctional from the standpoint of developing a consensus in new territorial political systems.[71]

## Value Differences, Absolute or Relative: The English-Speaking Democracies

In seeking to demonstrate that value analysis helps to account for systematic variations in the political and other social structures of nations, I have deliberately limited the primary scope of this paper to a discussion of the four most populous developed Western states, which varied in the extent of their polities' stability or instability. By doing so, I sought to move beyond the analysis of what seem to be the relatively rigid conceptions of the basic traits of "developed" and "underdeveloped" states that have crept into the literature of social science analysis and that imply that social change moves along a unilinear ladder of development. Rather, this paper has sought to demonstrate that there are not only "many roads to socialism," but "many roads to developed societies and polities."

In relating values to other structures, it is important to understand that a specification of value patterns cannot be made in *absolute terms* but must be perceived by *reference to the specific systems* being compared. To compare nations or societies that are highly similar in basic values may be even more fruitful analytically than to contrast those that are very different. As a final illustration of this mode of comparative inquiry, I shall briefly expand the analysis of the stable democracies to include Australia and Canada, nations that like the United States, are former colonies of Great Britain, were settled on relatively open continental frontiers, and are today continent-spanning federal states. There is general agreement that on a world-wide comparative scale these two large, predominately English-speaking states resemble the United States in stressing equalitarianism, achievement, universalism, and specificity. But if, compared to Britain and most other European countries, Canada and Australia share basic values with the United States, they differ with it also, and it is these differences that sharply illustrate the ways in which even relatively slight (when viewed on the scale of many nations) variations in value patterns help account for important differences among the stable and highly developed democracies.

The very tentative rankings that may be given to the four major, predominantly English-speaking democracies on the four pattern-variable dimensions discussed in this paper are presented in Table 1. It is obviously extremely difficult to be precise about such variations, and these rankings should be considered as at best an informed guess.

**Table 1. Tentative Estimates of Relative Rankings of the Four English-Speaking Democracies According to Strength of Certain Pattern-Variables (Rankings According to First Term in Polarity)**

|  | United States | Australia | Canada | Great Britain |
|---|---|---|---|---|
| Elitism-Equalitarianism | 3 | 4 | 2 | 1 |
| Ascription-Achievement | 4 | 2.5 | 2.5 | 1 |
| Particularism-Universalism | 4 | 2 | 3 | 1 |
| Diffuseness-Specificity | 4 | 2.5 | 2.5 | 1 |

According to my estimates, Australia differs from the United States in being slightly more equalitarian, but less achievement-oriented, universalistic, and specific. It seems, moreover, less universalistic but more equalitarian than Canada, but it is difficult to estimate the differences on the other two polarities. Canada differs from the United States on all four dimensions, while Britain in turn is much more elitist, ascriptive, particularist, and diffuse than Canada.

To demonstrate or even to argue strongly that such differences really exist would involve a considerable research program. I have drawn, however, on a considerable number of writings which have argued and given some evidence that these differences are as they are presented here and, for the time being, we must depend on such impressionistic evidence to support the discussion to follow. In this section, I shall first account for the differences by indicating the variations in the social development of these countries which presumably created and sustained structures carrying these values, and then "derive" differences in their political systems that seem related to value patterns.

The Canadian pattern seems to reflect the fact that Canada has been more conservative than the United States, that its early political history from 1776 on involved the defeat of various reformist efforts, and that consequently some of the traditionalist forces and values that declined in the United States continued in Canada. The Canadian historian, Frank Underhill, has described the situation in the following terms:

The mental climate of English Canada in its early formative years was determined by men who were fleeing from the practical application of the doctrines that all men are born equal and are endowed by their creator with certain inalienable rights amongst which are life, liberty and the pursuit of happiness. . . . In Canada we have no revolutionary tradition; and our historians, political scientists, and philosophers have assiduously tried to educate us to be proud of this fact. . . .[72]

One consequence of this varying value system is that Canadians. "are less imbued with the Horatio Alger myth and accept with less protest the facts of economic inequality and social stratification."[73] As the Canadian sociologist Kaspar Naegele put it in his excellent discussion of his society:

[T]here is *less* emphasis in Canada on equality than there is in the United States. . . . In Canada there seems to be a greater acceptance of *limitation*, of hierarchical patterns. There seems to be less optimism, less faith in the future, less willingness to risk capital or reputation. In contrast to America, Canada is a country of greater caution, reserve, and restraint.[74]

But if there is agreement that Canada lies somewhere between America and Britain on an equalitarianism continuum (although it is closer to America),[75] the generalizations about Australian values are somewhat different. The scanty available evidence, or more properly speaking, impressions, suggest that equalitarianism is stronger in Australia than in Canada or the United States but that, compared with the latter, universalism is weaker, particularly among the workers. The particularistic and equalitarian value of "mateship," the "uncritical acceptance of reciprocal obligations to provide companionship and material or ego support as required," is supposedly viewed by many Australians as contradictory to the the value of "success-ship" (achievement), although many feel that the latter value is "gradually gaining ascendency. . . ."[76] Frederick Eggleston argues that:

In Australia, there is little respect for wealth as such. . . . It is harder for an industrial magnate to enter politics than for a camel to pass through the eye of a needle. . . . The wealthy classes have never provided leaders or shown the community any guidance in political matters.[77]

A report by an Australian professor of education on the school system of his country complains that the equalitarian values and behavior patterns built into the school system prevent the emergence of any concern for leadership. Compare the comments on the British educational system cited earlier with these statements about the Sydney school system:

The almost century-old tradition of equalitarianism militates against class leadership of any kind. . . . Nowhere, thus in his education does he [the young Sydney citizen] receive inspiration and encouragement to strive for a position of leadership in the community. . . .

The general effect in secondary education here appears to have been a blurring of distinctions between different secondary schools [public and private]. . . . The tendency of the system appears to be towards the elimination of distinctions between schools and thus the elimination of characteristics, in so far as schools can provide them, distinctive of an upper class which has special knowledge, attitudes, or skills built into it by the schools.[78]

Leslie Lipson accounts for the differences between Australia (and New Zealand) and the mother country by the fact that nations which were settled "in large part by representatives of the laboring and lower middle classes could be expected to react instinctively against any whiff of the mother country's social stratification."⁷⁹ Australia was originally settled as a penal colony. As late as the 1850's, before its gold rush, the *majority* of the population consisted of convicts, ex-convicts, or the children of convicts. Many of the later "free immigrants" were people who had been involved in Chartist and other left movements in Britain.⁸⁰ It is also important to note that "Australia is one of the very few countries whose whole development has taken place since the beginnings of the Industrial Revolution," and consequently it developed its national ethos and class structure in a period in which traditional and aristocratic values were under sharp attack.⁸¹ Unlike Canada, Australia did not emerge from a vanquished democratic revolution, and has no history of defeated nineteenth-century reformist movements.⁸² If anything, the reverse is true: The "left" played the major role in defining political and social institutions in the periods in which national identity was established.⁸³

In a certain sense, the differences in outlook between Canada and Australia are reflections of the need of each country to dissociate from the major power that has had the most direct cultural and economic influence on it. Canadians, as the eminent elder statesmen of Canadian historians, Frank Underhill, put it recently in a public lecture, are the world's oldest and continuing "anti-Americans." Canadians have always felt their sense of nationality threatened by the United States, physically in earlier days, and culturally and economically in more recent years. Canadians have found it necessary to define why they are not and should not become Americans, and they have done so by disparaging various elements in American life, mainly those which seem to be outgrowths of mass democracy and excessive emphasis on equalitarianism.⁸⁴ Australian nationalism, on the other hand, has inspired efforts to dissociate itself from Britain, first politically and later in terms of societal values.⁸⁵ Britain has been perceived as the stronghold of rigid social inequality. Conversely, the United States and various American equalitarian patterns have been used

*Democracy and the Social System* [ 309 ]

as models to be emulated, particularly in the nineteenth century.[86]
Some quantitative indicators of the value differences among
the four major English-speaking nations, particularly in their
achievement values, may be deduced from variations in numbers securing higher education. In the United States, strong
and successful efforts to extend the opportunities to attend colleges and universities have to some considerable degree reflected
the pressures on those in lower-status positions to secure means

Table 2. **Students Enrolled in Institutions of Higher Learning
as Per Cent of Age Group 20-24 by Country,
about 1956**

| Country | Per Cent of 20-24 Total Population |
|---|---|
| United States | 27.2 |
| Australia | 12.05† |
| Canada | 8.0 |
| England and Wales | 3.7† |
| Scotland | 5.1† |
| Philippines | 14.5 |
| Jamaica | .7 |
| Puerto Rico | 11.9 |
| Western Europe | 4.5 |
| Denmark | 6.6 |
| France | 5.8 |
| Germany (West) | 4.1 |
| U.S.S.R. | 11.1 |

Source: The educational data for the first eight countries and the U.S.S.R. are calculated
from materials in UNESCO, *Basic Facts and Figures, 1958* (Paris: 1959), and *Demographic Year-
book 1960* (New York: Statistical Office of the United Nations, 1960). The data for the western
European countries other than Britain are taken from J. F. Dewhurst, *et al.*, *Europe's Needs and
Resources* (New York: Twentieth Century Fund, 1961), p. 315.
† The proportion of Britons and Australians attending institutions of higher education is
somewhat higher than the figures in the table, which include those in universities and teachers'
colleges only. Both countries have systems of technical colleges, most of which are designed
for vocational training in technical subjects for students who have not completed high school.
Some of these "colleges" do, however, give university level education in engineering and scientific subjects. No precise estimate of the size of this group has been located, but one report
indicates that in 1957, approximately 20,000 students were taking university level work in British technical colleges. See E. J. King, *Other Schools and Ours* (London: Methuen and Co., 1958),
p. 98. If this group is added to the English total, it would raise the figure to about 4 per
cent of the age cohort in higher education. Since there are more than 200,000 students in
Australian technical colleges, the "true" Australian figure may also be somewhat higher than
that presented in the table. On the other hand, it should be noted that a higher proportion of
students in English universities are foreigners (more than 10 per cent) than is true in any other
country. The Russian figure is probably a low estimate since it is based on educational enrollment for 1956, but on a population cohort taken from a 1959 census data. It, however, includes
many part-time and correspondence students.
Since definitions of higher education and methods of training for different professions vary so
much from country to country, it is necessary to stress the fact that statistics, such as these,
though derived from official national bodies and censuses, are subject to considerable error,
particularly when used comparatively.

to succeed—and the recognition by the privileged that American values of equality and achievement require giving to all qualified the means to take part in the "race for success." Perhaps the most striking evidence of the difference between American and British values is the variation in such opportunities.

If we relate the number enrolled in institutions of higher learning to the size of the age cohort 20-24, we find that almost seven times as large a group was attending such schools in 1956-57 in the United States as in England and Wales. The number attending institutions of higher learning (post-high school) has been related to the four-year age category 20-24 since in most countries, the bulk of such students are in this age group. The best category for such analysis would probably be 18-21, but the more or less standardized census categories are 15-19 and 20-24. Since these two groups are about the same size, using the category 20-24 probably gives as good an estimate of the national variations in the proportion attending schools of higher education of the relevant age cohort as is needed.

Some proof that these differences reflect variations in values, and not simply differences in wealth or occupational structure, may be deduced from the fact that the one major former American colony, the Philippines, has a much larger proportion enrolled in colleges and universities than any country in Europe or the British Commonwealth, a phenomenon which seems to reflect successful American export of the belief that "everyone" should be given a chance at college education. A comparison of the variation in enrollment in such institutions in the two major Caribbean nations long under the hegemony of Britain and the United States, Jamaica and Puerto Rico, also suggests the ways in which the values of metropolitan nations may influence the behavior of once colonial areas. Thus, Jamaica, like many other former British colonies in Africa and Asia, has a higher education system that seems premised on the belief that only a tiny elite should receive such training; while the system in Puerto Rico, like the one in the Philippines, clearly reflects the continued impact of American assumptions concerning widespread educational opportunity. Canada, though appearing to be so similar to the United States, has apparently not accepted its commitment to spreading educational advantages as widely; it has less than one-third the United

States' proportion in colleges and universities, twice that of the English, but amazingly less than the Filipinos or Puerto Ricans.[87] Australia is closer to the United States in this respect, particularly since the percentage reported for it is probably not based on as complete an estimate of those in higher education as the North American data. The assumptions made by various observers of the Australian scene that achievement values are gaining there seem to be congruent with the evidence that a much larger proportion of Australians than Canadians is enrolled in higher learning institutions. As Tocqueville, among others, has suggested, an emphasis on equalitarianism apparently fosters competition for higher position derivative from its assumption that all should have equal chances. Whether or not enrollment in higher education directly reflects variations in achievement-orientation is a moot question. The assumption, however, that it has some bearing on these differences seems to be warranted. Some indication that these differences operate within the United Kingdom can be seen in the fact that the Scots, whose society is both more equalitarian and achievement-oriented than the English, have proportionally many more students enrolled in universities than the English, even though they are much poorer economically.

It may be argued that American and Australian equalitarianism is most clearly reflected politically in the relative strength of "populist" anti-elitist movements, through which popular passions wreak their aggression against the structure of the polity. Most recently Australia and the United States have both sustained large-scale, popularly based efforts to drive suspected Communists out of key positions in unions and politics.[88] Conversely, in Canada as in Britain, such efforts were handled in a much more discrete fashion, reflecting in some part the ability of a more unified and powerful political elite to control the system. The Canadian sociologist S. D. Clark has explained these differences as derivatives of the variations in patterns of political integration:

[In the nineteenth century] Canada maintained her separate political existence . . . only by resisting any movement on the part of her population which had the effects of weakening the controls of central political authority [and thus encouraging the possibility of American take-over]. The claims to the interior of the continent were staked not by advancing frontiersmen, acting on their own, but by advancing armies and police forces, large corporate economic enterprises and ecclesiastical organizations supported by the state. The Canadian political temper, as a result, has run sharply counter to the American. Those creeds of American political life—individual rights, local autonomy, and limitation of executive power . . . have found less strong support within the Canadian political system . . . [the] conditions of rule in Canada required the maintenance of a highly centralized political community. . . .

Critics outside [the United States] might well pause to consider not the intolerance which finds expression in McCarthyism but the tolerance which makes it possible for McCarthyism to develop. In Canada it would be hard to conceive of a state of political freedom great enough to permit the kind of attacks upon responsible leaders of the government which have been carried out in the United States. More careful examination of the American community . . . would probably reveal that, in spite of the witch hunts in that country, the people of the United States enjoy in fact a much greater degree of freedom than do the people of Canada.[89]

Forty years earlier, James Bryce also called attention to these aspects of Canadian life:

Demagogism is supposed to be a malady incident to democracies. Canada has suffered from it less than any other modern free country except Switzerland. . . . The spirit of licence, a contempt of authority, a negligence in enforcing the laws, have been so often dwelt upon as characteristic of democracies that their absence from Canada is a thing of which she may well be proud. To what shall we abscribe the strength of the Executive, the efficiency of the police, the strict application of criminal justice, the habit of obedience to the law? . . . The habit was formed under governments that were in those days monarchical in fact as well as in name and it has persisted.[90]

The greater similarity between Australia and the United States, contrasted with Canada (and to a much greater degree with Britain), in the extent to which populist explosions and threats to systematic due process occur is reflected to some degree in their attitudes toward law and order. Again a reading of largely impressionistic literature suggests that the two seemingly more equalitarian nations are more willing to tolerate lawlessness. The reason may be that the absence of traditional and hierarchically rooted social control mechanisms in these societies has weakened the pressure to conform without coercion.[91] As the Australian historian Russel Ward has put it, the deferential "respect for the squire" that underlies the acceptance of authority and informal social controls in Britain is "based on traditional obligations which were, or had been, to some extent mutual." This respect was not easily transferred to new equalitarian societies, which emphasized the universalistic *cash nexus* as a source of social relations.[92] Complaints in the United States that corrupt means of achieving success are accepted have also been expressed by Australians.[93]

One indicator of the relative strength of informal normative mechanisms of social control, compared to restrictive emphases on legal sanctions, is the extent to which given nations need lawyers. Among the English-speaking democracies, the United States and Britain stand at polar extremes. As of 1955, the United States had 241,514 lawyers "of whom approximately 190,000 were engaged in private practice. This means there was one lawyer in private practice per 868 of population ... the total English legal profession seems to number about 25,000, and those in private practice can hardly be more than 20,000, or one lawyer per 2222 population."[94] The comparable ratio for Australia, considering all men reported in private practice as practicing lawyers, is one for every 1210 persons, while in Canada the figure is about one for every 1630.[95]

The emphasis on populist values derivative from equalitarianism in the United States, contrasted with the very different value emphases in Britain, is reflected in the differential status and role of judge and jury in the two countries. The American system has stressed the notion of the judge as a neutral "umpire" in a contest decided by a jury drawn from the population, while the British have placed more stress on the positive role of the judge and less on that of the jury. In a detailed study of changes in the British conception of the jury, Joseph Hamburger points out the relationship between these differences and the larger social systems:

The main difference between England and America that led to the different status of the jury system in the estimate of public opinion arises from the differences in social and political backgrounds. America, a new country in which people had a greater freedom to form their opinions without the restraints of tradition or the influences of an established class system, allowed wider range for populistic fantasies. There were, particularly in the frontier communities, few ancient traditions or vested interests of an established society to keep people from modelling their institutions on the popular democratic beliefs that seemed to emerge almost naturally in such an atmosphere. It is not surprising, therefore, that the jury was seen, not in its English historical context, but as a microcosm of the popular will, a positive instrument of democracy. Accompanying such an image, there were hostilities to any ideas or practices that spoiled the pure, democratic character of this picture; thus, the impatience with judges who asserted more authority than an umpire needed or who insisted on the authority of a law that was not only complex but also foreign. The jury appeared to be an ideal instrument for allowing the sovereign people to form and interpret the laws that regulated their conduct.[96]

The contempt for the law in Australia is expressed by the behavior of the trade unions, which "can reduce the law, or parts of the law to impotence. Practically every strike of any size in Australia is illegal, yet the Australian record of man-days lost per head since the war is challenged only by the United States."[97] Lack of respect for the police and for law-enforcement in general, an attitude linked not only to equalitarian attitudes toward authority but also perhaps to the country's penal-colony origins, is evident in the many press reports and editorials that report incidents and complaints that bystanders "refuse to help, in fact their inclination [is] to hinder a policeman in trouble."[98] A study of Australian national character states unequivocally that "Dislike and distrust of policemen . . . has sunk deeply into the national consciousness."[99]

This judgment may be contrasted with the emphasis in the report of a detailed questionnaire-based study of English national character on the great respect for the police in that country. Geoffrey Gorer describes "the enthusiastic appreciation of the police, disclosed by this study" and comments that he does "not think the English police have ever been felt to be the enemy of sizeable non-criminal sections of the population. . . ."[100] Similarly in Canada, the respect given to the national police force, the Royal Canadian Mounted Police, far exceeds that ever given to the police in the United States, and crime statistics for English Canada indicate a much lower rate of law violation than occurs south of the border.

If all these differences among the English-speaking nations discussed so far reflect their variations on the elitism-equalitarianism polarity, the strength and policies of their labor movements seem linked to alternative attitudes toward particularism. As was noted earlier, most commentators agree that Australia differs from the United States and to a lesser degree from Canada in the extent to which its social structure is tied to strong particularistic sentiments, the emphasis on "mateship." It may be suggested that the strength of Australian unionism (two-thirds of all workers belong to unions) and the early strong development of its Labor Party (a minority Labor Government held office in 1904, and the first majority Labor Government in the world was formed in Australia in 1910) reflect political values derived from the particularistic class-conscious "mateship" sentiments of a working class almost totally transplanted from the more ascriptive and particularistic society of the British Isles to a culture without a traditional elite supported by deferential norms.[101] That is, the particularistic values have prescribed class economic and political organization; the absence of aristocracy and elitism have undercut the supports for conservative institutions and parties inherent in traditional loyalties. The combination of equalitarian and particu-laristic value patterns apparently makes for successful and early lower-class economic and political organization.[102]

Canada is seemingly less particularistic than Australia and Britain but more so than the United States. Its political party system has witnessed the rise of a number of "particularistic" third parties, the Progressives, Social Credit, and the Cooperative Com-monwealth Federation (CCF). The latter socialist party has re-cently joined with the Canadian Labor Congress to form a new, larger group, the New Democratic Party. On the level of *ex post facto* interpretation, it may be suggested that this pattern of Canadian politics, that is, the continued presence of strong particularistic "third" parties (weaker than left class-parties in Australia and Britain but stronger than any formed in the United States) is to be expected from its relative ranks with regard to the strength of the different value patterns. It can not be urged too strongly that the attempt to link the complex traits of diverse political systems with one type of explanatory variable does not mean that this factor is the most important one in the causal process. As I indicated earlier, I have related many of the same behavior traits to variations in levels of economic development and to the "rules of the game" set by constitutional processes. This paper is designed to *illustrate* the potential utility of incorporating concepts such as those employed here in a fuller and more integrated complex analysis of comparative politics.

Quantitative evidence of the greater emphasis on particularism in Australian and British politics, compared to the two North American democracies, may be found in a detailed comparative analysis of the factors associated with electoral support for different parties in these four countries. Although there is a clear correlation between class and voting in each country (the poorer or lower the status of a group, the more likely it is to be "leftist" in its voting behavior), the relationship is "consistently higher in Australia and Great Britain than in Canada and the United States."[103]

To spell out further differences among the English-speaking democracies would go far beyond the scope of this paper. The differences already cited, however, should indicate the degree to which value analysis may help to account for variations among highly similar nations. In effect, the empirical generalization suggested by this section is that similarities in basic values derivative from comparable institutionalized historical experiences in Australia and the United States have made each more like the other than either is to Canada or Britain.[104] It has been postulated that similarities in core-value patterns override the influences derivative from the fact that Australia is in closer cultural contact with Brittain than with the United States or from the fact that Canada is in relatively intimate contact with the United States and has much less direct stimulation from Britain. Australian democracy is thus sustained by mechanisms comparable to those operative in the United States, while democracy in English-speaking Canada, though very different from that in Britain, continues to differ from Australia and the United States in ways that make it more comparable to Britain than either of the other large English-speaking democracies.


### Conclusions

The systematic use of basic societal values as explanatory variables is not designed to deny or challenge the usefulness of economic or technological variables in accounting for the variation in political or other social institutions. Clearly, as many people have demonstrated, a given level of economic development is a necessary condition for many institutional patterns. For example, I tried to show in my book, *Political Man*, that the form of democratic government that rests on competing parties has become institutionalized only in the most economically developed states.

A necessary condition is not a sufficient condition, however, and complex social institutions undoubtedly have more than one necessary condition. It is clear that economic change affects the form and character of political institutions, but societal values and class relations, to take only two examples, also have effects. (In addition, of course, economic change affects values and class relations, and values and class relations in turn affect the pattern of economic development). The task ahead, therefore, is to specify other necessary conditions which shape and mold political institutions. I suggest that this specification can best be accomplished by investigating the differences among nations at roughly similar levels of industrial development. To demonstrate the causal power of economic factors by comparing the patterns of behavior in economically developed states with those in underdeveloped states is to elaborate what has become the obvious. Social systems vary greatly in their political possibilities at roughly similar levels of economic development and with comparable sets of economic class relations. It is important to move beyond this pointing out of gross variations at different levels of technical development and to specify the key sources of differences among nations at comparable levels. This problem was recognized by that sociologically most prescient of the major formulators of Marxist theory, Friedrich Engels. He pointed to many of the factors differentiating industrialized nations which concerned men like Tocqueville and Bagehot. It may be worthwhile, in conclusion, to cite a few of Engels's descriptive comments on national polities:

It seems a law of historical development that the bourgeoisie can in no European country get hold of political power—at least for any length of time—in the same exclusive way in which the feudal aristocracy kept hold of it during the Middle Ages. Even in France, where feudalism was completely extinguished, the bourgeoisie as a whole has held full possession of the Government for very short periods only.

. . . A durable reign of the bourgeoisie has been possible only in countries like America, where feudalism was unknown, and society at the very beginning started from a bourgeois basis. . . .

In England, the bourgeoisie never held undivided sway. . . . The English bourgeoisie are, up to the present day, so deeply penetrated by a sense of their social inferiority that they keep up, at their own expense and that of the nation, an ornamental caste of drones to represent the nation worthily at all State functions; and they consider themselves highly honored whenever one of themselves is found worthy of admission into this select and privileged body. . . .

Parliamentary government is a capital school for teaching respect for tradition; if the middle-class look with awe and veneration upon what Lord John Manners playfully called "our old nobility," the mass of the working-people then looked up with respect and deference to what used to be designated as "their betters," the middle-class. . . .

Furthermore, in accounting for the behavior of the French and German workers, who were more "rebellious" according to Engels (writing in 1892) than those in Britain, he placed the chief responsibility, not on variations in economic development or class relationships, but on the strength of specific values. To keep the masses in line, once they are aware of their political rights, one must rely on *"moral means."* English society was more stable than various continental polities because it had not broken with traditional religion. "Religion must be kept alive for the people—that was the only and last means to save society from ruin. Unfortunately for themselves, they [the continental bourgeoisie] did not find this out until they had done their level best to break up religion forever."[105]

For Engels, as for other Marxists, of course, "juridical, philosophical, and religious ideas are the more or less *remote* offshoots of the economical relations prevailing in a given society." It is these ideas, which he subsumed under the heading "tradition," that accounted for variations in national social systems having the same "economical relations."[106] Such efforts to specify particular value elements and their social supports, while clearly outside the formal Marxist tradition of political and social analysis, may be viewed as attempts even by Marxists to systematize comparative analyses of variations *within* major historical epochs (within feudalism, capitalism, and socialism) and to go beyond the type of *ad hoc* description found in the writings of most Marxists or for that matter of most economists concerned with "noneconomic" factors.[107]

The sociological conceptual framework of which a focus on values and the specification of pattern variables are a part is, of course, much more ambitious in its intellectual concerns. It is not designed simply to supplement economic or Marxist analysis. Rather, Talcott Parsons and other major sociological theorists see economic analysis and "interest" analysis, of which class political theory is a part, as special aspects of the larger body of social system analysis. There is · abundant room and necessity for intellectual conflict at the level of the theory of social systems. At the same time that it is appropriate to stress the utility of one or another conceptual framework for integrating all the major problems of societal organization, it may also be worthwhile to indicate for those who work on specific aspects of given social organizations that different theoretical orientations often highlight sets of variables which those working in other traditions either ignore or treat in an *ad hoc* descriptive fashion. The fact that a given larger conceptual formulation, whether of Marx, of Weber, or of Parsons, may ultimately be supplanted or preferably subsumed in some later analytic formulation—or that much of what is postulated may prove to have been in error—obviously does not mean that present large-scale theoretical formulations cannot be fruitful catalysts for intellectual breakthroughs to new insights and knowledge. Whether or not one agrees with other elements in Parsonian analysis, it seems to me that the effort to specify the value and orientation polarities within which men act is an important contribution to the intellectual equipment available for comparative analysis. To further operationalize, systematize, elaborate, or supplant the categories suggested for such analysis is a major obligation for those interested in analyses of modern societies.

## Notes

1. This paper was written as part of a larger project designed to analyze the relationships between national value systems, institutions, and patterns of behavior in a comparative and historical context. The entire study is presented in S. M. Lipset, *The First New Nation: The United States in Historical and Comparative Perspective* (New York: Basic Books, 1963). The materials presented here form a part of Part III of the book.

I am indebted to Arthur Goldberg for research assistance on this project. I would like to gratefully acknowledge my indebtedness to the Political Science Department of Yale University for providing me with a year "free" from the ordinary responsibilities of the academic world as the Ford Visiting Research Professor of Political Science and Sociology during 1960-61. The comments of Neil Smelser and David Landes on an earlier draft of the paper were especially helpful.

2. Elsewhere, I have attempted to elaborate on these different lines of inquiry. For the relationship between economic development and democracy, see my *Political Man: The Social Bases of Politics* (Garden City: Doubleday, 1960), Chapter II; for the relationship between the legal structures of political systems and their stability, see *The First New Nation*, Chapter IX; for an analysis of the role of mediating organizations in sustaining democracy see S. M. Lipset, Martin Trow, and J. S. Coleman, *Union Democracy* (Glencoe: The Free Press of Glencoe, 1956; reprinted in an Anchor Books paperback edition, 1962), Chapters 1, 4-9, 18; and S. M. Lipset, *Agrarian Socialism* (Berkeley: University of California Press, 1950), Chapter 10. For a further elaboration of the first two approaches using similar concepts see Raymond Aron, "The Situation of Democracy: Western Political Institutions in the Twentieth Century," *Daedalus*, XC (1961), 350-370, and C. W. Cassinelli, *The Politics of Freedom* (Seattle: University of Washington Press, 1961). For a comprehensive survey of the third type see William Kornhauser, *The Politics of Mass Society* (New York: The Free Press of Glencoe, 1959).

3. An excellent discussion of the general assumptions underlying emphasis on the central value system of societies in sociological analysis may be found in Edward Shils, "Centre and Periphery," *The Logic of Personal Knowledge: Essays Presented to Michael Polanyi on His Seventieth Birthday* (London: Routledge and Kegan Paul, 1961), pp. 117-130.

Although many political analysts have attempted to relate various aspects of the polities of different nations to specific structural components that are part of the value system, no one has as yet formulated a general theory in this area. Perhaps the closest approximation to this may be found in Harry Eckstein, *A Theory of Stable Democracy* (Princeton: Center for International Studies, Princeton University, 1961). Eckstein does not describe his approach as an effort to relate general values to political systems but rather writes of the need for "propositions relating governmental authority to other forms of social authority" (p. xiii). He tries to relate the stability of political systems to their congruence or lack of congruence with authority relations in nonpolitical areas, *e.g.*, family, school, religion, and so forth (p. 6). Since authority relations are necessarily closely involved with the central value system, if they are not to be conceived as core components of that system, Eckstein is essentially engaged in what I would describe as value analysis.

4. *Structure and Process in Modern Societies* (New York: The Free Press of Glencoe, 1960), p. 172.

5. *Ibid.*, p. 173.

6. These classic categories are, of course, those of Ferdinand Tönnies. See his *Community and Society, Gemeinschaft und Gesellschaft* (East Lansing: Michigan State University Press, 1957). A somewhat more complex specification of the component elements of these two concepts may be found in Charles P. Loomis, *Social Systems: Essays on Their Persistence and Change* (Princeton: D. Van Nostrand Co., Inc., 1961), pp. 57-63. The pattern-variables may also be seen as derivative from Max Weber's types of social

action, especially the traditional and the instrumentally-rational. See Max Weber, *The Theory of Social and Economic Organization* (New York: Oxford University Press, 1947), pp. 115-118.

7. Parsons has three other pattern-variables which I ignore here, largely for reasons of space: affectivity-affective neutrality, self-orientation-collectivity-orientation, and the instrumental-consummatory distinction. For a detailed presentation of the pattern-variables see Talcott Parsons, *The Social System* (New York: The Free Press of Glencoe, 1951), pp. 58-67. Parsons' most recent elaboration of the relationship of pattern-variable analysis to other elements in his conceptual framework is "Pattern Variables Revisited," *American Sociological Review*, xxv (1960), 467-483; see also his article "The Point of View of the Author," in Max Black, ed., *The Social Theories of Talcott Parsons* (Englewood Cliffs: Prentice-Hall, 1961), pp. 319-320, 329-336.

8. Although all four polarity distinctions are important to the analysis of the political system, ascription-achievement and universalism-particularism seem more important than the other two. As Parsons has suggested, these two are the variables which have the most reference to the total social system, rather than to subparts or to the motivation of individuals. "They are concerned . . . with the type of value-norms which enter into the structure of the social system." Combinations of these pairs are also most useful to help account for "structural differentiation and variability of social systems." See Parsons, *The Social System*, p. 106. The other two pairs, specificity-diffuseness and equalitarianism-elitism, are to a considerable degree dependent on the particular combinations of the first two.

9. As Parsons has put it, "In a very broad way the differentiations between types of social systems do correspond to this order of cultural value pattern differentiation, but *only* in a very broad way. Actual social structures are not value-pattern types, but *resultants* of the integration of value-patterns with the other components of the system." *Ibid.*, p. 112 (Emphases in the original). Gabriel Almond has recently criticized the utility of pattern-variable analysis for the study of comparative politics on the grounds that it results in exaggerations of the differences among political systems, particularly between Western and non-Western and primitive ones. He argues that "all political systems—the developed Western ones as well as the less-developed non-Western ones—are transitional systems in which cultural change is taking place." Thus they both include elements of each polarity of the pattern-variable in many of their institutions. See Gabriel Almond, "Introduction: A Functional Approach to Comparative Politics," in Gabriel Almond and James S. Coleman, eds., *The Politics of Developing Areas* (Princeton: Princeton University Press, 1960), pp. 20-25. This criticism is useful if it is considered as a warning against reifying these concepts or tending to exaggerate the integrated character of societies, whether large or small. There is, however, no reason why use of the pattern-variables for analytic purposes need fall into these pitfalls, and Parsons himself repeatedly stresses that systems and structures are never wholly one.

A detailed criticism of Parsons' analysis of politics, which, however, does not touch on the concepts dealt with here may be found in Andrew Hacker, "Sociology and Ideology," in Max Black, *The Social Theories of Talcott Parsons*, pp. 289-310.

10. It is important to note also that the pattern-variables can and have been used to distinguish among and within different orders of social systems or structures. We may characterize total epochs (feudalism compared to

capitalism), total nations (the United States compared to Britain), subsystems within nations that may logically operate with different combinations of variables (the state or industry), subsystems within nations that must logically follow specific sets of pattern-variables (the family), and subsystems within which there is conflict between different pattern-variables (the French business system, to be discussed later.)

11. There have been other efforts at using the pattern-variables for political analysis. For the most part, however, they do so in the context of specifying differences between Western and agrarian societies and hence posit ideal-type integrated *Gemeinschaft* and *Gesellschaft* cultures. See Francis X. Sutton, "Social Theory and Comparative Politics" (mimeographed); Fred W. Riggs, "Agraria and Industria—Toward a Typology of Comparative Administration," in W. J. Siffin, ed., *Toward the Comparative Study of Public Administration* (Bloomington: Indiana University Press, 1959), pp. 23-116. A paper which does attempt to use the variables to analyze contemporary differences is William Evan, "Social Structure, Trade Unionism, and Consumer Cooperation," *Industrial and Labor Relations Review*, X (1957), 440-447.

12. For a justification of the utility of concentrating on an analysis of variations among highly similar units see the Introduction in *The First New Nation*.

13. See *Political Man*, pp. 21-41, 45-48; and my "Introduction" to a paperback edition of Robert Michels, *Political Parties* (New York: Collier Books, 1962), pp. 15-39, esp. 33-38.

14. "Introduction" to Michels, p. 33.

15. For a good discussion of the American value system see Robin Williams, *American Society* (New York: Alfred A. Knopf, 1951), pp. 372-442; Talcott Parsons, and Winston White, "The Link Between Character and Society," in S. M. Lipset and Leo Lowenthal, eds., *Culture and Social Character* (New York: The Free Press of Glencoe, 1961), pp. 98-103. I devote less space here to elaborating on American values since much of Parts I and II of *The First New Nation* deal with them in some detail.

16. Daniel Bell, ed., *The Radical Right* (Garden City: Doubleday, 1963).

17. See the essays in Charles Sellers, ed., *The Southerner as American* (Chapel Hill: University of North Carolina Press, 1960) for interesting insights on the difficulties faced by Southern whites before and after the Civil War in resolving the conflicts generated within the society and within themselves by the sharply varying dictates of alternative value systems.

18. Elitism explicitly affects the training given to prospective members of the British upper class. A description of the English public schools (private in the American sense) reports that "learning and the getting-fit are represented as part of the 'training for leadership' which many public-schoolmasters see as their social role. . . . It infects the whole set-up with a certain smugness and a certain frightening *elite* concept. The word 'breeding' is often on their lips. . . . Many of these boys go around looking for people to lead: they actually say at the university interviews that they feel they have been trained to lead. . . ." John Vaizey, "The Public Schools," in Hugh Thomas, ed., *The Establishment* (New York: Clarkson Potter, 1959), pp. 28-29. See Drew Middleton, *The British* (London: Pan Books, 1958), pp. 230-231. See also G. J. Renier, *The English: Are They Human?* (New York: Roy Publishers, 1952), p. 249, pp. 229-270; and Asa Briggs, *Victorian People* (London: Odhams Press, 1954), pp. 150-177; and Denis Brogan, *The English People* (New York: Alfred A. Knopf, 1943), pp. 18-56.

19. Writing in 1833, Tocqueville pointed out that what distinguished the English aristocracy "from all others is the ease with which it has opened its ranks. . . . [W]ith great riches, anybody could hope to enter into the ranks of the aristocracy. . . . The reason why the French nobles were the butt of all hatreds, was not chiefly that only nobles had the right to everything, but because nobody could become a noble. . . . The English aristocracy in feelings and prejudices resembles all the aristocracies of the world, but it is not in the least founded on birth, that inaccessible thing, but on wealth that everyone can acquire, and this one difference makes it stand, while the others succumb. . . .

". . . [O]ne can clearly see in England where the aristocracy begins, but it is impossible to say where it ends.

". . . [I]f you speak to a member of the middle classes; you will find he hates some aristocrats but not the aristocracy. . . .

"The whole of English society is still clearly based on an aristocratic footing, and has contracted habits that only a violent revolution or the slow and continual action of new laws can destroy. . . ." *Journeys to England and Ireland* (New Haven: Yale University Press, 1958), pp. 59-60, 67, 70-71. Similarly, the great French student of English history, Elie Halévy described the English upper class as "an aristocracy in which no rank was a closed caste, an aristocracy in which the inferior regarded the superior not with envy but respect. It was not impossible to climb into a superior class and those who respected those above them were respected in turn by those below them. . . ." *Halévy's History of the English People in the Nineteenth Century*, IV (London: Ernest Benn, Ltd., 1961), p. 345; see also I, 221-222.

20. See C. A. R. Crosland, *The Future of Socialism* (London: Jonathan Cape, 1956), pp. 232-237; and Raymond Williams, *The Long Revolution* (London: Chatto and Windus, 1961), pp. 318-321.

21. Hippolyte Taine, *Notes on England* (Fair Lawn: Essential Books, 1958), pp. 162, 164-165.

22. Clement Attlee, speaking as leader of the Labour Party in the House of Commons on July 9, 1952, opposed sweeping economies in royal expenditures on the following grounds: "It is a great mistake to make government too dull. That, I think, was the fault of the German Republic after the first World War. They were very drab and dull." Edward Shils and Michael Young, "The Meaning of the Coronation," reprinted from *The Sociological Review* (1953) in Lipset and Neil Smelser, eds., *Sociology: The Progress of a Decade* (Englewood Cliffs: Prentice-Hall, 1961), p. 221. See also Tom Harrison, *Britain Revisited* (London: Victor Gollancz, 1961), p. 232; George Orwell suggested that elitist sentiments are strong among British workers as well. See his *The English People* (London: Collins, 1947), p. 29.

23. Shils, *The Torment of Secrecy* (New York: The Free Press of Glencoe, 1956), pp. 37-51. This book deserves recognition as a minor classic of sociological analysis of a social problem, yet curiously it is not well known. There are few other books I know that are as illuminating concerning the interrelationships of American society and polity. The earlier article by Shils and Michael Young on the monarchy is also well worth reading in the context of problems raised in this paper. "The Meaning of the Coronation," pp. 220-233.

Other articles and books that present interesting case materials on significant differences between various aspects of British and American society are: Stephen Richardson, "Organizational Contrasts on British and American

Ships," *Administration Science Quarterly*, I (1956), 189-207; L. C. B. Gower and Leolin Price, "The Profession and Practice of Law in England and America," *Modern Law Review*, XX (1957), 317-46; Roy Lewis and Rosemary Stewart, *The Managers: A New Examination of the English, German, and American Executive* (New York: Mentor Books, 1961); P. S. Florence, *The Logic of British and American Industry* (Chapel Hill: The University of North Carolina Press, 1953); E. Lipson, *Reflections on Britain and the United States—Mainly Economic* (London: The Pall Mall Press, 1959), pp. 3-34; Crosland, pp. 238-257 and *passim*; and George Baron and Asher Tropp, "Teachers in England and America," in A. H. Halsey, Jean Floud, and C. A. Anderson, eds., *Education, Economy, and Society* (New York: The Free Press of Glencoe, 1961), pp. 545-557.

24. Baron and Tropp, p. 548.

25. Ralph Turner, "Modes of Social Ascent Through Education: Sponsored and Contest Mobility," in Halsey, *et al.*, eds., p. 122.

26. *Ibid.*, pp. 122, 125 (emphasis in original). For a discussion of the elitist assumptions and consequences of the English school system by a Labour Party leader who is much impressed by the egalitarian aspects of the American educational system, see Crosland, pp. 258-277 and *passim*.

27. *Ibid.*, p. 126. One of the key differences between England and the United States that has been noted as most clearly reflecting the contrast between an egalitarian society with a "common school," and an elitist society with a highly class segregated system of education is accent variations. As Crosland has put it: "[P]art of the reason why these differences [between classes in England] make so strong an impact is that they are associated with, and exaggerated by, the most supremely unmistakable of all symbols of social standing—differences of accent and vocabulary. In no other country is it possible in the same way to assess a person's social standing the moment he opens his mouth. . . ." (pp. 177-178). In a recent report on English life, the founder of Mass Observation (an organization that has studied mass behavior through systematic observation techniques since 1937), writing about working-class life, comments that, in spite of all the other major changes that have occurred since his group began its observations, "No voice changes can be detected between 1937 and 1960. Radio, television and other outside impacts oriented to a more standard English appear to have had little or no effect. A tiny minority have consciously altered their voices. But elocution and speech training are still not important here. An English master at one of the big local schools . . . gave his considered opinion that if anything the standard of speaking of what he called 'King's English' had gone *down*." Harrison, p. 32 (Emphasis in original).

28. For an analysis of the way in which variation in the status of elites, diffuse or specific, affects the position of intellectuals in England and America see my *Political Man*, pp. 326-328. See also A. G. Nicholas "Intellectuals and Politics in the U.S.A.," *Occidente*, X (1954), 47; and Gertrude Himmelfarb, "American Democracy and European Critics," *The Twentieth Century*, CLI (1952), 320-27.

A clear indication of the differences in the values of those in charge of English elite education and those of comparably placed Americans may be seen in the criticism of the views of the former president of the highest status American university, Harvard, by the Master of the Manchester Grammar School:

"When Professor Conant demands 'a common core of general education which will unite in one cultural pattern the future carpenter, factory workers, bishop, lawyer, doctor, sales-manager, professor and garage mechanic,' he is simply asking for the impossible. The demand for such a common culture rests either on an altogether over-optimistic belief in the educability of the majority that is certainly not justified by experience or on a willingness to surrender the highest standards of taste and judgment to the incessant demands of mediocrity." Quoted from E. James, *Education for Leadership*, in Michael Young, *The Rise of the Meritocracy* (London: Thames and Hudson, 1958), p. 40.

29. Harry Eckstein, pp. 15-16.

30. "France," in Arnold M. Rose, ed., *The Institutions of Advanced Societies* (Minneapolis: University of Minnesota Press, 1958), pp. 500-501.

31. "The Idea of Democracy and the Political Institutions," in Saul K. Padover, *French Institutions, Values and Politics* (Stanford: Stanford University Press, 1954), pp. 12-13.

32. See John E. Sawyer, "Strains in the Social Structure of Modern France," and David S. Landes, "French Business and the Businessman: A Social and Cultural Analysis," in Edward M. Earle, ed., *Modern France* (Princeton: Princeton University Press, 1951), pp. 293-312, 334-353. See also Lewis and Stewart, pp. 182-187. For a discussion of similar attitudes and consequences in Italy, see Maurice F. Neufeld, *Italy: School for Awakening Countries* (Ithaca: N.Y. State School of Industrial and Labor Relations, 1961), pp. 36 and *passim*.

33. Even Raymond Aron, who differs from most analysts of the French scene in arguing that there has been a rapid rate of growth in the total French economy during most of this century, agrees, however, that "the usual idea that France is still the nation of small business is, then, not false. . . . It is quite likely that in many sectors there are still large numbers of firms which are too small and more or less unproductive. Sometimes these marginal enterprises are protected rather than opposed by the larger ones, which thus ensure extra profits by maintaining prices at levels desired by the former.

"This relative slowness in concentration is attended by the survival of precapitalistic legal entities. . . .

"The French seem to attach importance to independence and at times to prefer it to higher income. Resistance (to incorporation into larger units) . . . expresses a characteristic of the national psychology just as it is a result of a policy adopted by governments under pressure from the electorate or grouped interests." *France Steadfast and Changing* (Cambridge: Harvard University Press, 1960), pp. 60-62.

34. In discussing the French businessman, Lewis and Stewart have pointed out these tendencies in detail: "The businessman is paternalistic and autocratic, treating his employees as 'mes enfants,' as much a part of his 'maison,' as his own children and domestics. In an age of rapid technological change, this has led not only to discontent among the children, but also to a failure to modernize. . . .

"Their labor relations are also prejudiced, and even French big business lacks 'industrial-relations sense.' The British businessman may be open to criticism on these grounds too. . . . But to the Frenchman, British employers seem to have accepted and adapted the role of the trade unions in a masterly manner, which has produced a moderate Labor Party. In France, the dogged anti-labor attitude of the businessman has ended not only with businesses paying for social welfare out of their own pockets directly, but also with an irreconcilably bitter anticapitalist feeling among the workers, who vote Communist often for that reason and no other. To some thoughtful French businessmen, American business ideals and classlessness in industry really begin when he crosses the Channel" (pp. 186-187).

35. See Raymond Aron, pp. 45-77.

36. "France," p. 478.

37. There is some evidence and opinion to sustain the belief that successfully mobile Frenchmen are more likely to hide this fact than would be true for comparable individuals in other countries. See Lipset and Bendix, *Social Mobility In Industrial Society* (Berkeley: University of California Press, 1959), pp. 19, 82-83.

38. Val Lorwin, *The French Labor Movement* (Cambridge: Harvard University Press, 1954), pp. 36-37.

39. See Herbert Luethy, *The State of France* (London: Secker and Warburg, 1955), p. 87; Val Lorwin, pp. 87-88; Henry W. Ehrmann, *French Labor From Popular Front to Liberation* (New York: Oxford University Press, 1947), pp. 169-232.

40. *Democracy in America*, I (New York: Vintage Books, 1956), p. 55.

41. Charles P. Kindleberger, "The Postwar Resurgence of the French Economy," in Stanley Hoffman, *et al.*, *In Search of France* (Cambridge: Harvard University Press, 1963), p. 133.

42. Stanley Hoffman, "Paradoxes of the French Political Community," in Hoffman, *et al.*, *In Search of France*, p. 61.

43. "Classes sans conscience ou préfiguration de la société sans classes," *European Journal of Sociology*, I (1960), 244-245.

44. *Ibid.*

45. It should also be noted that this alienation cannot be explained primarily by low wages. "In comparison with European wages, they are not low. Higher than in Italy or Holland, certainly not as high as in Sweden or Switzerland, a little lower than in Great Britain, they have been somewhat better in buying power than in Germany and are still at least equal in that respect." Aron, p. 49.

46. Peter Gay, *The Dilemma of Democratic Socialism. Eduard Bernstein's Challenge to Marx* (New York: Columbia University Press, 1952), pp. 254-55 and *passim*. See also Arthur Rosenberg, *The Birth of the German Republic* (Oxford: Oxford University Press, 1931), p. 48ff.

47. "From 1920 onward the history of the Weimar Republic was only a rearguard action against the revitalized social forces on which the German state structure had been built under Bismarck: Army, *Junkers*, big industrialists, and the higher strata of the Civil Service." J. P. Mayer, *Max Weber and German Politics* (London: Faber and Faber, 1956), p. 64.

48. Eckstein, pp. 17-18.

49. Dankwart Rustow, *The Politics of Compromise* (Princeton: Princeton University Press, 1955), pp. 65-85; Douglas Verney, *Parliamentary Reform in Sweden* (Oxford: The Clarendon Press, 1957), pp. 159-173, 202-214.

50. Perry Anderson, "Sweden," *New Left Review*, VII (January-February 1961), 6-7. For other objective factors that have served to reduce hierarchical differentiation and class tension in Sweden, see the second part of Anderson's article, *New Left Review*, IX (May-June 1961), 34-35.

51. Crosland, pp. 181-182 (emphasis mine).

52. "An Investigation of Class-Consciousness among Office Employees and Workers in Swedish Factories," *Transactions of the Second World Congress of Sociology* (London: International Sociological Association, 1954), Vol. II, 300-301, 305.

53. See Eckstein, p. 37.

54. Contemporary West Germany, of course, differs from Britain and Sweden in not being a monarchy. As I have tried to demonstrate in *Political Man*, pp. 78-79, this difference is not unimportant. It reflects the breaking of traditional legitimacy, of the loss of a felt "title-to-rule" on the part of the political system. To create legitimacy is much more difficult than to transfer the symbolic legitimacy of an older system to a new political system, as the monarchical democracies have done. It should be stressed that a variety of public opinion polls and studies of elite opinion indicate that attachment to democratic values is extremely fragile in Germany. For detailed summaries and discussion of such data, see Karl W. Deutsch and Lewis J. Edinger, *Germany Rejoins the Powers* (Stanford: Stanford University Press, 1959).

55. See *Political Man*, pp. 101-105, 109-114, for a summary of studies bearing on this problem. This attitude will, of course, not be found in countries in which democratic "rules of the game" have not been institutionalized. Where privileged classes are fighting to retain their traditional oligarchic rights and powers, they will strongly resist the claims for participation in the polity of groups based on the lower strata.

56. In an extremely interesting paper comparing life and social organization on ships in the American and British merchant marine, Stephen Richardson indicates that variations in basic national values deeply affect authority relationships within identical economic institutions. "Comparison of British and American crews suggests that the British realize and accept the authority of competent persons and are not as fearful of the misuse of authority as Americans. This acceptance of authority is closely related to acceptance of social stratification and the symbols of these differences. Status symbols functon as cues for self-regulation, in conformity with the status and role requirements of the ship. British seamen are conditioned before coming to sea to accept authority, and consequently the change in attitudes required when a man becomes a seaman is slight. . . .

"Among American crews a far greater fear and suspicion of authority appears to exist. Social stratification is not widely accepted and is often denied. Many symbols of social stratification have been removed, and, because they are suspect, the remaining symbols do little to enhance self-regulation of the men in conformity with the status and rule demands of the ship's social organization." Since the norms of the social structure undermine authority on American ships, there is a necessity for a "far greater formalization of the social system than [on] the British," and American ships have many more explicit rules and regulations. Richardson, pp. 206-207.

57. For a good discussion of the dysfunctions inherent in an elitist society, see Crosland, pp. 227-237.

58. The thesis that revolutionary socialism and transvaluational religion have served similar functions for oppressed groups was elaborated by Friedrich Engels, "On the Early History of Christianity," in K. Marx and F. Engels, *On Religion* (Moscow: Foreign Language Publishing House, 1957), pp. 312-320.

59. In France, for example, ecological studies that contrast degree of

religious practice with Communist strength show that the Communists are most successful in regions in which the "anti-clerical" wave had previously suppressed much of the traditional fidelity to Catholicism. See G. LeBras, "Geographie électorale et géographie religieuse," *Etudes de sociologie électorale* (Cahiers de la fondation nationale des sciences politiques, I ([Paris: Armand Colin, 1949]); and Goguel, *Géographie des élections Françaises de 1870 à 1951* (Cahiers de la fondation nationale des sciences politiques, XXVII [Paris: Armand Colin, 1951], pp. 134-135).

60. The various implications of the problems of "failure" in an open society, which in some ways are psychologically worse than in an ascriptive culture, have been analyzed by Robert K. Merton, *Social Theory and Social Structure* (New York: The Free Press of Glencoe, 1957), pp. 131-194.

61. "Economic development may then be considered as being associated with a transformation of social behavior from a form which in its economically relevant aspects is oriented towards ascription, particularism and functional diffuseness to a form ·of social behavior oriented towards achievement, universalism and functional specificity." Bert F. Hoselitz, *Sociological Aspects of Economic Growth* (New York: The Free Press of Glencoe, 1960), p. 59.

62. Lewis and Stewart, pp. 166-168.

63. Schumpeter addressed himself explicitly to this problem, but curiously put the responsibility for the differences between British and German political systems on the behavior of one man, Bismarck.

"But, why was it that the English methods and tactics did not prevail in Germany? . . .

"The fatal mistake was really Bismarck's. It consisted in the attempt, explicable only on the hypothesis that he completely misconceived the nature of the problem, at suppressing socialist activities by coercion. . . ." *Capitalism, Socialism, and Democracy* (New York: Harper and Brothers, 1950), pp. 341, 343.

In 1917, Max Weber saw the failure of Bismarck to share political power with the various opposition parties as a prime cause of their inability to function as a responsible and loyal opposition. See J. P. Mayer, *Max Weber and German Politics* (London: Faber and Faber, 1954), p. 78.

Addressing himself to the same problem, in terms of why Britain succeeded in avoiding major class tension, a French historian also credits the insight of individuals. G. E. Lavau urges that England avoided a revolutionary working class because of "the practical intelligence—at the right moment—of some Conservative [Disraeli, Randolph Churchill, Joseph Chamberlain] and Liberal [Asquith, Lloyd George] leaders." *Partis politiques et réalités sociales* (Paris: Armand Colin, 1953), p. 95.

64. *The Old Regime and the French Revolution* (New York: Anchor Books, 1955), pp. 82, 88-89.

65. "One often hears it said that the English nobility has proved itself more adroit, more worldly wise, more accessible to new ideas than any other. It would be truer to say that for a long time past there has been no nobility in England, if we use the term 'nobility' in the sense it has elsewhere." *Ibid.*, p. 83.

66. *Education of Nations* (Cambridge: Harvard University Press, 1961), p. 95. See also Nancy Mitford, "The English Aristocracy," in Nancy Mitford, ed., *Noblesse Oblige* (Harmondsworth: Penguin Books, 1959), pp. 36-37.

67. Ulich, p. 96. Bryce called attention to this attitude as a major force in building national solidarity. See *Modern Democracies I* (New York: Macmillan, 1921), pp. 30-32; see also Briggs, pp. 153-54.

68. Ulich, p. 96.

69. For detailed analyses of these problems in the new states see Edward Shils, "Political Development in the New States," *Comparative Studies in Society and History*, II (1960), 265-292, 379-411; S. N. Eisenstadt, "Soziale Entwicklung und Politische Stabilität in Nichtwestlichen Gesellschaften," *Koelner Zeitschrift für Soziologie und Sozialpsychologie*, XII (1960), 189-203; Eisenstadt, *Essays on Sociological Aspects of Political and Economic Development* (The Hague: Mouton and Co., 1961).

70. Max Weber, *Essays in Sociology* (New York: Oxford University Press, 1946), pp. 193-194.

71. Some of these ideas are discussed in more detail in *The First New Nation*, Chapter IX.

72. *In Search of Canadian Liberalism* (Toronto: The Macmillan Co. of Canada, 1960), p. 12. He goes on to point out that while Jacksonian democracy triumphed in the United States in the 1830's and "swept away most of the old aristocratic survivals and made a strong attack on the new plutocratic forces," its equivalent in Canada, the movements of Papineau in Quebec and Mackenzie in Ontario, were defeated and discredited. In Canada, unlike the United States, the "social pyramid . . . was *not* upset" (pp. 12-33). As another eminent Canadian historian put it, after the Revolution "colonial Toryism made its second attempt to erect on American soil a copy of the English social edifice. From one point of view this is the most significant thing about the Loyalist movement, it withdrew a class concept of life from the south, moved it up north and gave it a second chance. . . . Canada in time came to be almost as wide a popular democracy as the United States itself: though a much more conservative one, for a country founded to preserve the old order against the new must necessarily be conservative." A. R. M. Lower, *Colony to Nation: A History of Canada* (Toronto: Longmans, Green and Co., 1946), pp. 114, 120; see also Stuart Jamieson, *Industrial Relations in Canada* (Toronto: The Macmillan Co., 1957), pp. 8-9.

For a general discussion of the way in which historical factors affect national social structures, with specific reference to Canada and the United States, see my "A Sociologist Looks at History," *Pacific Sociological Review*, I (1959), 13-17; and *The First New Nation*, Chapters I and II.

73. Jamieson, p. 4. A sociological study made in the mid-1930's in English-speaking Montreal and based on a small sample of "seventy people, who were thought to be representative," reports that the "notion of a social elite, of a culture based upon the traditions and ideals of aristocratic Britain, reappears over and over again in the interviews." These attitudes, the authors note, are probably not characteristic of Canadian opinion much west of Montreal. S. D. Clark, assisted by C. A. Dawson and E. C. Hughes, "Opinions and Attitudes in English-Speaking Quebec," in H. F. Angus, ed., *Canada and Her Great Neighbor* (Toronto: The Ryerson Press, 1938), pp. 383-389.

74. "Canadian Society: Some Reflections," in Bernard Blishen, *et al.*, eds., *Canadian Society* (Toronto: The Macmillan Co. of Canada, 1961), p. 27. This article is the best effort to sum up the general value system of Canada. Naegele argues strongly for the thesis that on many matters Canada

lies "in the middle between America and England" and that it both attempts and rejects various aspects of the English and American models (emphases in original).

75. Fred Alexander, *Canadians and Foreign Policy* (Toronto: University of Toronto Press, 1960), p. 121.

76. Ronald Taft and Kenneth F. Walker, "Australia," in Arnold M. Rose, ed., *The Institutions of Advanced Societies* (Minneapolis: University of Minnesota Press, 1958), pp. 144-145. These two Australian social psychologists sum up Australian values as being militantly equalitarian, "set in the background of *politico-economic class consciousness.* . . . These equalitarian attitudes have taken the form of militant attempts to eliminate the material and prestige liabilities of the working class. . . . Thus a high value is placed on activities aimed at protecting and promoting the standing of the 'underdog' by abusing privileged or would-be privileged persons. Although, as we have seen, middle-class Australians avoid identifying themselves as workers, they nonetheless typically share this militant equalitarianism against authority or prestige figures. . . . Thus the middle class, by and large, supports the welfare state, maintains the right of workers to strike and to look after their own interests, and eschews the servility associated with certain necessary occupational roles. Australians are poor at providing personal service and are reluctant to demand it" (emphasis in original).

77. "The Australian Nation," in George Caiger, ed., *The Australian Way of Life* (London: William Heinemann, 1953), p. 11; see also A. P. Rowe, *If the Gown Fits* (Melbourne: Melbourne University Press, 1960), pp. 59-67; and J. D. B. Millet, *Australian Government and Politics* (London: Duckworth and Co., 1954), pp. 22-24.

78. W. F. Connell, "Education and Social Mobility in Australia," *Transactions of the Third World Congress of Sociology*, V (London: International Sociological Association, 1954), 75-76.

79. *The Politics of Equality* (Chicago: The University of Chicago Press, 1948), pp. 487-488.

80. Russel Ward, *The Australian Legend* (Melbourne: Oxford University Press, 1958), pp. 14-16, 157-158.

81. *Ibid.*, p. 18.

82. Canadian unification in 1867 is associated with the Conservative Party, while the federation of Australia around the turn of the century was pressed by the Labor Party, which existed in most states. It is noteworthy that the "conservative" party in Australia has constantly changed its name to avoid association with traditional and privileged elements. "Not by accident but by design the term conservative early in the twentieth century disappeared from the nomenclature of parties in Australia and New Zealand. It could not obviously win enough varied backing among the surviving elements of conservative opinion. . . . In Canada a conservative outlook in many respects found great favor." Alexander Brady, *Democracy in the Dominions* (Toronto: University of Toronto Press, 1958), p. 528.

83. It is also important to mention one major objective difference between Australia and North America. Carter Goodrich has suggested that "the United States owes its individualism largely to its small man's frontier; I think it not fanciful to suggest that Australia owes much of its collectivism [particularism] to the fact that its frontier was hospitable to large men instead." See "The Australian and American Labour Movements," *The Economic Record*, IV (1928), 206-207. In Australia, unlike the United States

and Canada, frontier farms were immensely large and employed large numbers of workers. This pattern reflected, to a considerable degree, the difficulties of desert farming and ranching: "The typical Australian frontiersman in the last century was a wage-worker who did not, usually, expect to become anything else." Ward, p. 226. Large groups of land laborers developed a sense of group consciousness, and very early formed a major trade union, now the largest in the country, the Australian Workers' Union. See also Fred Alexander, *Moving Frontiers* (Victoria: Melbourne University Press, 1947).

84. In an earlier paper, Underhill pointed to "the effect of British influences in slowing down all movements throughout the nineteenth century in the direction of the democratization of politics and society. Inevitably, . . . the urge towards greater democracy was likely to appear in Canada as an American influence; and since the survival of Canada as a separate entity depended on her not being submerged under an American flood, such influences were fought as dangerous to our Canadian ethos" p. 15. More recently, even Conservative Canadians cited McCarthyism as a reason for "suspicion" of the United States. Fred Alexander, p. 132.

85. James Bryce was struck by these attitudes before World War I. He reports, "I was amazed to find in 1912 how many Australians believed Britain to be a declining and almost decadent country." *Modern Democracies,* I (London: Macmillan and Co., 1921), p. 268.

86. See Robin Gollan, *Radical and Working Class Politics: A Study of Eastern Australia* (Melbourne: Melbourne University Press, 1960), esp. pp. 113-115. In drawing up their constitution, the Australians consciously modeled it "upon the American rather than the Canadian model." See Brady, p. 153.

87. The assumption is often made that Quebec, which is a more traditionalist and Catholic area, shows lower proportions on statistics like these. This assumption is not valid in the case of university education. In the academic year 1959-1960, the proportion of the population aged 18-21 attending universities was higher in Quebec than in Canada as a whole or than in the neighboring, predominantly English-speaking province of Ontario. See Dominion Bureau of Statistics, *Fall Enrollment of Universities and Colleges, 1959* (Ottawa: Queen's Printer, 1960), p. 9.

88. There have been a number of cases in recent Australian history of restrictions on academic freedom and outside political interference in the life of universities. Perhaps the most scandalous involved the refusal of the University of New South Wales to appoint an important scholar, Russel Ward, to its faculty because of objections by government security officers. He had apparently belonged to the Communist Party in the 1940's. See "Security in the Quad," *Nation* (Australia), December 3, 1960, p. 7; see also W. M. Bell, "Secure No More," *Nation,* October 8, 1960, pp. 6-8.

89. "The Frontier and Democratic Theory," *Transactions of the Royal Society of Canada,* XLVIII (1954), Series III, Section Two, 71-72; see also S. D. Clark, *Movements of Political Protest in Canada* (Toronto: University of Toronto Press, 1959), esp. pp. 3-10.

90. Bryce, I, 559-560.

91. On the contrast between Britain and the United States, see E. Lipson, pp. 7-10.

92. Ward, p. 27.

93. James Bryce, II, 276-277; see also *The First New Nation,* Chapter V, for a discussion of pressures toward law violation in America.

94. Gower and Price, p. 317.

95. The Canadian estimate of about 11,000 practicing lawyers (and notaries in Quebec) is from a study by the Taxation Division of the Department of National Revenue, reported in a letter from the Information Officer of the Canadian Embassy in Washington; the Australian data were supplied by the Australian References Library in New York City.

96. "Trial By Jury and Liberty of the Press," in Harry Kalven, ed., *The Public Image of the Jury System* (Boston: Little, Brown and Co., forthcoming); see also Hamburger's chapter in the same volume on "Decline of the Jury Trial in England."

97. Hugh Clegg, *A New Approach to Industrial Democracy* (London: Basil Blackwell, 1960), p. 22.

98. Ward, p. 6.

99. *Ibid.*, p. 149.

100. Geoffrey Gorer, *Exploring English Character. A Study of the Morals and Behavior of the English People* (New York: Criterion Books, 1955), p. 295.

101. The fact of a Labour government in England from 1945 to 1951 has led many people to forget how basically powerful conservatism has been historically in Great Britain compared to other countries, particularly Australia and New Zealand. As the Labour M.P. Woodrow Wyatt points out: "Only twice this century, or for that matter since 1886, have either Liberals or Labour had an overall working majority in the House of Commons, over the Tories and the others. Once in 1906, once in 1945. The 1945 Labour victory was not a majority demand for socialism but a post-war revulsion against the Tories and a desire for a new deal. Even in the 1945 election the Labour Party got only 48.01 per cent of the total votes cast." And he goes on to suggest that, "The general acceptance by the British of the hierarchical system based on the monarchy and snobbishness of every kind makes it inevitable that Britain should frequently be a Conservative country." See "My Plan for a Lib-Lab Pact," *The New Statesman*, LXIII (January 26, 1962), p. 110.

The seemingly greater strength of the British Labour Party compared to leftist parties on the European continent is largely a function of the fact that the second largest party in what is fundamentally a two-party system almost always receives a larger proportion of the vote than in a multiparty system using proportional representation. For a discussion of some of the factors affecting the weakness of British Labour, see my "The British Voter," I and II, *The New Leader* (November 7 and 21, 1960).

102. The same emphasis on equalitarianism and particularism has been suggested as the major cause for Australia's much lower wage differential for skill compared to the United States and Canada. This lower differential not only applies among manual workers but between manual workers and the stratum of company executives. Kenneth F. Walker, *Industrial Relations in Australia* (Cambridge: Harvard University Press, 1956), pp. 329-330; Taft and Walker, p. 141. A more elaborate discussion of differences among trade unions in these four countries which are related to value differences may be found in *The First New Nation*, Chapter V. Among other variations are the much greater reliance of American and Australian unions on paid officials, contrasted with British and Continental organizations, which have many fewer full-time leaders proportionate to membership. Many British

and Swedish national labor leaders are chosen for *life*, a pattern reflecting other aspects of their national structures.

103. Robert Alford, *Social Class and Voting in Four Anglo-American Democracies* (Berkeley: Survey Research Center, University of California, dittoed, 1961), p. 89.

104. It has been suggested by some that these similarities and differences in values showed up in vivid form in reactions to the demands that military life have made on civilian conscripts in the four countries. The British and, to a lesser degree, the Canadians accepted the need to conform to the rigid hierarchical structure of the military; while Australians and Americans showed deep resentment at having to exhibit deference to superiors. I have been told by nationals of different countries that in London bars during World War II, Americans and Australians tended to associate with each other, while Canadians were more likely than the Australians to prefer British companions to Americans. I am indebted to Professor Frank Underhill for first calling my attention to such behavior patterns.

105. Friedrich Engels, "Introduction," *Socialism Utopian and Scientific* (Chicago: Charles H. Kerr and Co., 1912), pp. 37-43. This area is one of considerable scholarly controversy.

106. *Ibid.*, p. 43 (emphasis mine).

107. Engels's emphasis on values may not be as "heretical" as it appears. Marx himself once stated that "We know that the institutions, manners and customs of the various countries must be considered, and we do not deny that there are countries, like England and America, . . . where the worker may attain his object by peaceful means." Cited by Hacker, *op. cit.*, p. 289. Hacker goes on to say that "It is remarks like this which turn scholarly heads gray."

# INDEX

Abbas, Ferhat, 146
Achievement-ascription distinction,
    and democracy, 267-333
Agriculture, in French economy and
    culture, 188-189, 201-202
Algeria, internal war in, 104, 136, 146
Almond, Gabriel A., 321n
American War of Independence,
    recruitment in, 105
"Analysis," in social science, 21-22
Arendt, Hannah, 83
Arnold, Theodor, 90
Aron, Raymond, 325n
Attlee, Clement, 323n
Australia
    conservatism in, 330n, 331n
    value system in, 307-309, 311-316
Authority, cultural differences in
        response to, 327n
    elements of, 131-33
    patterns of struggle for, 133-137
    role of in internal war, 130-140
    transfer of, 137-139

Bagehot, Walter, 271
Blanksten, George, 19
Blanqui, 2
Bolivia, 149
Bourricaud, François, 279
Brinton, Crane, 25
Bryce, James, 312, 331n
Burma, 165, 175

Canada
    conservatism in, 330n, 331n
    value system in, 305-316
Capitalism, and French Revolution,
    187-190

Catholic Church, in France, 280
China, internal war in, 104, 136, 148
Clark, S. D., 311-312
Classes, and rebellion, 153
Classification of internal wars, 16-21
Clausewitz, Carl von, 16, 140n
Cohn, Norman, 97n
Colombia, 104
Colonial insurgency, 79
Comte, Auguste, 2
Conservatism
    in Canada and Australia, 330n,
        331n
    in Great Britain, 332n
Constitutionalism, and rebellion,
    149-151
Conventional warfare, in revolution,
    90-95
Crosland, C. A. R., 290-291
Crozier, Brian, 89-91

D'Annunzio, Gabriele, 2
Democracy
    and minority systems, 251-261
    political definition of, 270-271
    theory of stability of, 320n
    and value orientations, 270-292
DeTocqueville, Alexis, 184-185, 273-
    274, 282, 300, 311, 323n
Durkheim, Emile, 2-3

Economics, of revolution, 180-204
Education
    as indicator of value systems, 309-
        311
    and political awareness, 215, 217,
        225-226
Edwards, L. P., 25

Egypt, internal war in, 148
Elites, value systems of in stable democracies, 292-296
Elitism, and democracy, 267-333
Engels, Friedrich, 203n, 317-318, 327n
England, internal war in, 150, 153
Equalitarianism, and democracy, 267-333

Feudalism, in France, 181-184
Force
  and authority, 132-134
  military and civic, 11
  and power system, 57-61
  and social control, 11, 37-40
  in social process, 33-70
  and systems of normative order, 33-37
France
  business ethos in, 280-282, 284-285
  Communists in, 283
  economic development in, 182-190, 203n
  internal war in, 150, 153, 181-193
  Poujadist movement in, 283
  social change in, 297-298, 300-301
  union movement in, 280-281, 284-285
  value system of, 278-285
French Revolution, 13, 203n
  and capitalism, 187-190

Gause, G. F., 105
Germany
  authoritarianism in, 288-289
  business ethos in, 285-288
  Nazi rise in, 148, 149
  political instability in, 278-279, 285-292
  social change in, 298-302
  union movement in, 286-288
  value system of, 278-279, 285-292
Goguel, François, 280
Goodrich, Carter, 330n
Gorer, Geoffrey, 314
Great Britain
  attitude toward violence in, 179n
  conservatism in, 332n
  economic development in, 203n

revolution of 1688, 203n
social change in, 297, 299-301
stability of democracy in, 271-278
value system of, 271-278, 305, 309-316
Greece, internal war in, 104
Guerrilla warfare, 90-94, 105
Guevara, Che, 87

Halévy, Elie, 323n
Hamburger, Joseph, 313-314
Heer, Friedrich, 95n
Hitler, 135
Hungary, rebellion of 1956, 103
Huntington, Samuel, 19

India, internal war in, 145
Indonesia, internal war in, 165
Industrialization
  and conflict generation, 119-122
  and social change, 124-126
Internal war
  advocates of, 2
  "analysis" of, 21-23
  classification of, 16-21
  components of, 22
  contagion of, 100-101
  course of, 26-27
  delimitation of concept, 8-16
  external involvement in, 15-16, 107-108, 100-110
  measures of morale in, 106, 107
  outcomes of, 27-29
  and political alienation, 228-231
  and political attitudes, 205-232
  political framework of, 130-140
  pre-theoretical concerns in study of, 7-32
  problems of, 23-32
  quantitative aspects of, 104-107
  recruitment and attrition in, 104-106
  and social science methodology, 5-6
  and social science theory, 1-7
  techniques of, 17
  types of, 17
Italy
  economic development in, 187, 190-191
  Fascist rise in, 148-149

internal war in, 152
political attitudes in, 208-209,
212-231
socio-economic structure of, 209

Jacobins, 186
Japan, internal war in, 148
Jaurès, Jean, 185

Kaplan, Abraham, 19
Kenya, 108
Korea, 102-103
Kropotkin, 82-87

Labrousse, C. E., 184
Lasswell, Harold, 19
Latin America, pattern of rebellion
in, 154-155
Lavau, G. E., 328n
Lebanon, 1958 crisis in, 103
Lefebvre, Georges, 185, 187-188
Legitimacy
and authority, 132-134.
of new elites, 302-304
Lewis, Roy, 298-299
Lower, A. R. M., 329n

Malaparte, Curzio, 2
Malaya, internal war in, 89-90, 165,
175
Mao Tse-tung, 105
Marczewski, Jan, 203n
Marxists, 2, 135, 181
Mathiez, Albert, 185
McCarthyism, 273, 311-312
Mexico
internal war in, 104
political attitudes in, 208-210, 212-
231
revolution of 1910-1920, 207-210
socio-economic structure of, 209
Michels, Robert, 301-302
Mosca, Gaetano, 2
Mussolini, 135

Naegele, Kaspar, 306-307
Napoleon, 135

Nationalism, in rebellion, 144-146
Netherlands, national development
of, 145-146
New states, strife in, 13
Northrop, F. C. S., 9

Pareto, Vilfredo, 2
Parsons, Talcott, 119, 267-269, 319,
312n
Pirenne, Henri, 152
Political alienation, and internal violence, 228-231
Political attitudes, classification of,
210-211
Political competence, and national allegiance, 224-228
Political development, and course of
internal war, 25-26
Politics
exposure to, and political attitudes,
217-221
growth of involvement in, 206-207
violence as introduction to, 206
Prerevolutionary conditions, 24-26

Rapoport, Anatol, 105
Rebellion
American attitudes toward, 158-
159
authority objects of, 143-144
British attitudes toward, 159-161
categorizations of, 162-166
and centralization, 146-149
Chinese attitudes toward, 161
and citizenship, 151-154
and class privileges, 153
and constitutionalism, 149-151
government foreknowledge of, 176-
177
government strategy toward, 157-
179
and independence, 144-146
in Latin America, 154-155
and minority rights, 153
nationalism in, 144-146
and organization of society, 163-
164
organizational form of, 164-165
and political context of, 142-156
reasons for lack of study of, 162

Rebellion (*cont'd*)
  role of succession in, 149-150
  sequence of causes of, 154-155
  traditionalism in, 145
Recruitment, in internal war, 104-106
Revolution
  economic aspects of, 180-204
  Marxist view of, 181
  potential for, and value conflict, 122-123
  predictability of, 111-128
Richardson, Stephen, 327n
Richelieu, Cardinal, 103
Riesman, David, 85
Romeo, Rosario, 190-191
Russia
  economic development and revolutions in, 191-202
  government effectiveness in, 204n
  internal war in, 104, 148, 149
  Revolution of 1905, 191-198
  Revolution of 1917, 3, 136-7, 198, 202
Russian peasantry, and economic development, 191-195, 199-200, 201-202

Schumpeter, Joseph, 328n
Segerstedt, Torgny, 291
Shils, Edward, 275-276
Smelser, Neil, 119
Smith, Adam, 190
Social change, 111-128, 296-304
  and revolutionary potential, 118-119
Social force
  institutionalized, 14, 28
  in internal war, 11-12
  nature of, 11
Social mobility, in United States, 272-273
Social science theory, and internal war, 1-7
Sorel, George, 2
Spain, internal war in, 104
Specificity-diffuseness distinction, and democracy, 267-333
Stalin, 201
Stewart, Rosemary, 298-299
Stolypin, 193-196

Succession, role in rebellions, 149-150
Sumner, William G., 237
Sweden, political and cultural ethos of, 289-291

Taft, Ronald, 330n
Taine, Hippolyte, 184
Taylor, Edmond, 83
Terror, 27, 71-95
  counterreaction to, 96n
  definition of, 73-82
  discrimination in use of, 81-82
  extranormality of, 75-77
  incumbent and insurgent, 72-73, 95n
  objectives of, 82-88
  place of in internal war, 88-95
  and political behavior, 73-75
  psychological effects of, 97n
  responses induced by, 80-81
  symbolism in, 77-78
  tactical considerations of, 78-82
  targets of, 78-81
  violence in, 75
Thirty Years' War, 103, 110
Tönnies, Ferdinand, 234-240, 249
Totalitarian societies, and minority systems, 251-261
Traditionalism, in rebellion, 145
Turgot, 197-199
Turkey, internal war in, 148
Turner, Ralph, 275-277

Union movement
  in France, 280-281, 284-285
  in Germany, 286-288
United States
  stability of democracy in, 271-278
  value system of, 271-278, 305, 309-316
Universalism-particularism distinction, and democracy, 267-333

Value system
  in Australia, 307-309, 311-316
  in Canada, 305-316
  in France, 278-285
  in Germany, 278-279, 285-292

in Great Britain, 271-278, 305, 309-316
in United States, 271-278, 305, 309-316
Value systems
anti-elitist movements as indicators of, 311-312
and attitudes toward law and order, 312-314
and democracy, 267-333
education as indicator of, 309-311
of elites in stable democracies, 292-296

and third parties, 315-316
unionism as indicator of, 314-316

Viet Cong, 96n, 98n
Violence
initiation of, 167-178
role of in internal war, 130-140

Walker, Kenneth F., 330n, 332n
Weber, Max, 2, 31, 268, 303, 328n
Witte, 197-199, 204n

111-129